Trailer Life

RX for RV Performance & Mileage

OTHER BOOKS BY TRAILER LIFE

RV Repair & Maintenance Manual

John Thompson & the Editors of *Trailer Life* magazine

The best, most complete RV information source for repairing and maintaining your RV's systems. This book explains, step-by-step, how to repair and maintain these systems on your own and cut costs of repairs.

8¼ × 10¾, 288 pages
$12.98 cover price   ISBN: 0-934798-00-1

Secrets of Successful RVing

John Thompson and the Editors of *Trailer Life* magazine

The RVer's encyclopedia. Here in one handy book are all the facts you need to know to buy, maintain, and enjoy camping trailers, campers, motorhomes, trailers, and van conversions, including rental information.

7¼ × 9¼, 309 pages
$12.95 cover price   ISBN: 0-934798-03-6

Rider's Complete Guide to Motorcycle Touring

Dick Blom & the Editors of *Trailer Life* magazine

This guide brings you the tips and techniques that will make your tours worry-free—whether you're day tripping or touring from coast to coast. You'll find out how to buy a touring motorcycle that fits your needs—and your budget—and how to maintain your motorcycle on and off the road. Hundreds of photos (including sixteen pages in full color!) and drawings.

7½ × 9½, 207 pages
$12.95 cover price   ISBN: 0-934798-02-8

These books are available at fine bookstores everywhere. Or, you may order directly from Trailer Life. For each book ordered, simply send us the name of the book, the cover price, plus $2 per book for shipping and handling (California residents please add 6½% sales tax). Mail to:

Trailer Life, PO Box 4500, Agoura, CA 91301

You may call our Customer Service representatives if you wish to charge your order or if you want more information. Phone, toll-free, Monday through Friday, 7:30 A.M. to 6:00 P.M.; Saturday, 7:30 A.M. to 12:30 P.M. Pacific Time, **1-800-423-5061**. In California call **1-800-382-3455**.

Trailer Life's

RX for RV Performance & Mileage

John Geraghty and Bill Estes

Editor in Charge: Alice M. Dauro

Published by TL Enterprises, Inc.
29901 Agoura Road, Agoura, California 91301

Book Division TL Enterprises, Inc.

Richard Rouse
President

Ted Binder
Vice President/General Manager

Bill Estes
Vice President/Technical Editor

Michael Schneider
Publisher, Book Division

Rena Copperman
General Manager, Book Division

Cindy Lang
Assistant Manager, Book Division

Composition by: Publisher's Typography
(A Division of TL Enterprises, Inc.)

Production Management: Robert S. Tinnon
Book Design: Robert S. Tinnon
Cover Design: Joe Cibere
Chapter Opening Art: Ken Roberts
Technical Art: Randy Miyake
Associate Editor: Sheryl Davis
Editorial Assistant: Virginia Huffstetter

Published by TL Enterprises, Inc.
29901 Agoura Road, Agoura, California 91301

Library of Congress Cataloging in Publication Data

Geraghty, John, 1930-
     RX for RV: Trailer Life's RX for RV performance & mileage.

     Includes index.
     1. Recreational vehicles—Maintenance and repair.
2. Recreational vehicles—Fuel consumption.   I. Estes,
Bill.   II. Dauro, Alice M.   III. Trailer Life.
IV. Title.   V. Title: R.X. for R.V.
TL298.G47   1983   629.28'76   83-4397
ISBN 0-934798-06-0

Printed in the United States of America

10 9 8 7 6 5

Contents

Contents

John Geraghty

Bill Estes

Introduction

"If you know the theory, you can fix anything."

That's one of the euphemisms used for many years by automotive mechanics instructors.

Possibly it's waning in popularity because it never was quite true, and is even less so in these days of complex emission controls, computerized ignition and carburetion systems and necessity for special diagnostic equipment to electronically "read" the signals given out by various probes and monitors that sniff out an engine's malfunctions.

However, it still has some validity for the RV owner. It's part of what this book is all about—the reasons why an engine performs poorly and why it doesn't produce the fuel economy of which it is capable. It isn't enough for you to be told that one possible reason is an in-

operative mechanical spark advance system, or that a carburetor float has become partially saturated with fuel. You need to know how that spark advance system works, so you can appreciate its function in the total spark advance picture. And you need to know how a partially saturated float affects fuel economy.

The Book

The word "theory" may be intimidating, since it implies highly technical terminology. You won't find that here. This book is written for the average RV owner with an *interest* in how his or her engine works, plus at least a minimum of do-it-yourself backyard mechanical experience. As with any endeavor, experience helps. If we're talking about how the power enrichment system of a carburetor works, it helps if you've done any kind of work on your own carburetor. But it isn't a necessity. This book will help you improve your ability to perform modifications that will help mileage and performance, and to diagnose problems, many of which have perplexed mechanics and even factory representatives.

That's one part; another is direct mechanical experience—information on how to fix specific problems. Still another is information on how to correct deficiencies built into a vehicle at the factory—not necessarily factory goofs (although many are) but ways to compensate for compromises that the factory found necessary due to the extremely wide variation in possible uses and abuses to which their engines could be subjected. This book will help you get closer to the most ideal calibration for best fuel economy and performance.

The Authors

TL Enterprises is confident that RVers throughout North America will agree that the two individuals most highly qualified to do this today are the authors of this book: John Geraghty and Bill Estes.

Geraghty has operated an automotive diagnostic and repair shop for nearly 30 years; he has specialized in RVs since 1970. He has written articles for many national automotive publications, including *Trailer Life* and

MotorHome magazines, and he has lectured before groups of automotive mechanics as well as before large groups of RVers interested in learning more about their RV engines. Throughout the past 10 years in particular he has collaborated with Estes on many performance and mileage-related articles which have appeared in the publications of TL Enterprises.

Estes has been associated with TL Enterprises since 1969, when he joined Trailer Life, already a convinced RV enthusiast himself, to become the editor of the then popular *Camper Coachman* magazine. He was soon technical editor of both *Trailer Life* and *MotorHome* magazines, eventually becoming editor. In these capacities, spanning many years, Estes has written literally hundreds of articles based on his personal tests and research; many of them have been reprinted for dissemination to RV readers throughout the country. In addition to engine performance and fuel economy, Estes' research and testing has extended to all aspects of RV travel.

The Content

Much of the material in the pages that follow is completely new, written particularly for this book. Some, however, appeared previously in *Trailer Life* or *MotorHome,* as part of the Estes and Geraghty columns. Some of the material reprinted here from those columns (the facts have not changed or the material involved has been completely updated for appearance here) was written solely by Geraghty, some solely by Estes. There is also material written by Estes in the past about Geraghty's research and modifications to engines. Consequently, in most sections of this book the authors use the collective "we" in referring to their research and recommendations. However, in some of the reprinted material as written originally by Estes alone, Geraghty will be quoted. This does not affect the validity of the material presented or your ability to use it; the explanation is intended only to outline the way the authors worked together in assembling the extensive chapters that follow.

For More Facts

Of course, no single book can provide all the information you'll need about your engine. This book does not go into detail on standard procedures for automotive repair, such as how to replace a water pump, how to replace a starter, how to clean out a radiator. It specializes in the RV topics and problems you won't find in most other books. As a supplement to this book you might purchase the factory shop manual for your vehicle. It includes detailed mechanical repair information as well as helpful routine diagnostic information.

A variety of specialized products designed to improve engine fuel economy and performance are available through shops specializing in that equipment. Beyond that, more attention paid to regular maintenance will provide assurance that your RV engine is operating as efficiently as possible—and you can have the satisfaction of taking part of the credit.

Parts Availability

One final note on the information contained in this book. Since it was written in 1983, a few of the specific parts mentioned are no longer available. These include the engine tuning kits described in some chapters and the Vari-Flow water injector. Specialized engine tuning is available at shops equipped with chassis dynomometers. Such shops are listed in the Yellow Pages of your telephone book. Water injectors of other brands are available at specialty shops.

Trailer Life

RX for RV Performance & Mileage

How an Engine Works

1

The inefficiency of the internal combustion engine is notorious. Since its invention in 1680, numerous improvements have been made and fuel economy has improved dramatically. But miracles have not happened; it still requires fuel to move weight, particularly when the weight is higher than normal. With the various types of recreational vehicles, fuel economy figures are dramatically lower than those recorded with late-model lightweight passenger cars.

Due to weight, the RV owner largely sticks with the V-8 engine, which may be the chief dinosaur in a breed of power plants facing extinction as soon as suitable replacements can be produced on a mass scale. Of course, that's the rub. Many engine designs—some dating back to the 1800s—seem to offer more

promise than the internal combustion engine. One such is the Stirling engine, invented by a Scottish clergyman in 1816. It's an *external* combustion engine. Thus, heat losses are dramatically reduced, emissions are less toxic and noise is reduced, compared to internal combustion engines.

Why, then, haven't several more efficient designs been marketed, and why hasn't the internal combustion engine lapsed into oblivion a long time ago?

The answer involves cost and practicality. Although it is possible to build more efficient engines, costs are high and inherent design problems may limit their application. The internal combustion engine, with all its faults, is versatile.

Rather than wait for the advent of an engine that will cut our fuel bills to a

RV owners and other motorists tend to take the modern V-8 engine for granted due to its well-known deficiencies, but it is a sophisticated machine that relies on very close tolerances, clean lubricants, proper air/fuel ratios and spark advance characteristics that change with engine load. Readers who are not familiar with internal design of the V-8 might take note of how the cam is situated (in the center of the cutaway section) and how the cam is driven by a chain powered by the crankshaft. Valve lifters are operated by the cam, and pushrods open and close the valves. All this happens in proper sequence with rise and fall of the pistons in a 4-stroke combustion cycle (intake, compression, combustion and exhaust). Illustration Courtesy of Chevrolet.

fraction of their current status, let's set out to improve what we have. It is possible to create worthwhile fuel economy improvement while also improving performance. The two may seem mutually exclusive. They are not, and the key word is *efficiency*. When we improve the efficiency of an engine we improve its fuel economy potential and it's possible to improve performance potential as well. In addition, we can improve our driving habits. And we can pay more proper attention to maintenance. For example, many studies have shown that most RV owners do not inflate tires properly. This has been pointed out for many years, but little improvement is apparent.

To better understand the concepts and recommendations included in this book, it's necessary to have a basic understanding of how an internal combustion engine works. Few readers may be interested in the really fine details of engine design, so this explanation will be very basic, and will relate specifically to what we'll be dealing with in this book.

The 4-Stroke Engine

All gasoline V-8 engines used in RVs are 4-stroke engines. That is, each combustion cycle includes 4 strokes: intake, compression, power and exhaust. During the intake stroke, the intake valve is open and downward movement of the piston draws air/fuel mixture in. This mixture is created when air passes through the carburetor, mixing with

fuel. The piston, in effect, creates the suction to make this happen. How fast and how well it happens depends on design of carburetor, intake manifold and the ports in the cylinder heads through which the gases pass, and timing of the valves. What happens when the piston moves down on its intake stroke and the throttle is closed? A partial vacuum is created in the intake manifold. Measurement of this vacuum, by means of a *manifold vacuum gauge*, gives us our most important visual indicator of engine operation and fuel economy. Later in this book you'll see more on use of the vacuum gauge.

Following intake is the compression stroke. Length of this stroke in proportion to the size of the combustion chamber determines *compression ratio*. You may recall that compression ratios were much higher in the 1960s than they are now. The reason is fuel octane—the resistance of fuel to spark knock or ping. Fuel quality was better in the 1960s. Detection and prevention of ping is another important item we'll deal with.

During the power stroke, the compressed gases are ignited and they create downward force to propel the vehicle. Then the piston makes another upward stroke to expel the burned gases through the exhaust valve. Design of the exhaust system has much to do with performance and efficiency of RV engines, since they operate under heavier throttle than do engines in the average passenger car. An engine with restricted exhaust passages obviously will be restricted in performance and will be more inclined to ping. More information on ping is in a later chapter.

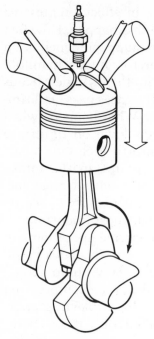

INTAKE STROKE

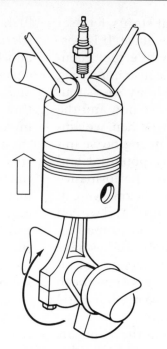

COMPRESSION STROKE

SPARK PLUG FIRING

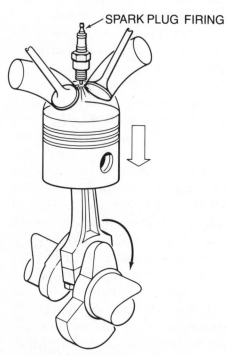

POWER STROKE

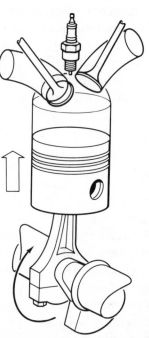

EXHAUST STROKE

Combustion in the typical 4-stroke engine is affected by a variety of factors including intake and exhaust efficiency and cam timing.

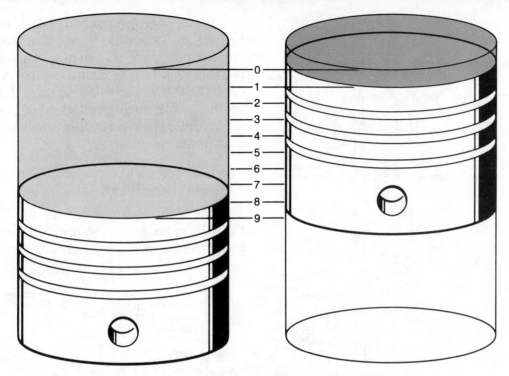

Compression ratio is the amount of change in cylinder volume between the piston at the bottom of the stroke, and the piston at the top.

Driving for Maximum Efficiency

It's natural for RV owners to seek dramatic ways to improve fuel economy. Unfortunately, few, if any, exist. In our quest for dramatic fuel economy improvers we overlook what is possible today without major cost: a combination of small measures which can be very worthwhile.

We all know that speed increases fuel consumption. It is a more important factor in RVs than in the average passenger vehicle, because most RVs offer more resistance to wind. The average RV is streamlined like a brick, although that is gradually changing. The result

is that additional speed creates more fuel penalty in RVs than in passenger vehicles. A manifold vacuum gauge will tell you just how much. A later chapter tells just how a vacuum gauge can be used; suffice it to say here that the vacuum readings for lightly loaded vehicles may drop only moderately when speed increases, but readings for RVs will drop dramatically. Low readings mean poor fuel economy.

Weight has its effect, too, but on a percentage basis it's not as great as in passenger vehicles. Add 150 pounds to a 5000-pound passenger car and the fuel economy penalty may be ¼-mpg. Add that much to a 10,000-pound RV and

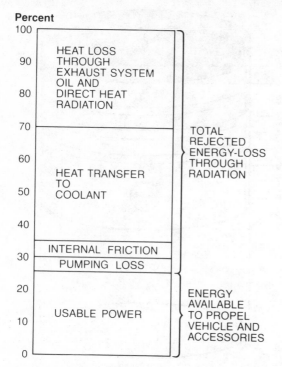

Only a portion of each gallon of gasoline is directly applied to propelling the vehicle. The remainder is lost through direct heat radiation.

mountains a cruise control cannot anticipate and otherwise think ahead. And it does not back off when a vacuum gauge tells it to. The cruise control can open the throttle to wider settings than are desirable during hill-climbs. Consequently, driver control of throttle is best in the mountains.

Vacuum Readings

The most efficient way to handle the throttle is to keep vacuum readings above seven inches of mercury where

the difference is barely noticeable. However, RV owners are prone to add great amounts of weight, merely because the space is available, and the addition of 1000 pounds or more can be very noticeable on hill-climb speeds. Anything that makes a noticeable effect on hill-climb speeds will be even more noticeable at the gas pump.

It's common knowledge that steady pressure on the accelerator pedal produces best fuel economy, as opposed to erratic acceleration and deceleration. But it's a common misconception that cruise control improves fuel economy. It may, under level-highway conditions if the driving is erratic. However, in the

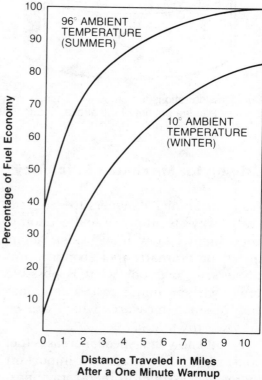

Engine warm-up affects fuel economy and overall engine efficiency in the first few miles of driving. The duration of carburetor choke actuation and of atomization of fuel are affected (colder fuel is more difficult to atomize).

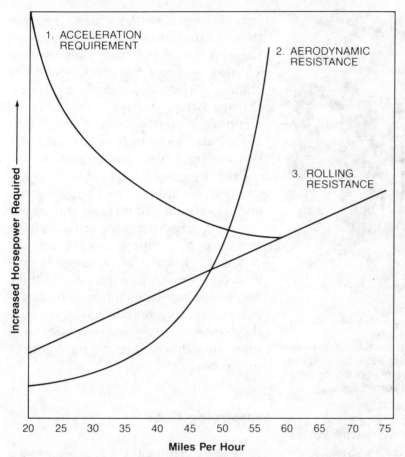

Curve 1 represents the approximate power required to accelerate a vehicle rapidly to 55 mph, illustrating an advantage of gradual acceleration. **Curve 2** represents the typical aerodynamic resistance of RVs, demonstrating the required increase of power to sustain higher speeds. **Curve 3** illustrates the typical rolling resistance as it increases with speed.

possible. This means allowing speed to drop as low as the driver can tolerate without going below seven inches. Then, rather than applying additional throttle, downshift to second gear and still keep vacuum at seven inches or above. Then and only then, if road speed drops below tolerable levels, use more throttle to go below seven inches. When the crest of the hill is reached, return to seven inches or higher as quickly as possible, and to higher gears. Pick up speed (within your personal limits) down the hill to get as much of a run at the next hill as possible. The most efficient speed for an RV usually is about 38 mph. Few of us want to drive that slowly, but you get the idea.

7

Fuel quality has dropped since the 1960s when octanes exceeding 100 were available. Engines must be protected against preignition or detonation (ping) possible with current fuels.

On initial starts, move away gradually, again keeping vacuum above seven inches. Particularly during cold starts the vehicle should be accelerated gently, because a cold engine means poorly vaporized fuel. The result is that much of the fuel is blown out the exhaust unburned. More throttle is used to make up for it and a cold engine gets worst fuel economy during the first few minutes of operation.

By planning routes and times for travel, fuel can be saved. Fuel economy suffers in hot weather, not only due to more use of air-conditioning, but also because engine temperatures are higher than normal and the air which enters the carburetor is hotter, thus thinner. Thin air reduces the efficiency of the engine by richening the air/fuel ratios. During a trip, starting very early and stopping by mid-afternoon can result in fuel savings as well as less wear and tear on the vehicle and on nerves.

Best time to fill fuel tanks is in the morning because the fuel is more dense and its volume will increase during the day as it grows warmer in the vehicle fuel tank. When filling, always raise the nozzle to drain it after stopping fuel flow. Never attempt to fill a tank all the way to the top when a nozzle has a vapor recovery system attached, because the vapor recovery system often will route fuel that you're paying for back to the tank.

Choosing Fuel

How to determine the fuel quality you'll need is a simple proposition: buy the least expensive fuel which does not ping in your engine.

This is particularly true in high altitudes. Many drivers believe they need high-octane premium fuels in high altitude because those fuels are hotter and will produce more power. The opposite is true. A premium fuel is not hotter; rather, its burn rate is more controlled. In high altitude, a faster burn rate is desirable to counteract the effect of lower atmospheric pressure.

Preventive Maintenance 2

Many maintenance factors ranging from wheel alignment to condition of fuel filters can affect fuel economy. Often we check some obvious items and miss others. A check list of periodic inspection/maintenance items would include all these actions:

- Engine oil and filter: Change every 3000 miles in short-distance driving, every 6000 on extended trips.
- Transmission oil and filter: For automatic transmissions, change every 20,000 miles unless oil temperatures above 250 are frequently encountered (monitor oil temperatures in the oil sump); change manual-transmission lube oil every 20,000 miles.
- Engine air filter: Change every 10,000 miles under normal conditions—less often if dusty conditions are rarely, if ever, encountered.

- Engine fuel filter: Change every 10,000 miles.
- Tire pressure: Check every 30 days during commuter driving; check weekly during trips; inspect tires daily.
- Tread depth: Check every 30 days.
- Wheel alignment and steering system: Check every six months or 24,000 miles, unless abnormal tire wear is evident. If so, check immediately.
- Spark plugs: Change plugs every 10,000 miles.
- Points and condensor (ignition system): Change every 10,000 miles. (This is not applicable for electronic ignition systems.)
- Connectors in electronic ignition systems: Check and lubricate with dialectric grease every 10,000 miles.
- Wheel bearings: Repack every 25,000 miles or every 2 years.

- Brakes: Check every 24,000 miles for wear on pads and shoes.
- Battery and battery cables: Check all connections annually. Corrosion should be prevented through use of silicone grease or petroleum jelly.
- Engine compression: Check every 10,000 miles.
- Timing chain wear: Check every 20,000 miles.
- Valve adjustment (if applicable): Check every 20,000 miles.
- Tightness of various engine bolts, particularly intake manifold bolts: Check when vehicle is new and every 24,000 miles or annually thereafter.
- Rear axle: Change rear axle lube every 25,000 miles.
- Vacuum hoses and connectors: Check every 10,000 miles.
- Coolant hoses: Inspect for leakage weekly, or more often, during trips.
- Exhaust gas recirculation (EGR) valve: Check every 10,000 miles.
- Positive crankcase ventilation (PCV) valve: Check or change this every 10,000 miles.
- Engine coolant thermostat: Change thermostat annually. Change coolant every other year.
- Initial spark advance setting: Check every 10,000 miles.
- Mechanical spark advance system: Check every 10,000 miles.
- Vacuum spark advance system: Check every 10,000 miles.
- Air-conditioning: Check refrigerant pressure every other year.
- Fuel lines: Inspect weekly during trips. Examine for cracking of neoprene hoses and replace as necessary.
- Fuel tanks: Check weekly during trips for leakage; use alcohol-base fuel additive 5 percent per volume annually to eliminate water that has accumulated due to condensation.
- Shock absorbers: Check monthly during trips for oil leakage.
- Suspension and drivetrain lubrication (grease) fittings: Lube annually or every 6000 miles.

Wheel Alignment

Wheel alignment affects fuel economy while also reducing tire life, so two important reasons exist for maintaining proper settings. Generally, factory-recommended settings can be followed, except we like to increase the caster setting 1.5 degrees beyond the maximum factory specifications, if the vehicle tends to wander. The additional caster usually will correct it. When alignment is set, be sure to have the vehicle loaded as for a trip, as loading generally will change the degree of suspension compression and this affects the alignment settings. Have wheel bearings checked and lubricated at the same time and have shock absorbers checked. It's common to find shock absorber mounting bolts missing, and even to find entire shocks missing. Steering gears should be adjusted for best possible steering control, and least tendency of the driver to over-correct.

Insufficient tire pressure wastes fuel by increasing rolling resistance, and it increases tire wear and the possibility of blowout. Graduated load/inflation

Left: Checking tire pressure is apparently routine, but too many RV owners neglect it, use an inaccurate gauge or do not have sufficient knowledge of proper pressures. **Above:** Periodic measurement of tread depth is important in order to detect irregular wear patterns.

tables are included in the chapter on tires, so you can weigh your vehicle wheel by wheel and inflate precisely for the load being carried. In other words, a tire that is not loaded to its maximum need not be inflated to its maximum. However, inflation pressures that are higher than the minimums will increase fuel economy by slight margins, due to reduced rolling resistance. Those higher-than-necessary inflation pressures tend to wear the tire in the center faster than on the outsides, reducing tire life. The tradeoff probably favors accurate inflation for the load, for best tire life, but overinflation certainly

beats underinflation for a variety of reasons. When in doubt, inflate to the maximum pressure stamped on the tire sidewall. When a tire tends to run hot even if inflation pressure is at the maximum, the load may be in excess of what the tire is rated for. Tires normally won't run so hot that it's impossible to keep one's hand on them comfortably for more than a few seconds, except in very hot weather.

Many RVers are prone to install oversize tires, which tend to handle loads better. This is well and good, except that it changes the effective gear ratio (see Chapter 7 on axle ratios).

Among preventive maintenance procedures often neglected is the changing of automatic transmission oil and filter. Here, the transmission pan has been removed.

Lubrication

Great strides have been made in durability of chassis components during the past several years; as a result, chassis lubrication is not required as often. It's necessary to lube chassis fittings at least once a year for light service, and at least once every 6 months for heavy service. Or, once every 6000 miles.

A manual transmission should have its oil changed about every 20,000 miles, using low-friction lube. An automatic trans should have an oil change about every 20,000 miles as well, unless the vehicle is equipped with a very efficient trans oil cooler and a trans oil temp gauge with the sensor installed in the oil pan. Since trans oil is not subjected to the same contamination as is engine oil (combustion by-products, fuel, moisture), it will last a long time unless overheated. When the oil retains its reddish color and clarity—the appearance of new oil—it's in good shape. When it becomes brownish and dirty, it has been overheated and should be changed, along with the filter. Removal of the oil pan is necessary to change the filter.

Most transmissions do not have drain plugs for the torque convertor, so only a portion of the oil is changed when the pan is removed. For a complete change, drain the oil in the pan, replace the pan and refill with an approximately equal amount of oil to that which was drained. Then add an extra quart. Remove the transmission output line from the oil cooling tank in the radiator, attach an appropriate length of flexible oil line or fuel line to it and place the line in a bucket. Start the engine and allow it to idle while oil flows into the bucket. Allow about two quarts to flow into the bucket. Stop the engine and pour two quarts into the transmission. Repeat the process until the oil entering the bucket is clear and appears like new oil. Through this process, you can flush the torque convertor. Normally, the burned oil in the torque convertor returns and is mixed with the new oil after an oil change. Reconnect the transmission line and check for leaks.

Prior to the oil change you can determine which trans line is the output by disconnecting the line and having someone crank the engine for just a second. If the disconnected line is the output, oil will issue from the line. If it's the input, oil will pour from the point where the line was disconnected.

Critical Oil Level

When checking transmission oil level, it's important, even critical, that you do it properly. Most vehicle owners don't, and overfilling occurs. As a result, the oil is high enough that gears run in it and aerate it, causing overheating. Aerated oil cannot be cooled properly. The overheated oil then foams more and possibly is pushed out the dip stick tube or out a vent tube. Often the oil gets onto an exhaust manifold and causes a lot of smoke.

If the oil level is up to the full mark when the trans is cold, it is *too high.* When the trans is cold, the oil level should be slightly *below the add mark.* This allows for heat expansion of the oil. If the oil is checked when it is up to normal operating temperature, it should be about halfway between the add and full marks. If the oil is checked after a hill climb, temperature supposedly will have reached the highest level and the oil should be at the full mark.

The differential (rear axle) lubricant should be changed about every 25,000 miles, or sooner if the differential is equipped with a positive traction (no-slip) device. Clutches in those devices

depend on special additives in the lubricant. If chattering or any other abnormal behavior occurs, change the oil, making sure the new oil is labeled as suitable for differentials with positive traction devices. An oil change will not keep a faulty positive traction device from going bad, but if the device is in good condition and if the additives in the oil were minimal to begin with, an oil change certainly will do no harm. Check to make sure the axle vent is clear of obstructions. Check oil level about every 10,000 miles, more often if any oil leakage is apparent.

The worst operating condition for engine oil is stop-and-go driving and short trips in cold weather. Under such conditions, maximum moisture enters the oil through condensation, and the maximum fuel dilution of the oil occurs. Long trips are not hard on oil, unless it is overheated. Ideal oil temperatures are between 180 and 220 degrees F. It's not uncommon to see transmission oil temperatures in that range if a good auxiliary cooler is used. Engine oil temperatures usually will be higher, which is not disastrous since the oil is changed more often. Engine oil temperature ideally should not exceed 250 under the most severe conditions (measuring temperature in the oil pan).

Oil Quality

Be sure to use oil that is labeled "SF." This means it is suitable for extreme service. Until recently, the oils labeled "SE" were the best, but the SF rating

Engine oil should be checked to make sure it has SF rating; for diesel, check for CC or CD ratings.

which have built up on the oil, and which will go to work on bearings during the storage period.

Many manufacturers of synthetics and other expensive friction-reducing oils recommended oil change intervals ranging up to 50,000 miles. We don't believe in those extended intervals, because these oils do not eliminate the causes of oil contamination—condensation and fuel contamination. Even though the oil may be higher in quality than normal, it is not reasonable to assume it can soak up all those contaminants over a 50,000-mile period without some loss of effectiveness. And when you consider the cost of the special oils ($4 to $6 a quart), cost-effectiveness is not good unless oil changes are greatly reduced. It's safer to use conventional oils rated for SF service, many of which now have friction-reducing additives, and change more often.

has replaced the SE rating. We recommend SAE 20W-40 or 20W-50 oil for temperatures above 32 degrees F, and 10W-40 for temperatures less than 32 degrees. When long trips are involved, change oil and filter about every 6000 miles, unless temperatures are very high. If so, change about every 3000 miles. For round-town use in moderate weather change oil every 3000 miles, and for excessive stop-and-go use, change every 2000 miles. Use a six-month interval if those distances are not reached, unless the vehicle is in storage.

When storing a vehicle for several months, change the oil *before* it goes into storage. This gets rid of the acids

Cold Starts

Even though the oil is high quality, engine lubrication is very marginal at one point: when starting cold. When an engine has sat overnight, only a thin oil film remains on moving parts; the rest of the oil has returned to the pan. It is necessary to avoid racing the engine immediately after startup. Allow it to run at a fast idle for at least 30 seconds without putting the transmission in gear. Make sure oil pressure reaches the maximum in about 5 seconds. If longer time is required, and if the gauge is electric, have a mechanic check with a mechanical gauge (engine cold). If oil pressure does not rise within 5 seconds, the oil pump is faulty or the oil pickup screen is clogged.

Every 25,000 miles, front wheel bearings should be cleaned in solvent, inspected for wear and relubricated. After installation, they should be tightened properly. Grease seals should be replaced each time this occurs. Bearings on rear axles usually are lubricated by the differential oil, but check your owner's manual for lubrication recommendations to make sure.

Periodically, drum brakes require cleaning of backing plates and moving parts, which tend to bind and prevent the shoes from moving away from the drums, creating brake drag. Master cylinder free travel should be checked to assure it is adequate to prevent brake application through pressure caused by temperature rise and expansion of the fluid. But it shouldn't create excessive pedal travel.

Disk brake pads should be inspected for thickness. Edges should be chamfered (rounded). If the pad is floating free on the brake piston, a special adhesive available at brake shops should be applied to prevent dragging of the pads. Brake drag is difficult to feel while driving, since it is consistent, but a rough measure of whether or not it's occurring can be gained during an on-the-road check. While driving on an interstate or other highway where braking is not required for at least 20 miles, watch for a safe area and coast to a stop, using gears for braking. Feel

the brake discs and drums for heat. They should be no warmer than the wheels or hubs.

Electrical Maintenance

Electrical connections largely are taken for granted, but they require periodic maintenance, especially battery connections. Battery cables should be removed and the battery should be cleaned with baking soda and water. The battery tray should be cleaned and repainted if it was subject to corrosion. Connections on the battery, as well as the terminals on the battery cable, should be scraped to remove corrosion and assure good metal-to-metal contact. Silicone dialectric compound or petroleum jelly should be applied to

Battery care should include keeping the top clean; leakage of power can occur between top posts through accumulation of oil and dirt. Posts and connectors should be cleaned and coated with grease or silicone dialectric compound.

prevent future corrosion. Coat any surface subject to corrosion. The silicone compound or petroleum jelly prevents the exposure of metal to oxygen which enables corrosion to occur. An engine starting battery and an auxiliary (RV) battery may both be grounded to the chassis. Ground connections must be clean and corrosion-free.

Electrical connectors should be separated and inspected for corrosion. Lightly rough up the contact surfaces with sandpaper or emery paper, coat lightly with silicone compound and then reconnect.

Compression Check

Engine periodic maintenance should include a routine annual check of compression. This can be performed with a compression tester available at any auto parts store. Such checks will provide a record of engine progressive condition.

It's best to check compression when the engine is warm, with all spark plugs removed. Easiest time to do it is when replacing spark plugs (recommended about every 10,000 miles). With the plugs removed, spin the engine to clear the combustion chamber of static gases. Prop the throttle open and use the tester to check each cylinder. Record compression. Then inject about 2 squirts of oil into each cylinder, and again check compression. No more than about 10 percent difference in compression should occur between cylinders, or between the "dry" and "oiled" compres-

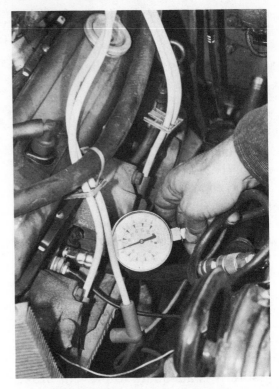

Periodic checking of cylinder compression will detect valve leakage and piston ring leakage.

sion checks. If greater than 10 percent differential occurs when the cylinders are dry, but is reduced when they're oiled, this is not uncommon and indicates only a temporary loss of ring seal due to excessive fuel intake. Re-check compression after about 500 miles. If a single cylinder shows higher compression than others, inspect the spark plug from that cylinder for signs of oil residue or heavy carbon deposits. That cylinder probably will have a valve seal problem.

Timing chain wear should be checked every 20,000 miles. A worn timing chain will affect throttle response, requiring additional throttle to move the same weight. Chapter 16 explains how the check can be made.

Valve settings normally don't need periodic checks. Most engines have non-adjustable valve components and hydraulic valve lifters. However, some (such as the Chevrolet V-8 engines) have adjustable valve rocker arms and these should be checked. When new, the factory adjustment leaves a lot to be desired. It calls for the adjustment at one turn down from zero lash, and we believe a one-quarter to one-eighth turn works best and prevents valve "float" at high rpm due to pump-up of the lifters. The adjustment procedure is described in the Chevrolet material later in this book.

It's critical that all engines with hydraulic lifters receive regular oil changes, and that detergent-type SF oils be used after the break-in period to keep them clean. Dirty oil usually causes problems first in the lifters.

Getting Loose

After initial break-in, ideally the bolts which secure cylinder heads, intake manifolds and exhaust manifolds should be retorqued. Usually this step is omitted with new vehicles, but it's easy to retighten intake manifold and exhaust manifold bolts, plus valve cover bolts. Failure to cinch down intake manifold bolts can cause oil leakage into the intake manifold and dramatic increases in oil consumption. It's indi-

Loose manifold bolts may permit vacuum leakage between the manifold and the cylinder head.

cated by rough idle and loss in idle vacuum.

It's best to retighten intake manifold bolts about once a year. A box end wrench can be used, tightening bolts from the center outward, since tightening to precise torque figures is not necessary here. When retightening exhaust manifold bolts, use of a torque wrench is wise as overtightening can crack manifolds.

A check of all vacuum lines and connections should be made every 10,000 miles or once a year, since vacuum lines deteriorate, split at the ends and may fall off the connectors. Any time idle characteristics change, or a vacuum gauge shows an unexplained reduction in average readings, check for a faulty vacuum connection.

A defective positive crankcase ventilation (PCV) valve also will change

Vacuum lines and fuel lines should be checked frequently for cracks that will lead to leakage. All neoprene lines eventually age and crack.

Cooling Systems

Draining, flushing and servicing the cooling system should occur every 2 years. All makers of antifreeze offer directions for use of their products. Avoid mixing antifreeze brands.

Replacing the thermostat every year is a good practice that may prevent a stuck thermostat during a trip. In cool climates a 190-degree thermostat can be used. Thermostats rated lower than 180 degrees should not be used because they do not provide adequate engine temperature for good fuel vaporization during cool weather. Never operate the vehicle without a thermostat, as it acts as a flow regulator for coolant, allowing it to be exposed to the radiator's cooling surfaces for the prescribed time. Check all hoses and belts, particularly the water pump and fan belts. Slippage can lead to overheating, and slippage is more prevalent in hot weather when the engine fan operates in its locked-up mode more of the time.

vacuum readings, as can a faulty exhaust gas recirculation (EGR) valve. A faulty EGR valve can also cause rough idle. The valve is not supposed to open, permitting recirculation of exhaust gases into the intake manifold, until engine rpm rises above idle. A faulty spark delay valve also can cause erratic engine operation.

When a cruise control system is engaged, manifold vacuum readings should immediately return to those which occurred when the engine was manually controlled. Otherwise a vacuum leak inside the cruise control may be indicated. The vacuum line for the vacuum gauge should not be connected to the same port as the vacuum line for a cruise control unit.

Air-Conditioning

Freon should be checked each year and more added as needed. Every 2 years the system should be evacuated and recharged as recommended by the factory. If the mechanic sees signs of moisture in the system during the evacuation, a drying agent should be used. It's best to operate the air-conditioning system about once a month, even in winter, to prevent deterioration of seals and shortened component life.

Neglected fuel filters may become so dirty that they will pass only small amounts of fuel.

Fuel System

Each tune-up at 10,000-mile intervals should include fuel filter inspection and, in most cases, replacement. Once a year, methanol or ethanol should be added to fuel, generally 5 percent by volume, to remove condensation—especially after prolonged storage.

All fuel lines should be checked for cracks which indicate eventual failure and possibly dangerous fuel leaks. Neoprene fuel lines will last 3 to 5 years, depending on location (amount of ozone in the air). If contamination of the fuel system (other than water) is ever detected, a full-flow fuel filter with a sediment reservoir that can be drained frequently should be installed. Fuel bypasses some filters when they become restricted. If a small piece of debris gets past a filter which has by-pass capability, the debris could lodge in a small passage inside the carburetor and require a complete carburetor overhaul. The additional filter should be placed under the vehicle near the fuel tank, away from any heat source so it does not act as a heat sink and induce vapor lock.

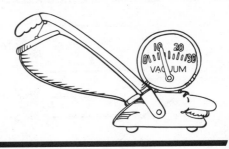

The Vacuum Gauge

3

Repeated reference to use of a vacuum gauge is made in this book. The importance of this gauge cannot be overemphasized, for two reasons:

a) The gauge helps the driver improve fuel economy, and

b) It is relatively inexpensive.

It's possible to spend several hundred dollars on equipment which doesn't produce as much improvement in fuel economy as the vacuum gauge, *properly used.* Those words, *properly used,* are critical. Any gauge that the driver ignores will have no effect. And lack of understanding of what the gauge readings mean can render the gauge useless. Let's see what the vacuum gauge has to offer.

First, what is it? A vacuum gauge is one that measures the partial vacuum inside the intake manifold. That's the vacuum created when the pistons create suction on their intake stroke, but the throttle is closed or partially closed. Thus, the vacuum gauge serves as an indicator of throttle position. But it has more important functions, related to carburetor performance.

When a vacuum gauge monitors vacuum, the results are indicated by a needle on a scale of numbers which represent inches of mercury. That's a common method of measuring vacuum and we needn't explain it here. The scale usually is calibrated from zero to 30. Most RV engines will make use of the area between zero and 25. Zero indicates no vacuum (atmospheric pressure). Trucks and motorhomes usually will cruise between 10 and 14 inches of vacuum on level highway (depending on weight and wind resistance and engine condition). A passenger car towing a heavy trailer often will cruise on lower

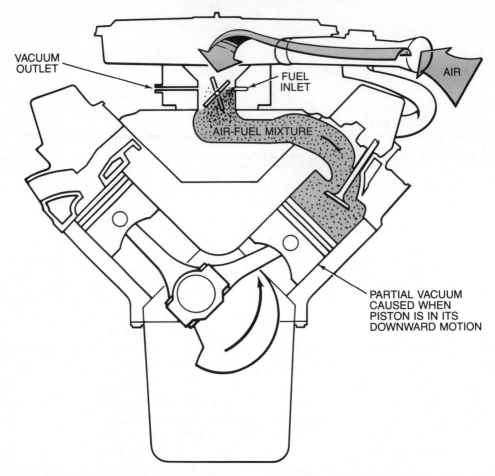

VACUUM
OUTLET

FUEL
INLET

AIR

AIR-FUEL MIXTURE

PARTIAL VACUUM
CAUSED WHEN
PISTON IS IN ITS
DOWNWARD MOTION

When the piston moves downward on the intake stroke, partial vacuum is created, drawing in the air/fuel mixture. The amount drawn in depends on position of the throttle. Unless the throttle is fully open, partial vacuum is created between the piston and the throttle valve.

readings because cars seldom are as low-geared as pickup trucks and motorhomes, and the engines must work harder to make up for it. A passenger car or pickup truck cruising without a load will produce vacuum readings in the 14 to 18 range. Vacuum at idle usually will be 18 to 20. And vacuum on a downhill grade (throttle closed, but the vehicle weight is pulling the engine) may vary up to 25 inches.

If you have a vacuum gauge, suck on the end of the tube and see how much of a reading you can create. Not much. So, you can appreciate the amount of suction that must be applied to valve guide oil seals and gaskets when vacuum on a downhill grade exceeds 20 inches. Faulty valve guide seals will permit the high vacuum to draw oil into the combustion chambers, as will a faulty intake manifold gasket.

The vacuum gauge is the most valuable aid to improved fuel economy. To be effective, it must be mounted where it can be easily seen by the driver—preferably on the instrument panel.

Keep Readings High

Generally, it's best to keep vacuum readings as high as possible, for they're synonymous with best possible fuel economy. However, one point on the vacuum gauge is more important than any other: *7 inches.* It is at 6½ to 7 inches that conventional carburetors change from cruise fuel mixtures to power fuel mixtures. The difference in air/fuel ratio usually is from about 14 to 1 (cruise) to 12 to 1 (power). The concentration of fuel in the air thus changes from 7.14 percent to 8 percent. Not a great difference, you say. But it can make as much as 25 percent difference in fuel economy, depending on road, load and driving conditions.

The general rule is simple: stay above 7 inches unless road speed drops more than you can tolerate. As described earlier, in the chapter on most efficient driving, hold vacuum at 7 inches or above while road speed drops on hills; then shift to second, while still holding above 7 inches. Only when road speed drops more than you can tolerate should vacuum drop below 7 inches. Often, the difference between 5 inches and 7 is only slight in road speed, but it can be substantial in fuel economy, and the driver who doesn't know the difference simply wastes fuel.

A prime example of the value of a vacuum gauge occurs when facing a headwind. During several hours of a headwind, a great deal of fuel can be used if the driver attempts to maintain usual speed. The best way to handle a headwind, with minimum fuel economy loss, is to hold vacuum at 7 inches and let speed fall where it may, if your driving schedule affords the time.

When driving in high altitude, it's not always possible to keep vacuum readings above 7 inches, because speed may drop too rapidly. Altitude robs horsepower at the rate of about 4 percent per thousand feet of rise. However, the carburetor doesn't know the difference and still begins to enrich fuel mixtures at about 7 inches. So the rules still apply, although vacuum readings at really high altitudes (8000 feet and up) with heavy loads may never get above 7 inches except at idle or when going downhill.

Diagnosing Problems

A vacuum gauge, used consistently, will diagnose engine problems and deficiencies. The driver will become accustomed to seeing certain readings under specific driving and load conditions. When the readings drop suddenly, a leaking vacuum line, faulty spark plug or other such malfunction may be the cause. A leaky valve may create a pulsating reading on the gauge.

A vacuum gauge also can help diagnose the causes of engine detonation or pre-ignition (ping). If ping only occurs at about 8 inches or above, the cause usually is too much vacuum spark advance (see the chapter on carburetor/distributor tuning). To confirm this, the vacuum spark advance line may be temporarily disconnected and plugged. This should stop the ping problem. However, the line should be reconnected, as proper vacuum advance is needed for best possible fuel economy. Correction should be made.

If vacuum readings drop when cruise control is engaged (same speeds), an internal leak in the cruise control is indicated and this will result in premature enrichment of air/fuel ratios and reduction in mileage.

Distributor and Carburetor

4

How any engine operates—even a new one with computerization—is determined by ignition and carburetion systems. That is, by the systems which control how and when the spark plugs are fired, and how and when the fuel is mixed with air and fed into the engine.

It's not possible for the layman to do much with computerized systems, which require expensive diagnostic machinery for identification of malfunctions. But earlier systems are not difficult to modify and correct. And many of them need a lot of correction.

We're including in "earlier systems" all those without computer controls. Most engines made since 1976 have electronic ignition systems, but they do not prevent modification and correction. Most of these systems are a definite improvement over points and condenser systems, although they may be unreliable at times. Not until 1979 did some passenger cars get computerized systems (except Chrysler Lean Burn). Trucks didn't get them until the 1981 and 1982 models—and not all trucks were so equipped.

These computerized systems alter spark and fuel mixture characteristics in response to information fed to a computer from probes at various points on the engine. *Theoretically*, they match spark and fuel mixtures more precisely to operating conditions—when they're working correctly. When they're not, problems are possible because, in too many cases, dealership personnel don't know how to troubleshoot and repair the systems adequately.

This situation surely will improve.

The distributor turns at half engine speed; the rotor tip transmits high voltage to the spark plug cables.

But in the meantime RV owners with the older conventional systems are less likely to have problems for which they can not find adequate help. One system we must exempt from this is Chrysler's Lean Burn system, used in a variety of models from 1975. It was a poorly designed system with very little flexibility that most mechanics do not know how to modify for proper operation. It tends to cause severe engine ping under medium to light throttle.

The Distributor

The distributor of any engine is just what the word implies—it distributes the spark to all cylinders at appropriate times. The distributor does this with a rotating pointer (rotor) that circles inside a cap, to which eight spark plug cables (V-8 engine) are attached. As the rotor circles, it sends an electrical charge of 30,000 to 50,000 volts to each spark plug. A set of breaker points (pre-1976) or a magnetic triggering system (post-1976 electronic ignition) times the charge just at the milli-second when the rotor is directly in front of one of the eight terminals inside the distributor cap.

In addition to this, two systems determine just how far in advance of the piston's top of stroke (TDC) the electrical charge should be delivered. As piston speed increases, the spark plug must be fired farther in advance, or the fuel burn will occur well after the piston is into its downward stroke. This so-called *spark advance* is critical to the power an engine produces and how much fuel it uses.

The two systems that control spark advance are: mechanical advance (also called centrifugal advance) and vacuum advance. Here's how they work.

To improve power and mileage, engines are fitted with an automatic system to match spark advance to engine rpm. At slow speeds (left), weights in this system are at rest. As rpm increases, centrifugal force causes them to spread, thereby advancing the spark. How fast the weights spread is determined by their mass and by the tension of the retaining springs. Any change in springs or weights will alter the spark advance curve.

The mechanical advance system must automatically change the amount of spark advance in direct proportion to engine speed. If advance were static, the engine still would run, but not nearly as well. Small engines on lawn mowers and other such implements do not have automatic spark advance systems. They could benefit from such systems, but cost precludes their use.

The automatic mechanical advance system in a distributor operates like a small centrifuge. As the distributor spins faster, weights move outward against spring tension and change the position of devices which determine when the spark plug charge should be delivered. This change in position due to the automatic system can be as much as 30 degrees of crankshaft rotation. In late-model engines, it's usually around 20 degrees.

An engine can use even more spark advance under light throttle than under heavy throttle. Thus, vacuum

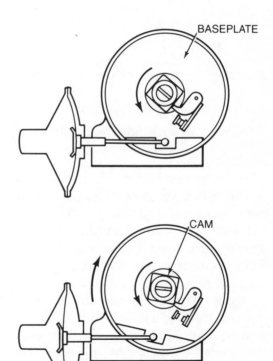

Under light throttle, a vacuum diaphragm advances the spark. Diaphragm action begins around 8 inches vacuum and ends around 12.

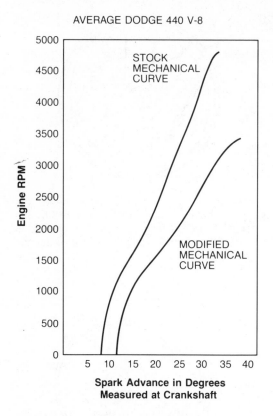

AVERAGE DODGE 440 V-8

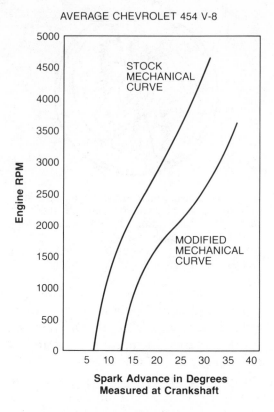

AVERAGE CHEVROLET 454 V-8

These spark advance curves indicate how spark advance changes in response to engine rpm.

advance comes into play. The vacuum advance is a vacuum diaphragm connected to a metal rod, attached to those same devices that determine when the spark plug charge is delivered. At manifold vacuum readings of about 7 to 8 inches, the vacuum diaphragm begins to move. As the throttle closes, more vacuum is applied to the diaphragm and vacuum spark advance increases. The basis for this is that an engine will tolerate more spark advance at light throttle than at heavy throttle, without pinging. For this reason, RV owners who have installed special perfor-

mance-type distributors which do not have vacuum advance units have limited fuel economy potential. The sole purpose of a vacuum spark advance unit is fuel economy under medium-to-light-throttle conditions.

Static Spark Advance

Those two described above are the *variable* spark advance systems. The *static* spark advance factor is initial spark timing. That's the one most owners and most mechanics deal with. When you

Initial spark timing, checked with a timing light, is one of three sources of spark advance. The timing light can also be used to check automatic and vacuum advance.

is about 2400. Initial spark advance is set at 10 degrees BTDC (Before Top Dead Center). That miniature centrifuge in your distributor is spinning at a sufficient speed to have advanced the timing another 15 degrees, for a total of 25 degrees. That's usually referred to as *total* advance. Vacuum advance usually is figured separately. Since cruise conditions at light throttle produce high manifold vacuum readings, the vacuum advance unit is subject to about 14 inches vacuum, which was sufficient to raise the spark timing another 15 degrees. Vacuum advance units vary in calibration so they may be capable of a minimum of about 10 degrees, or a maximum of 20 or more. The vacuum source used to operate the vacuum advance diaphragm usually is a *metered* vacuum source. The term *metered* refers to the fact that it is created by the velocity of air passing through the carburetor venturi. Thus, its characteristics are slightly different from straight manifold vacuum. For example, with metered vacuum source there is no vacuum at idle.

take your vehicle to a garage and they "set the spark," they're setting the initial spark timing. Rarely do they even check the automatic mechanical or vacuum advance systems to see if they're working. (We describe how to do that here.) Unfortunately, these systems do become rusted or gummed up, and when they're inoperative, performance as well as mileage suffer greatly.

Let's look at an example of how much spark advance your engine might be using, under differing conditions.

Example 1: You're cruising, lightly loaded (no trailer or other RV) at 55 mph on fairly flat terrain. Engine rpm

Example 2: Your trailer is hitched, or you're driving a motorhome instead of a lightly loaded tow vehicle. You're still cruising at 2400 rpm (55 mph), but your foot is much heavier on the throttle due to the additional load. What changes? Initial advance? No, that's fixed. Mechanical advance? No, it responds only to engine rpm—not to your load. Vacuum advance does change. As throttle pressure becomes heavier, vacuum drops and the vacuum spark advance unit backs off. Rather than 15 degrees vacuum advance, you may now have 5 degrees, or less. Most vacuum advance units are programmed to begin affecting spark timing at about 8 inches vacuum.

Example 3: The situation is the same as in the previous example (high weight) but now you're climbing a hill in second gear. Engine rpm is 3300 and you're using about two-thirds throttle. Has initial advance changed? No. But mechanical advance has changed. You're now getting about 20 degrees of mechanical advance. Due to heavy throttle pressure, you're getting no vacuum advance.

Numbers quoted here are merely examples, because the amount of spark advance created by the two changeable systems (mechanical and vacuum advance) varies widely. In the early 1970s and before, it was not uncommon for mechanical advance capability to be as high as 28 degrees. Vacuum advance could be as high as 20 degrees. However, in the past few years fuel quality has dropped substantially and motor companies have had to reduce the spark advance capability in an attempt to keep engines from pinging. Unfortunately, they have not been too successful. Many new vehicles ping severely on fuels identified as suitable (by octane number), and the owner seems to have no choice but to reduce initial spark timing to reduce or eliminate the problem. This reduces performance and fuel economy and increases the tendency of the engine to overheat. However, there is a solution: an effective water injec-

tion system is designed to reduce an engine's fuel octane requirements, allowing retention of stock spark advance settings. Or, in a case where the engine does not ping when set at stock timing, addition of a water injector will permit use of more aggressive spark advance. Performance is substantially improved in most cases. Mileage often improves slightly, or remains about the same.

Advantages of Proper Calibration

As you can see, improper design of either the mechanical or vacuum spark advance systems can cause problems. If the mechanical system advances the spark too fast, ping may occur in medium to heavy-throttle operation, unless initial advance is reduced. If the mechanical system is too slow, power and fuel economy suffer. If the vacuum advance system is too fast, ping may occur at light throttle (above 10 inches manifold vacuum). This is very common with the Chrysler Lean Burn systems because they have too much vacuum advance. If vacuum advance is too slow by design (rare), fuel economy will suffer. It is fairly common for diaphragms inside vacuum advance units on vehicles at least three or four years old to rupture. Thus the vacuum advance unit is inoperative, possibly for several years if the mechanic does not cover all the bases and check all systems.

How to Check
Spark Advance Systems

If you have a timing light, checking the automatic and vacuum spark advance systems is easy. The vacuum system can be checked even without a light.

Mechanical Advance. Connect the timing light. Temporarily disconnect the vacuum line to the vacuum advance unit and temporarily plug the vacuum port. While watching the timing marks on the engine vibration damper, increase engine speed slowly. As rpm increases, you should see the timing mark begin to move up the scale. That tells you the automatic mechanical advance system is working. If you know the specifications for your particular engine (the manufacturer's service manual includes them), you can check to see if your distributor meets the specifications.

To check for proper mechanical advance, set initial timing temporarily to zero. This serves no purpose other than to allow use of the full length of the engine's timing scale on the pulley. Have an assistant increase engine rpm to desired levels mentioned in your specifications while you check the timing. If your shop manual calls for 7 degrees advance at 1500 rpm, you should see 7 degrees on the scale.

Important: when reading specs, make sure they apply to timing read at the *crankshaft* timing marks. The distributor turns at half-crankshaft speed. Consequently, if your specs indicate seven degrees at 1500 rpm reading at the crankshaft, that translates to 3.5 degrees if the distributor were out of the engine, being tested on a distributor tuning machine.

Vacuum advance. With your vacuum advance line still disconnected for the previous step, and initial spark advance still set at zero (solely for the purpose of using the degree scale), idle the engine while you disconnect and reconnect the vacuum advance line to a *source of manifold vacuum.* That's a vacuum source with *suction at idle.* The line to which your vacuum advance normally is connected *may not* have suction at idle. Regardless, make sure you properly mark the normal vacuum connection so you can go back to normal when these procedures are all completed.

When the vacuum advance line is disconnected, your timing should be where you set it: zero degrees. When you connect it to manifold vacuum, timing should jump to the full potential of your vacuum advance unit. That will be at least 10 degrees. Most timing scales are only 10 to 16 degrees in length, so the timing mark may jump well ahead of your scale. If so, you at least know the vacuum advance is working properly. If you have a ping problem at light throttle, the tuning kits described elsewhere in this book include information on replacement vacuum advance units or modification of existing units, to solve the problem.

Reset initial timing to the desired setting, and reconnect the vacuum advance line to the original vacuum source.

It is *very* common for many distributors, particularly General Motors High Energy Ignition (HEI) systems, to rust and cease to advance the spark properly. This can happen in as little as 10,000 miles, but more often it happens about every 20,000 miles. It's important to make these mechanical advance and vacuum advance checkups about every 10,000 miles.

Electrical Connections

Electronic ignition systems utilize computerized modules and other components which are subject to failure, but more often the problem may be in an electrical plug. Corrosion between the connectors inside the plug may create electrical resistance and the engine may run erratically or fail to start. Unplug all connectors, clean them and rough up the connector surfaces with emery paper. Apply silicone dialectric compound, available at most dealership parts counters, and reassemble. The silicone improves electrical conductivity, and keeps oxygen from getting to the surfaces. Without oxygen, corrosion will not occur. Repeat this about every 10,000 miles. If this is done, one common cause of engine unreliability will be eliminated.

Ignition Troubleshooting

Until introduction of computer-controlled systems, troubleshooting even the electronic ignition units was fairly

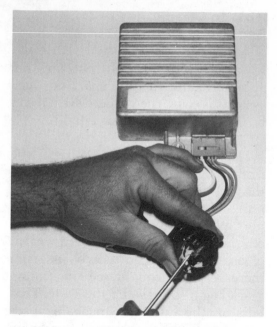

A primary cause of electronic ignition components failure is electrical resistance in connectors. The contacts should be cleaned, roughed with emery paper and coated with silicone dialectric compound.

simple and did not require special, expensive test meters. The General Motors HEI system is simple to diagnose, as are Ford and Dodge and American Motors electronic ignition systems. To do so, buy a service manual from your dealer. The information is too voluminous to be included here, although we'll cover faults that are not brought out in the manuals.

The common fault of the General Motors HEI system is use of excessively large spark plug gaps, which create very high voltage buildup in the system. Any time you increase spark plug gap, voltage in the spark plug cable and in the

Excessively large spark plug gaps cause very high voltage levels in the General Motors Energy Ignition system; the voltage can go to ground on the distributor shaft by burning through the rotor.

Spark plug gaps should not be larger than .042-inch, even for electronic ignition systems.

distributor cap must build up to higher levels to bridge (ionize) the gap. In the case of the GM system, spark plug gaps of .060 were recommended until GM recognized the problems and reduced gap recommendations. With such a large gap, voltage may have to build to 50,000 volts to ionize it, whereas with a .042-inch gap, (.032-inch for Chrysler products), voltage must build only to about 30,000 volts.

The higher voltage would be fine, *if* the GM system could contain it. It cannot. The voltage wants to "leak" anywhere it can, and it manages to wander around inside the distributor cap, eating through the distributor rotor at certain points. After a couple of years, voltage is prone to leak from spark plug cables and boots. The voltage may go

to ground, causing the engine to miss, or it may cross to another cable, causing erratic operation and backfiring.

The solution is to use .042-inch spark plug gaps, and replace the distributor rotor about every two years or 20,000 miles.

In all electronic ignition systems, wiring connections cause many of the problems. With age, corrosion forms between a connector and a terminal and retards the flow of current. The corrosion may be so slight as to be invisible to the naked eye. Periodically, connectors should be removed and all contact surfaces should be cleaned, roughed with emery cloth, coated with silicone dialectric compound and reassembled.

When a problem occurs with a Ford electronic ignition system (other than connector problems), it's often a faulty amplifier module. When a problem occurs with a Chrysler product, often it's the ballast resistor. By carrying spares, you can avoid costly delay on the road when parts aren't available. Shop manuals for the various vehicle brands include specific and easy-to-understand procedures for troubleshooting electronic ignition systems; often the tools required are merely hand tools plus a volt-ohm-milliameter.

Carburetion

How a carburetor works may seem very elusive to some RV owners. In fact, the concepts are rather simple and by understanding how the carburetor responds to engine demands, you'll be much more able to diagnose your own problems—at least where conventional carburetors are concerned. The new computer-controlled units require special diagnostic equipment.

Conventional, non-computer-controlled carburetors are still used on most trucks and vans, and their design is similar to what has been in use for the past 20 years or more. Models vary in how fuel reservoirs (float bowls) are arranged and they vary in design from single-venturi (1-barrel) to 4-venturi configuration. Most RV engines are (or should be) equipped with carburetors of at least 2-venturi size, unless the engines are straight-6 cylinder design. Regardless of the number of venturi, the carburetor functions the same. Here's how it works.

The key to operation of the carburetor is the action of a venturi and the velocity of air passing through it. For proper combustion to occur, fuel must mix with air in proportions varying from 14.5 to 12.2 parts air to one part fuel. The leaner mixtures occur at light throttle, and the richer mixtures at heavy throttle.

A 2-barrel carburetor has two different metering systems to change the air/fuel ratios according to engine load, and the 4-barrel carburetor has three different systems.

But first, how does the fuel get out of the carburetor, mixed with air and into the engine? What follows is greatly oversimplified, but will aid your understanding of the engine tuning concepts described in this book.

If you look down into the venturi of a carburetor, you'll see a metal protrusion located roughly in the center of the bore. This is the fuel distribution nozzle. Holes are located in its underside, connected to passages which lead to the fuel bowl. As air flows rapidly past the nozzle, a low-pressure or suction action is created in the area where fuel flow holes are located. The air sucks the fuel out of the nozzle. The amount of fuel is determined by the amount of airflow and by size of passageways leading to the fuel bowl. In the passageways are metering jets in some cases, and a combination of metering rods and jets in other cases. Still others have vacuum-operated valves which open and close. Also, there is the circuit which meters fuel to the engine at idle. But in recalibrating a carburetor, changes are rarely needed in that circuit—only simple external adjustments.

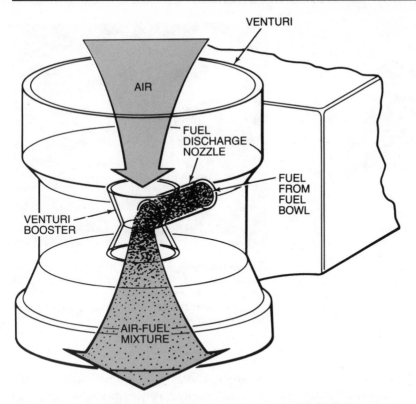

The increased velocity of air passing through the restricted portion of the venturi creates a low pressure area, siphoning off the fuel from the discharge nozzle.

Under cruise conditions with a 2-barrel carburetor, airflow past the nozzle usually draws fuel from the nozzle in a proportion of about 14 parts air to one part fuel. This proportion remains about the same as throttle opening increases. Airflow increases, but so does fuel flow, on a roughly proportional basis. All the while, the primary metering jets are controlling fuel flow.

At medium throttle (more precisely, at 6.5 to 7 inches manifold vacuum) the carburetor's power enrichment system begins to affect air/fuel ratios. Depending on carburetor design, it may occur when a vacuum-operated valve opens and allows the fuel distribution nozzle to draw fuel from a new source in addition to the aforementioned primary metering jets. Or, in many carburetors using metering rods, all the fuel flows through the primary metering jets, but at 6.5 inches a pair of tapered metering rods positioned in the jets begin to lift, allowing more flow. As the rods lift higher, more fuel is passed because the rod is tapered. Position of the rods is controlled by a small vacuum-operated piston to which they're attached. A spring pushes up on the piston (at-

Fuel enrichment is created in different ways in various carburetors. A power valve is used in Holley and in certain Motorcraft 2-barrel carburetors. Four-barrel carburetors, except Holley, use metering rods.

tempting to lift the rods) while manifold vacuum pulls down. The balance between the two permits the rods to begin lifting at about 6.5 inches manifold vacuum.

The value of a manifold vacuum gauge is easy to see. When the primary enrichment system goes fully into action, fuel mixtures are enriched about 26 percent. Obviously, it behooves us to know when that happens.

The 4-Barrel Carburetor

We've just described the way a 2-barrel carburetor works, with two metering systems. A 4-barrel carburetor has yet another system, for the secondary venturi. In a 2-barrel, mixtures in the enrichment circuit must be rather rich,

because that's the circuit which handles all power requirements from 6.5 inches manifold vacuum down through full throttle. In a 4-barrel, the secondary power system handles heavy and full throttle, so the primary power system needn't be so rich. The result is more precise fuel flow for varying conditions.

One confusing aspect of a 4-barrel carburetor is when the secondary venturi open. Many drivers believe full throttle automatically opens the secondaries. Not true. Secondary venturi in all 4-barrel carburetors used on RVs are controlled by engine demand. When engine rpm rises sufficiently to require more air and fuel than the primary venturi can provide, a secondary air valve opens and the secondaries go into action. Secondaries usually do not open

In a decision between 2-barrel and 4-barrel carburetors, cost must be balanced against improved performance under heavy throttle.

below about 2500 rpm (3000 rpm with some carburetors) regardless of throttle position, and they do not open unless more than about three-fourths throttle is used, regardless of engine rpm. Again, this varies with carburetors and engines, but you get the idea.

On many engines it's difficult to tell when the secondaries open. On others, the engine makes a definite howling sound, which is more audible with an open (360-degree air intake) air cleaner than with stock air cleaners. Air cleaner restriction has a substantial effect on heavy-throttle performance; information is included later on how to correct the restriction. If you're looking for evidence of when the secondaries open, one way to gauge it is to temporarily wire the secondary air valve linkage immobile (make sure the throttle move-

Most 4-barrel carburetors have vacuum-operated secondary venturi. That is, the secondaries don't open automatically with full throttle. Engine demand determines when the secondaries open; it's usually under heavy or full throttle at more than 2500 rpm. The secondary air valve of the Quadrajet carburetor shown here is spring loaded.

ment is not restricted) and check the difference in performance under full throttle.

Over the years, a 4-barrel carburetor has gained the reputation of a gas hog. In fact, it's a more efficient design (if calibrated properly) than is a 2-barrel. The 4-barrel indeed will use more fuel at heavy or full throttle. But it delivers more power. It will use less fuel in the mid-throttle range. The RV owner who uses the 4-barrel carburetor properly (driving with a vacuum gauge, using heavy throttle only when needed) will have an engine that is more responsive and a vehicle that is more fun to drive.

Conversion from 2-barrel to 4-barrel carburetion is possible with most V-8 engines, although increases in prices of the carburetors and in manifolds have made the change less cost-effective in recent years. Specific 4-barrel conversions are covered in later chapters on specific engines. Suffice it to say here that a 4-barrel carburetor must be calibrated properly for the engine in question, and it must be of the proper cfm size (cubic feet per minute air flow volume), or money is wasted and engine efficiency is reduced.

Carburetion Troubleshooting

Many RV owners wish their engines could talk, to tell them what is wrong. In fact, they do. You just have to understand the language. One of the best interpretive aids is a vacuum gauge.

This is not to say you can accurately diagnose all carburetor problems while driving, simply by looking at a vacuum gauge. But you can detect several very common ones.

A very common problem with many carburetors is excessively lean fuel mixtures in the cruise range. You might recall our previous discussion; the cruise mixtures are controlled by metering jets. The cruise range extends from light to medium throttle, down to 6.5 inches of manifold vacuum where the carburetor transitions to the primary power enrichment system.

Engines that are too lean often lag, stumble, backfire and generally run poorly when medium throttle is applied. To determine if this is caused merely by excessively lean primary jets, accelerate from a stop, gradually increasing throttle until the vacuum reading drops to 7 inches. Don't go to 6.5 or the power system may begin to open. If the engine runs well (although fairly flat) above about 9 inches of vacuum, but surges at light throttle, lags, stumbles and possibly backfires as you approach 7 inches, fuel mixtures in the cruise range are too lean. The specific tuning kit for your engine, described in later chapters, will solve the problem. If one is not available, the problem may be solved merely by drilling the primary jets slightly larger (usually .002-inch). Unfortunately, this may create fuel mixtures that are a bit too rich in the other operational ranges.

A given carburetor may have an excessively lean cruise system and a very rich power system. It's common for Detroit to run lean cruise mixtures and then dump in a bunch of fuel to cool things down when the power system comes in. By drilling main jets larger, the cruise problem is corrected, but the already rich power system mixtures will be made even more rich. Using tuning kits, each metering system is corrected individually. If the cruise system is lean, it's opened up a bit, while a rich power system would be leaned down. Calibrations for this kind of tuning are not possible on the street, but the common problem of part-throttle lag due to lean cruise ratios can be easily detected.

If a sudden change occurs in engine performance, and fuel economy drops, there is the possibility that the power valve or primary metering rods are not operating properly. One or the other of these devices is responsible for additional fuel flow when manifold vacuum drops below 6.5 inches. If the valve leaks, the engine will operate on rich mixtures during cruise conditions. If a pair of metering rods sticks in the up position, again the mixtures will be too rich for cruise conditions. If the rods stick in the down position (not common), no enrichment will occur under medium to heavy throttle and the engine will lag and possibly backfire.

If the power enrichment system is working properly, the cruise fuel mixtures will be overly rich in very few cases. However, the natural inclination of many RV owners is to assume they can reduce jet sizes and automatically improve fuel economy. It often produces opposite results; the engine runs poorly and is prone to ping. Lean mixtures will create more combustion chamber heat.

Any time jet changes are made, jet sizes must be precise. Jets are difficult to buy from motor company dealers, but changes can be made if the owner has an accurate set of drill bits or reamers, and a micrometer. Again, it's better and easier to go with a tuning kit backed by extended dyno testing.

When evaluating engine performance, always make sure the choke is fully open. In some cases a choke may stick and enrich fuel mixtures.

Fuel Level

Most late-model carburetors equipped with plastic fuel bowl floats may cause hard starting in hot weather. The problem is partial saturation of the float with fuel, which raises fuel level enough that the fuel percolates into the engine when the key is turned off. The engine is flooded and becomes difficult to start. The solution is replacement of plastic fuel floats about every two years, and calibration of fuel level 1/32-inch below the factory recommendation.

Any of a number of problems can prompt a mechanic to recommend a carburetor "boil-out" when the solution to the problem is not obvious. In most cases, a carburetor does not accumulate gum and varnish until at least 50,000 miles have passed, unless the vehicle is operated in particularly dirty conditions or is regularly subjected to several months of storage. Fuel evaporates and leaves residue which can partially block small orifices and metering passages. Water in fuel also can cause problems by blocking orifices. Addition of methanol to the fuel about once a year, or when the vehicle is taken out of storage, gets rid of the water by mixing it with the fuel and allowing it to be burned without collecting in the carburetor.

Hard Starting

Some carburetors have leakage problems which create hard starting after they have been parked overnight. In such cases, the fuel bowl drains dry overnight and the engine must be cranked until the fuel pump can fill the bowl. So much cold cranking is hard on the engine.

To determine if this is a problem, let the vehicle sit overnight, or for several days (the amount of time which normally produces the hard starting problem). Remove the air cleaner and, using a flashlight, look down the primary venturi of the carburetor. Crank the throttle once or twice. You should see strong streams of gasoline from small nozzles in the venturi. Crank the throttle three or four times and the streams of gasoline should be equal in volume. If little gasoline flows from the nozzles, the fuel bowl may be empty.

Evaporation of fuel does occur after a vehicle sits for more than a week. In addition, volatility of the fuel left in the carburetor is reduced, so more cranking usually is necessary. But the GM Quadrajet carburetor is prone to leak from soft plugs in the bottom of the bowl. Recesses into which these plugs fit can be cleaned and filled with epoxy glue to stop the leakage. The plastic fuel bowl of the Carter ThermoQuad used on many Chrysler Corporation vehicles may have cracks in the bottom of the bowl, near the main metering jets. The cracks may be filled with epoxy. Most other carburetors are not prone to leak. But when leakage is suspected, disassemble the carburetor, fill the bowl with paint thinner or solvent and visually inspect for leaks.

Hard starting also can be caused by a faulty accelerator pump. The procedure mentioned in the previous paragraph can be used to check effectiveness of the accelerator pump, which primes the engine with gasoline prior to starting. Each stroke of the throttle creates a stroke of the accelerator pump. Usually, only a couple of throttle strokes are needed to prime the engine for a cold start, but this will vary with the engine, the choke setting and temperature. The initial throttle movement sets the choke to maximum position, which enriches fuel mixtures and aids starting. Pumping the accelerator pedal excessively can flood the engine, especially if the choke is set to a rich position. When the engine is flooded, letting it sit for a few minutes allows excess fuel to partially vaporize from the spark plugs and the engine often will start. When a flooded condition occurs, it's helpful to prop the choke valve open. A clothespin is handy for this. Whatever is used should be large enough that it can not fall through the carburetor.

Effect of Altitude

RV owners are particularly concerned about the effect of altitude on carburetion. Indeed, fuel mixtures become rich in high altitude, and fuel is wasted. The reason mixtures become rich is that atmospheric pressure is reduced—less air is available for mixing with the fuel.

Ideally, fuel flow should compensate for this. And it does, on some of the late-model computer-controlled vehicles with fuel injection systems or altitude-compensating carburetors. However, those systems in many cases leave something to be desired in performance with heavy RVs, so the conventional carburetor may not be as bad a choice as it seems.

It's usually not practical to change carburetor jets everytime we go from low altitude to high altitude, and back down. But at least we can eliminate one problem which worsens the altitude-enrichment of fuel mixtures. A restrictive air cleaner causes even more enrichment. Changing the air cleaner to a non-restrictive arrangement (either a 360-degree air cleaner, or modification of the existing air cleaner for more air

Many air cleaners are restrictive. Here, a spacer has been used under the air filter to create 360-degree air intake around the lid of cleaner.

flow) will assure best possible air flow and minimum enrichment of fuel mixtures.

That, combined with use of aggressive spark advance, assures best possible performance in high altitudes. While it is possible to change carburetor jets for high-altitude running, it isn't practical for short duration. If the vehicle will be used in high altitude for several months, or has been moved there permanently, primary jets can be reduced .002-inch in size for each 4000 feet altitude difference.

How to Avoid the Cost

A New Tow Vehicle

5

Remember a few short years ago when a new, fully equipped car or pickup truck suitable for trailer-towing or hauling a camper would cost $3500 to $5000? Today, that's just a down payment.

For $12,000 to $18,000 you get a limited selection of axle ratios and engines which produce performance that is, at best, marginal. Mileage often is high while not towing, but it rarely is higher while towing.

Although there appears to be no way around the high cost of gasoline, there is a way around the high cost of the vehicle. Would you believe, for one-half to one-fourth the price of a new truck or car you can have a fine tow vehicle or camper hauler with increased performance, good dependability and reduced operational costs? No waving of

a magic wand is necessary. It's possible through the proper selection and modification of a used vehicle—one that has been the property of a proud owner for several years—an owner who, not realizing the potential of upgrading Old Faithful, has traded her in.

The thought of spending over half the original purchase price on modifications and reconditioning a vehicle you have had around for several years may be hard to accept. But it is cost-effective. How many times have you heard the not-so-proud owner of a new vehicle say, "I wish I had my old one back! It out-performed this new one and got better mileage."

Passenger car suspensions and axle assemblies usually are not as well suited to towing, but passenger cars can be used if trailer weight is not too high.

You'll find some of the best bargains in passenger cars—specifically in the luxury cars of the late 1960s and early-to mid-1970s. These cars are not economical during solo driving, compared to the new models. But hitching a trailer to one of the new fuel-efficient cars has a way of bringing the mileage down to just about what you'd get with an older luxury car. And with that older car you get much better performance due to the larger engines used in those years. The purchase price of a mid-1970s luxury car may be low enough that you can justify using it for nothing but towing. You can use a newer, small economy car for round-town duties.

Pickup trucks, vans and the Suburbans have held their value somewhat better but they still are bargains compared to new models. In addition, some of those new models are more limited in performance due to use of catalytic convertors in their exhaust systems, and many require lead-free gasoline which is more costly than regular.

The selection of brands described here is not all-inclusive because of the availability of aftermarket accessories, parts, and the response of the vehicles to the modifications.

Determine Priorities

When considering a used vehicle, first determine your basic priorities and requirements. Buying a vehicle to tow a 20-footer and later going to a 30-footer doesn't make much sense. Some people are well-organized and can comfortably exist in small quarters. Others require more room and find restricted areas impossible to accept. You should, of course, be comfortable, but it isn't advisable or cost-effective to pull around a 30-foot unit if it is not functional for your requirements.

If possible, choose a vehicle that does not have a catalytic convertor on the exhaust system, unless the RV weight situation is minimal. Ideally the vehicle should have dual exhausts. A single exhaust system with catalytic convertor creates more heat retention in the combustion chambers than is ideal. Convertor-equipped cars and trucks can be used, but they are not often as desirable as vehicles without convertors.

In GM vehicles for applications under 10,000 pounds with campers or motorhomes, or up to 5000 pounds trailer weight, the 350 and 400 small-block Chevrolet or GMC engines are good choices. The 350 is preferred over the 400 due to the ability of the 350 to respond to extensive modifications. Both have the same size rod and main bearings, which is a slight disadvantage to the 400 when looking for 100,000-mile life expectancy. The Turbo Hydramatic 400 transmission is stronger and is adaptable to the 350. The 350 transmission, when equipped with adequate cooler and serviced properly, will handle the job very well.

The 350 engines respond very well to most modifications, especially to use of special pistons that increase compression to 9.2 to 1. That compression in most cases is not compatible with today's regular leaded fuel. However proper use of water injection is recommended.

Retaining the original heads, and *not* replacing them with high-performance heads usually fitted in 350 modifications, is important. That's because the increased valve size destroys low-speed torque which the modifications described here are designed to obtain. We are not attempting to build a race car. Dual exhausts and a restricted-flow header system will work very well. The exhaust must be 2 or 2¼ inches in diameter on all 350 modifications.

Full floating Teflon valve seals should be used in conjunction with the stock valve seals to control excessive oil travel through valve guides. A high-volume oil pump should be used. The 350 cylinder head castings are generally rough at the point where the combustion chamber meets the head surface and coarse emery paper should be used to remove any sharp edges which might retain heat and cause preignition. Special attention should also be paid to the exhaust valves. If the valve heads become less than approximately .050-inch from regrinding, they should be replaced to prevent premature valve jobs.

On the later 350 engines the standard Quadrajet carburetor with proper modifications work as well as any. Correcting the distributor advance curve, and selecting the proper spark plug heat range completes this engine modification, producing performance equal to the later standard larger engines and excelling at altitude.

For heavier loads, the 454 Chevrolet/GMC engine is suitable. Criticism has been leveled at its excessive oil usage and valve lifter and valve train problems of the 1970s. However, these are easily corrected; after modifications the engine is strong and dependable.

The 454 engine responds exceptionally well, with increases in actual rear wheel horsepower in excess of 50 percent being possible with a compression increase to 9 to 1. A special set of pistons is used for this application, and a correction of deck height (distance from top of piston to top of block) is required. The 454 cylinder block varies greatly from crankshaft center to head surface from side to side and this must be corrected to attain the same compression on all cylinders. After boring cylinders to correct piston size, the crankshaft is temporarily placed in the block and number one and six piston assemblies are installed. The engine is rotated to absolute top dead center. This places both pistons at the top of the block for surface measurements. The deck height is checked and the amount of material to be removed from the block surface is determined. Deck height of .012-inch is ideal and with the stock cylinder heads will provide the required compression ratio. It is not uncommon to find as much as .020-inch variance between sides. The maximum material to remove is .040 from either side even if it would be necessary to violate the .012-inch requirement or misalignment of the manifold will result.

The valve lifter oil galley plugs located in the front of the block in the timing cover cavity must be removed and modified. A .032-inch hole should be drilled through each of the plugs to release the trapped air from oil galleys and eliminate erratic lifter operation and noise. The larger-body heavy-duty oil pump should be used. It's standard on the early high performance engines. Use only the original General Motors rear main seals, as many of the after-market seals do not supply adequate tension to eliminate seepage; that results in premature failure.

The Cloyse double-row timing chain and sprocket should be used, as 454 timing chains tend to stretch early, retarding camshaft timing and affecting low-speed torque. A combination of special full floating Teflon valve guide seals and the viton GMC special exhaust valve seals must be used on all valves to reduce the excess oil flow through the valve guides. Reference to proper valve grinding procedures should be taken. The stock intake manifold and carburetor are sufficient. Dual exhausts are a prerequisite. Headers are optional. A restricted header with a 2¼-inch collector cone and 2½-inch-diameter exhaust system is best. Headers should be used on the 454 only when the compression is increased. Headers will add to the mid-range torque and increase valve life by reducing operational temperatures under sustained load conditions. There will be no effect on mileage.

To achieve the full benefit of the wide operational torque curve of the 454 and other engines, final tuning procedures are most important. Precise control of fuel mixture throughout the entire operational range, proper timing control matching the various load conditions and correct spark plug head range selection will produce maximum results.

Ford Choices

The most impressive modification deals with the 360 and 390 Ford engines. This combination produces results which fall right between the 350 and 454 conversions.

Rear wheel power is more than doubled, mileage is increased and engine life extended. The 360 is fitted with a standard 390 crankshaft and rods. Both the 360 and 390 are fitted with special pistons, increasing compression to 9 to 1. A reground camshaft, special 4-barrel intake manifold and modified 600 cfm Holley carburetor are used. Headers and dual exhausts with 2-inch diameter pipes are a prerequisite. Teflon valve seals and a reworked distributor are included.

The result is the most impressive overall package available, that will outperform any new unit on the market. This combination never requires lower axle gearing than 3.70 to 1, and delivers impressive mileage. Experience shows a life expectancy exceeding 100,000 miles with normal maintenance procedures.

All the engines mentioned previously have been available in cars as well as pickup trucks in the late 1960s and early 1970s, up through current models for the Chevy 350 and 454. Ford discontinued the 360 and 390 in favor of the 351 and 400 engines, apparently for emission reasons; these engines generally aren't any more efficient than the 360 and 390 in stock conditions, and they do not respond to modification as well as the 360 and 390.

When looking at specifications for the late 1960 engines and those of the early 1970s, you'll see quite a difference in horsepower and torque ratings. There were real differences, but not as dramatic as the figures indicate.

Changes in Test Methods

In 1970, compression ratios of many engines were lowered due to the advent of low-lead gasoline and tighter emission rules. A few 1970 engines retained their high compression ratios. All the high compression ratios were gone by the 1971 model year. During the changeover period horsepower did drop. But the methods by which horsepower and torque were rated changed also. So, the figures show more horsepower loss than actually occurred. What did occur was substantial enough.

Throughout the '60s the factories had claimed horsepower and torque based on tests of blueprinted engines running on test stands and not saddled with accessories. When the change was made, only stock engines with no special preparation were tested, and all the normal accessories were used. The figures were more realistic.

When choosing a passenger vehicle, you might look at models dating up to 1975 because that's when catalytic convertors appeared. Also, very high axle ratios in the area of 2.50 to 1 began to appear then. Prior to that, most stock axle ratios in full-size passenger cars were 2.75 to 1 or 3 to 1. We used to consider that fairly high, but stock axles in many cases now are as high as 2.21 to 1 and they are quite unsuitable for trailer towing.

With almost any of the pre-1975 cars, a stock 2.75 to 1 gearset can be changed to something in the 3.23/3.31 range, for good performance with a fairly heavy trailer.

A few comments on certain passenger car engines: In 1968 to '70, Cadillac had very short cam timing plus 10 to 1 compression. These cars would not be good choices for towing on today's fuel. Also, parts are increasingly difficult to obtain.

In 1971 the Cadillac 500-cubic-inch engine had 8.25 to 1 compression making these cars excellent tow vehicles. The 472-cubic-inch engine also was available throughout those years. But the 472 had a tendency to overheat and pistons tended to lose shape and break.

In Chevrolet, the 1969 to 1970 350-cubic-inch 300hp engine was possibly the best small-block engine ever made. It was rated at 10.25 to 1 compression but actually was about 9.8 to 1. Compression needs to be cut down a bit for today's poor-quality gasoline.

In 1970, the Chevy 454 had 10.5 to 1 compression and this is a problem due to our low octane fuel. The 1971 and later engines are 8.5 to 1 and make better tow vehicles. If an early or late 454 is to be overhauled, it can be modified for the proper compression ratio that is compatible with regular gas while using a water injector.

Of the smaller-displacement Chrysler Corporation engines, the 360 Dodge is famous for requiring premature valve work but it responds quite well to modification.

In 1970 and 1971 the Chrysler/Dodge 440 was a strong engine. Compression actually was 9.4 to 1 and cars with those engines made great tow vehicles. In 1972 to 1975 compression was rated at 8.2 to 1. Actually it was 7.8 to 1, which left a lot to be desired. Pistons can be changed to rectify this compression ratio drop. The lower compression was accomplished by lowering the piston head down in the cylinder, resulting in a loss of turbulence and cooling in the combustion chamber.

Even though the 1970 and 1971 440 is capable of good service with fairly large trailers, the suspensions of the passenger cars were somewhat soft for towing the heavier trailers. But that can be corrected, providing trailer hitch weight is not more than about 800 pounds.

The Ford 360 and 390 engines were mentioned previously as being good choices. Pre-1973 Ford 460s also were good choices. Compression ratios were moderated in 1971. When considering a 460 previous to that year, make sure you don't get a compression ratio higher than about 9 to 1.

Two of the most popular Ford engine conversions of the 1970s were installation of 429s and 428s into passenger cars replacing smaller engines and in trucks replacing the original 352, 360

and 390 engines. Installation of the low-mileage larger-displacement engine was suggested to be more cost-effective than overhauling the smaller engine.

The 429, which was produced from 1968 through 1973, had 11 to 1 compression from 1968 through 1970. The 1971 engine had 10.3 to 1 and none of these engines were stable and dependable when required to sustain power during RV travel. Preignition was a major problem. Valve guide problems were bothersome and the availability of performance modification equipment was limited. The 1972 and 1973 429 engines were 8.5 and 8 to 1 compression, which eliminated the preignition problem; but overall, any modification program on those engines was disappointing.

The 428 engine was available from 1966 through 1970 and when high octane fuels were available, the 10.5 to 1 compression ratio worked very well. The equipment for 360 and 390 engines was interchangeable and impressive results could be obtained through properly selected modifications. As the fuel octane dropped, it became necessary to reduce compression, destroying the efficiency of the 428 combustion chamber and creating restrictions which made it more desirable to modify a 390.

Lincoln and Mercury 460s

The 1972 to 1974 Lincoln and Mercury 460 engines had 8.25 to 1 compressions (actual). Suspensions were excellent for towing. Earlier Lincoln steering boxes gave a lot of problems with wandering, which could be corrected.

The 1972 to 1975 Olds 455 had 8.5 to 1 compression and was one of the most dependable of the large displacement engines. It responds very well to minor modifications. Suspensions are excellent, and the transmission is good for towing.

Pontiac and Buick 455 engines had the power, but oil distribution problems and a history of overheating would eliminate them from preference.

Passenger cars usually will need some suspension work as in many cases their springs have lost some of their strength. Air shocks might be added in the rear and the front coils might be replaced with heavy-duty coils available or on order from the factory dealership. Good shocks are a prime item. Adding a stabilizer bar is a good idea if one is not already used. Obviously, a load-distributing hitch with sway control will be needed when trailer hitch weight exceeds 200 pounds.

Check the radiator. It should have a minimum of three rows of cores. If not, change it. Four-core radiators are available for most cars and light trucks.

A large auxiliary transmission oil cooler is needed.

Inspect the front suspension for bushing wear, idler arm wear and install lube fittings on ball joints if the fittings are not already there.

Install a coolant temperature gauge calibrated in degrees Fahrenheit. If any heating problems occur, you might suspect the automatic clutch on the engine fan. The clutch fans are the best choices providing the clutches work properly.

In selecting a used vehicle, buying from a private party generally is best. Overall appearance generally relates to the type of maintenance and use it has had. Suspension, steering, body and overall chassis tightness are main considerations. Engine condition is least important if you can buy the vehicle cheaply enough to justify engine work.

Most clean, used recreational vehicles have received exceptional care and have usually served only limited use. The year is not as important as overall condition. Have your local mechanic check the chassis thoroughly for previous damage and overall condition. After your selection and purchase, locate a qualified and well-established independent mechanic for the modification.

How to Choose Equipment

6

If you own or are planning to buy a tow vehicle, no one has to tell you that trucks, vans and truck-based wagons are prime choices. And you know the choice may be confusing, since the federal government began to measure emissions relative to miles traveled several years ago. Many late-model trucks and vans are equipped with engine/axle combinations that are suitable only for lightweight trailers, and knowledge of proper drivetrain combinations is helpful. It's helpful also in choosing a motorhome, although the engine/axle ratio choices usually are predetermined.

Continued reduction in trailer-towing ability of passenger cars makes trucks and vans not only the best tow vehicles for heavier trailers, but the only choices in many cases. The equipment choices are similar whether the vehicle is new or used. It's just as important for the buyer of a used truck or van to check the axle ratio and engine size as it is for the new-vehicle buyer to make sure the proper equipment is specified on the order. Unfortunately, proper ratios may not be available on specific vehicles, and the owner may have to consider a different model just to get the proper ratio. Or, an axle ratio change may be considered, although it's expensive ($400 to $600).

Let's define a few terms:

The only example of a truck-based wagon is the Chevrolet/GMC Suburban. International Harvester made one several years ago, called the Travelall. But it was more like a heavy-duty truck than the Suburban and didn't survive. The Suburban was rather trucky in the

Manufacturer's RV and trailer-towing literature is an excellent source of information on engine and axle ratio combinations for various RV loads, as well as recommendations on optional equipment. Dealers should have the literature. If it is not available at a dealership, write to the motor company's public relations department.

early 1970s but redesign in 1973 enlarged the seating area and the engine compartment and revamped suspension packages so ride and handling are excellent for the truck-oriented buyer.

The truck-based wagon is an overgrown station wagon in one sense; it has a large body with ample seating and a cargo area in the rear. But that body is installed on a chassis designed originally for pickup trucks; hence its handling and road clearance are quite different compared to that of conventional station wagons. The ride isn't usually as cushy as that of a conventional wagon, but neither does the tail end sag when only a moderate load is placed in it.

Until the mid-1970s, vans were not renowned for their towing abilities.

Early vans were built on short wheelbases and they were top-heavy. Suspensions did not offer good control. Engine sizes were limited. But the advent of the mini motorhome, built on a cutaway van chassis, brought the van makers into view of a huge new potential market—and they quickly produced the improvements necessary to make the van something other than a barebones box on wheels.

One worthwhile advantage of trucks and vans with gvw ratings exceeding 8500 pounds is that they can be ordered without catalytic convertors and the need to burn lead-free gasoline. While the lead content in gasoline is gradually diminishing, significant cost differences remain between regular and unleaded fuels. The cost factor, combined with the fact that a catalytic convertor in a single-pipe exhaust system restricts performance (compared to an engine equipped with dual exhausts and no catalytic convertor), offers incentive for the buyer to seek a nonconvertor-equipped vehicle. If that's not possible, proper choice of equipment for the weight being towed still can assure good performance.

Towing Vs. Hauling

Selection of a vehicle for towing requires several equipment choices that can be critical to proper performance, fuel economy and ride comfort. A pickup truck, van or truck-based wagon is not *hauling* a trailer. The trailer is being *towed*. Super-heavy frames,

A tow vehicle need not be sprung as stiffly as a vehicle used to haul a camper; to do so will produce a stiff ride. This truck has a rear-spring package for an 8600-pound gross vehicle weight (gvw) rating, suitable for camper hauling. Buyers who want to avoid the catalytic convertor must order 8600-pound rating even if vehicle will be loaded lightly.

All light-duty trucks and truck-based passenger vehicles have plates or stickers on their door frames indicating gvw rating, to help owners determine suitable loading.

tires and springs are not necessary except with the largest of trailers, although it may be necessary to accept a higher-than-necessary gvw rating (stiffer springs) if your desire is to avoid the catalytic convertor. Example: a half-ton pickup truck may weigh 4200 pounds, with options and full gasoline tanks. Add the weight of passengers, supplies, a camper shell, about 60 percent of the trailer hitch weight (the rest is transferred back to the trailer axles by the action of the load-distributing hitch), plus any optional equipment that might be added, such as a step bumper. The

added weight might be 1600 pounds, for example; 4200 plus 1600 equals 5800. It's good to have a modest margin of safety, and the proper gvw rating in this case might be 6200 pounds. Again, a truck with this gvw rating will have a catalytic convertor, but it will ride better than one with a gvw rating exceeding 8500 unless the truck bed is loaded with at least 1000 pounds of equipment in addition to hitch weight.

In the case of a fifth-wheel trailer, loaded ride would be OK but the ride without the trailer would be rather stiff. Fifth-wheel trailers require trucks with higher gvw ratings than do conventional trailers because fifth-wheelers have higher hitch weights.

Springs have been improved in recent years, so a stiff-sprung late-model truck will ride better when empty than

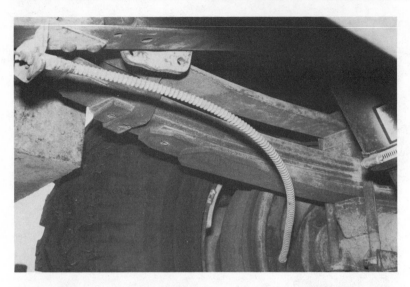

Ride stiffness problems in older vehicles with short rear leaf springs may be improved by inserting Teflon pads between spring tips. Competent suspension repair shops can do this work. Pads were used on Dodge motorhome chassis in the late 1970s.

will an earlier model. The earlier models can be improved, however. It's possible to have Teflon pads inserted between spring leaves, to reduce friction and make the spring more flexible. The pads were used by Dodge on motorhome chassis.

The choice between a so-called half-ton model and a three-quarter-ton model is a tough one for many buyers. They're attracted by the heavier components of the higher-rated vehicle but they like the lower price and lower weight of the lesser-rated vehicle. Theoretically, the gvw rating should provide the answer. If you can get the gvw rating you need for your particular load situation, the vehicle should be suitable. But there is one complicating factor: axle ratio availability. In some cases

you can get only the numerically lower ratios in the so-called half-ton vehicles. Thus, you must choose a larger engine than you may feel comfortable with, to compensate for the "tall" gearing. In those cases it's usually better to move up to the heavier vehicle to get the engine/axle combination you feel is right for your situation.

Drive Train Choices

How do you know what is right? To a limited extent, it's a guessing game. But the motor companies have issued guidelines. In most cases they're pretty close, but a single guideline cannot possibly serve with precise accuracy for all the varying conditions RVers encounter. The trailerist who spends most of his time in the high mountains will not find the guidelines quite as realistic as the person who tows mostly in low elevations over fairly flat terrain. Generally, the motor company guidelines are more closely suitable for the low-altitude/moderate terrain trailerist than for the high-mountain traveler. Also entering the picture is the human element—the fact that each of us will differently define what is "acceptable" performance. If your driving will be in mostly flat terrain, the factory recommendation should suffice. If you plan a lot of mountain driving, you might choose an engine/axle combination suitable for about 1000 pounds more weight than you will have.

Dealers often don't even have the motor company trailer-towing literature available for customers. In all too many cases, they don't even read the towing recommendations in their own data books. Many dealers come up with some really incorrect recommendations that result in tow vehicles that won't do the job. The buyer is the unwitting victim.

We hear repeatedly from owners of vehicles with inadequate power because the dealer recommended an axle ratio that is numerically too low, despite a specific recommendation of a different ratio that is right in front of him in his data book. Moral: Do your homework so you have a good idea of what you want and so you'll know when your dealer is steering you wrong. In many cases he'll do that simply to sell a vehicle he already has in stock rather than having to order one.

On the other hand, dealers tell of owners who are adamant about ordering specific equipment that is erroneous and the dealers can do nothing to convince the buyers otherwise.

The trend nowadays is to order engines that are too small for the loads being carried or towed, and many owners have found out to their dismay that their vehicles are inadequate. A smaller engine doesn't automatically mean better fuel economy. If the load is more than the engine can handle with the axle ratio that was ordered, the engine will have to work at nearly full throttle to do the job. When working an engine that hard, fuel economy will be no better than with a larger engine running easier, and the result is poor performance as well as poor fuel economy. If we must suffer poor fuel economy, we may as well have decent performance.

Engine size is a compromise between solo driving and towing. Too large an engine will result in lower-than-normal solo fuel economy. The usual procedure is to shoot for the happy medium, which means somewhat lower levels of towing performance than are ideal, in favor of slightly improved fuel economy while solo driving.

Obviously, the proportion of solo distances to towing distances will affect the compromise. In all cases, 4-barrel carburetors are more suitable for trailering performance than 2-barrel carburetors, although in some cases you have no choice. The 4-barrel acts as a 2-barrel except under heavy throttle. If the driver can use a light foot on the accelerator pedal, the 4-barrel will deliver fuel economy as good as or better than the 2-barrel, while offering better top-end performance for passing and hill climbing.

Obviously, the heaviest radiator available is the one you'll want for towing. Auxiliary transmission oil cooling is wise in many cases with trailers, but the decision depends on a number of factors, including efficiency of the oil cooling circuit inside the radiator, gross weight, towing conditions (mountains, hot weather) and the amount of towing the vehicle does. A vehicle used for 10 percent towing and 90 percent around-town use obviously would be less of a candidate for auxiliary oil cooling than would one with the opposite kind of use.

Choosing Tires

A popular choice for pickups, vans and wagons in the ¾-ton class is 8.75-16.5 D. It's a good choice, although the tire is not renowned for long wear. Its cousin, the 8.00-16.5, doesn't seem to perform well. It's a very hard tire which promotes vehicle vibration and a rough ride. And the tire is more prone to skate when traction is marginal. Excellent choices are the P-metric radial tires such as LT 235/85R16E, available on the heavier duty models, and P235/75R15 on the lighter models. Both tires are designed for reduced rolling resistance. Radials are quite suitable on all types of RVs, assuming they are not over-loaded and that vehicle weight distribution is proper. Radial-ply tires improve traction on slippery surfaces.

Radial-ply tires with metric size designations have grown popular for RVs. Tires such as the LT235/85R16 used on pickup trucks and for Suburbans are suitable for towing and camper hauling.

Also improving traction is the optional limited-slip device for the rear axle. It's designed to prevent one-wheel spinouts and is worthwhile if the vehicle will be driven frequently on slippery surfaces. There is no other benefit so it's an unnecessary expense if most driving is on terrain that offers good traction.

Transmission Choice

The choice of a transmission used to be fairly simple. But now Detroit offers so many different types that a wrong choice can create problems. The old

Automatic transmission is favored among most RV owners because manual transmissions with floor-mounted shift levers often are clumsy. Manual transmission offers a very slight fuel economy advantage over an automatic.

standby 3-speed automatic still is valid. Four-speed manual transmissions (floor-mounted shift levers) are still offered and are valid if the buyer doesn't mind the clumsy shift patterns and stiff clutches. Nowadays, 4-speed automatic transmissions are offered with overdrive fourth gears when medium-size engines are used. These transmissions are rated for about 250 lb.-ft. torque. Also, 4-speed manual overdrive transmissions are available. There are several critical differences.

The 4-speed automatic with OD (overdrive) top gear is a good choice for trailer towing. The OD gear does not see much use while towing, unless the trailer is lightweight. The role of the OD gear is to provide improved fuel economy during light cruising (without the trailer). The OD ratio usually is too "tall" for towing a heavy trailer; the transmission will automatically downshift from OD gear (usually around .7 to 1) to third gear (1 to 1—the traditional "high" gear) in response to the heavy foot on the accelerator pedal that is required when trying to move a lot of weight with excessively high gearing.

The 4-speed manual overdrive transmission usually is not suitable for trailer towing, except for trailers less than 2000 pounds, because its first gear is too high and the clutch is not heavy-duty. The result is considerable "feathering" or slipping of the clutch to get the vehicle and trailer moving. Clutches don't tend to last long. It's particularly a problem in high altitudes on uphill grades when there may not be enough gear reduction (torque multiplication) to get the

Engine/Axle Ratio Recommendations for Recreation Vehicles

Net Engine Horse-power	Gross Combined Weight in Pounds													
	4500	5000	5500	6000	6500	7000	7500	8000	8500	9000	9500	10,000	10,500	11,000
80	3.4	3.7												
90	3.4	3.7	4.1	4.1										
100	3.0	3.4	3.7	3.7	3.7	4.1								
110	2.7	3.0	3.2	3.4	3.4	3.7	3.7	4.1						
120	2.7	2.7	3.0	3.2	3.2	3.5	3.7	4.1	4.1	4.5				
130	2.5	2.7	2.7	3.0	3.2	3.2	3.5	3.5	3.7	3.7	4.1			
140		2.5	3.0	3.0	3.0	3.2	3.2	3.5	3.5	3.7	3.7	3.7	4.1	4.1
150			2.5	2.7	3.0	3.0	3.2	3.2	3.5	3.5	3.7	3.7	3.7	4.1
160				2.5	2.7	2.7	3.0	3.0	3.2	3.2	3.5	3.5	3.7	3.7
170							2.5	2.7	3.0	3.0	3.2	3.2	3.4	3.7
180									3.2	3.2	3.5	3.5	3.7	3.7
190										3.0	3.0	3.2	3.2	3.5
200														3.2
210														

rig rolling. The result may be an embarrassing call for help. Automatic transmissions don't have very low first-gear ratios, either, but they have torque convertors that multiply those ratios. The new 4-speed manual OD transmissions are akin to the 3-speed manual transmissions of the earlier years in their suitability for towing trailers—not very good.

Vans Vs. Pickup Vs. Wagon

Should you choose a van or a pickup or a Suburban for towing a trailer? That is a question only you can answer, since all three can be equipped to tow heavy trailers. The decision rests on which type will be more practical for you.

The pickup has an advantage in ease of engine maintenance and repair due to good accessibility, in addition to better legroom than most vans have. But the van offers lots of passenger hauling capacity that can quickly be converted to carrying space for equipment. Van versatility is hard to beat. A car-top boat can be carried on any of the three vehicles (on the truck if a camper shell is used). The Suburban has an advantage of passenger hauling capacity plus load-carrying capacity, plus being more car-like in appearance than either the truck or a van.

Engine/Axle Ratio Recommendations for Recreation Vehicles, *(continued)*

Net Engine Horse-power	Gross Combined Weight in Pounds													
	11,500	12,000	12,500	13,000	13,500	14,000	14,500	15,000	15,500	16,000	16,500	17,000	17,500	18,000
80														
90														
100														
110														
120														
130														
140														
150	4.1													
160	4.1	4.1												
170	3.7	4.1	4.1	4.5										
180	3.7	4.1	4.5	4.5	4.5									
190	3.5	3.7	3.7	4.1	4.1	4.5	4.5							
200	3.5	3.5	3.5	3.7	3.7	4.1	4.1	4.5	4.5	4.5	4.8	4.8		
210		3.2	3.2	3.5	3.5	3.7	3.7	4.1	4.1	4.1	4.1	4.5	4.5	4.8

Dealing with the Compromises

Selection of an engine/axle combination unfortunately involves many compromises and variables. Consequently, it is important for you to know that this table is *not* a precise guide.

The compromises include engine/axle combinations that are ideal for towing but not for fuel economy while driving solo (and vice-versa) between high altitude and low altitude operation. There is a personal choice between best possible performance and performance that is merely adequate. Another important variable is tire size. For example, in the 1970s buyers were offered pickup trucks with tire sizes ranging from 8.00-16.5 to 7.50-16. As you can see in Chapter 7 on axle ratios, overall tire diameter can substantially affect torque multiplication (gear reduction). The difference between 8.00-16.5 and 7.50-16 tires is about the same as the difference between a 3.54 axle and a 4.00 and that is a substantial difference. Ideally, we should not offer an engine/axle ratio guide if it cannot be more specific than that. However, for many years we have encountered cases in which RV owners have made errors in engine/axle combinations that were *much worse* than the variance just mentioned. For example, we'll hear from a trailerist whose pickup truck has a 2.73 axle although his trailer weight suggests he should have a 3.73 ratio.

With that in mind, we offer this *approximate* engine/axle ratio selector; we have tried to place our recommendations roughly in the middle of the range of possible tire sizes from which the vehicle owner can choose. Keep in mind, assuming the same axle ratio, smaller-diameter tires mean more power; larger-diameter tires mean less power. The opposite may be true for fuel economy, but other criteria enter that picture, as explained in Chapter 7.

Critical Aspects of Using This Table

Another very important aspect of using this table is recognition that the engine listings are in HORSE-POWER, not cubic inch displacement (cid). Most of us are accustomed to dealing with cid in discussing engines, so why must we make it difficult here by relating to horsepower? The reason is that two engines of identical cid may have dramatically different horsepower ratings due to differences in engine design. Horsepower and torque are the only common denominators, and we chose horsepower.

We repeat: DO NOT think cid when reading the engine net horsepower figures at the left of the table or serious error may result.

Further, before making an engine/axle ratio choice

for a new vehicle, obtain a copy of the manufacturer's trailer-towing guide. All U.S. manufacturers offer the guides, and they can be more specific than is possible for us here since they do not have to cover engines of all brands.

Since 1971 all domestic engines have been tested for horsepower output to the same standard: SAE J-245. The figures are termed "net horsepower." Prior to 1971, gross horsepower figures were issued. To adjust pre-1971 figures to the more recent procedure, subtract 25 percent for an approximation.

Engine net horsepower ratings are determined by vehicle manufacturers and are listed in dealers' new-vehicle data books. Also listed in Chilton's *Motor Manual* for the given year, often available in public libraries and book stores.

Diesel Engines

Horsepower is horsepower, and a diesel engine that develops about the same horsepower and torque as a gasoline engine theoretically should be assigned the same gross combined weight rating. However, diesels develop most of their power in the first one-half of throttle travel, whereas gasoline engines may require 80 to 90 percent of throttle travel to pull the same load uphill, with the same axle ratio and tire size. The result is that the diesel feels stronger than the gasoline engine. Truck-type diesels last longer, while delivering 80 percent or more of their power for long periods. In using this table to select an axle ratio for a light-truck or medium-truck diesel, add 25 percent to the horsepower rating of the engine. This table is not applicable to diesels limited to less than 3300 rpm.

Axle Ratios

7

Performance and fuel economy of an RV are heavily dependent upon engine efficiency, weight, wind resistance and other factors, but one of the primary items is axle ratio. Anyone who orders a new trailer-towing vehicle from the factory must choose an axle ratio. The buyer who leaves this important choice up to the salesman may regret that decision, for most car and truck salesmen have little understanding of the performance needs of the RV owners—or any other RV needs.

The motorhome buyer usually is not offered an axle ratio choice. Nevertheless, understanding of the effect of axle ratio on performance and fuel economy is important.

The data table accompanying Chapter 6 lists a wide range of engine and axle ratio combinations that we believe

are suitable for RVs of specific weight. However, any set of recommendations must be general; it cannot take into account the fact that one RV owner prefers to travel mostly in high altitudes while another stays primarily on flat roads in low altitudes, or that one owner may be very critical of performance while another is not. Still another variable is tire size (overall diameter), which affects torque mutiplication (gear reduction) much the same as does axle ratio. If you understand how axle ratios and tire diameter affect performance and fuel economy, your choice of a new or used vehicle will be much more accurate. If you're not ready for a vehicle change, you'll understand your present vehicle better and may be prompted to consider an axle ratio or tire size change.

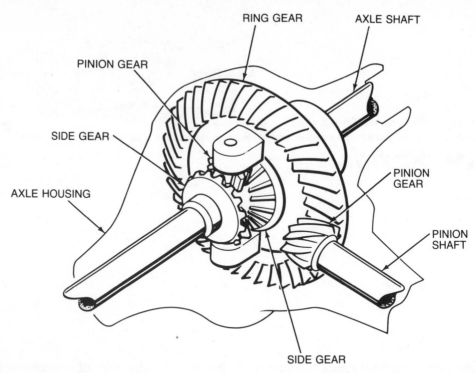

RING GEAR

AXLE SHAFT

PINION GEAR

SIDE GEAR

PINION GEAR

AXLE HOUSING

PINION SHAFT

SIDE GEAR

Gear ratio or axle ratio refers to how many times the pinion gear (attached to driveshaft) revolves for each turn of the ring gear. Ring gear revolves at the same rate as wheels. A 3.5 to 1 axle ratio means pinion gear revolves 3.5 times for each ring gear revolution. When visually inspecting a differential, divide number of pinion gear teeth into ring gear teeth to determine axle ratio.

Torque Multiplication

When we talk about axle ratio, we're actually talking about torque multiplication, more commonly known as gear reduction. Torque is measure of twisting force. When a small gear is used to drive a large one, torque is multiplied.

These days in a passenger car, light truck, van or motorhome, the range of axle ratios varies from 2.41 to 1 up to 4.88 to 1. The numbers describe the proportion between the driving gear (pinion gear) and the driven gear (ring gear). For example, if the pinion gear turns 2.41 times for every revolution of the ring gear, it's a 2.41 to 1 ratio—a very high ratio. It's found only in late-model passenger cars.

The driveshaft is connected to the pinion gear. The wheels are attached to the ring gear, via axles. Most transmissions operate in 1 to 1 ratio (direct drive) in third (or high) gear. So, a 2.41 to 1 ratio means the engine is turning 2.41 revolutions for every single revolution of the drive wheels. If the axle ratio is 4.1 to 1, the engine turns 4.1 revolutions for every wheel revolution (in high gear).

Numbers Denote Gearing

When thinking about axle ratios, the most important item to remember is that *higher numbers mean lower gearing*—or more torque multiplication. A vehicle with a 3.50 to 1 axle ratio will be more powerful than one with a 3.00 to 1 ratio, assuming engine performance is the same.

Obviously, for the sake of performance alone it would behoove us to choose the numerically highest axles available. Unfortunately, axle ratio affects mileage. As an engine turns faster, it may use more fuel. However, there is an important trade-off point: *an engine working under excessive throttle usually will consume more fuel than one turning more rpm but operating under less throttle*. This complicates the axle selection process.

Mathematical formulas can be used to determine how much horsepower is needed to move a given load at a given speed with given gearing, when the load has a certain amount of wind drag. The problem is, how can we accurately determine all those factors for each RV? Most of it is not too difficult, but the wind drag question injects some doubt. And it's necessary to have access to a horsepower curve for the engine in question. Listings in most sales literature are for maximum horsepower. This usually occurs between 3200 and 4200 rpm. If the vehicle cruises at 2700 rpm, we would need to know the available horsepower at that rpm level.

Let's talk instead about a measurement method that is much more practical. In testing hundreds of different RV combinations, we have found that a proper axle ratio choice is one that allows the engine to develop manifold vacuum readings in the area of 10 to 12 inches while crusing at 55 mph on level highway in low altitude and with no headwind. Again, we're back to that important manifold vacuum gauge described in an earlier chapter. If you don't have one, it would be one of the most important additions you could make for best possible fuel economy.

If a vehicle has an axle that is numerically too high (low gearing), vacuum readings at cruise generally will be in the 13- to 15-inch range. This is rarely the problem. Much more common is an axle ratio that is numerically too low (high gearing). This results in the engine working harder than it should to overcome the lack of torque multiplication. Manifold vacuum readings are lower, and the engine operates below 7 inches manifold vacuum more of the time. As you may recall from Chapter 3, at about 6.5 to 7 inches the carburetor enriches fuel mixtures about 27 percent. Thus, an axle ratio that is numerically too low (high gearing) causes more fuel consumption.

RV owners who live in high altitudes will generally find vacuum readings low most of the time, for reasons stated in Chapter 3. And it may not be beneficial to change the ratio. But by knowing which ratio is being used, and by knowing the general level of manifold vacuum readings, concrete reasons for poor performance and poor fuel economy can be determined.

How to Check Axle Ratio

The dealer invoice issued with a new vehicle or a sticker in the glove compartment may identify the axle ratio if it is optional. If it is standard, the numbers may not be listed, but the dealer's data book will list standard ratios.

Still, it's best to be sure and check it yourself, because it's so easy. This method is possible with vehicles that have conventional exposed driveshafts. It cannot be used with front-drive vehicles because the relationship between wheel revolutions and driveshaft revolutions cannot be visually inspected.

• Jack up both rear wheels, or raise the vehicle on a lift.
• Have two assistants turn both rear wheels exactly one revolution. (Or, if the vehicle has sufficient ground clearance, have an assistant roll it slowly forward for one tire revolution while you scoot along underneath, counting driveshaft revolutions. Obviously, do this on flat pavement where there is no danger of the vehicle picking up speed. If you count 3½ revolutions, your ratio is 3.50 to 1. If you count 2¾ revolutions, your ratio is 2.75 to 1.

To be more accurate, have the assistant roll the vehicle 2 tire revolutions; then divide your results by 2. Small errors in your count and in turning of the wheels will be less significant with more tire revolutions.

Now you know what your axle ratio is. While you were checking, it may have occurred to you that tire size (overall diameter) could affect the outcome. Indeed it can.

Tire Diameter Affects Results

With different tire sizes, your axle ratio does not change. If you have a 4.1 to 1 ratio, your driveshaft always will turn 4.1 times for every wheel revolution, no matter how large or small your tires.

However, a larger diameter tire will make you *travel more distance in one tire revolution*—or in 4.1 driveshaft revolutions.

Example: The 8.75-16.5 tire commonly used on pickup trucks and vans has an outside circumference of 29.46 inches, while the 8.00-16.5 tire has a 28.34-inch circumference. The larger tire will take you 1.12 inches farther per revolution. It would be easy to calculate the effect of this, per mile, but because a tire will deflect or flatten a bit at its tread contact with the pavement, overall circumference is not used in the calculations. Tire engineers test each tire they market and assign a tire *revolutions per mile* figure under loaded conditions. It's easiest to use those figures while calculating how one set of tires will affect torque multiplication.

Making a substantial change in tire size can affect torque multiplication much like a change in axle ratio. However, in most cases tire size changes are subtle. Most RV owners don't make radical tire size changes because it's not possible without dramatically affecting load-carrying ability.

In general, changing to larger diameter tires is like changing the axle ratio to one that is numerically a bit lower; you have less power, but fuel economy may improve a bit if your manifold vacuum readings are not lowered too much.

The reverse also is true: Changing to smaller-diameter tires will improve power a bit, and this may even improve mileage if the vehicle currently operates with manifold vacuum readings that are lower than ideal. The engine turns a bit faster but is not using as much throttle.

Let's use a simple mathematical formula to equate a change in tire diameter to axle ratio:

$$R = \frac{RPM \times 60}{MPH \times M}$$

R = axle ratio
RPM = engine speed
60 = a constant
M = tire revolutions per mile

Example: 8.00-16.5 tires turn 735 revolutions per mile
9.50-16.5 tires turn 700 revolutions per mile

This formula normally is used to determine the ideal axle ratio based on engine governed speed in medium-duty trucks. If engine governed rpm is 2800 and desired road speed is 55 mph, the axle ratio would be 4.15 to 1 with 8.00-16.5 tires. With the same rpm and road speed but with 9.50-16.5 tires, the axle ratio would be 4.36 to 1.

Thus, changing from 8.00-16.5 to 9.50-16.5 tires would be about equal to a change from a 4.36 axle ratio to a 4.15.

Those particular ratios don't exist in light trucks, but you get the idea. In one-ton trucks and motorhomes, 4.1, 4.55 and 4.88 ratios are offered. In three-quarter-ton trucks and vans, axle ratios range from 3.08 to 4.1. In half-ton trucks, axle ratios range from 2.75 to 3.73 (4.1 available on older models). Passenger cars use axles in a range from 2.41 to 3.08. In the mid-1970s and earlier, passenger-car ratios extended to 3.23 and 3.42.

Parts Availability

If it is determined that an axle change is needed, and you have checked to see what ratio exists in the vehicle, the next step is to find out about parts availability. Check with your dealer. Replacement gear-sets may be available; the changeover costs $350 to $600. If the lack of performance is only marginal, the money would be better spent in improving engine performance. If the performance deficiency is drastic, an axle change to a numerically higher ratio is necessary. If the vehicle is substantially *over*powered, a change to a numerically lower axle may be justified. Addition of an overdrive would serve the same purpose, but in most cases overdrive units are too expensive to be cost-effective and gear ratio selection is limited.

Possibly the most economical way to change axle ratios in a pickup truck is to buy a different third-member (the housing that holds the ring and pinion gears) at a wrecking yard. But if the axle housing does not have a removable third-member, the entire housing would have to be changed. Still, wrecking-yard prices are worth checking. To determine the ratio of gears while at the wrecking yard, count the number of teeth in the pinion and ring gears and divide the pinion teeth number into the ring gear teeth number. Example: 40 ring gear teeth ÷ 13 pinion gear teeth = 3.08 to 1 axle ratio.

Effect on Fuel Economy

Fuel economy is an important consideration when considering an axle ratio change. It's not possible to accurately predict the effect of a ratio change on fuel economy, but the effect is hardly ever more than 2 mpg because most RV owners don't make dramatic changes in axle ratio.

When a vehicle is underpowered (traveling with manifold vacuum below 7 inches much of the time), a change to a numerically higher ratio (lower gearing) will reduce the engine's load, although engine rpm is raised. The result usually is power improvement with no change in fuel economy, while in a few cases fuel economy improves slightly. Solo fuel economy may drop .5 to 1 mpg, depending on the situation.

When the owner believes the vehicle has excess power due to a numerically high axle ratio (low gearing) and intends to change, it usually will improve fuel economy .5 to 1 mpg unless the change is too severe and causes the engine to run much of the time below 7 inches manifold vacuum. In that event, fuel economy would drop.

In most cases an axle ratio change is too expensive to be justified on fuel economy alone. Performance improvement usually must be one of the goals.

Axle Ratio and Road Speed

If you don't have a tachometer, have you ever wondered how fast your engine is turning as you cruise at 55 or 60 mph? It may be more interesting to know engine rpm in second gear during an uphill climb. The best source of information of course is a tachometer. But rpm can be calculated if you know the revolutions per mile/figure for your tires. Many tire rpm figures are listed with the tire load/inflation tables in Chapter 10.

Here is the formula for calculating engine rpm at specific road speeds:

$$RPM = \frac{R \times M \times MPH}{60}$$

R = Transmission gear ratio x axle ratio
M = Tire revolutions per mile (see Chapter 10)
MPH = Road Speed
60 = A constant

All transmissions have 1 to 1 top gears unless they are overdrive transmissions, so the R listing merely is your axle ratio unless you have an overdrive transmission. In this example, let's use 9.50-16.5 tires with a tire rpm figure of 700, axle ratio of 3.73 and road speed of 55 mph.

Example:

$$\frac{3.73 \times 700 \times 55}{60} = \frac{143605}{60} = 2393 \text{ RPM}$$

If, for example, you want to calculate engine rpm in second gear at 45 mph, the second-gear ratio is added (we'll use the 1.52 ratio of the GM Turbo-Hydra-matic 350 transmission).

Example:

$$\frac{1.52 \times 3.73 \times 700 \times 45}{60} = \frac{178592}{60} = 2977 \text{ RPM}$$

Engine rpm at 45 mph in second gear is 2977, disregarding any "slip" in transmission's torque convertor.

Axle Ratio Vs. Torque Curve

As you can see from the previous discussion, axle ratio and tire selection determine the engine rpm at which your vehicle will cruise at 55 mph—or whatever speed you choose. By checking your axle ratio and using the engine rpm formula you may find that your engine rpm at 55 mph does not match the peak torque rpm listed for your engine.

Example:
Chevrolet 305-cubic-inch V-8 (federal emissions)
Peak net torque, 240, lb.-ft. @ 2000 rpm
Peak net horsepower, 165 @ 4400 rpm

Now, we've all heard that we should cruise at the rpm level where peak torque occurs. This has been recommended by dealership salesmen for years, although they're of little help to the customer in actually figuring how to do it, if indeed it is desirable.

It is *not* desirable in many cases, depending on weight. If you're able to cruise at 55 mph at the peak torque figure for your engine, it's an accidental perfect combination of gross weight and peak torque rpm.

Torque is a measurement of twisting force exerted at the crankshaft by the engine. The pound-foot unit of measure is the force of 1 pound acting at right angles at the end of an arm 1 foot long. Horsepower is a measure of the rate at which engine power is produced—the amount of work done by a certain torque over a period of time.

If you don't understand that difference, don't feel alone, because the difference between horsepower and torque is very elusive when one attempts to relate it to on-the-road performance. Let's look at it this way: Torque is what we feel in high gear when cruising or accelerating moderately. Horsepower is what gets us up the hill in second gear under heavy throttle.

Let's see what happens if we try to choose an axle ratio that will allow us to cruise at 55 mph with rpm at 2000, which is the torque peak rpm of the Chevy 305 engine.

If the vehicle is a Chevy/C-10 pickup truck, we might choose P225/75R15 tires, which have a revolutions per mile specification of 737. Using the formula listed earlier (R = axle ratio), we come up with these figures:

Formula	Calculation	
$R = \dfrac{RPM \times 60}{MPH \times M}$	$R = \dfrac{2000 \times 60}{55 \times 737}$	$R = 2.96$

Thus, we must choose a 2.96 axle ratio, or whatever is available in that area,

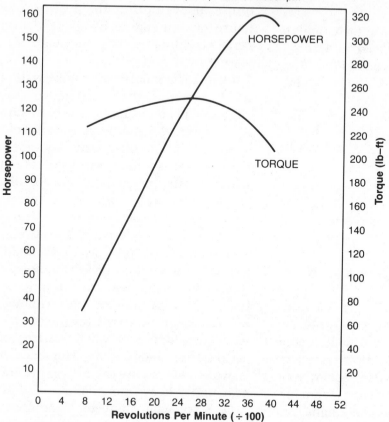

All states except California (8501 lbs GVWR and above)
SAE net horsepower (85°F)   160 @ 3800 rpm
SAE net torque, lb-ft (85°F)   250 @ 2800 rpm

HORSEPOWER

TORQUE

Horsepower

Torque (lb-ft)

Revolutions Per Minute (÷ 100)

Torque/horsepower graphs such as this one on the Chevrolet 350 V-8 (1982) appear in dealers' data books and can help in axle ratio selection.

to cruise at 2000 rpm at 55 mph with the aforementioned tires. Chevrolet offers a 3.08 to 1 axle in that truck, so we could come close to the target.

What would we achieve? The combination would be fine for solo driving and light- to medium-duty towing. But what if a 6000-pound trailer were hitched to it? Performance would be insufficient in the mountains. The 3.73 axle would be the proper choice in that

instance. But what of the torque peak? The torque peak is out the window—forget it, and choose the axle ratio that will do the job properly.

The Proper Choice

The point of all this is that running an engine at its torque peak under usual cruise conditions is fine if gross weight permits it, but when weight is too high, performance as well as fuel economy will suffer even though the engine *is* running at its torque peak. With a heavy load, the engine will be laboring against the tall axle ratio and manifold vacuum readings will drop, causing enrichment of fuel mixtures. The efficiency of running at the torque peak will be more than cancelled out by the excessive load on the engine.

Still, by knowing how all this works, you can do a better job of tailoring the engine and axle ratio for the load. For example, the Chevy 350 engine has a 2800 rpm torque peak. By plugging that figure into our formula, the result (R) is 4.14. If we chose the 3.73 axle we would cruise at 55 mph just under the engine's torque peak—fine for towing or hauling 4000 pounds or more. But again, it would limit fuel economy potential if the truck were mainly used in solo driving. The proper axle ratio for solo driving would have the engine running well *under* its torque peak.

Horsepower is where it's at. Of course, we don't want to cruise at the engine's maximum horsepower, because the horsepower peak usually is at maximum rpm. The engine usually will turn faster, but the horsepower curve starts going downhill at that point (4400 rpm for the Chevy 305). Horsepower peaks vary widely. Compare that 4400 figure for the Chevy engine with the 3200 rpm horsepower peak of the Ford 351 V-8 (1982 light-duty model).

The rpm figures at which horsepower and torque are derived vary greatly among the various brands. Regarding horsepower, part of this is due to the difference between 2-barrel and 4-barrel carburetion. But other important factors include cam characteristics, length of piston stroke and spark advance characteristics.

It's obvious, when choosing an engine that gets its peak horsepower at 3200 rpm, that power available for passing will be minimal if a numerically high axle ratio is ordered.

When choosing a replacement vehicle, check horsepower figures and the rpm at which maximum horsepower occurs. Use the engine rpm to calculate engine rpm in second gear at 50 to 60 mph, or whatever maximum speed you consider usual during passing situations. Higher peak horsepower rpm allows higher speeds in second gear. Also check the torque peak and see how well it coincides with 55 mph cruise conditions. If you can match the torque peak to your cruise speed, so much the better. If not, don't worry about it.

Alternate Fuels

8

There is nothing like a gasoline shortage to spark renewed interest in alternate motor vehicle fuels. The market for propane motor fuel conversion kits has gone up and down like a yo yo in the 10 years since the 1973 fuel crisis, alternating between boom periods in which the conversion equipment was back-ordered for several months and times when dealers could hardly give it away. In 1982, diesel engines finally became viable for RV usage with the Chevrolet and GMC introduction of the 6.2-liter diesel. Sales of the optional diesels appear capable of wide fluctuation as well.

In either case, it's necessary to make a cost versus benefits decision. This is true with any fuel economy improver, whether it be an optional diesel engine, a propane conversion or an add-on overdrive unit. Let's examine the practicality of these alternate fuels and list a few math calculations that are necessary to make a decision on cost effectiveness.

The GM 6.2-Liter Diesel

Although the 6.2-liter diesel isn't the only diesel practical for RV applications, it's a valid choice up to about 13,500 pounds gross combined weight (total weight of tow vehicle and trailer). Ford offers a 6.9-liter diesel engine with 26 more horsepower; see more about it later in this chapter. We have experienced more than 15,000 miles with the 6.2-liter diesel in three different vehicles: A C-2500 GMC Suburban, a Chevrolet K-10 Blazer and a Chevrolet

The Chevrolet/GMC 6.2-liter diesel is used in pickup trucks, vans, Suburbans and motorhome chassis. This engine is designed for heavy service, unlike the 5.7-liter diesel previously offered in GM passenger cars and half-ton GM pickup trucks.

motorhome chassis. In all three vehicles, optional cost of the diesel engine and the accompanying equipment package was $2500 to $2700. That's the nut the buyer must crack, from the standpoint of cost-effectiveness—how long the improved fuel economy takes to pay off the engine cost in the distance the buyer expects to drive.

Although the 6.2-liter diesel is not the first offered by GM in light trucks, it is the first diesel suitable for RV service. The previous diesel, the 5.7-liter (350-cubic-inch) Oldsmobile-built engine, was designed for passenger car use, and

GM limited the trailer-tow rating to 2000 pounds. Although not as beefy as engines built by GM's Detroit diesel division for tractor-trailer rigs, the 6.2 is advertised as a real truck diesel designed for medium- and light-duty applications—i.e., it is quiet enough for most pleasure-oriented drivers, yet it can be driven under heavy throttle for extended periods without accelerated wear or mechanical problems.

Indeed, the 6.2 is relatively quiet, reasonable in weight (about 100 pounds heavier than the gasoline 454) and has enough rpm range (3600 maximum) to make it compatible with 3- and 4-speed automatic transmissions favored by RV owners. Heavy truck diesels have much narrower power bands (many are governed at 2000 rpm) and multi-speed manual transmissions are necessary to make up for it. They are also much more noisy. The 6.2 is a "civilized" diesel.

How well does it work, and how well does it support the price tag—in other words, initial cost versus fuel economy, performance and durability (maintenance)? At this point we can only assume durability will be good.

Accompanying technical specifications list the horsepower and torque output of the 6.2-liter diesel as similar to those of the five-liter (305 cubic-inch) gasoline engine. That may come as something of a shock, since diesel tends to be synonymous with power in the big tractor-trailer rigs that haul such heavy loads at fairly high speeds. Not everyone takes into account the sheer size of those engines plus the gear versatility with which they're coupled.

If the low horsepower of the 6.2 is a surprise, the 13,500-pound gross combined weight (gcw) trailering rating may be as well. That rating is available only when the 4.56 to 1 axle ratio is specified in a C-2500. The test Suburban was equipped with a 4.1 to 1 axle that rated it for 12,000 pounds gcw.

Since the test vehicle weighed 5980 pounds with a load-distributing hitch and full 40-gallon fuel tank, we acquired a trailer that would enable us to test the 12,000-pound rating. Although loaded weight of the test 32-footer would require the 4.56 axle ratio,

its dry weight put us right at 12,000 pounds gcw, and that's the way the test was conducted. We also briefly towed a 34-footer (6500 pounds dry weight), and found that the test Suburban would handle it well in fairly level terrain. However, the real challenge for the 6.2 engine, even with realistic trailer weight, is mountains. Here's how it fared with the test trailer:

Hill-Climb Challenge

At low altitudes, traveling level highway combined with low hills, the Suburban with 6.2 engine is a very pleasant tow vehicle. With the cruise control in use it will maintain the desired speed within two mph, with excellent consis-

Various appliances around the intake manifold of the 6.2 engine include vacuum pump and fuel filter immediately behind manifold air inlet, crankcase ventilation tubes immediately in front, fuel injection pump in front and another fuel filter at upper left.

tency. The engine has most of its torque right at the start of throttle travel, so it feels responsive when pulling away from a stop at part throttle. And it climbs hills, towing the trailer, with only modest apparent effort. But when it encounters a 3- to 4-percent grade, more throttle is applied and nothing much happens. That's when one begins to believe the horsepower and torque ratings. Full throttle is little different from half throttle and speed drops fairly rapidly with a load. The three-speed automatic transmission is downshifted to second, and speed holds at 45 mph. Additional power is noticed from the downshift but not the kick that occurs at full throttle in second gear with a gasoline engine of similar displacement.

As the road became more mountainous, hill-climb ability dropped. We climbed the well-known "Grapevine" grade on Interstate 5 between Bakersfield and Los Angeles, California, at 27 to 30 mph in second gear, full throttle. The grade is 6 percent and peaks at about 4000 feet. Many major-highway grades throughout the nation and particularly in the West are 6 percent.

On up to 7400 feet we went, on five- to 6-percent grades. Speeds stayed around 27 to 30 mph in second gear. The transmission will downshift to low at 27 mph if full throttle is applied. That downshift speed will change with different axle ratios, since the relationship between engine rpm and road speed changes with axle ratio (and tire size).

It's apparent that travel with heavy trailers is slow in mountains when judged by standards of large gasoline engines. Most 18-wheelers passed us on the 6-percent grades. How much of the slow hill-climb pace can be tolerated will depend on individual situations. The 6.2 engine, used to tow a heavy trailer, may require more patience than the mountain-dweller can muster, while the flat-lander who travels mountains only occasionally should find it an acceptable compromise. Again, it should be emphasized that our situation was a worst-case test with maximum trailer weight. By choosing a vehicle that is overrated for the trailer involved, performance would be improved. The test vehicle's mountain-climbing ability without a trailer was quite good.

While towing, the situation at least is very relaxed. Since almost all the power is available within half throttle and is controlled by the cruise control system, no help is needed from the driver, who just steers, enjoys the scenery and downshifts or upshifts when necessary. This kind of pace with a gasoline engine may be more frustrating, because in many cases the engines are not developing the power of which they're capable, due to the effect of emission controls, catalytic convertors and the like. With the diesel, that's all there is.

Undoubtedly some of the established add-on turbocharger manufacturers will produce kits for the 6.2 diesel but the cost-versus-benefits ratio may be questionable. Turbo kits cost upwards of $2500 for gasoline engines these days.

Fuel Consumption

If the 6.2 is slow in the mountains, at least it is burning less fuel—and on flat highway as well. While towing the 32-footer in low altitudes on 50/50 flat highway and low hills, we recorded an average of 12.12 mpg. While we towed the trailer from 800-foot elevation through mountains to the 7400-foot level and back, fuel economy dropped a mere 1.23 mpg, to 10.89.

Most owners of gasoline engines are accustomed to seeing quite a difference between flat-highway fuel consumption and that which occurs in heavy going through the mountains. We may be surprised at the fuel economy that can be recorded with gasoline engines when maintaining the same pace as that dictated by the 6.2 diesel, but undoubtedly the diesel will come out substantially ahead. During our tests, headwinds were not a factor; ambient temperature was 60 to 80 degrees F and No. 2 diesel fuel was used.

During solo driving at 60 to 63 mph (Detroit to Los Angeles) the Suburban ranged from a low of 14.49 in a run from Henderson, Nebraska, to Cheyenne, Wyoming (uphill much of the way), to 18.01 while driving from Cedar City, Utah, to Los Angeles (downhill some of the way). Cruise speeds were 60 to 63 mph. In later tests at 55 mph the Suburban delivered an 18.60 mpg average at 55 mph. Again, this is with a 3-speed automatic transmission.

After reading our fuel economy figures, one might be inclined to ask,

"Where's the 30 mpg they're advertising?" It's there, but in different vehicles that are not equipped to tow heavy trailers. The GMC C-2500 and Chevy C-20 models are not available with the overdrive transmissions that are offered in C-1500 and C-10 models. The overdrive top gear is the key to further improved fuel economy while cruising without a trailer.

In tests with a K-10 Chevrolet Blazer equipped with the 4-speed automatic overdrive transmission and 3.73 axle ratio, solo mileage varied between 22 and 24 mpg while towing a 5000-pound low-profile 29-foot trailer. Mileage on flat highway was slightly better than 15 mpg. Overdrive (.70 to 1 ratio) was usable on flat highway but the transmission automatically downshifted to third (1 to 1 ratio) on slight hills or in headwinds, while towing.

In a motorhome chassis (gross weight 13,500 pounds), fuel economy of 10 to 11 mpg was common in reasonably level terrain.

Cost Vs. Benefits

Assuming our fuel economy figures are fairly representative of what RV owners will get when moving similar weight, let's calculate a hypothetical 10,000-mile cost-benefit situation.

As an example, let's figure the C-2500 Suburban is used to tow a 6000-pound trailer about 40 percent of the time, and is driven solo 60 percent. Let's estimate average towing fuel economy at 11.5

mpg and average solo fuel economy at 17 in combined city-highway use. We'll figure fuel cost at $1.15 per gallon, which is the average of what we paid during our test in late 1981, when the engine became available. The price has changed and the buyer should adjust fuel cost figures used here for a more accurate picture of the cost-benefit ratio of a diesel. For 4000 miles of trailer towing we would use 348 gallons at a cost of $400. For 6000 miles of solo driving we would use 352 gallons at a cost of $405. Total diesel fuel cost for each 10,000 miles would be $805.

Now let's see what a gasoline engine in similar use would do. Speculation must be used here because we didn't test a gasoline rig under identical circumstances. Let's estimate towing mileage at eight mpg and solo mileage at 11 mpg, with fuel cost at $1.27 per gallon, which was the average price we would then have paid for regular gasoline. For 4000 miles of towing we would have used 500 gallons, at a cost of $635. For 6000 miles of solo driving we would have used 545 gallons at a cost of $692. Total gasoline cost for each 10,000 miles would have been $1327.

Difference between diesel and gasoline in this case would be $522 per 10,000 miles.

We're assuming use of regular fuel. Lead-free would add about 10 cents per gallon and make the diesel versus gasoline cost difference around $600 per 10,000 miles.

Assuming the vehicle is driven 20,000 miles a year, the diesel would pay for itself in fuel savings at the rate of $1044

to $1200 a year in this example. The cost figures and payoff will change with every individual situation, which means the prospective buyer must evaluate fuel costs and other factors and make his or her own calculations.

Obviously, the RV owner who already plans to buy a new vehicle is in the best position to benefit from the optional diesel. To buy a new vehicle that costs $16,000 to $18,000 just to get improved fuel economy of a diesel engine doesn't make financial sense; $16,000 to $18,000 will pay for a lot of fuel and a lot of mechanical improvement on the presently owned vehicle, if that vehicle is suitable for the role it is required to fill.

Refining the Fuel

When the 6.2 engine first was introduced in the fall of 1981, diesel fuel prices generally were somewhat less than those of regular gasoline, and considerably less than lead-free gasoline. But higher demand for diesel was expected to raise prices. From every barrel of crude oil, specific proportions of diesel fuel, gasoline and other fuels can be refined. Consequently, increased refining of diesel fuel causes more gasoline to be produced. If the demand for gasoline is down, this tends to limit diesel fuel production because only so much gasoline can be stored. Limited diesel production creates higher prices, which in turn reduces demand. It's the free-enterprise system in action.

In other areas of the diesel's performance and suitability for towing, sound level is not offensive at low elevations. It's hardly noticeable at cruise speeds but makes itself evident at slow speeds. The 6.2 seems to become more noisy as altitude is gained, apparently due to enrichment of air/fuel mixtures that occurs when atmospheric pressure drops. It also is more noisy during cold starts due to a cold advance feature on the fuel injector pump. Injection of the fuel is advanced three to 4 degrees beyond normal (in relation to top dead center of the piston on its compression stroke).

Issuance of black smoke from the exhaust is not noticeable at low altitudes by watching tail pipes in the mirrors, even under heavy load, but it becomes noticeable at high altitudes. GM will offer altitude compensation calibration for the engine in vehicles sold in areas above 5000 feet.

Oil consumption has ranged from a quart in 700 miles to a quart in 1500 miles, depending on the vehicle. Engineers said normal consumption should be around a quart in 1400 miles.

Chevrolet engineers designed a new cooling package for the 6.2 engine and it includes a special large cross-flow radiator with oil cooling tanks in each end, one for the automatic transmission and another for engine oil. Coolant circulates around the tanks to absorb heat from the oil. Temperatures were reasonable (see accompanying performance figures) during our test in 80-degree weather and the 6.2 should have no trouble in hot weather. The engine is fitted with a 180-degree thermostat. We monitored temperatures in the left cylinder head, and recorded normal operating temperature without a trailer of 185, and 190 to 192 while towing. When the temperature reached 200 degrees, the thermostatically controlled engine fan went into its high-speed phase, drawing more air through the radiator and reducing the temperature.

Diesels Much Stronger

Function of a diesel engine is quite different in many ways from a gasoline engine, and similar in others. However, in general its construction is much stronger, to withstand the 21.5 to 1 compression ratio. Gasoline-engine compression ratios usually are around 8.5 to 1.

Features that create this durability include a heavier cast-alloy iron block, with webbed areas in the lower end to maintain rigidity, 4-bolt main bearing caps (light-duty gasoline engines usually have two-bolt caps), stronger crankshaft, camshaft, pistons and rods. Bulkheads are solid (no metal cored out) to give more rigid support for crankshaft bearings. Piston rod as well as crankshaft bearings are larger. Forces exerted on bearings are much higher, but because the bearings are larger, potential for wear is about the same or possibly better. This was one aspect of the Olds diesel engine that precluded its use in RV service; bearings would not stand up to forces created when the engine was operated at heavy throttle for long periods. The 6.2-liter engine also has heavier-duty pistons, with pis-

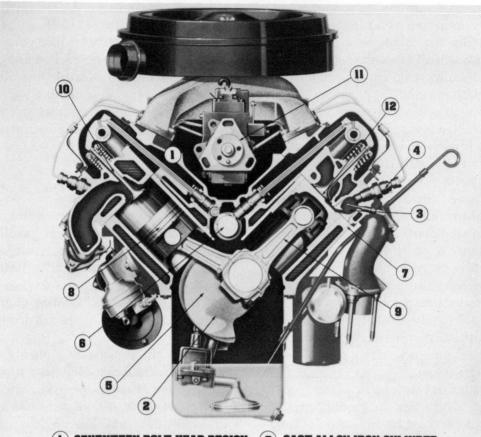

1. **SEVENTEEN-BOLT HEAD DESIGN.** For a tight gasket seal all around.

2. **FOUR-BOLT MAIN BEARING CAPS.** Provide rigid support for the crankshaft.

3. **RICARDO COMET V PRE-COMBUSTION CHAMBERS.** For high efficiency and low noise levels.

4. **PINTLE-TYPE INJECTOR NOZZLES.** With fuel lines made of high-pressure steel tubing.

5. **NODULAR IRON CRANKSHAFT.** With external torsional damper for reduced vibration.

6. **FORGED-STEEL CARBURIZED CAMSHAFT.** For strength and durability.

7. **CAST ALLOY IRON CYLINDER BLOCK.** For overall strength. Cylinder walls are reborable.

8. **CAST ALUMINUM PISTONS.** Combine light weight and strength.

9. **FORGED HEAT-TREATED STEEL CONNECTING RODS.** For strength and rigidity.

10. **SILCHROME® STEEL INTAKE VALVES.** With full-chrome stems.

11. **STANADYNE® MECHANICAL DISTRIBUTOR FUEL SYSTEM.** Which feature a full mechanical governor with friction damper ring.

12. **STELLITE-FACED EXHAUST VALVES.** With full-chrome stems and positive valve rotators.

Components of the 6.2-liter engine are illustrated in this cutaway drawing from Chevrolet.

ton crowns about 100 percent thicker than gasoline-engine pistons.

When driving a vehicle with a diesel engine, the sound of the engine indicates why all this is necessary, even in the 6.2 engine, which is comparatively quiet. A diesel makes a rattling sound somewhat similar to that of detonation or preignition ping in a gasoline engine. The principles are not dissimilar; the diesel knock is caused by very rapid combustion pressure rise, compared to a gasoline engine. In a gasoline engine the fuel burns at a progressive rate, with a sparkplug-ignited flame front moving across the combustion chamber. When ping occurs, a second flame front, one caused by spontaneous ignition, meets the normal flame front and the pressure rise is very high, sending shock down through the piston, rod, crankshaft, and possibly even slapping the piston against the cylinder wall. This happens on a more modified and controlled scale in a diesel, but the engine is designed much heavier to withstand the shock of rapid pressure rise that "excites" all the structure elements of the engine and produces an audible knock. It's one reason SAE 30 oil is emphasized by Chevrolet/GMC for the 6.2-liter diesel, whereas multigrade oils are emphasized for light-duty gasoline engines. The owner's manual recommends SAE 30 oil for operation above 32 degrees F.

Other similarities between gasoline and diesel engines include the fact that both have intake and exhaust valves and intake, compression, power and exhaust strokes. At least, the 6.2-liter diesel has four strokes. Some commercial-truck diesels are 2-stroke, but we needn't get into that here.

Other than much higher compression and substantial difference in volatility of the fuels, a diesel differs from a gasoline engine mainly in the way fuel is delivered to combustion chambers. In a gasoline engine, downward movement of pistons (intake stroke) draws air through the carburetor. The air, moving rapidly past fuel distribution nozzles, pulls fuel out of the carburetor. It mixes with air and is drawn into the combustion chamber. The amounts of air and fuel are controlled by a throttle. In a diesel, there is no driver control over the amount of air drawn into the engine. It changes only with engine rpm. The engine's speed is controlled by how much fuel is injected through small nozzles directly into the combustion chambers. The accelerator pedal is linked to an injector pump and the fuel is accurately measured under pressure to the precombustion chambers. Compression super-heats the air and combustion occurs spontaneously—no spark plugs. Combustion spreads to the combustion cavity on top of the piston. When fuel is injected, the piston already has progressed through much of the compression stroke.

With all that compression, one wonders why a diesel engine does not have as much power output per liter of displacement as a gasoline engine. The five-liter gasoline engine, for example, develops 165 hp at 4400 rpm while the 6.2-liter diesel develops 135 hp at 3600 rpm. The higher rpm limit is an advantage for full-throttle passing but wouldn't be much of a factor in routine driving and hill-climbing since most RV owners rarely sustain rpm higher than 3500 for hill climbing.

Reason for the horsepower-per-liter disparity lies in characteristics of diesel fuel versus gasoline and in valve timing. The heavier diesel fuel, sprayed into the precombustion chamber 4 to 12 degrees before piston top dead center (depending on rpm), does not atomize as finely as gasoline, and thus does not mix as thoroughly with air. The diesel particles cannot "find" the oxygen as readily. Some of the fuel may be blown out the exhaust only partially burned, hence the tendency of a diesel to produce black smoke (carbon) on heavy acceleration. A gasoline engine will react the same way if the choke sticks; more fuel is fed to the engine than can be combined with available air for combustion.

Bore of the 6.2-liter diesel is similar to that of the gasoline 5.7-liter engine (3.98 inches versus 4 inches) but the diesel engine has longer stroke (3.80 versus 3.48 inches). An engine with long stroke usually has good torque at lower rpm (an example is the straight 6-cylinder engine design) but doesn't have much power at the top end when the driver downshifts and pulls out to pass. In addition, due to diesel combustion characteristics, almost all the apparent power is available in the initial one-half of throttle travel.

Other mechanical features of the 6.2 engine that contribute to durability are roller cam followers in the hydraulic valve lifters, and a double-row cam chain. Conventional valve lifters ride

The 6.2 as it looks with air cleaner in place, in a 1983 Chevrolet Blazer.

directly on the cam lobes, protected from sliding friction only by oil film. In the 6.2, rollers are mounted in the bottoms of the lifters, reducing potential for wear on cam lobes. The double-row cam chain should be more resistant to wear, which elongates the chain and gradually retards cam timing.

Protection Against Water

Water is a no-no in diesel engines because it tends to adversely affect operation of the injector pump and the injectors. Same goes for dirt, which is a more serious problem. Consequently engineers included two filters in the system—one more than was used with the Oldsmobile diesel engine. The filter used in the Olds engine, a 10-micron unit, is used along with an 80-micron filter attached to the bulkhead on the passenger side. A petcock permits draining of that filter if any water is

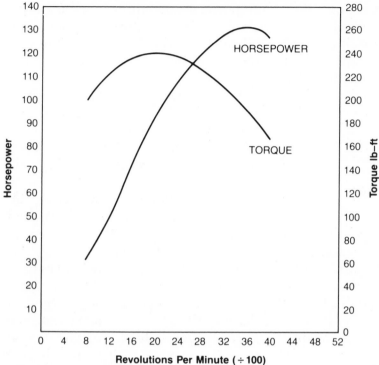

Horsepower and torque curves are illustrated on a graph from Chevrolet literature.

detected by an electronic water sensor in the fuel tank. A water separator sock of 180-micron mesh is used on the fuel pickup inside the tank, and a siphon access can be used to draw water out if it is detected. Protection against water as well as dirt seems quite thorough in the 6.2-liter engine.

As for maintenance, a change of fuel filters is recommended each 15,000 miles. Oil-change interval is 5000 miles or 12 months for normal use, or 2500 miles or three months for more severe use such as trailer towing, stop-go driving in cold weather and high-speed runs

at high temperatures. Additives are available to prevent formation of algae. The oil sump holds 6 quarts plus one quart for the filter. Oil-change intervals for gasoline engines are 7500 miles or 12 months for moderate service and 3000 miles or three months for more severe use, so the diesel will cost more for oil maintenance. However, there is no carburetor to service, no spark plugs to replace and no spark timing to set— no need, in fact, for any kind of regular tune-up procedures. No service intervals are listed for the injector pump or nozzles.

An engine block heater is provided, to aid in cold-weather starting. Glow plugs powered by the 12-volt electrical system preheat the precombustion chambers for cold starts, with only a short delay in moderate weather. The engine does not have cylinder sleeves, and may be bored .030-inch oversize for overhaul.

Ford/IH 6.9-Liter Diesel

With introduction of a new 6.9-liter diesel engine and re-introduction of the 7.5-liter (460-cubic-inch) gasoline V-8 in pickup trucks, vans and mini-motor-home chassis, Ford appears to be taking new aim at prospective customers who plan to tow or haul large amounts of weight.

In the case of the new 6.9-liter diesel (420 cubic inches), the highest rating is 15,700 pounds gross combined weight. If that seems a lot, consider that the engine also will see action in medium-duty International Harvester trucks with load ratings up to 26,000 pounds. RV usage of the engine may be rather tame by comparison.

If it seems improbable that an engine rated at 161 hp (compared to 202 hp with the 460 V-8), can do all that, a quick inspection of the new 6.9-liter diesel in a dealer's showroom should bring reassurance. With its battleship-gray paint, the engine in our F-250HD test vehicle looked like it meant business. On the road, it maintained that image, with good power throughout its rpm range, good throttle response and a very civilized nature that should not offend RV owners accustomed to gasoline engines. In short, it is very impressive.

Although Chevrolet took much of the pizazz out of diesel-engine introductions by being the first to introduce a workhorse diesel (6.2 liters) in light-duty trucks and vans, the Ford introduction was also a major event because it gave the RV owner another significant way to go in reducing operational costs. And its higher power output qualifies it for heavier loads.

In view of how diesel fuel prices have increased, compared to the cost of regular gasoline, one may logically wonder how the 6.9 engine can be expected to reduce costs. But even at the current (mid-December 1982) price penalty, the 6.9 still comes out on the positive side of the ledger, and the price spread may narrow in the future. We'll deal with prices and cost-effectiveness in more detail later.

International Harvester designed the 6.9 engine specifically for medium-duty service. The engine gives every promise of excellent durability under the most severe RV service, which is probably what it will see, in view of the $2500 optional cost of the engine and the fact that it probably will appeal strongly to owners of heavy RVs who travel considerable distances. As is the case in the trucking industry, the "buy-out" time depends on travel distances. If one drives only 5000 miles a year, it will

The Ford/IH 6.9-liter diesel is a heavy-duty design that is used in medium-duty trucks up to 27,000 pounds gvw.

take twice as long for the fuel savings of a diesel engine to equal the optional cost of the engine than if one drives 10,000 miles a year. Since the optional 460 engine is priced at $476—and since most RV owners who are interested in the 6.9 engine are also considering a large gasoline engine, actual optional cost of the 6.9 would be closer to $2000. A similar situation exists with the Chevrolet 6.2-liter diesel and the division's 454-cubic-inch gasoline engine.

In comparing RV sales literature from the two companies, the 6.9 has the edge in rated weight-moving capability, with a 15,700-pound gross combined weight rating (combined total of vehicle, trailer and all their content) with 4.1 axle, while the 6.2 is rated at 13,500 pounds gcw with a 4.56 axle ratio. The 6.2 gets a 15,500-pound rating in motorhome chassis with 5.86 axle.

To put the diesels into perspective with gasoline engines that may also be under consideration, consider these specifications:

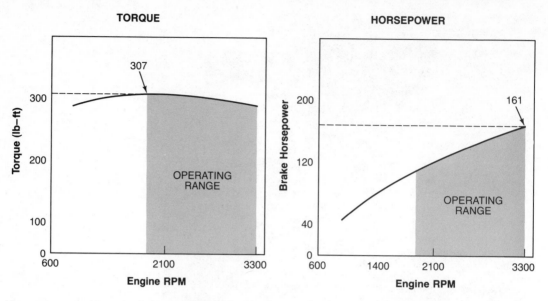

Horsepower and torque characteristics are illustrated in graphs provided by Ford.

	HP @ RPM	Torque @ RPM
Ford 6.9 Diesel	161 @ 3300	307 @ 1800
Ford 460 Gasoline	202 @ 4000	331 @ 2200
Ford 351 Gasoline	147 @ 3200	276 @ 2000
Chevrolet 6.2 Diesel	135 @ 3600	240 @ 2000
Chevrolet 454 Gasoline	230 @ 3800	360 @ 2800
Chevrolet 350 Gasoline	160 @ 3800	250 @ 2800

(All listings are for 1983 heavy-duty emissions—vehicles with gross vehicle weight ratings over 8600 pounds. Figures for light-duty emissions vehicles may differ slightly.)

As you can see, the diesels are strong in torque but no match in horsepower for the big-block (460 and 454) gasoline V-8s. The 6.9-liter Ford/IH diesel has a substantial margin over the 6.2-liter Chevrolet diesel. However, both share the diesel characteristic of producing most of their power with light to medium throttle, whereas with many gasoline engines heavy throttle is required before power output feels substantial. This doesn't make the diesels any stronger but it makes them *seem* stronger.

Design of the 6.9

Regardless of how the 6.9-liter diesel stacks up against any other engine, it is impressive in its own right—even rated with a clumsy 4-speed manual transmission. (Ford used the 4-speed with this engine until modifications of the C-6 automatic would be completed.

The 6.9 engine is an all-new design by International Harvester, although based on that company's many years of diesel-engine design and manufacture. In late 1982 Ford had an exclusive on its use in pickups, vans and other vehicles with gvw ratings below 14,000 pounds, as part of a $500 million contract. IH planned to use the engine in some of its own medium-duty vehicles; other uses might include marine, military and re-power (replacement of gasoline engines in existing vehicles).

The engine weighs 780 pounds without flywheel, flywheel housing, fuel filter, alternator or starting motor, so the actual weight is upwards of 1000 pounds, which is about 200 pounds more than the 460 gasoline engine. Ford's excellent I-beam front suspension handles the additional weight without any noticeable difference. The 6.9 engine is similar to most automotive-style diesels in that it uses a pre-combustion chamber, heated by glow plugs, to facilitate starting and to improve combustion characteristics. Valves are equipped with rotators and valve lifters have roller camshaft followers that minimize wear on the cam. The cam is gear-driven, as are the oil pump and injector pump; consequently the timing chain, one source of premature wear in a gasoline engine, is eliminated.

The engine is fitted with an unusual oil cooler—a tube attached to the block (see page 86). Oil is drawn from the pan, routed through the tube, into the oil filter and then into the main oil gallery. Engine coolant circulates around the oil passages in the oil cooler and prevents oil temperature from greatly exceeding coolant temperature. As you might imagine from the size of the radiator, coolant temperature is held tightly in check. Oil jets direct continual streams of oil upward under each piston, for cooling.

The block is designed to withstand the loads of diesel operation in high-weight situations and utilizes a 4-bolt main bearing setup, with five main bearings. Connecting rods are forged steel and pistons are aluminum alloy. The block is not fitted with sleeves but can be bored overside during overhaul. Overhaul probably is more of a consideration for commercial users, since it's difficult to imagine many RV owners encountering the need for one.

The fuel injector pump is a Stanadyne, used in concert with a conventional fuel pump, whose only role is to lift fuel to the injector pump that supplies fuel under high pressure to the injector nozzles. Injector timing is very precise, with the fuel charge being sprayed from the nozzle into the precombustion chamber slightly after top dead center (ATDC) of the piston stroke.

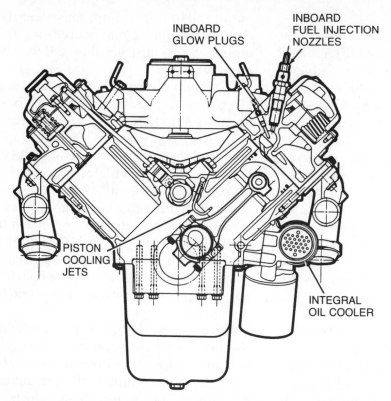

INBOARD
GLOW PLUGS

INBOARD
FUEL INJECTION
NOZZLES

PISTON
COOLING
JETS

INTEGRAL
OIL COOLER

Special features of the 6.9 engine include special oil jets for piston cooling, integral oil cooler. Engine holds 10 quarts of oil.

This contrasts with a gasoline engine, in that spark plugs fire prior to top dead center. The 6.9 injectors are timed at 4 to 6 degrees ATDC for low altitude and from 5 to 7 degrees ATDC for altitudes above 3000 feet. Degree variance depends on burning rate of the fuel (cetane value). When diesel fuel is injected, it burns very rapidly compared to gasoline, hence the ATDC fuel injection timing. The higher the cetane number, the shorter the time lag from the point when fuel enters the chamber to the time it ignites. By contrast, higher octane numbers for gasoline mean a slower, more controlled burning rate and better resistance to spark knock. Normally we use Number 2 diesel fuel and it is rated for about the same cetane value as Number 1 fuel: a value of 40. Nowever, Number 1 has a flash point of 100 degrees F or lower, while the flash point of Number 2 is about 125 degrees F. Number 1 is more suitable for use in cold climates, although when it is not available, the Number 2 fuel usually has been "winterized." A nonwinterized fuel may partially turn to wax in low temperatures.

The truck is fitted with two starting batteries, wired in parallel.

Water, a deadly enemy of any diesel engine, is prevented from entering the injector pump by a fuel filter/water separator attached to the rear wall of the engine compartment. Every 5000 miles the operator must open the top air vent and the bottom drain vent to permit escape of any water trapped in the unit. We performed this routine on two occasions and noticed only small amounts of water in the fuel that was drained. A warning light is activated when the amount of water in the separator becomes excessive. A change of fuel filter is called for every 15,000 miles. The filter is priced at $13.10. The oil change interval is 5000 miles or six months for normal service, 2500 miles or three months for heavy service, such as trailer towing. The engine holds 10 quarts and the oil filter is priced at $13.35. In our first 7000 miles of driving oil consumption averaged 1600 to 1800 miles per quart. Change interval for engine coolant is three years.

No periodic service is required for the fuel injection system. Since a diesel does not have a throttle valve, each piston draws in a full charge or air with each intake stroke. The volume of air is the same as that of a gasoline engine of equal size, running under full throttle all the time. The amount of fuel injected into the diesel determines power output. Thus, air cleaner maintenance

is important. Replacement of the air cleaner is called for every 30,000 miles, or more often if the truck is operated in dusty conditions.

Cooling

Diesels are not supposed to run hot. Engineers put a top limit of 245 degrees on the 6.9 and even included an engine-heat warning light in addition to the coolant temperature gauge. Ideally the engine should run much cooler, and it probably will, since Ford has included what appears to be the largest radiator ($136.70 option) ever used in a pickup truck. It has 585 square inches of frontal area and four rows of tubes to conduct coolant from one end tank to the other. There are 11 heat-dissipation fins per inch without air-conditioning and

The 6.9-liter engine is fitted with an exceptionally large radiator to hold coolant temperatures below 245 degrees even under the most severe conditions.

Ford/IH 6.9-liter engine has Stanadyne fuel injector pump immediately in front of screened inlet to intake manifold.

On the Road

Although the design is that of a medium-duty truck engine, noise level and operational characteristics of the 6.9 engine are excellent. That is to say "civilized." Engine noise is clearly audible but is not annoying. Smoke is visible after cold starts but very little is noticed afterward. Even in high altitudes, when a diesel will smoke more and be more noisy, smoke was negligible and noise level was tolerable. Ford has done a very good job with sound deadening. No diesel fuel smell is noticeable except during re-fueling.

Our first experience with the engine was a drive from Detroit to Los Angeles with the test vehicle, an F-250 HD with 3.54 axle ratio, in early October, 1982. We took major routes and drove at a brisk pace. Fuel consumption ranged from a low of 16.19 to a high of 18.12, depending on the situation. The 18.12 figure was similar to what we recorded with the Chevrolet 6.2-liter engine under similar conditions.

Using cruise control, the truck is very comfortable to drive on long trips with one exception: due to the 8600-pound gross vehicle weight rating (gvwr), stiff rear springs are required and the rear suspension is very stiff when the truck is unladen or unattached to a trailer. In fact, it's intolerably stiff. On some of the rougher sections of interstate highways in the Midwest, it was necessary to wear a seat belt for reasons other than safety—to keep one's head from hitting the roof. Later tests indicated

12 fins with air-conditioning. By comparison, the radiator used with the 460 gasoline has 537 square inches of frontal area, three rows of tubes and 10 to 13 fins per inch, depending on equipment ordered.

During our test with 6500-pound (dry weight) Silver Streak trailer in 60 to 65 degree weather, coolant temperature would rise slowly during heavy-throttle climbs on 6-percent grades until temperature reached 205 degrees F. At that point the thermostatically controlled fan would go into full engagement and pull temperature down to the normal for flat-highway running (195 to 200 degrees) and the process would be repeated until the summit was reached. Hot weather is the real test but I would not expect this engine to have a cooling problem regardless of load or weather conditions.

that a load of about 1000 pounds in the bed would produce a reasonably decent ride (without a trailer).

The truck is still rough and a moderate amount of bounce occurs when a trailer such as our test Silver Streak 34-footer is towed with the empty truck. The ideal situation is a permanent load of at least 1000 pounds in the truck bed. (Springs were redesigned in April 1983, solving the problem.)

Steering characteristics were excellent during solo driving as well as (later) towing. The truck requires very little steering correction to maintain a straight course; it responds properly to steering input. Turning angles are good, which aids parking and backing.

During the solo drive from Detroit to Los Angeles we crossed Wolf Creek Pass near Durango, Colorado, at 10,857 feet altitude, and the vehicle climbed most of the grade in high gear on cruise control, seldom dropping below 55 mph. On most grades while driving the truck without a trailer, the cruise control would hold speed very accurately. However, more speed loss occurs with a trailer and the cruise control annoyingly quits (disengages) when road speed drops 10 mph below the pre-set speed. That probably is intended as a safety feature but it should be corrected since it forces the trailerist to return to manual throttle operation on mountain grades. The engine is fitted with a vacuum pump to operate the cruise control and other vacuum-powered accessories such as heater doors. The cruise control will apply almost all the power of which

the 6.9 liter engine is capable.

After we hitched to the 34-foot Silver Streak, the pace dropped, as one might expect. A 34-foot conventional trailer is a *big* trailer, although this specimen is of excellent design and handles well. Even though the trailer's frame has recently been lightened, the new design is equally as solid (if not more so) and the trailer frame does not flex, encouraging the tow vehicle to bounce or porpoise. A moderate amount of bounce was encountered while towing, but it was the result of the over-stiff truck rear suspension.

Stability While Towing

The Ford/Silver Streak combination was quite stable in varied driving conditions, including strong crosswinds. While descending grades, large trucks overtaking from the rear can cause severe problems for marginally stable vehicle/trailer rigs, but the effect could be felt in the test rig only slightly, prompting very minor steering correction. Gusting crosswinds also called for very minor steering correction. The Eaz-Lift friction-brake sway control used on the test vehicle contributed to the excellent stability by effectively damping lateral motion of the truck/trailer at the hitch ball. Rapid lane changes (simulating evasive maneuvers) had to be made with deliberation because the weight mass was considerable. Still, the truck/trailer combination felt manageable and safe.

We drove the Ford/Silver Streak combination over the same route traveled earlier with a diesel-powered Chevy Suburban and 32-foot Alfa. The Chevy was equipped with a 4.1 axle (3.54 axle with the Ford). And the Silver Streak weighed 600 pounds more than the Alfa (dry weight). On 5-percent grades climbed at 27 to 30 mph in second gear (three-speed automatic) with the Chevrolet, the Ford did 43 to 45 mph in third gear of the 4-speed manual transmission. Gear ratios were similar. The automatic is not as efficient as a manual in such a situation but the difference in hill-climb speeds would be marginal. The Ford/IH 6.9 engine's additional horsepower is evident in the mountains.

Fuel economy with the Ford during that trip was 11.90. While driving at 55 mph on mostly level highway the Ford/Silver Streak combination produced fuel economy of 14.8 mpg.

Ford's sales literature indicates that the 6.9 engine in our test truck (3.54 axle) will do 19.9 mpg in solo cruising. We recorded 19.2 mpg. The same literature indicates mileage at 17.5 mpg with the 4.1 axle, 19.1 mpg with a 3.73 axle and 21.4 mpg with a 3.07 axle. The 3.73 axle apparently was not available at the time of our test as it was not listed in the dealer data book, although the engineering department apparently had done some testing with that axle. In a city/suburban driving test, the Ford literature indictes 12.7 mpg for the 4.1 axle, 14.2 mpg for 3.73, 14.1 for 3.54 and 15.5 with 3.07. (Figures are for an unladen F-350.) The F-350 is only marginally heavier than our test F-250HD, so the figures should be applicable. EPA fuel economy figures are not available for vehicles with gvw ratings over 8500 pounds.

Auto Vs. Manual

Although shifting characteristics of the 4-speed manual transmission used in our test truck left much to be desired, the transmission does offer a slight efficiency edge over a conventional automatic trans (not equipped with torque convertor lockup), in that no excessive heat is generated in the transmission oil—which is the medium through which torque is multiplied in the torque convertor. Thus, no external cooling is required and the manual 4-speed has proven reliable. Most RV owners prefer the automatic for the sake of driving ease. Just one stint in a traffic jam with the 4-speed will illustrate the wisdom of that attitude. On the highway, it's no problem because not that much shifting is done—no problem at least unless three persons occupy the cab, in which case the middle passenger must straddle the shift lever. Ford initially introduced the 6.9 engine only with the 4-speed manual, to get the engine on the market and to appeal to farmers and ranchers, many of whom seem to prefer a manual.

The 6.9 in a truck properly geared for towing heavy trailers cries out for an overdrive for solo cruising. At introduction Ford is offering the 3-speed automatic C-6 transmission and the stump-puller 4-speed-manual Warner T-19. Gear ratios of the T-19 are 5.11, 3.03, 1.70 and 1.00. The C-6 automatic has 2.46, 1.46 and 1.00 ratios. As you can see, second gear of the C-6 is slightly faster than third gear of the T-19. Our test engine reached its rpm limit (3300 rpm, controlled by a governor), at about 50 mph but road speed would be slightly faster with the C-6.

Optional trailer-towing items for a 6.9-equipped truck include a 60-amp alternator, dual extended RV mirrors and heavy-duty turn signal flasher. The super cooling package and gauge package are listed separately. The extended mirrors were inadvertently omitted from our test truck. Base price for our test vehicle was $9189. Options, including the $2543 diesel engine, pushed it into the low-$15,000 range. Warranty on the engine is 36 months or 50,000 miles.

Tow Ratings

Trailer-tow weight ratings vary among the different models. Our F-250HD with 3.54 axle ratio was rated by Ford for maximum gross combined weight (gcw) of 13,700 pounds. With the truck weighing approximately 5300 pounds (with hitch but without camper shell), that leaves 8400 pounds for weight of trailer, accessories, supplies and equipment. Our test truck was well suited to that weight rating. Other gcw ratings range from 10,400 to 15,700 pounds, depending on truck model and axle ratio. Axle ratio selection includes 3.07, 3.54 and 4.10.

Cost-Effectiveness

After lengthy consideration of just how well the 6.9-liter diesel serves as a trailer-tow vehicle, we must now discuss what businessmen call the *bottom line*—whether or not the savings in fuel costs are large enough to justify the optional cost of the engine and any other disadvantages inherent in the engine.

Unfortunately, one aspect of this requires a crystal ball. When we completed our test of the Chevrolet 6.2-liter diesel late in 1981, diesel fuel cost averaged $1.15 per gallon and regular gasoline averaged $1.27 during our travels. With the Ford/IH 6.9 engine (late in 1982) diesel fuel cost averaged $1.22 and regular gasoline pricing was about $1.10—and dropping. Although the price comparison between diesel fuel and regular gasoline may change by the time you read this, let's take a look at cost-effectiveness. Our figures may differ from yours, based on how you travel, so you'll have to utilize your own figures.

Let's assume the test vehicle is used to tow the trailer about 40 percent of the time. Let's estimate average towing mileage with the test trailer at 12 mpg, average solo mileage at 16 and diesel fuel cost at $1.22. For 4000 miles of trailer towing and 6000 miles of solo driving fuel cost would be $863.

Let's estimate the appetite of the Ford 460 at 7.5 mpg while towing our test trailer and average solo fuel consumption at 10 mpg, with fuel cost at $1.10 per gallon. Cost of fuel per 10,000 miles would be $1246.

Thus, the 6.9-liter engine would be $383 less costly to drive per 10,000 miles, considering fuel costs alone. Of course, maintenance costs affect the equation. Estimating that maintenance will cost about $30 more per 10,000 miles with the 6.9 engine, it brings cost-per-10,000 miles advantage for the diesel engine down to about $350. Thus, the vehicle would have to be driven about 60,000 miles before fuel savings would equal the $2000 out-of-pocket cost of the diesel (assuming the buyer otherwise would have ordered the 460). In fact the maintenance cost difference may favor the gasoline engine somewhat more, due to the diesel engine's high oil capacity and filter cost.

If the 6.9 engine suffered from marginal quality or performance—or any other kind of defect—the bottom line might be rather doubtful. However, the engine is an excellent performer, is apparently durable, fits into the truck quite well and generally is quite a piece of work. Couple that with the usual good design of the F-250, and Ford Pickups with 6.9-liter diesels qualify as prime tow vehicles or camper haulers.

Diesel Conversions Vs. Propane

In past years, diesel conversions (replacement of a gasoline engine with a diesel) sold for $10,000 to $15,000 (including a 4-speed Allison transmission), which put them in a rather poor cost-effectiveness category. Cost may come down a bit with availability of the International Harvester 6.9-liter engine being used by Ford in light trucks and vans, so the cost benefits of diesel versus propane must be measured using the methods described in the previous section on the GM 6.2-liter diesel.

Propane still stands up well as an RV motor fuel and the price has been consistently lower than that of gasoline, although availability is more limited and convenience is questionable, depending on personal circumstances.

To evaluate the practicality of a propane conversion, calculations must include fuel cost (including state license, if applicable), cost of the propane conversion, and effect on fuel economy. Since propane has less heat content than gasoline, fuel economy usually drops. Performance drops with many dual-fuel setups, partially due to the heat content problem, but also due to inefficiency of the fuel mixing setup. The propane fuel mixing apparatus must be positioned on top of the gasoline carburetor, and this often affects performance while using propane as well as gasoline although latest equipment reduces this loss.

With dual-fuel setups of older design the performance loss usually is around 20 percent. The fuel economy loss will vary from 10 percent to 20 percent, due to the combination of restrictive conventional fuel mixing equipment and the difference in heat content. Performance on gasoline may be restricted by the gasoline shutoff valve. When operating on propane, an electrically controlled valve stops gasoline flow to the carburetor. The problem is that inside diameter of the valve is less than that

Propane motor fuel can be cost effective—but usually isn't with small fuel capacity such as this 20-gallon tank. Minimum capacity should be 40 gallons.

of the fuel line and fuel flow is restricted under heavy throttle. By using two of the valves in a manifold arrangement (parallel), with quarter-inch pipe fittings, the problem can be eliminated.

Gas Vs. Liquid

Propane is theoretically an excellent motor fuel, primarily because it enters the engine as a gas, whereas gasoline must be vaporized. Vaporization of gasoline usually is incomplete, which reduces engine efficiency. Propane has a high octane rating (anti-knock) and the ideal propane engine has higher compression than can be used if the vehicle is to be operated on gasoline. An

engine converted to propane could meet gasoline performance if effective equipment is used and if compression is raised to about 10.5 to 1. Then, and only then, can the owner get full benefit from the excellent fuel.

How It Works

One or two tanks feed propane into special hoses leading to the propane lock-off. It's either electrically or vacuum operated and forms a positive shutoff anytime the ignition key is turned off or the propane control switch is moved away from the propane position. The lock-off includes a filter that traps a good deal of debris when new tanks are

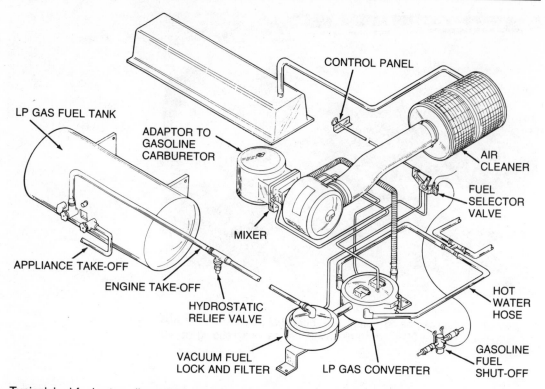

CONTROL PANEL

LP GAS FUEL TANK

ADAPTOR TO GASOLINE CARBURETOR

AIR CLEANER

FUEL SELECTOR VALVE

MIXER

APPLIANCE TAKE-OFF

ENGINE TAKE-OFF

HYDROSTATIC RELIEF VALVE

HOT WATER HOSE

VACUUM FUEL LOCK AND FILTER

LP GAS CONVERTER

GASOLINE FUEL SHUT-OFF

Typical dual-fuel setup allows driver to change from propane to gasoline with control handle or electrical switch.

put into service but gets little use after that. Tanks are hydrostatically tested (water pressure) for strength and the remaining water may create some rust before the tank is put into service.

Propane exits the bottom of a motor fuel tank in liquid state and passes through the fuel lock and into the regulator, which drops the pressure in two stages from a maximum of about 200 pounds (full tank) to about 1.5 pounds in the area where it's ready to exit on its way to the propane mixer. When propane in liquid state at minus 44 degrees F is allowed to expand into a vapor, it creates refrigeration. Thus, hot coolant from the engine is circulated

through the regulator to counteract the refrigeration and more quickly vaporize the fuel.

The reason that running propane as a single fuel is more efficient than a dual-fuel situation is that propane, as a gas, displaces more air than does gasoline as a vaporized liquid when passing through the carburetor venturi. In a straight LP-gas carburetion setup the propane is introduced *downstream* of the air valve (the equivalent of the venturi in a gasoline carburetor) and thus displaces none of the air passing through the air valve.

Late-model pickups have a good deal of room under the hood. The propane

Dual-fuel applications are possible even in vans with limited under-hood clearances.

Among the more effective propane mixers is the Impco CA300A-50, shown here in offset and straight applications.

equipment can be sandwiched into almost any pickup or motorhome. The fuel propane lock and convertor are permanently mounted, but the propane carburetor and air horn are easily and quickly removable after three hoses are disconnected from the regulator. The regulator responds to demand. During engine cranking, a partial vacuum is created in the propane carburetor and in the fuel line connecting it with the regulator. The regulator senses the vacuum and responds with the proper amount of fuel.

Impco literature makes it clear that operating temperatures must be lower

with propane than with gasoline because the dry propane does not have the heat-quenching effect on exhaust valves that gasoline provides. Engine temperature should be 170-180 degrees F during normal cruise conditions and should not exceed 220 under more severe conditions. Also, fans with fluid-drive clutches usually are calibrated to actuate in the 220- to 230-degree range (water temperature), which is higher than desirable with propane. The thermostatic coils on the faces of the fan clutches sometimes can be adjusted for lower actuation; either that or replace it with a solid fan, which tends to be noisier.

Temperature Monitoring

It's wise to install a coolant temperature gauge calibrated in degrees F and a solid fan, unless you can hear fan roar even with outside air temperature below 70 degrees, or you can adjust the thermostat on the fan so it will fully engage at about 190 degrees water temperature.

Ignition is critical with propane because the ability of the spark to cross the spark-plug gap is decreased. Consequently, the electrical charge that fires the plug builds to higher levels in the spark-plug cables before the gap is bridged. The spark, meanwhile, is looking for a place to jump to ground, and a faulty spark-plug cable, a leaky spark-plug boot or a worn distributor cap will allow this to happen. Or, the spark may jump to an adjacent wire. Proper routing of wires is important. Routing is indicated in most service manuals for specific vehicles. When wires are routed improperly, a charge from wire 7 may jump to wire 8 and fire that cylinder 120 degrees prematurely.

Temperature of the air ingested by the carburetor also is important. A propane-fuel vehicle suffers more from hot intake air than does a gasoline engine and free breathing is necessary. Addition of cool-air induction to the air cleaner is a must. It's difficult in many older trucks to find the room for a 4-inch air tube leading from an air horn on the propane carburetor to an air filter ahead of the radiator, but where space permits, it's worthwhile. Cool-air intake appears critical only when ambient air conditions exceed 70 degrees. Below that, air-conditioning normally is not used and the amount of heat thrown back into the engine compartment is reduced.

Impco found detonation a problem during tests with commercial trucks in summer temperatures of 90 to 105 degrees. They measured temperature of the carburetor inlet air and found it to be 180 degrees F. After ducting 90- to 100-degree air from the outside, the detonation ceased and the vehicle picked up 11 horsepower (measured at the rear wheels). The weight of air (oxygen content) is reduced one percent for each 10-degree temperature increase. Thus a temperature decrease of 50 degrees of inlet air will add five percent or 7.5 hp to a 150-hp engine.

The enrichment system in a propane mixer is activated at about 3 to 4 inches. Consequently, the engine doesn't run on enriched mixtures as much of the time on propane, even though more throttle is used than on gasoline. Also, the mixtures produced by the gasoline carburetor tend to get richer with increasing altitude, due to the decrease in atmospheric pressure. At 8000 or 9000 feet the gasoline mixture is quite fat, unless the carburetor has been re-jetted to compensate for it, and this is not practical unless the vehicle is continually used in high altitudes. But the propane regulator compensates automatically for changes in atmospheric pressure and mixtures remain the same regardless of altitude.

Another mechanical consideration with propane is its effect on valves. Recession (wear) of exhaust valve seats has been a problem in older engines, especially in industrial usage where engines are operated under heavy throttle most of the time. This is less prevalent since 1971, when manufacturers introduced hardened valves and valve seats that are necessary for durability with lead-free gasoline. Hardness of valves and valve seats has continued to improve since 1971. Lead is often thought to provide a lubricant to valves and seats, thereby extending their life, but the effect is different at least in regard to propane. The lead particles in gasoline perform a sort of shimming effect. They keep the face of the valve from actually resting fully on the seat; the distance is microscopic. Propane does not do this. The result is that the exhaust valve comes to rest fully on the seat. It's quite hot and in certain cases with specific metals, the valve welds itself to the seat at microscopic points. When it lifts, it takes the particles of the seat with it, causing recession.

When recession becomes a problem, the seats can be machined out and new hardened seats installed. Or the heads can be replaced. But it's not a prevalent problem.

Propane stations usually are more difficult to locate, not usually being located on main routes as are gasoline stations. Also, they usually perform no maintenance functions such as checking the oil and wiping the windows. They're usually open five and a half days a week from about 8:30 a.m. to 5 p.m. on weekdays and until noon on Saturdays. Truck stops licensed to sell propane as motor fuel often are open 24 hours a day, seven days a week.

While driving through unfamiliar areas, finding propane stations is tedious. But when driving familiar areas where the propane stops already have been located, it is not usually a problem to go off the regular route a few blocks. In many small towns the propane station is right on the main street. In mountainous areas and other locations not served by natural gas, propane availability is at its best.

Most stations are very conscientious about avoiding overfilling of the tanks (as indicated by the 20 percent or "bleeder" valve). Overfilling can cause the pressure relief valve (safety valve) of a tank to open and release enough gas to limit tank pressure to the maximum specified by the manufacturer. LP-gas motor-fuel tanks are normally frame-mounted and any gas escaping in this manner dissipates quickly. Safety valve releases should be prevented by avoiding tank overfilling. It's a matter of watching the serviceman to make sure he stops filling when white liquid appears at the bleeder valve.

Safety with propane always has been of prime concern and some RV owners tend to distrust the fuel. It's a safe fuel if the owner will follow basic safety procedures, such as checking the fuel lines periodically for leaks, with a soap and water solution. Actually, more hazard exists inside the coach with the propane appliance system than from a motor-fuel system, because the gas must grow in volume to a specific minimum mixture with air before it becomes explosive. Gas leaking from a motor-fuel system often dissipates quickly because the lines and appliances usually are fully exposed. There are specific precautions, such as not parking a propane-fueled vehicle inside a closed garage with a water heater.

In case of an accident, the Manchester tanks are equipped with automatic flow limiter devices that cut the flow to a very small volume (that passing through a "weep" hole) if a line is severed.

Propane belongs to a category commonly described as liquefied petroleum gas (LP-gas). So does butane. Both fuels remain in liquid state when compressed but "boil" into gas when pressure is reduced. The amount of pressure reduction determines how rapidly the gas is formed. Propane's advantage is that it is vaporized in temperatures as low as minus 40 degrees F. Below that, you carry it around in a bucket like water. Butane will not vaporize below 32 degrees F, hence its unsuitability in cold climates.

LP-gas is refined from crude oil, as gasoline, although in a different refining process. Propane has 91,500 BTUs per gallon and gasoline has 119,000. Propane weighs 4.25 pounds per gallon and gasoline weighs 6.3 pounds.

The propane tanks and other equipment as well last practically forever, so it's not necessary to amortize the investment during the life of one vehicle. The equipment usually can be easily transferred from one vehicle to another at minimal cost.

Weighing Your RV

9

Among the many important aspects of safe and economical RV travel, few that are so critical receive such casual attention as weight.

Most RV owners have only vague notions of what their vehicles weigh, even when they're attempting to diagnose and cure a handling problem that might be caused by improper weight distribution. Those vague notions come, in most cases, from the manufacturers' published dry weights. In the early 1970s and before, those figures were notoriously erroneous. They're better in more recent years, but still undependable in many cases. And, they do not take into account the load added to the vehicle by the owner.

It's up to the RV owner to weigh his vehicle and find out if the equipment, supplies, water, gasoline, and such, add

up to violations of chassis and tire load ratings, or if distribution of the load is improper. It's doubtful that one in a hundred will have done so. The weight figures also relate to fuel economy and performance, since every pound that must repeatedly be hauled up and down hills adds to fuel consumption and reduces performance.

Weighing procedures for motorhomes, campers and van conversions are basically simple, but the trailer-weighing procedure can be a bit more involved. Ideally, RVs should be weighed on individual wheel scales. But these are rare, and most owners will use the local commmercial scale, which is a platform scale normally used by heavy trucks and truck-trailers. You'll find these scales at grain elevators, equipment rental yards, trucking com-

Knowledge of RV weights allows the owner to determine tire inflation pressures accurately.

Trailers

Trailer gross vehicle weight (gvw) ratings have been listed since the early 1970s. Owners of trailers manufactured prior to that date can only hope that axles, wheels, suspension and frame are adequate for the loaded weight of the trailer. They usually are, if trailer weight does not exceed the rating(s) of the tires with which the trailer was originally equipped. But if heavier tires have been installed, wheel or axle ratings may be violated.

Choose a time when the trailer is loaded for a trip (water and LP-gas tanks full) and drive the car and trailer on to the scale for a reading on gross combined weight (gcw). Then drive ahead until the car is off the scale and get a reading for the trailer wheels alone. Action of the load-distributing hitch will result in trailer weight figures slightly different from those you'd get by unhitching the trailer on the scale. But the *hitched* figures are what you'll use to determine proper tire inflation. An important word of caution: The figures can be affected if the apron at the end of the scale is not level.

Next, position only one side of the trailer on the scale, by driving so that the right- or left-side trailer wheels are only an inch or so off the edge. Of course, the car should still be off the end. Alternate this action so that you'll have left and right side figures, in order to carry more tire pressure in one side than the other if the trailer is heavier on one side.

Now that you have right-side, left-

panies and a variety of other points. Look in the *Yellow Pages* of your phone book under Weighers, Public. If none is listed there, phone several grain elevators or equipment rental yards and ask if they know of a nearby commercial scale.

Fees for an RV weigh-in will vary, but they're usually not more than $3 for each reading. Even at that price this is a bargain for information that can help prevent failures and accidents, or aid you in improving stability through redistribution of weight. Platform scales will accommodate heavier weights than you'll record, so don't expect precise accuracy even though they're state-certified. For instance, you might weigh each wheel of a motorhome, as well as the entire RV, and find that the total of the weights does not precisely match the gross weight. But it should be close.

To check hitch weight, disconnect spring bars and allow coupler to rest on ball mount as dead weight. (Support tow vehicle with jack if neces-

sary.) Then position tongue jack on scale and move tow vehicle away. Subtract the difference between the two weight figures.

side figures, all you need is tongue (hitch) weight. Position the car and trailer so the tongue jack and trailer wheels are on the scale but rear wheels are off. Position a jack or block under the rear of the tow vehicle, so it will not sag excessively when you drop the spring bars. (This often is not necessary with trucks.)

Follow your usual unhitching procedure in removing spring bars, but leave the coupler on the ball. In other words, leave the trailer hitched, but without spring bars, so the coupler will rest as dead weight on the ball. By blocking up the rear of the car, make sure the trailer is in the position normal for travel. In other words, if the trailer travels perfectly level, that's the position it should have on the scale. If it

travels with the front several inches lower than the rear, weigh it that way. When a trailer is nose-down, hitch weight increases. When it's tail-down, hitch weight decreases. Trailers should be level for best towing stability.

Get a weight figure on the trailer wheels with the tongue resting on the tow vehicle off the scale. Then, lower the tongue jack to the scale, raise the coupler off the ball, drive the vehicle away and leave the trailer on the scale. You'll have two readings. Subtract to determine hitch weight.

A logical question might be, "Why go through all that when you can just set the tongue jack on the scale and get a hitch weight figure?" The answer is: Commercial scales are more accurate with higher weight. You'll get a much better figure by subtracting the difference, say, between 4000 and 4500 pounds than by weighing a 500-pound trailer tongue on a scale that may be calibrated for as much as 80,000 pounds.

If you expect tongue weight to be less than 300 pounds, use a bathroom scale or other portable scale.

Tongue weight should not be less than 10 percent of the gross trailer weight. That's gross dead trailer weight. From this procedure you'll have a *hitched* trailer weight and a *dead* trailer weight. For purposes of hitch weight relevancy, use the dead trailer weight. Hitch weight may be as high as 20 percent. In small and medium trailers, around 15 percent is desirable for good towability as long as the tow vehicle and hitch are capable. The owner often can manipulate hitch weight to some degree by shifting supplies.

Here's a sample list of figures derived for a trip-ready, 19-foot Aljo using the above procedure:

1. Gross combined weight
   truck and trailer   8460 lbs.
2. Gross trailer weight
   (hitched)   3540
3. Left side (hitched)   1790
4. Right side (hitched)   1750
5. Trailer dead weight
   minus hitch weight
   (spring bars removed
   but coupler resting on
   ball, vehicle off scale)   3220
6. Gross trailer dead
   weight   3660
7. Hitch weight   440

If your stability is good, you can get along without all seven of these figures. But you should have No. 2, and it would be best to have Nos. 5, 3 and 4, for proper tire inflation. All tires should be inflated according to weight and need not carry the maximum pressure unless they're loaded to the maximum.

Motorhomes, Chassis-mounted Campers, Vans

The weighing procedure is much simpler for these vehicles.

If you can manage with only axle weights, drive one axle off the scale while a reading is taken on the other. Follow the same procedure with side weights, to determine lateral balance. Or, you can weigh each wheel individually. This is the best method and results in the most accurate figures for purposes of tire inflation. When weighing one wheel at a time, (the right front wheel for instance), it would be on the scale while the left front wheel would be an inch or so off the side of the scale and the two rear wheels an inch or so off the end of the scale.

Motorhome and camper owners often have the mistaken impression that a vehicle must be exactly half on and half off a scale if the axle weight readings are to be accurate. Actually, it makes absolutely no difference, as long as the scale and the aprons surrounding the scale are level. If the aprons are *not* level, it's important that wheels *not* being weighed are positioned very close to the edge of the scale, as this is about

Motorhome or trailer left-side/right-side weights can be checked by positioning one side on scale. If the scale apron is not level, it's important to position wheels just off scale. Weighing an un-level RV will produce error in readings.

the only way to get the coach level without using blocks or boards as you would in a campground.

Here's an example of how a loaded 25-foot motorhome might weigh in. Of course, no two motorhomes are exactly alike in weight and weight distribution after the owner's equipment has been added.

1. Gross weight   12,780 lbs.
2. Right front wheel   2230
3. Left front wheel   1970
4. Right rear wheel   4350
5. Left rear wheel   4230

Motorhomes with generators and refrigerators mounted on the right usually are right-heavy when dry. But tankage often helps balance the rig. The owner can help by carrying heavy supplies and equipment on the left.

Compare your weight readings to gvw, tire and axle ratings to determine if overloads exist. Compare your axle or wheel readings to ratings for your tires; follow inflation recommendations outlined in the tire inflation guide mentioned previously. Items to watch for are motorhome front axle overloads, camper rear axle overloads and imbalance to one side of more than 5 percent of gross weight. If an imbalance is not enough that the vehicle obviously leans more in a right-hand turn than when turning left, or vice-versa, it's usually not enough to warrant suspension alterations. But tire inflation on the heavy side should be correspondingly higher. Perfectly balanced vehicles are rare—and they need not be perfectly balanced. But side imbalances in excess of 1000 pounds are common in large motorhomes.

Slide-In Campers

The procedure for weighing a truck carrying a slide-in camper is identical to that described above. But in addition you'll want to weigh the empty truck to determine the payload it's carrying and how it affects balance of the truck.

With the camper loaded for a trip (including passengers), watch for high rear axle loadings. Some slide-in campers are tail-heavy to the point that the rear axle, in addition to carrying 100 percent of the camper weight, also carries some poundage lifted from the front axle in the seesaw action created by the tail-heavy condition. Obviously, in these cases it's time to shift weight forward by moving supplies and mounting the spare tire on the front of the truck. To determine weight distribution of a truck camper, get axle weights and a gross weight on the truck and camper (as well as side weights). Then, return at a future date when the camper is removed from the truck. By subtracting the loaded front axle weight from that recorded for the empty truck, you'll find how much weight transfer (if any) from front to rear has occurred. It usually does not occur in campers shorter than 10½ feet.

Here's how an 11-foot camper on a three-quarter-ton truck might weigh in:

1. Gross loaded weight,
   camper and truck   8200 lbs.
2. Left front   1290
3. Right front   1370
4. Left rear   2715
5. Right rear   2825
6. Gross weight empty
   truck   4600
7. Front axle empty truck   2670
8. Rear axle empty truck   1930

Unless special equipment has been added, most empty pickup trucks are almost evenly balanced side to side.

Check the truck's gvw rating and tire ratings to make sure overloading has not occurred.

Many camper owners overload and underinflate rear tires but overinflate and underload front tires. While the overload/underinflation situation is much more serious, overinflation can result in reduced traction and accelerated tire wear.

Weighmasters and Scales

When planning a trip to your local commercial scales, show consideration for the weighmaster. Phone him and ask him to recommend a slack period. If your procedure is lengthy, move off the scale and allow his commercial customers to pass through. Of course, plan your weigh-in on a day when you have adequate time. And take someone with you to help you position the vehicle on the scale without endless jockeying back and forth while the weighmaster waits.

Knowledge of RV weights is extremely important in preventing equipment failures (particularly tires) and assuring good handling through proper load distribution. A few dollars spent at a local scale may be the best investment you ever make in RV safety.

How to Make Them Last Longer

RV Tires

10

They're black (in most places). They're round (except when the air departs from them—usually at the most inopportune times). And they cost money to replace (which is more often than we like).

The average motorist knows little more than that about his tires. RV enthusiasts are better informed, but we don't always have the knowledge necessary to prevent tire problems—the consequences of which usually are quite dramatic because of the bulk and weight of our vehicles.

Care and feeding of the rubber on motor vehicles is not ideally simple. The owner cruises blissfully along for 10,000 miles or so. Then one morning he suddenly notices funny little craters in his tires (improper balance). Or maybe one side of the tire looks like new while the other has its underwear showing (improper alignment).

When we increase the strain by towing or hauling our homes-away-from-home along the sun-heated superhighway for 200 to 400 miles at a stretch, our rubber-footed monster may develop a severe limp.

What can the RV owner do to avoid these misfortunes? He can get acquainted on a more intimate basis.

The most important knowledge you need in order to keep on the good side of your RV tires is how much you're asking them to carry. Weight in relation to inflation pressure will determine whether or not your beast of burden will develop a limp or head for the ditch, barring manufacturing defects. The owner who doesn't know his weights doesn't have any basis for determining

105

Tread depth gauges may be purchased at auto parts store and will help determine proper time for tire rotation, based on measurement of tread wear.

correct inflation pressure or whether his tires are overloaded.

In most cases we just run the maximum recommended for the tire, or near it, and this keeps us out of trouble. But it doesn't keep us out of accelerated, uneven tire wear and decreased ability of the tire to absorb road shock without injury.

Most problems occur when a tire is loaded beyond its rated capacity. If it's underinflated at the same time, this compounds the problem. What happens? The tire flexes more than it should. This creates friction and heat. Heat is a tire's worst enemy. It softens the tire and increases wear and the tendency to blow out.

Tire overloading has a secondary, lesser-known effect. In many cases when you overload a tire, you're also overloading the wheel.

Obviously, knowledge of the weight of your vehicle is important in order to accurately determine proper inflation pressure for your load. The maximum pressure for the tire is not necessarily the proper pressure for your needs. In many cases, you'll want to carry more pressure than that recommended for your load. (See tables which are part of this chapter.) But you should know your weights and determine the recommended minimum inflation. Then you can determine how far above that recommended inflation you can go for improved stability.

Let's look at a typical example. The owner of a tandem-axle 27-foot travel trailer has 7.00-15D tires, rated at 2040 pounds each tire at 60 psi. By weighing his trailer this owner has found that the right two tires carry 3150 pounds and the left two 3000. Each of those figures divided by two equals 1575 and 1500, respectively. By checking the load/inflation tables (see page 112) we find that the proper inflation for the tires carrying 1575 pounds would be 40 psi, and for the tires carrying 1500 pounds each, 37 psi. That's possibly getting more exact than necessary. Few trailerists will weigh each side unless the trailer appears to be seriously unbalanced. So just weighing the trailer hitched to the tow vehicle is sufficient to determine weight for proper tire inflation.

Those inflation pressures are the minimum for the loads being carried.

Most of us like to carry more pressure than the minimum, but certainly the load in this case does not justify the full 60 psi for which these tires are suitable when load is at the maximum.

Why? The intent of load/inflation tables is to improve tire wear and handling characteristics. An overinflated tire will wear faster in the center, and will be less resilient on rough road surfaces. An underinflated tire will wear faster throughout the tread, especially at the outsides, and will run warmer—more subject to tread separations and blowouts. This applies to radial-ply tires as well as bias-ply (conventional), although with radials a visual inspection of the tire is more inclined to produce the impression that it's underinflated, when it may not be, due to the bulge where the tread meets the road. The metric radials that began to appear on new vehicles in 1981 don't have quite as much bulge, since one of the design concepts with those tires is higher inflation pressures for a given amount of load, in the interest of reduced rolling resistance.

Let's look at one more example—one that involves a chronic problem or rough ride and poor traction. Many mini motorhomes and vans have been equipped with 8.00-16.5 D or E tires. The design of this tire is poor—limited ability to absorb road shock due to very short sidewalls—and the tire transmits much road shock to the vehicle. In addition, it is more prone to skate on wet pavement and slippery surfaces than are tires with more flexibility.

Typically, the owner will inflate to the maximum pressure stamped on the tire sidewall. If the tire is an E load range, that means 75 psi. If the tire is loaded to its maximum (2330 pounds each tire), the pressure is fine. The tire will still ride hard but nothing can be done about it. Usually the weight doesn't go that high. Often the rear axle may carry about 7000 pounds and the front axle 3500.

By consulting the load/inflation table we find that the 8.00-16.5 E used in dual configuration is rated at 2050 pounds each tire. Used as a single it's rated at 2330. (Tires used as duals are downrated because, under some circumstances, one wheel may carry more weight than the other.)

The rear axle weight of 7000 pounds divided by four tires is 1750 pounds on each tire. The table calls for minimum inflation pressure of 60 psi for each rear dual—not a large reduction from the 75-psi maximum inflation pressure, but it will help. For the front, each tire again carries 1750 pounds, but the single-tire ratings call for about 47 psi. The difference between that pressure and the 75-psi maximum will be significant in ride as well as wet traction. All pressures are for cold tires.

Load/inflation recommendations are just that—recommendations. They are not 100 percent accurate for all situations. For example, some tires of passenger-car design tend to wear the outside tread ribs excessively when minimum inflation pressures are used. Tires from various manufacturers are different. The load/inflation figures quoted here are from the Tire and Rim

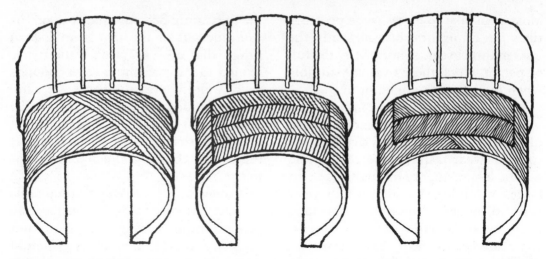

Various methods of tire construction have been used, but radial-ply has become the most common. Bias-ply (left) has cords cross the tire at an angle. Radial-ply tire cords (center) run straight across and an additional layered belt of fabric is placed between the plies and tread. Bias-belted tires (right) combine the two concepts. *Illustration courtesy Goodyear.*

Association, to which most tire manufacturers belong. But tire designs vary considerably, and it's possible to see variations in overall diameter and section width between two brands in the same size.

Everyone is after maximum stability. Stability is improved by using greater inflation than is required by the load being carried. But how far can you go above recommended maximum pressures?

The Tire and Rim Association warns that pressures should not be above those stamped on the sidewall of the tire. The association further states: "The load and cold inflation pressure . . . must not exceed the rim or wheel manufacturer's recommendation, even though the tire may be approved for a higher load." That may be a difficult recommenda-tion for most of us to follow, since wheel load ratings usually are not stamped on the wheel. Suffice it to say, the tire, loaded and inflated to maximum pressure, will not exceed the load rating of the wheel if that tire is the same size prescribed by the vehicle manufacturer. If an oversize tire is installed, a violation may indeed occur. The load and inflation pressures still should not exceed those of the highest-rated optional factory-installed tire that could be used on that wheel.

Wheels may be identified as "D" for diagonal (bias-ply or bias-belted only) or "R" for radial-ply or bias-ply usage. Wheels used on most light trucks and motorhomes since 1976 are made for radial-ply tires. One exception is that Dodge does not recommend radial-ply tires on motorhome chassis using 8-17.5

tires. Dodge chassis made in 1976 or later using 8-19.5 tires are approved for radial tires, as are 6.75 x 16.5-inch wheels used on the mini motorhomes of 1976 and later.

Motorhomes tend to have uneven wear with dual-rear tires, even when load and inflation pressures are correct; many remedies have been suggested. One remedy suggests that an axle with dual wheels places slightly more weight on the inside duals than the outside, and that the outside tires slip more and wear faster. If tire diameters are unequal, tires of the largest diameter should go on the outside. Ten percent more inflation pressure should be used in outside tires.

A word or two about appropriate load ranges. The old ply rating classifications of the 1960s were replaced by load ranges identified by alphabetical letters, such as 9.50-16.5D, or L78-15B.

Here's how that scheme works:

Ply Rating/Load Range Conversion Table

Load Range	Replaces Ply Rating
A	2
B	4
C	6
D	8
E	10
F	12

The old size—7.75-14, for instance—indicated the distance across the widest point in the tire (7.75 inches) and the wheel-diameter (14 inches).

The 7.75-14 tire became the F78-14.

The F means the tire is capable of carrying an equal amount of weight as any other F tire, regardless of other size factors. The letter is a load-carrying capacity designation. The numbers following the letter represent the aspect ratio of the tire. The height of the tire from the point where it meets the rim to the tread surface is 78 percent of the tire's width, giving it an aspect ratio of 78. The wider the tread, the lower the aspect ratio. A 70-series tire is wider and lower than a 78-series. A 60-series is widest and lowest. The last numbers still represent wheel diameter.

More recently, metric tires use a different load range indicator: SL means standard and XL means extra load.

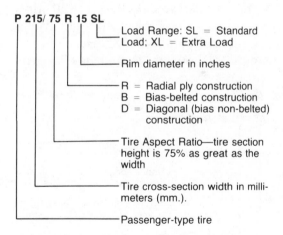

P 215/ 75 R 15 SL

Load Range: SL = Standard Load; XL = Extra Load

Rim diameter in inches

R = Radial ply construction
B = Bias-belted construction
D = Diagonal (bias non-belted) construction

Tire Aspect Ratio—tire section height is 75% as great as the width

Tire cross-section width in millimeters (mm.).

Passenger-type tire

Following is an indicator of how the metric designations relate to the earlier alphabetical and numerical designations, although the tires cross-referenced here are not necessarily precisely equal:

P-Metric Size	Max. Load Capacity (1 tire)	1979 Alpha-Numeric Size	Max. Load Capacity (1 tire)	Numerical Size (outdated)
P195/75R 15 SL	1338 lbs.	F78-15B	1363 lbs.	7.75-15
P205/75R 15 SL	1452 lbs.	GR60-15B & GR78-15B	1472 lbs.	8.25-15
P215/75R 15 SL	1583 lbs.	H78-15B	1609 lbs.	8.55-15
P225/75R 15 SL	1703 lbs.	JR78-15B	1690 lbs.	8.85-15
P235/75R 15 SL P225/75R 15 XL	1843 lbs.	L78-15B	1790 lbs.	9.15-15
P235/75R 15 XL	1984 lbs.	L78-15C & LR78-15C	1909 lbs.	9.15-15

It isn't any wonder that people become confused. As soon as we became accustomed to thinking in letters instead of numbers, an entirely new system is thrown at us. The latest code (metric) is an international one that will last a while, we can hope.

LT metric steel-belted radial tires were introduced for many light trucks and motorhomes in 1982. Here's an example of how the light truck identification system works:

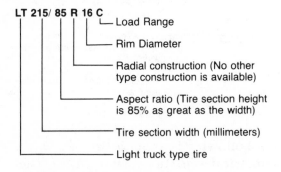

LT 215/ 85 R 16 C
— Load Range
— Rim Diameter
— Radial construction (No other type construction is available)
— Aspect ratio (Tire section height is 85% as great as the width)
— Tire section width (millimeters)
— Light truck type tire

Suitability of radial tires for RV service has been questioned repeatedly through the years since they first began to grow popular (early '70s), due to their more flexible sidewalls. While it is true that radials may have an adverse effect on handling of an RV that is marginally stable, they work out quite well on rigs that are balanced properly and handle well. They offer improved traction and improved wear. Reduced rolling resistance undoubtedly means slightly improved fuel economy, but the improvement usually is so slight as to be undetectable. RVs that have inherent stability problems usually benefit from bias-ply tires that have stiff sidewalls—more plies in the sidewalls.

As mentioned before, wheels used on light trucks and motorhomes were not specifically designed for radials prior to 1976, and manufacturers caution against use of radials on those vehicles due to the possibility of wheel breakage. A radial-ply tire exerts more pressure on the bead seat of the rim (lip which retains the tire on the rim) where a breakage problem normally would occur. However, few breakage problems have been reported. A few occurred with radials on early GMC motorhomes. Load is a factor in wheel break-

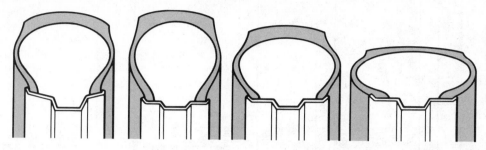

The "profile" of a tire more accurately refers to aspect ratio. It's the ratio between height and width. In the tire designation P215/75R15, the numerals 75 mean the tire section height is 75 percent as great as the width. Left to right, late-model tire with a 75 aspect ratio, an earlier tire (100 aspect ratio) a 70 aspect ratio and a 65.

age, but inflation is a factor as well. All wheels have maximum load as well as maximum inflation pressure ratings. For example, the 15 x 6-inch wheel used on 1982 C-10 Chevrolet pickup trucks is rated at 1585 pounds load and a maximum 40 psi inflation.

Wheel breakage is more common with single-axle trailers made in the 1960s—trailers that should have been built on tandem axles because they weigh 4000 pounds or more. Owners of most vehicles, especially late models, needn't worry about wheel breakage if load and inflation recommendations are not violated.

Tire rotation may be something of a problem with radial tires, since it is recommended by some companies that their direction of travel not be changed. Others disagree. For many years Michelin has been saying that direction of travel may be changed if necessary to correct uneven wear. However, Michelin also says tire rotation is necessary *only* to correct uneven wear.

On the other hand, Goodyear recommends against changing the direction of travel of a radial tire unless it appears necessary during attempts to correct uneven wear. Otherwise, Goodyear recommends moving tires from front to rear and vice-versa on the same side of the vehicle.

Since many RVs don't accumulate high mileage, the effect of storage on tires is important in areas where deterioration occurs due to the effect of sunlight and ozone in the air. Cities like Los Angeles are notorious as places where small cracks appear in sidewalls exposed to the sun. At least some of this can be prevented by covering the tires, removing weight off them (position the vehicle on jack stands if possible), and reducing inflation pressure to about 20 psi. However, ozone in the air still will cause some cracking. Unless the most severe cracks reach the cord in the tire sidewall, the tires usually are still serviceable. Use of preservative products such as Armorall is helpful.

"P" Type Tires Used on Passenger Cars and Station Wagons
(Tire and Rim Association Standard)

Tire Load Limits in Pounds at Various Cold Inflation Pressures (psi)

Tire Size Designation		17	20	23	26	29	32	35	38	41
13 Nominal Diameter (80 Series)										
P135/80*13	Standard load	540	584	628	661	694	728	761	–	–
P145/80*13	Standard load	606	661	705	750	783	827	860	–	–
P155/80*13	Standard load	683	739	783	838	882	926	959	–	–
P165/80*13	Standard load	761	816	871	926	981	1025	1069	–	–
P175/80*13	Standard load	838	904	970	1025	1080	1135	1179	–	–
P185/80*13	Standard load	915	992	1058	1124	1190	1246	1301	–	–
13 Nominal Diameter (70 Series)										
P175/70*13	Standard load	739	794	849	893	948	992	1036	–	–
P185/70*13	Standard load	805	871	926	992	1036	1091	1135	–	–
P195/70*13	Standard load	882	948	1014	1080	1135	1190	1246	–	–
P205/70*13	Standard load	959	1036	1113	1179	1235	1301	1356	–	–
14 Nominal Diameter (75 Series)										
P175/75*14	Standard load	827	893	959	1014	1069	1124	1168	–	–
P185/75*14	Standard load	904	981	1047	1113	1168	1235	1290	–	–
P195/75*14	Standard load	992	1069	1146	1213	1279	1345	1400	–	–
P205/75*14	Standard load	1080	1168	1246	1323	1400	1466	1532	–	–
P215/75*14	Standard load	1179	1268	1356	1433	1521	1587	1664	–	–
P225/75*14	Standard load	1268	1367	1466	1554	1642	1720	1797	–	–
14 Nominal Diameter (70 Series)										
P205/70*14	Standard load	1014	1091	1168	1235	1301	1367	1433	–	–
15 Nominal Diameter (75 Series)										
P185/75*15	Standard load	948	1025	1102	1168	1235	1290	1345	–	–
P195/75*15	Standard load	1036	1124	1201	1279	1345	1411	1477	–	–
P205/75*15	Standard load	1135	1224	1312	1389	1466	1532	1598	–	–
P215/75*15	Standard load	1224	1323	1422	1510	1587	1664	1742	–	–
P215/75*15	Extra load	1224	1323	1422	1510	1587	1664	1742	1808	1874
P225/75*15	Standard load	1334	1433	1532	1631	1720	1797	1874	–	–
P225/75*15	Extra load	1334	1433	1532	1631	1720	1797	1874	1951	2028
P235/75*15	Standard load	1433	1543	1653	1753	1852	1940	2028	–	–
P235/75*15	Extra load	1433	1543	1653	1753	1852	1940	2028	2105	2183

Size	Load type										
15 Nominal Diameter (70 Series)											
P205/70*15	Standard load	1058	1146	1224	1301	1367	1433	1499	—	—	—
P215/70*15	Standard load	1146	1246	1323	1411	1488	1554	1620	—	—	—
P225/70*15	Standard load	1246	1345	1433	1521	1598	1675	1753	—	—	—
15 Nominal Diameter (60 Series)											
P195/60*15	Standard load	849	915	981	1036	1091	1146	1190	—		
16 Nominal Diameter (50 Series)											
P255/50R16	Standard load	1190	1279	1378	1455	1532	1609	1687	—		
13 Nominal Diameter (60 Series)											
P195/60*13	Standard load	761	827	882	937	981	1036	1080	—	—	—
P205/60*13	Standard load	827	893	959	1014	1069	1124	1179	—	—	—
P215/60*13	Standard load	904	970	1036	1102	1168	1224	1279	—	—	—
13 Nominal Diameter (50 Series—Radial Ply)											
P215/50R13	Standard load	772	838	893	948	992	1047	1091	—	—	
P235/50R13	Standard load	893	970	1036	1102	1157	1213	1268	—	—	
14 Nominal Diameter (70 Series)											
P185//70*14	Standard load	849	915	981	1036	1091	1146	1201	—	—	
P195/70*14	Standard load	926	1003	1069	1135	1201	1257	1312	—	—	
P215/70*14	Standard load	1102	1179	1268	1345	1411	1488	1554	—	—	
P225/70*14	Standard load	1190	1279	1367	1455	1532	1609	1675	—	—	
P235/70*14	Standard load	1279	1378	1477	1565	1653	1731	1808	—	—	
P245/70*14	Standard load	1378	1488	1587	1687	1775	1863	1940	—	—	
14 Nominal Diameter (60 Series)											
P215/60*14	Standard load	948	1025	1091	1168	1224	1290	1345	—	—	
P235/60*14	Standard load	1102	1190	1279	1356	1422	1499	1565	—	—	
P245/60*14	Standard load	1190	1279	1367	1455	1532	1609	1675	—	—	

*Load/inflation statistics established by the Tire and Rim Association, Inc., 1982, unless otherwise indicated. Standard load figures are converted from metric values (not included here) and rounded to the nearest pound.

Important: Minimum cold inflation pressures are indicated for speeds below 75 mph. Cold inflation pressures may be increased above those specified for various tire loads, but *not to exceed the maximum pressure molded on the sidewall of the tire.* Check inflation pressure when tire is cold. Pressure will increase as tire temperature increases while traveling.

Source: All data except the tables on pages 120–121 is adapted from tables courtesy of the Tire and Rim Association, Inc., Akron, Ohio.

"P" Type Tires Used on Passenger Cars and Station Wagons, *(continued)*
(Tire and Rim Association Standard)

Tire Load Limits in Pounds at Various Cold Inflation Pressures (psi)

Tire Size Designation		17	20	23	26	29	32	35	38	41
14 Nominal Diameter (50 Series—Radial Ply)										
P245/50R14	Standard load	1014	1091	1168	1246	1312	1378	1433	–	–
P265/50R14	Standard load	1157	1257	1345	1422	1499	1576	1642	–	–
15 Nominal Diameter (75 Series)										
P175/75*15	Standard load	871	937	1003	1058	1124	1179	1224	–	–
15 Nominal Diameter (70 Series)										
P235/70*15	Standard load	1334	1444	1543	1642	1731	1808	1896	–	–
P245/70*15	Standard load	1433	1554	1664	1764	1852	1951	2028	–	–
P255/70*15	Standard load	1543	1664	1775	1885	1984	2083	2183	–	–
15 Nominal Diameter (60 Series)										
P225/60*15	Standard load	1080	1157	1246	1312	1389	1455	1521	–	–
P235/60*15	Standard load	1157	1246	1334	1422	1499	1565	1642	–	–
P245/60*15	Standard load	1246	1345	1433	1521	1609	1687	1753	–	–
P255/60*15	Standard load	1334	1433	1532	1631	1720	1808	1885	–	–
P275/60*15	Standard load	1521	1642	1753	1863	1962	2050	2149	–	–
15 Nominal Diameter (50 Series—Radial Ply)										
P265/50R15	Standard load	1213	1312	1400	1488	1565	1642	1720	–	–
P275/50R15	Standard load	1290	1400	1499	1587	1675	1753	1830	–	–
P295/50R15	Standard load	1455	1576	1687	1786	1885	1973	2061	–	–

*Load/inflation statistics established by the Tire and Rim Association, Inc., 1982, unless otherwise indicated. Standard load figures are converted from metric values (not included here) and rounded to the nearest pound.

Light Truck Tires for Trucks, Busses, Trailers and Multipurpose Passenger Vehicles Used in Normal Highway Service

(Tires Mounted on 5° Drop Center or Semi-Drop Center Rims, Tire and Rim Association Standard)

Diagonal (Bias) Ply

Tire Size Designation	Dual (D) Single (S)	Tire Load Limits in Pounds at Various Cold Inflation Pressures (psi)									
		30	35	40	45	50	55	60	65	70	75
6.50-16LT	D	1120	1225	1320	1420	1500	1590	1670	1750	1830	1900
	S	1270	1390	1500	1610	1710	1800	1900	1990	2080	2160
6.70-15LT	D	1060	1170	1265	1355	1440	1520	1600	1670	1750	1820
	S	1210	1320	1430	1530	1630	1720	1810	1900	1980	2060
7.00-15LT	D	1190	1310	1420	1520	1620	1715	1800	1870	1960	2040
	S	1350	1480	1610	1720	1830	1940	2040	2130	2220	2320
7.50-16LT	D	1430	1565	1690	1815	1930	2040	2140	2245	2345	2440
	S	1620	1770	1930	2060	2190	2310	2440	2560	2670	2780

Radial Ply

Tire Size Designation	Dual (D) Single (S)	Tire Load Limits in Pounds at Various Cold Inflation Pressures (psi)									
		35	40	45	50	55	60	65	70	75	80
6.50R16LT	D	1120	1225	1320	1420	1500	1590	1670	1750	1830	1900
	S	1270	1390	1500	1610	1710	1800	1900	1990	2080	2160
6.70R15LT	D	1060	1170	1265	1355	1440	1520	1600	1670	1750	1820
	S	1210	1320	1430	1530	1630	1720	1810	1900	1980	2060
7.00R15LT	D	1190	1310	1420	1520	1620	1715	1800	1870	1960	2040
	S	1350	1480	1610	1720	1830	1940	2040	2130	2220	2320
7.50R16LT	D	1430	1565	1690	1815	1930	2040	2140	2245	2345	2440
	S	1620	1770	1930	2060	2190	2310	2440	2560	2670	2780

Light Truck Tires For Trucks, Busses, Trailers and Multipurpose Passenger Vehicles Used in Normal Highway Service
(Tires Mounted on 15° Drop Center Rims, Tire and Rim Association Standard)

Diagonal (Bias) Ply

Tire Size Designation	Dual (D) Single (S)	Tire Load Limits in Pounds at Various Cold Inflation Pressures (psi)									
		30	35	40	45	50	55	60	65	70	75
8-14.5LT	D	1210	1330	1430	1540	1640	1730	1820	1910	2000	—
	S	1380	1510	1630	1750	1860	1970	2070	2170	2270	—
9-14.5LT	D	1410	1540	1660	1780	1890	2010	2110	2220	2310	—
	S	1600	1750	1890	2020	2150	2280	2400	2510	2620	—
8-17.5LT	D	1445	1575	1700	1820	1935	2050	2155	2260	2360	2460
	S	1640	1790	1940	2075	2205	2335	2455	2575	2685	2795

Radial Ply

Tire Size Designation	Dual (D) Single (S)	Tire Load Limits in Pounds at Various Cold Inflation Pressures (psi)									
		35	40	45	50	55	60	65	70	75	80
8R17.5LT	D	1445	1575	1700	1820	1935	2050	2155	2260	2360	2460
	S	1640	1790	1940	2075	2205	2335	2455	2575	2685	2795

Diagonal (Bias) Ply Tires for Trucks, Busses and Trailers Used in Normal Highway Service

(Tires Mounted on Type I, II, and III Rims, Tire and Rim Association Standard)

Tire Size Designation	Dual (D) Single (S)	Tire Load Limits in Pounds at Various Cold Inflation Pressures (psi)								
		55	60	65	70	75	80	85	90	95
7.50-15TR	D	2050	2160	2260	2360	2460	2550	2640	2730	2820
	S	2070	2210	2340	2460	2580	2690	2800	2910	–
7.50-17	D	2230	2350	2460	2570	2680	2780	2880	2980	3070
	S	2270	2410	2540	2680	2800	2930	3060	3170	–
7.50-18	D	2310	2430	2550	2670	2780	2890	2990	3090	3190
	S	2350	2500	2630	2770	2910	3040	3170	3290	–
7.50-20	D	2490	2620	2750	2870	2990	3100	3210	3320	3430
	S	2530	2680	2840	2990	3140	3270	3410	3530	–
8.25-15TR	D	2440	2570	2700	2810	2930	3040	3150	3260	–
	S	2470	2630	2780	2930	3080	3200	3340	–	–
8.25-17	D	2650	2790	2930	3060	3180	3300	3420	3540	–
	S	2690	2860	3020	3180	3340	3490	3630	–	–
8.25-20	D	2960	3120	3270	3410	3550	3690	3820	3950	–
	S	3010	3190	3370	3560	3730	3890	4050	–	–
9.00-15TR	D	2920	3070	3210	3360	3490	3630	3760	–	–
	S	2950	3150	3330	3500	3660	3830	3980	4140	4290
9.00-20	D	3510	3690	3870	4040	4200	4360	4520	–	–
	S	3560	3770	4000	4210	4410	4610	4790	4970	5150

Diagonal (Bias) Ply Tires for Trucks, Busses and Trailers Used in Normal Highway Service

(Tires Mounted on 15° Drop Center Rims, Tire and Rim Association Standard)

Tire Size Designation	Dual (D) Single (S)	Tire Load Limits in Pounds at Various Cold Inflation Pressures (psi)										
		55	60	65	70	75	80	85	90	95	100	105
8-19.5	D	2230	2350	2460	2570	2680	2780	2880	2980	3070	–	–
	S	2270	2410	2540	2680	2800	2930	3060	3170	3280	3400	3500

Tire Size Designation	Dual (D) Single (S)	60	65	70	75	80	85	90	95	100	105	110
8R19.5	D	2230	2350	2460	2570	2680	2780	2880	2980	3070	–	–
	S	2270	2410	2540	2680	2800	2930	3060	3170	3280	3400	3500

Light Truck Metric Tires for Trucks, Busses, Trailers, and Multipurpose Passenger Vehicles Used in Normal Highway Service

(Tires Mounted on 5° Drop Center Rims, Tire and Rim Association Standard)

Diagonal (Bias) Ply and Bias Belted

Tire Load Limits in Pounds at Various Cold Inflation Pressures (psi)

Tire Size Designation	Dual(D) Single (S)	29	36	44	51	58	65	73	80	87
LT215/75 15	D	1257	1422	1587	1742	1896	—	—	—	—
	S	1378	1565	1742	1918	2083	—	—	—	—
LT235/75 15	D	1422	1620	1808	1984	2149	—	—	—	—
	S	1565	1786	1984	2183	2359	—	—	—	—
LT215/85 16	D	1389	1587	1764	1918	2105	2271	2425	2557	2734
	S	1532	1742	1940	2127	2315	2491	2668	2822	2998
LT235/85 16	D	1587	1808	2006	2205	2381	2579	2778	2932	3108
	S	1742	1984	2205	2425	2623	2844	3042	3219	3417

Radial Ply

Tire Load Limits in Pounds at Various Cold Inflation Pressures

Tire Size Designation	Dual (D) Single (S)	36	44	51	58	65	73	80	87	94
LT215/75R15	D	1257	1422	1587	1742	1896	—	—	—	—
	S	1378	1565	1742	1918	2083	—	—	—	—
LT235/75R15	D	1422	1620	1808	1984	2149	—	—	—	—
	S	1565	1786	1984	2183	2359	—	—	—	—
LT215/85R16	D	1389	1587	1764	1918	2105	2271	2425	2557	2734
	S	1532	1742	1940	2127	2315	2491	2668	2822	2998
LT235/85R16	D	1587	1808	2006	2205	2381	2579	2778	2932	3108
	S	1742	1984	2205	2425	2623	2844	3042	3219	3417

Light Truck Wide Base Tires for Trucks, Busses and Trailers Used in Normal Highway Service

(Tire and Rim Association Standard, Tires Used as Singles Mounted on 5° Drop Center Rims)

Diagonal (Bias) Ply

Tire Size Designation	Tire Load Limits in Pounds at Various Cold Inflation Pressures (psi)								
	20	25	30	35	40	45	50	55	60
7.9-14LT	790	900	1000	1090	1180	1260	1340	1420	1490
9-15LT	1230	1400	1560	1710	1850	1980	2100	2220	2340
10-15LT	1390	1580	1760	1930	2080	2230	2370	2510	2640
11-14LT	1430	1630	1820	1990	2150	2300	2450	2590	2730
11-15LT	1500	1710	1900	2080	2250	2410	2560	2710	2850
12-15LT	1780	2020	2250	2460	2660	2850	3030	3200	3370

Radial Ply

Tire Size Designation	Tire Load Limits in Pounds at Various Cold Inflation Pressures (psi)								
	25	30	35	40	45	50	55	60	65
8.5R14LT	885	1005	1120	1225	1325	1420	–	–	–
9R15LT	1230	1400	1560	1710	1850	1980	2100	2220	2340
10R15LT	1390	1580	1760	1930	2080	2230	2370	2510	2640
11R15LT	1500	1710	1900	2080	2250	2410	2560	2710	2850
12R15LT	1780	2020	2250	2460	2660	2850	3030	3200	3370

Tires Used as Singles on Passenger Cars/Station Wagons and Travel Trailers

Tire Load Limits in Pounds at Various Cold Inflation Pressures

Tire Size Designation	20	22	24	26	28	30	32	34	36	38	40
6.00-13	770	820	860	900	930	970	1010	1040	1080	1110	1140
6.50-13	890	930	980	1030	1070	1110	1150	1190	1230	1270	1300
7.00-13	980	1030	1080	1130	1180	1230	1270	1310	1360	1400	1440
8.20-15	1470	1570	1630	1710	1780	1850	1920	1980	2050	2110	2170
8.90-15	1700	1810	1880	1970	2050	2130	2210	2290	2360	2430	2500
6.45-14	860	910	960	1000	1040	1080	1120	1160	1200	1240	1270
6.95-14	950	1000	1050	1100	1140	1190	1230	1270	1310	1350	1390
7.35-14	1040	1100	1160	1210	1260	1310	1360	1400	1450	1490	1540
7.75-14	1150	1210	1270	1330	1390	1440	1500	1550	1600	1650	1690
8.25-14	1250	1310	1380	1440	1500	1560	1620	1670	1730	1780	1830
8.55-14	1360	1430	1510	1580	1640	1710	1770	1830	1890	1950	2000
8.85-14	1430	1510	1580	1660	1730	1790	1860	1920	1990	2050	2100
6.85-15	950	1000	1050	1100	1140	1190	1230	1270	1320	1360	1390
7.35-15	1070	1130	1180	1240	1290	1340	1390	1440	1480	1530	1570
7.75-15	1150	1210	1270	1330	1380	1440	1490	1540	1590	1640	1690
8.25-15	1250	1310	1380	1440	1500	1560	1620	1670	1730	1780	1830
8.55-15	1360	1430	1510	1580	1640	1710	1770	1830	1890	1950	2000
8.85-15	1430	1510	1580	1650	1720	1790	1860	1920	1980	2040	2100
9.00-15	1460	1540	1620	1690	1760	1830	1900	1970	2030	2090	2150
9.15-15	1510	1600	1680	1750	1830	1900	1970	2030	2100	2160	2230

Tires Used as Singles on Passenger Cars, Station Wagons, and Travel Trailers

Tires Mounted on 5° Drop Center or Semi-drop Center Rims

Tire Load Limits in Pounds at Various Cold Inflation Pressures (psi)

Tire Size Designation	30	35	40	45	50	55	60	65	70	75
6.00-16LT	1130	1230	1330	1430	–	–	–	–	–	–
6.50-16LT	1270	1390	1500	1610	–	–	–	–	–	–
6.70-15LT	1210	1320	1430	1530	–	–	–	–	–	–
7.00-13LT	1000	1090	1170	1260	1340	1420	1490	–	–	–
7.00-14LT	1030	1130	1220	1310	1390	1470	1550	1620	1700	1770
7.00-15LT	1350	1480	1610	1720	1830	1940	2040	–	–	–
7.00-16LT	1430	1560	1680	1800	1910	2030	2130	–	–	–
7.10-15LT	1320	1440	1560	1670	–	–	–	–	–	–
8.25-16LT	1980	2160	2330	2500	2660	2820	2960	–	–	–
9.00-16LT	2250	2460	2660	2850	3030	3210	3370	–	–	–

Early Tire and Rim Association specifications, no longer necessarily approved; many tire sizes obsolete

Dimensions of Selected Tires Used on Drive Axles of Recreational Vehicles

Size	Maximum Inflation Pressure (lbs.)	Unloaded Outside Diameter (in)	Section Width (in)	Loaded Radius (in)	Revolutions Per Mile @ 45 mph
Passenger Car-Type Tubeless Tires					
E78-14	32	26.00	7.65	12.4	798
F70-14	32	26.24	8.30	12.5	793
FR78-15	32	26.74	8.10	12.0	779
P195/75R14	35	25.50	7.90	11.5	817
P205/70R14	35	25.30	8.20	11.5	822
P205/75R14	35	26.10	8.20	11.7	796
P205/75R15	35	27.13	8.19	12.2	769
P215/75R15	35	27.68	8.50	12.3	753
P225/75R15	35	28.31	8.78	12.5	737
P235/75R15	35	28.86	9.05	12.8	722
LR60-15	32	27.86	10.30	12.6	740
P235/75R15	41	28.86	9.05	12.8	722
Truck-Type Tubless Tires					
8-19.5	90	33.82	8.00	16.0	613
8.00-16.5	60	28.34	8.00	13.2	734
8.75-16.5	75	29.46	8.75	13.9	712
8.75R16.5	80	29.46	8.45	13.7	703
LT215/85R16	65	30.39	8.50	14.1	682
LT235/85R16	80	31.73	9.25	14.6	653
10R-15	35	30.42	10.40	13.9	685
Truck-Type Tube-Type Tires					
7.50-16	45	31.80	8.65	15.0	652

Not Tire and Rim Association standards; specifications will vary from one tire brand to another. When in doubt, check with dealer for specific tire brand.

Wide Base Tires for Trucks, Busses, Trailers and Multipurpose Passenger Vehicles Used in Normal Highway Service

(Tires Mounted on 15° Drop Center Rims, Tire and Rim Association Standard)

Bias Ply

Tire Size Designation	Dual (D) Single (S)	Tire Load Limits in Pounds at Various Cold Inflation Pressures									
		30	35	40	45	50	55	60	65	70	75
8.00-16.5LT	D	1195	1310	1415	1520	1620	1710	1800	1885	1970	2050
	S	1360	1490	1610	1730	1840	1945	2045	2145	2240	2330
8.75-16.5LT	D	1380	1515	1630	1750	1855	1970	2070	2175	2260	2360
	S	1570	1720	1850	1990	2110	2240	2350	2470	2570	2680
9.50-16.5LT	D	1635	1785	1925	2070	2200	2330	2445	2570	2685	2790
	S	1860	2030	2190	2350	2500	2650	2780	2920	3050	3170
10-16.5LT	D	1620	1770	1910	2050	2180	2310	2420	2540	2650	2760
	S	1840	2010	2170	2330	2480	2620	2750	2885	3010	3135
10-17.5LT	D	1680	1840	1990	2135	2270	2400	2525	2650	2765	2880
	S	1910	2095	2265	2425	2580	2730	2870	3010	3140	3270
12-16.5LT	D	2090	2280	2460	2640	2810	2970	3120	3275	3420	3560
	S	2370	2590	2800	3000	3190	3370	3550	3720	3885	4045

Radial Ply

Tire Size Designation	Dual (D) Single (S)	Tire Load Limits in Pounds at Various Cold Inflation Pressures (psi)									
		35	40	45	50	55	60	65	70	75	80
8.00R16.5LT	D	1195	1310	1415	1520	1620	1710	1800	1885	1970	2050
	S	1360	1490	1610	1730	1840	1945	2045	2145	2240	2330
8.75R16.5LT	D	1380	1515	1630	1750	1855	1970	2070	2175	2260	2360
	S	1570	1720	1850	1990	2110	2240	2350	2470	2570	2680
9.50R16.5LT	D	1635	1785	1925	2070	2200	2330	2445	2570	2685	2790
	S	1860	2030	2190	2350	2500	2650	2780	2920	3050	3170
10R16.5LT	D	1620	1770	1910	2050	2180	2310	2420	2540	2650	2760
	S	1840	2010	2170	2330	2480	2620	2750	2885	3010	3135
10R17.5LT	D	1680	1840	1990	2135	2270	2400	2525	2650	2765	2880
	S	1910	2095	2265	2425	2580	2730	2870	3010	3140	3270
12R16.5LT	D	2090	2280	2460	2640	2810	2970	3120	3275	3420	3560
	S	2370	2590	2800	3000	3190	3370	3550	3720	3885	4045

Note: Tire and Rim Association specifications prior to 1982

Diagonal (Bias) Ply Light Truck "78 LT Series" Tires

(Tires Mounted on 5° Drop Center or Semi-drop Center Rims, Tire and Rim Association Standard)

Tire Size Designation	Dual (D) Single (S)	Tire Load Limits in Pounds at Various Cold Inflation Pressures (psi)						
		30	35	40	50	55	60	65
E78-14LT	D	1000	1090	1180	1270	1350	1430	1500
	S	1140	1240	1340	1440	1530	1620	1710
G78-14LT	D	1110	1210	1310	1400	—	—	—
	S	1260	1380	1490	1590	—	—	—
G78-15LT	D	1150	1260	1360	1460	1550	1640	1730
	S	1310	1430	1550	1660	1770	1870	1960
H78-15LT	D	1270	1390	1500	1610	1710	1810	1910
	S	1440	1580	1710	1830	1950	2060	2170
L78-15LT	D	1410	1540	1670	1790	1900	2010	2120
	S	1600	1750	1900	2030	2160	2290	2400
L78-16LT	D	1470	1600	1740	1860	1980	2090	2200
	S	1670	1820	1970	2110	2250	2380	2500

Tire Size Designation	Dual (D) Single (S)	Tire Load Limits in Pounds at Various Cold Inflation Pressures (psi)						
		35	40	45	50	55	60	65
ER78-14LT	D	1000	1090	1180	1270	1350	1430	1500
	S	1140	1240	1340	1440	1530	1620	1710
GR78-15LT	D	1150	1260	1360	1460	1550	1640	1730
	S	1310	1430	1550	1660	1770	1870	1960
HR78-15LT	D	1270	1390	1500	1610	1710	1810	1910
	S	1440	1580	1710	1830	1950	2060	2170
LR78-15LT	D	1410	1540	1670	1790	1900	2010	2120
	S	1600	1750	1900	2030	2160	2290	2400
LR78-16LT	D	1470	1600	1740	1860	1980	2090	2200
	S	1670	1820	1970	2110	2250	2380	2500

Engine Overheating

11

If you know how the internal combustion engine uses fuel, you can better appreciate why its ability to get rid of excess heat is critical. The typical internal combustion engine wastes about 70 percent of the energy it consumes by blowing it out the exhaust, or by transferring it to the radiator where it's carried away by air. Other losses due to friction, accessories (such as alternator, fan) make up about 10 percent. So we have 20 percent of the energy left to do the work. If, for instance, you used 1000 gallons in 10,000 miles of travel, 700 gallons went up in smoke, so to speak.

There has been a lot of research in past years into other engine designs that put more of the energy to work, but so far none have proved practical enough to be in actual production. Without going into actual designs, suffice it to say that there are several engines that do a much better job in theory. One is the Stirling engine, which is an *external* combustion engine. In this design, heat is applied to a cylinder containing a piston and trapped gases. The heat is applied much the same as it would be in a boiler, Consequently, much less is lost.

But that's rather off target here, since we're dealing with what's available today. It's ironic that this chapter deals with ways to improve your engine's ability to *get rid* of heat since that's exactly how it uses so much fuel. But of course we can't simply reduce the heat losses and automatically improve mileage. An engine that runs too hot loses performance and that translates directly to reduced fuel economy.

How It Works

When troubleshooting an automotive cooling system, it helps to know the theory. Briefly, the coolant (water and antifreeze) acts as an agent to absorb heat generated by the engine. The coolant is exposed to air through the function of the radiator and air removes heat from the coolant.

An accurate engine water temperature gauge calibrated in degrees Fahrenheit is essential for the RV owner who has a heating problem. The gauges with color bands help, but they don't provide the information needed to determine whether or not you really do have a problem.

In some cases, gauges or lights may be faulty and signal a heat problem when none exists.

Obviously, the vehicle needs help if the owner can hardly make it up a low hill in hot weather without radiator boilover. But the repair may be an inexpensive one if the owner knows how to diagnose the situation.

Gauge accuracy has two aspects: one, actual accuracy of the needle on the scale, within the normal operating range, and two, the ability of the driver to read the scale in the most accurate gradients possible.

For the second reason, mechanical gauges are better than electrical gauges. A mechanical gauge actually is a pressure gauge, in which the sensor, mounted on the engine, is connected to the meter by a capillary tube. An increase in temperature increases pressure of the fluid or gas inside the tube,

A coolant temperature gauge calibrated in degrees F is a necessity in diagnosing an overheating problem. This Stewart-Warner mechanical gauge is a good choice, as are electrical gauges of the same and other brands.

and the gauge indicates the results with a wide-sweeping dial. Modern electrical gauges of good quality are accurate, but most have short scales, while the needle on a mechanical gauge may sweep almost a full circle. The difference is that gradations on the electrical meter may be 15 degrees while on the mechanical they may be 5 degrees. Smaller gradations can be read with more accuracy by the driver.

Ideally, the installation of an additional engine water temperature gauge should not render the stock gauge or warning light inoperative. On most engines, a plug can be found near the engine water outlet, or in one of the heads. Head temperature usually is similar to temperature at the water outlet.

With a gauge installed, the next step

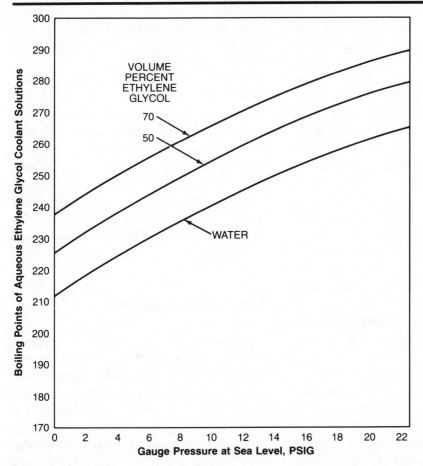

This graph from Prestone illustrates how use of antifreeze in water raises boiling point. Boiling point increases 2.5 degrees with every pound of pressure added, and drops 2 degrees with every 1000 feet of increase in altitude. Concentrations of antifreeze higher than 60 percent in water are not recommended.

is to monitor it first under cruise conditions and then during a hill climb in warm or hot weather. The conditions should be typical of the most severe that will be encountered during the usual summer RV trip, although not to the extent that it will produce an engine boilout during the test. It's not wise to operate near the boilout point, but it's good to know at about what temperature boilout will occur.

Boiling Points

The graph on this page indicates boiling point of a water and antifreeze mixture in various concentrations at sea level and with no pressure other than atmospheric. Add 2.5 degrees for every pound of pressure your radiator cap will hold, and subtract 2 degrees for every 1000 feet of altitude at which you're traveling.

For instance, a 50/50 percent solution of antifreeze and water will boil in an open container at 227 degrees F. Under 14 pounds of pressure, the boiling point is raised to 262 degrees—at *sea level*. At 5000 feet altitude, the boiling point has decreased to 252 degrees. Antifreeze manufacturers such as Prestone recommend a 50/50 percent solution of antifreeze and water. Prestone says greater concentrations of antifreeze can provide increased boiling points, but overall heat transfer efficiency is reduced. For that reason, higher concentrations than 60 percent antifreeze are not recommended. Prestone also notes that antifreeze does not last forever. Its anti-rust properties gradually dissipate. Antifreeze should be drained and the engine flushed with a 10-minute cleanser every two years.

With an accurate gauge installed and with boiling point established, you're ready to find out if you really do have excessive engine heat. That brings up the question, "How hot is hot?"

That will vary depending on one's vantage point. People who sell equipment designed to combat overheating tend to give low figures and the motor companies tend to be high, since they don't want any more customer complaints than necessary. But a middle-of-the-road posture would say 215 to 220 degrees should be about the maximum continuous level-highway coolant temperature. Late-model cars have 195-degree thermostats that don't open fully until about 205 degrees. So continuous level-highway readings usually will be at least 205 in those cases, since most vehicles running in hot weather will increase temperature until their thermostats open fully.

With older pickup trucks and vans, lower-rated thermostats are used and the usual level-highway temperatures will be somewhat lower, as they should be. Fuel economy and performance are not improved by running an engine that hot, but it does help reduce emissions—which is why it is done. On the other hand, the engine begins to lose efficiency when coolant drops below about 180 degrees.

Temperature Limits

Coolant temperatures on uphill grades ideally shouldn't exceed the figures given here. But unfortunately they do in many cases —particularly with passenger cars that are more limited on their cooling than trucks and vans. Since antifreeze and pressure both raise the boiling point of water, radiators with 50/50 antifreeze and water held in a system by a 15-pound pressure cap usually will not lose coolant until temperatures get to around 260 degrees at sea level. However, it's not good for the engine to run that hot, even if ping doesn't occur.

When you see 240 on the gauge, it's time to pull over and cool down—earlier if ping occurs. At about 245 to 250 is where most of the warning lights on late-model vehicles are calibrated to actuate. These are upper limits. Obviously, it's best to stay below them if possible.

To cool down properly, it's necessary to park safely away from the stream of traffic, raise the hood and run the engine at about twice idle speed. To turn the engine off when it's hot invites something called afterboil and loss of coolant. When circulation stops with a too-hot engine, coolant flow stops, and the hottest parts of the engine often can send the coolant over the 260-degree mark described previously. Afterboil usually does no harm, but is annoying and may produce coolant loss that can cause trouble later if not noticed. Running the heater will help prevent engine overheating—if you can stand it.

Motor companies usually state that the engine will not be damaged as long as coolant is retained in the system, but they caution against operating with the gauge needle in the red zone, or with the heat indicator light on. This allows quite a bit of variance, in addition to permitting excessive temperatures under cruise conditions for long distance—excessive if the engine is expected to "live" very long, but not a dramatic problem on short-term basis. When engine water temperature is continually high, combustion chamber temperatures and temperature of the engine oil are increased. The engine tends to detonate (ping) easily which can contribute to burned valves.

Inexpensive Items First

After determining that there is indeed an overheating problem, the most logical way to approach the problem is to tackle the least expensive items first. Many radiator shops automatically prescribe a radiator overhaul, especially for a vehicle that's several years old, when in fact the radiator cap might be the culprit in a premature coolant loss situation. Although a faulty radiator cap that is not holding adequate pressure wouldn't normally raise engine temperatures, the boilover point would arrive earlier on your temperature gauge . . . down in the 230- to 240-degree range, assuming you're running the proper coolant mix.

Pay attention to coolant concentration and to proper cooling system maintenance. When coolant level drops a little, too many of us just dump in a little water. Before long the concentration is too low to prevent corrosion, It's possible to completely renovate a radiator that has been partially clogged by corrosion, but corrosion inside the engine block is not easy to handle. Proper preventive maintenance is the answer—the only answer—if you expect to use your vehicle for many years.

Radiator caps can be removed and checked on a test device at many service stations or at any radiator repair shop. In some cases the radiator neck has been deformed and the cap might check out OK even though it is relieving prematurely, which permits premature loss of coolant. In such a case a pressure gauge can be connected to one of the threaded fittings in the intake manifold for a pressure check—with the thermostat open, since higher than normal pressures build in the block before the thermostat opens.

Special testers can check radiator cap performance.

A hand pump pressurizes cooling system to check for pressure retention ability.

Always use a thermostat. When overheating occurs, removal of the thermostat is a thought that occurs to many RV owners. In fact, that is a harmful move. The thermostat, even when it is wide open, operates as a governor on the coolant flow rate. The cooling system is designed for a specific flow rate so the coolant will be exposed to the engine and radiator surfaces for a prescribed minimum amount of time. Removal of the thermostat upsets the design.

If a thermostat problem is suspected, it can be removed and tested in a pan of water on a stove using a cooking thermometer. Increase temperature of the water until the thermostat begins to open. Remove the thermostat from the water and insert a piece of string so the valve closes on the string. Use the string to hold the thermostat off the bottom of the pan. Adjust the burner so the temperature is just below the rating of the thermostat (about 175 degrees for a 180-degree thermostat, for instance). Then slowly increase temperature until the valve opens and releases the string and the thermostat drops to the bottom of the pan. Increase temperature to make sure the thermostat appears to open fully.

While the thermostat is removed, check inside the water jacket for signs of corrosion. Use a heavy-duty cooling system cleanser if needed.

Erratic engine overheating may be associated with a sticking thermostat. A thermostat that sticks once will do it again, and can stick in any position. A radiator that is low on coolant also will create erratic overheating, as steam periodically blocks movement of the coolant.

A thermostat may be checked in a pan of water, using a thermometer, to make sure it opens at its labeled temperature level, and that it opens fully.

Another item that can affect cooling ability of the radiator is a coolant recovery system. It's installed as standard equipment on most late-model vehicles and consists of a radiator overflow container connected by a hose to the overflow tube at the radiator neck. The primary purpose is to prevent coolant loss due to radiator afterboil, but the recovery system improves radiator efficiency by eliminating the usual air space at the top. The air mixes with the coolant and cuts its efficiency.

Check the front surface of the radiator for clogging by insects. This is a common cause of impaired cooling in older vehicles because rarely if ever is a radiator cleared properly of insects and debris.

To do this properly, it's best to remove the radiator. That's less work than it may seem. With the radiator removed, it's much easier to clear the air-conditioner condensor of insects. Direct a strong stream of water or air at the back of the radiator to force the debris out the front. Take care not to hold the water or air nozzle so close as to bend the delicate fins.

Next, the fan. Engine fans are necessary in any RV because ram air (the air which flows through the radiator due only to vehicle speed) rarely is sufficient during a hill-climb situation in hot weather. Three types of fans are used commonly: clutch-type, solid metal and solid fiberglass. All will do the job. But they require trade-offs in performance.

The clutch-type fan is used most commonly—on all cars and trucks equipped with factory air conditioning. The advantages are that the fan partially free-wheels when weather is moderate, resulting in minimum horsepower loss and minimum noise. A solid fan, whether fiberglass or steel, pulls air all the time, even if temperature is low and extra cooling is not needed. The horsepower loss is noticeable, and everything counts these days.

The Fan Clutch

Operation of the fan often puzzles the driver, and its sound often is mistaken for mechanical problems in the transmission or engine. A clutch-type fan will stay in its semi-freewheeling mode most of the time. When engine coolant temperature increases to 220 to 230 degrees, the fan clutch locks up and creates a roar for a few minutes while it is pulling more air through the radiator. If weather is quite hot, the fan may stay in the locked mode for quite some time. If it's more moderate, the clutch may disengage and the noise level will drop. It sounds like engine rpm is changing, when actually it isn't. Many drivers mistake the changing sound for transmission slip.

The actuation points of most fan clutches are rather high. They should be in the 210- to 220-degree coolant temperature range, because even a modest increase in engine temperature can cause an engine to ping on a hill-climb, due to the poor grades of gasoline we must use these days. Allowing an engine to increase in temperature to 225 or 230 degrees invites engine ping, which in turn increases the overheating problem by cutting power. It also cuts mileage and can seriously damage an engine.

Many RV owners have solved the problem by changing to a fixed fan (no clutch) that pulls maximum air through the radiator all the time. This is fine for hot-weather driving, providing the fan's blades have as much size and pitch as those of the stock clutch fan. For RV use, the proper solid fan is one whose blades flatten very little, Many replacement fans have blades which flatten, reducing air flow, when engine rpm increases.

Worn-out fan clutches are a major cause of engine overheating in vehicles that have at least 50,000 miles on their odometers. Inoperative clutches are found even in newer cars, due to mechanical defects.

Checking the Clutch

One of the most important diagnostic procedures for the RV owner with an overheating problem is to determine if the fan clutch is working. Here's how: After the vehicle has been driven for at least 30 minutes in moderate or cool weather, rotate the fan by hand (engine shut off) and you'll note that it rotates with very little effort. Block the radiator with a blanket or cardboard and run the engine at a fast idle (1200 rpm) until higher than normal operating temperature is reached. Shut the engine off. If you have a temperature gauge, increase to about 230 degrees. Use a rag to keep from burning your hand, and rotate the fan blades. It should take considerably more effort to rotate the fan when the engine is hot. If the fan free-wheels easily under those conditions, the clutch should be replaced.

Actually, if the vehicle is equipped with an accurate temperature gauge, the aware RV owner can determine if the clutch is working, merely by sound. As temperature increases during a hill climb in second gear, there should be an easily identifiable difference in engine noise when the fan engages at 220 to 230 degrees. The sound won't be as easy to detect when operating in high gear with a vehicle that has a numerically low axle ratio because engine rpm and fan rpm are low. Vehicles with nu-

Thermostatically controlled fan clutches such as this one from a GM vehicle use coils or bi-metal strips to detect temperature of air passing through the radiator. Most go into high-speed mode at about 225 to 230 degrees. This one can be put into continual high-speed by moving spring out of normal position.

merically high axle ratios are less prone to overheat because fan and water pump rpm are higher.

Vehicles equipped with fan clutches that use exposed coil springs for thermostatic control offer the best of both fan types: They can be left in standard condition for moderate weather, and they may be locked up, functioning like a solid fan/in hot weather. To do so, the tip of the coil spring is merely removed from its anchor slot and moved counterclockwise until it stops. The tip no longer is anchored but it usually will remain in that position. Automatic engagement point of the clutch can be changed by bending the thermostatic spring, but it's an experimental procedure that often requires repeated adjustments.

Other Overheating Causes

Another cause of engine overheating is slipping belts, which reduce engine and water pump rpm.

If loss of coolant is evident, it is generally traced to a defective pressure cap or seepage in the cooling system. Seepage can be statically checked at a radiator shop by pressurizing the system. If the leak cannot be detected and is accompanied by a rough engine on cold starts—feeling as though two cylinders are not firing until the engine begins to warm up—this will generally produce an overheating problem under acceleration or sustained power application.

A sticking automatic spark advance system in the distributor will cause too much advance to be applied. Usually this will cause ping, which can lead to overheating.

Combustion Leak Test

If the engine overheats only under application of power, and a leaking head gasket is suspected, drain the cooling system. If the coolant is reasonably new, save it. Flush the system with water and fill with water only (do not perform this procedure in below-freezing weather or a cracked block could result). Drive the vehicle for a few miles, drain again and refill with water. Then drive about 200 miles or several days. Locate a local radiator shop equipped to perform a combustion leak test. This test is done simply with a chemical placed in a device attached to the radiator neck to detect presence of combustion gases in the cooling system. The draining and flushing makes sure all antifreeze is out of the system, as it creates error in the test. Radiator shops often fail to adequately flush out antifreeze and for that reason the tests are often inconclusive.

If it's determined that the engine has a combustion leak, the most common problem is a head gasket. In some cases there is a crack in a cylinder head, but very seldom is it a cracked block. Loss of coolant usually does not show up until late in the failure of a head gasket, so the combustion leak might be detected even though the engine loses no coolant. If removal of a cylinder head is needed to correct a head gasket leak, it's a good idea to change the gasket on the other head (V-8 engine) as well, as it may fail in the near future.

Before removing cylinder heads, observe closely the exhaust manifold bolts for signs of coolant seepage or rust. In some cases the coolant can be exposed to high temperatures through the threads of the exhaust retaining bolts. If this is suspected, drain the system, remove the bolts and seal the threads. Drive the vehicle again to accumulate possible exhaust contamination in the coolant and retest.

A restricted radiator will produce overheating at high speeds. This is easily checked by looking through the radiator fill cap with a flashlight, with coolant level low enough to permit inspection of the cooling tubes. If these tubes are crusted over, producing restriction of more than about 20 percent,

this indicates need to have the radiator rodded out. If you have had this procedure done recently, chances are the tubes will appear clear, even though you still have a heating problem. The radiator shop may have removed only one radiator tank. Both tanks must be removed in order to properly clear the tubes at both ends of the radiator.

Radiator Size

If the vehicle did not run high temperatures when it was new, a larger radiator should not be required. A larger radiator may be needed when the vehicle is subjected to harder use than before, such as towing a larger trailer or addition of accessories such as air conditioning. When a larger capacity radiator seems necessary, remember that the tubes must be equal to or larger than those in your system. Some aftermarket 4-core radiators with small tubes don't provide any better cooling than the standard 2-core radiators.

It's often possible to buy a heavier-duty replacement radiator from your dealer. First you need to positively identify what you have, and then compare that part number with what your dealer says is available.

However, it's often just as effective, and no more expensive, to have a good radiator shop convert your present radiator to one that has more cooling capacity. Radiators vary in cooling capacity depending on the number of cores, or rows of tubes that carry coolant from one side tank to the other in

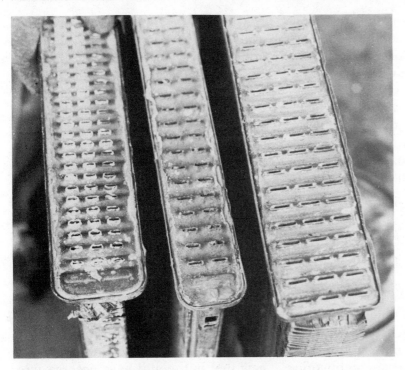

Tubes that channel coolant from one radiator end tank to the other often become clogged and must be cleaned. This is known as "rodding out" the radiator. Radiators with more rows of large tubes offer additional cooling capability.

a cross-flow radiator, or from the top tank to bottom in a down-flow radiator. Normal radiator configuration is two or three rows of ½-inch cores. If a 2-core radiator with ½-inch cores is changed to a 4-core radiator with ⅝-inch cores, cooling capacity is dramatically increased. The ultimate is the 4-core ⅝-inch, but a 3-core ⅝-inch is a definite improvement—or a 4-core half-inch. A 3-core ⅝-inch will cool as well as a 4-core half-inch. If measurements determine that the radiator is a 2-core with ½-inch cores, it's a foregone conclusion that improvement in radiator capacity will be necessary.

Next step is to be sure the exhaust is not plugged by a partially plugged muffler or rusted heat riser valve. The simple test for restriction is to install a manifold vacuum gauge. Increase engine rpm. If the gauge drops as rpm increases (transmission in neutral), it indicates a restriction. Exhaust blockage can cause engine overheating.

When radiator hoses are replaced, the metal coil normally included in the bottom radiator hose often is omitted. The result is that the bottom hose may collapse during high rpm operation, partially or fully restricting coolant flow. Simply by squeezing the hose (engine cold) you can determine if the coil is present. Once an engine gets hot, pockets of steam may form in the heads, which makes the situation worse. The only solution is full cool-down.

Retaining a several-year-old vehicle that's in good mechanical shape is tempting these days in view of high replacement costs. But in many cases an older vehicle will run hotter than when it was new, due to factors other than improper cooling system maintenance.

In many cases this is blamed on a generally "tired" engine condition. One item contributes significantly to this: timing chain wear. Chapter 16 deals with this.

Carbon plays a role in high operating temperatures. Heavy carbon deposits retain heat and act as an insulator that prevents cooling of the combustion chamber. Carbon is (or should be) removed from heads and pistons during a valve job. Use of proper valve guide oil seals and proper attention to valve guide wear will reduce oil consumption if it has been a problem. Reduction of oil consumption will prevent future heavy buildup of carbon.

Vapor Lock

Vapor lock often is related to engine overheating, but it can occur in many vehicles even when engine coolant temperature is normal or only slightly above normal.

Symptoms include loss of power and bucking of the engine, and/or refusal to start until it cools down.

Attempts to eliminate such problems range from repeated visits to dealers and independent mechanics, installation of electric fuel pumps, use of wooden clothes pins on the fuel lines, wrapping fuel lines, bottles of water carried for the sole purpose of pouring over the fuel pump and lines, traveling with the hood blocked partially open, and others.

All these have some theoretical basis. One is rather imaginative. The owner of a 4-wheel-drive vehicle used a borrowed hot water bottle attached to his radio antenna and connected via a rubber hose to the carburetor. Filling the hot water bottle with fuel, he was able to make his way through Baja California's hot, rough terrain 90 miles into Calexico. There he was able to get a new fuel pump and have necessary repairs completed.

Most fuel supply complaints can be traced directly to vapor lock. The term can best be described as the termination of fuel flow to the carburetor by vaporized fuel pockets or bubbles caused by expansion from overheating of the fuel at some point between the tank and carburetor.

The more volatile the fuel, the greater the tendency for it to vapor lock. Vapor lock is encouraged by high temperature, hard driving, high engine coolant temperatures and high altitude. Weak fuel pumps and partially restricted fuel filters will increase the tendency toward vapor lock.

A mild case of vapor lock will cause intermittent engine missing, stumble, hard starting when warm or hot. As the condition progresses, the engine will stop running and restart will not be possible until the engine has cooled.

Vapor lock is generally believed to be associated with the fuel pump and carburetor supply line. This is not the case. A condition known as heat soak lock is most common in these areas. True vapor lock is generally developed in the tank-to-fuel pump supply line.

When the temperature of gasoline reaches 86 degrees, a condition known as reed pressure expansion creates a pressure through vaporization, overcoming the flow of fuel from the tank to the pump, which is totally dependent on gravity and atmospheric pressure for its supply. When the temperature of the gasoline drops, the pressure lock will subside and allow fuel to flow again.

The output side of the pump and carburetor supply line, although exposed to greater heat, is under positive pressure and requires greater fuel expansion to overcome the supply pressure, producing a vapor lock. In other words, pressure raises the vaporization point of the gasoline and reduces the problem, just as pressure raises boiling point of the water and coolant in the radiator.

After a hot engine is shut off, the pressure in the pump-to-carburetor line drops. The fuel stops moving and absorbs more heat. This is known as heat soak. The pressure created by this heat soak and vaporization of the fuel in the already pressurized line can create a stall shortly after a hot restart, as well as carbuetor flooding while the engine is shut off.

Check Filters

Before directly attacking the vapor lock problem, the fuel filters should be removed and checked to be sure they're clear of restrictions. The fuel pump should be checked to ensure its capability of supplying adequate flow and pressure.

Two tests are necessary to establish the fuel pump condition, each made with a pressure gauge and a pint measuring container.

The pressure test is taken by connecting the gauge directly to the output side of the fuel pump. Start the engine. At idle an 8-cylinder engine should register a minimum of 5 pounds pressure. When shutting off the engine, a slow return to 0 should occur.

The volume test is made by connecting a line to the ouput side of the pump and feeding the line into the container.

A fuel pump should register a minimum of 5 psi with engine at idle.

With engine idling, the fuel pump should half-fill a pint measuring container in 12 seconds or less.

With the container held at carburetor height, start the engine. The container should be half full in 12 seconds, with the engine at normal idle. Obviously, take care with gasoline and do not fail to keep a fire extinguisher nearby. A spill or a leak could create some excitement.

The pressure gauge is important in diagnosing a vapor lock problem—and separating it from other types of problems that produce the same power loss symptoms. The pressure gauge should be spliced into the line between the fuel pump and carburetor.

When driving in cool weather, you'll quickly find out the normal pressure created by your fuel pump. It should be 5 to 7 pounds under cruise conditions, and may drop slightly under heavy throttle.

When a vapor lock or fuel delivery problem occurs, causing fuel starva-

tion, pressure will drop to less than 1 psi. A crimped fuel line, restricted fuel filter, or restricted fuel inlet line inside the tank will create the same symptoms, but usually in cool weather as well. (Possibly they won't be as severe.) A partial vapor lock condition combined with restricted fuel delivery may be the problem.

One common power loss problem occurs in GM vehicles due to over-rich fuel mixtures in the primary power metering system. Many vehicle owners think it's vapor lock; indeed, the symptoms are somewhat similar. The vehicle loses power on hills in warm or hot weather. It also blows black smoke out the exhaust—a telltale sign of excessive fuel delivery to the engine. Under these conditions, the fuel pressure gauge will indicate whether the problem is fuel delivery or something else. Restrictive air cleaners add to the over-rich carburetion problem.

Heat Sources

Once you have eliminated the possibility of a pump or filter problem, the vehicle should be placed on a lift and all fuel supply lines should be carefully checked, keeping in mind any heat source which could contribute to a vapor lock condition by being too close to a fuel line. Exhaust systems, transmission cooler lines, floor panels—all are heat sources. Unfortunately, many add-on fuel tanks, tank selector valves and additional fuel lines are installed in such a manner as to create the problem.

While inspecting the system, make sure no ⅛-inch pipe fittings have been used in the add-on system.

When a line is attached to any heat source, insulate it or reroute. Avoid all areas that prevent flow of air. Pay attention to the area of the exhaust manifolds. Inspect engine compartment fuel lines. Many vehicles, including Chevrolet and GMC, route lines behind the alternator and next to the water pump; the lines may actually come in contact with water hoses. Reroute.

Keep in mind when rerouting fuel lines that they are a source of fire danger. This is an important consideration; a fuel line that is rerouted so it rubs against a belt, gets into the fan or falls onto an exhaust manifold can cause very serious problems.

The first item many RV owners think of when vapor lock or other fuel delivery problems occur is addition of an electric fuel pump. In fact it is a good idea if the procedures mentioned here have been performed previously. No point in adding another fuel pump if the fuel intake line is restricted. Occasionally, foreign matter blocking fuel flow will be found inside the tank.

When other items have been checked and corrected and the problem still persists at least to a minimal degree, an electric fuel pump used as a "pusher" will help, because it raises pressure in the fuel line. Again, increased pressure raises boiling point of the fuel.

For an auxiliary fuel pump to work properly in solving a vapor lock problem, it *must* be mounted at the tank, and as low as possible. In vehicles with

The Carter P4070 electric fuel pump is an excellent choice as a "pusher" fuel pump for vapor lock problems. The pump should be installed as close to the tank as possible.

two or more tanks, owners often mount the pump at the tank selector valve so it will boost the feed from both tanks. This often does little good. Mount it at the tank that produces the worst fuel delivery problem. When vapor lock is prone to occur, use that tank. If the pump doesn't solve the problem on that tank (it should if you've isolated fuel lines from heat sources and made sure there are no crimped fuel lines or clogged filters), mount it at the other tank.

A good electric fuel pump is the Carter P4070. It can be wired to a switch on the dash so you can turn it on only when fuel delivery problems occur. The stock mechanical fuel pump (which is engine-mounted) will usually pull fuel through this pump.

Many electric fuel pumps are of inadequate size and flow capability. They actually restrict the flow capacity of the stock pump. When selecting a pump, make sure it has at least 1/4-inch pipe inlet and outlets and the fittings selected have 5/16-inch inside diameter. When adding fuel filters, be sure they're full flow and have adequate inlet and outlet sizes. Mount pumps and filters in such a manner as to prevent them from soaking up any more heat than necessary.

The electric pumps can be connected to operate either on demand or continuously. Under no circumstances should you delete the stock pump (unless defective and in need of replacement).

An oil pressure-sensing switch *must* be used in the electrical feed to the pump, to shut off the pump automatically when the engine dies.

A few more helpful hints might be in order here. Occasionally we hear from someone who has changed radiator coolant and is having trouble getting the air out of the cooling system. The solution is to remove the thermostat. (While it is out, check the temperature rating—install a 180-degree unit if it is rated at any other temperature.) Drill a couple of 3/16-inch holes in the outer flange and replace the thermostat. This will allow the air to escape and the cooling system then can be initially filled more completely.

Installing a fuel pump on Chevrolet V-8 engines can be a hassle since the fuel pump push rod slides down, blocking the pump arm. To simplify the job, smear some clean wheel bearing grease on the exposed end of the push rod. Then push it up into place. The grease will hold it up while you install the pump.

Fuel Bypass

Another useful item is stock on some late model engines: a fuel vapor bypass or return line, which is either attached directly to the carburetor fuel inlet line or to a fuel filter positioned near the carburetor. It has a metered outlet which allows a continual flow of vapor and fuel to return to the tank while the engine is running. This keeps the entire fuel supply moving through the lines more rapidly, reducing soak time and relieving pressure in the engine compartment line. Helping eliminate carburetor flooding allows better restarts.

The fuel bypass line which returns to the tank must not be confused with the carburetor vent return, which also attaches to the carburetor float bowl. This line only vents the bowl area, not the fuel supply. If your engine is not equipped with a fuel bypass system, and if you suffer vapor lock problems, a fuel filter with a metered bypass can be purchased and installed as close to the carburetor as possible. AC makes one, part No. 6F73, available at most parts houses.

If there are no unused connections on top of the tank for the fuel return, remove the tank gauge unit, drill an additional hole in the plate and silver-solder a fitting in the plate to accept the return line.

Late-model vehicles have fuel vapor return systems, but the AC 6F73 filter, utilizing a bypass, can be added to one that is not so equipped. A vapor return fitting must be soldered into the removable plate on the fuel tank.

If more than one tank is used, it's only necessary to connect the return to the main tank. Remember to run the main tank nearly dry first, or the fuel return will overfill it when you're using the auxiliary tank.

How about a fuel pressure regulator? It is not a necessity, since automotive fuel pumps are designed for the proper pressure output. However, one may be helpful in controlling occasional surges in pressure, and if the tank venting system allows too much air pressure to build up in the fuel tank. The only worthwhile regulator is the Holley 12-803. Many fuel pressure regulators are sold with claims that they will dramatically improve fuel economy by reducing pressure to the carburetor. The dramatic improvement does not usually occur, because a properly operat-

ing carburetor fuel inlet valve will maintain fuel level with reasonably good consistency. Some of these regulators reduce pressure to 2 or 3 psi. This much reduction isn't necessary if the fuel inlet valve is in good shape.

Engine Overheating, Q & A

Coolant Loss

I have a 1976 Ford F-250 with a 400 engine. It has only 26,000 miles, as I use the vehicle only for recreation. There has been a problem that has grown progressively worse in the last year. I have loss of coolant. It does not appear to have leaked on the ground. I have had a combustion leak test performed to check for a leaking head gasket. The thermostat has been checked and replaced. The mechanic and I have given up.

Glen Atkins
Dallas, Texas

One possible cause for loss of coolant could be a hairline crack on the tappet galley wall. Generally, if this is the case, evidence of moisture can be found in the crankcase breather, dip stick tube or PCV system. Look for a crack on the tappet galley wall about 4 or 5 inches long, about an inch above the tappets. Usually the crack will be located between either cylinders No. 2 and 3 or 6 and 7. Another way of checking is to pressurize the cooling system with a pressure tester for about 30 minutes and watch for pressure drop.

Overheating

Just before summer I had my tow vehicle serviced to be ready for our vacation. It was tuned up, fully lubricated and all new hoses and belts were installed. Since that time I have had an overheating problem which never existed before. I have since changed the thermostat, checked the radiator and had the engine checked for internal combustion leaks. I have checked the timing and carburetion. I'm stumped.

John Wells
Philadelphia, Pennsylvania

Assuming you have made sure the belt driving the water pump is of the proper width and is tight, the cause should be the lower radiator hose.

The replacement hose may be collapsing, shutting off or severely restricting coolant supply to the engine. While in park, run the engine rpm up with the engine at operating temperature and observe the lower hose. See if it collapses. Many lower radiator hoses are fitted with steel wire inside to prevent collapse but your mechanic may have used one that did not have this wire.

Heavier Fan Clutch

I have a fan clutch problem. During the past four years the clutch has been replaced four times. I have tried the original-equipment clutch as well as aftermarket replacements. I refuse to change to a conventional fan due to the noise, and obviously there are advantages to a fan that operates on demand.

William Marks
Carlsbad, California

The fan clutch assembly is a more economical and quieter means of controlling engine temperature. Most parts houses or mechanics are unaware that three categories of clutch units exist. In many cases these hubs are coded with letters designating the categories. D.D., which is most common, indicates a medium-duty application. D.H. indicates heavy duty—the proper selection for recreational vehicles.

Performance Loss

Last summer while towing my 5000-pound trailer with my 1979 Ford F-250, I lost the coolant through a radiator hose that developed a small hole. The engine, the 460, gradually overheated and the warning light did not come on until the engine began to slow up and bind up. I was not aware of the problem. I pulled off the freeway as soon as possible and the engine died. It would not turn over with the starter. I allowed it to cool with the hood up for about an hour, drained some water from my trailer and after restarting the engine slowly, I filled the radiator. Other than rocker cover gaskets seeping and three cooked spark plug wires, one additional problem has occurred.

The engine refuses to accelerate to high rpm. It flattens out and will backfire through the carburetor. My mechanic has not been able to find the problem. He has replaced the other spark plug wires, distributor cap and rotor, spark plugs, timing chain and cam sprocket. The compression runs from 130 to 150 pounds. His last effort was to check fuel supply and overhaul the carburetor. There is no sign of internal problems. The engine idles smoothly and I have only noticed a slight increase in oil consumption while towing.

Robert Dean
Midland, Texas

Severely overheating an engine is very unfortunate. The warning light often does not operate when the temperature sensor is not immersed in coolant. It's good that you allowed the engine to cool and used the proper procedure in refilling the radiator.

Installation of a temperature gauge at this point is like locking the barn door after the horse is out, but it would certainly be a good idea.

It's probable that your problem is valve spring failure. Often when an engine is heated to the point of seizure, the springs which are compressed when the engine stops will lose tension due to heat absorption. The tension is no longer adequate and the valve train cannot follow the camshaft profile, causing loss of valve timing control.

A simple method of checking involves a manifold vacuum gauge. Increase engine speed in neutral and you will notice an erratic reading, or dramatic loss in vacuum when you reach the rpm where your backfire problems occur.

Exhaust Systems

12

When improved fuel economy or performance is desired (and when aren't they?) one of the first targets for improvement is the exhaust system. Most RV owners who seek advice from performance shops invariably receive the recommendation that they install exhaust headers. That's not necessarily valid. But suffice it to say that most stock exhaust systems can be improved.

Why should the exhaust system be improved? A restrictive exhaust system creates too much back-pressure and that creates too much combustion chamber heat, which in turn restricts power and makes the engine more prone to ping. However, total elimination of back-pressure is not desired. A certain amount is needed or low-rpm torque will be reduced. Most exhaust systems designed for racing have large-diameter header tubes (2 inches or larger) and large-diameter exhaust systems and mufflers (2½ inches). Almost any muffler shop will recommend 2½-inch exhaust pipes and tail pipes. After all, bigger is better, isn't it?

Yes, for racing. No, for RVs. For RV situations one of the most important criteria is to retain or improve torque in the area of 2000 to 2500 rpm, where most of us cruise in high gear at 55 mph. And we need good torque for pulling away from a stop, especially in high altitude on uphill grades. We also want good power for climbing grades in second gear, which puts our rpm in the 3000 to 3500 range. And we want good power at the top end (3500 to 4000 rpm) for passing other vehicles. Top end for a racing engine is 5000 to 6000 rpm.

Dual exhaust systems on many Ford pickup trucks with tanks mounted admidship must have one leg of system outside the frame. 40-inch glass-pack mufflers and headers have been used in this installation.

Unfortunately, we can't have it all. The wide-open racing exhausts are best for maximum power from 3500 rpm up. But since we use that rpm band only occasionally, we must concentrate on mid-range performance.

Sustained Load

In general, any vehicle with a stock single exhaust system can benefit from installation of a dual exhaust system, assuming at least light to medium RV service. Passenger cars and pickup trucks that are not used for RV service can get along quite well with single exhaust systems because those vehicles usually are not operated under sustained load at heavy throttle.

That is the important factor in RV service. When climbing a hill in hot weather, the engine works hard for many miles, while heat climbs, and lightly loaded vehicles never are subjected to this kind of service. That's why the factories use single exhaust systems. It's a cost-cutting move they can get away with based on average use of the vehicles. Ideally, dual exhausts should be included in every RV special equipment package. Of course, the situation is complicated by the fact that many vehicles are equipped with catalytic convertors, and it is illegal to remove them, although there is no enforcement in most states at the owner level. Dealers and garages are subject to penalties and most will stay away from it.

The catalytic convertor, unfortunately, is very performance-restrictive and causes much heat buildup in the combusion chambers. Nothing legal can be done about it, short of installing dual exhausts with a second catalytic convertor (which helps, but usually is not cost-effective). So we'll concentrate here on vehicles that can accommodate non-convertor-equipped dual exhausts. When changing vehicles, try to get one for which the catalytic convertor is not required.

For all engines 400 cubic inches or less, 2-inch exhaust and tail pipes should be used. For those in excess of 400 cubic inches, pipe size can either be 2 inches or 2¼. Even with 2¼-inch pipe size, 40-inch glasspack mufflers with 2-inch cores are preferred. The mufflers are not restrictive, and they help create the right amount of back-pressure for good low-end performance.

On motorhomes in excess of 26 feet, two 40-inch glasspacks and two 30-inch glasspacks may be used to prevent resonance, although this may not be necessary. Some motorhomes have tail

In dual-exhaust conversions on Dodge motorhome chassis, stock system (top) has a single tail pipe exiting at rear. Dual-exhaust conversion utilizes 40-inch mufflers with tail pipes exiting ahead of rear wheels.

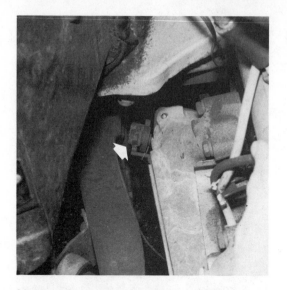

Many engines are equipped with heat riser valves that partially restrict exhaust flow, forcing exhaust through the heat passage in the intake manifold to help vaporize fuel. When the valve becomes stuck, severe exhaust restriction can result. Valve should be checked frequently for free movement and should be propped open for hot-weather driving.

pipes exiting at the rear of the coach and this tends to cause retention of exhaust gases at the rear. Also, it dirties the back of the coach. It's best to run tail pipes out the side, either in front or in back of the wheels. Pipes can be routed side by side if a fuel tank or other obstacle prevents routing one pipe on each side. Maintain at least 6 inches between any exhaust pipe or tail pipe and any fuel tank or the floor of the vehicle.

A slight fuel economy improvement often will occur when installing dual exhausts. In other cases, fuel economy may remain about the same. But performance usually increases. For example, we recorded horsepower improvement of about 10 percent at 4000 rpm with a dual exhaust conversion on a Dodge 440 in a motorhome. The improvement fell to about 6 percent at 2500 rpm. No mileage increase was noticed. With the Chevrolet 350 in a Blazer, performance increased about 10 percent at 4000 rpm. and 5 percent at 2500 rpm, and fuel economy increased a half-mile per gallon.

It's often not possible to buy a dual exhaust kit that can be merely bolted on. If that is the case, any muffler shop equipped with a tube bender can fabricate a dual exhaust system.

The Choice

Whether or not to add headers must depend on the vehicle—how well the engine in question responds to headers. In general, most big-block engines such as the Chevrolet 454, Ford 460 and Dodge 440 show performance increases, but only at high rpm, so installation of headers often is not cost-effective. Mileage improvement usually does not occur on those engines, despite what the header makers advertise. Installation of headers on a motorhome or van dramatically increases under-hood temperatures, which is another reason to stay with the stock exhaust system. Headers help the small-block engines more consistently.

With exceptionally heavy RVs that fall off badly in speed on uphill climbs, headers definitely are one way to boost power. Motorhomes longer than 30 feet, powered by the Dodge 440, are a case in point. Headers do improve power, especially in combination with aggressive engine calibration and use of a water injector; that combination can usually make an important difference to the 440 owner. Many of the less expensive headers will burn out and we have found Gemini chrome-plated headers about the only way to go on the 440. Spark plug cables and boots must be positioned as far from header tubes as possible and should be changed to high-temperature silicone, to keep the higher heat output of the headers from burning the cables and boots. Also, high temperature valve cover gaskets should be used on the Dodge 440. They're described in the question/answer section devoted to Dodge engines.

The theory of headers is associated with control of flow through the carburetor and intake manifold. It is something the RV owner should understand if he is contemplating buying headers.

In 4-cycle engines there is an overlap period in which intake and exhaust valves are open at the same time. Exhaust pressure being greater than atmospheric pressure, the exhaust pressure tends to reverse the intake flow and push the air/fuel mixture back out of the engine, destroying low-rpm torque. However, at higher rpm this overlap period tends to create a scavenging effect, improving intake flow. When the exhaust gases have picked up momentum, they help draw the air/fuel mix into the engine during the overlap period. For this reason a racing cam-

shaft has greater overlap because high rpm operation is usual.

At low rpm, the overlap creates a surge back and forth in the exhaust. Put your hand over a tail pipe with the engine at idle and you can almost feel the push-pull action. By lengthening the passageway through which the exhaust gases pass, the surge or reversing action can be reduced or eliminated. In other words, the exhaust from each cylinder is strung out in a long tube, with headers, and reversal of its direction is not as likely as when the exhaust immediately leaves the cylinder head and is collected in a common manifold with the gases from other cylinders. The long tube is called the primary tube. Each tube of a set of headers is a primary tube.

Installation of the desired length of primary tube is not possible in most chassis. Therefore, by joining the primary tubes together and restricting the flow with a cone that is pointed in the direction of the exhaust flow, a similar effect can be accomplished and a more uniform exhaust flow can be created. The cone is provided with a set of headers and in the case of RV headers, the cone is 2 or 2¼ inches in diameter. Many shops cut it to larger diameter but this should not be done.

The fundamentals of header design were worked out in the days of the great German Auto Union racing teams and Dr. Porsche; headers are not just an add-on gimmick. A prime example of a totally engineered exhaust system is evident in the original normally aspirated Ford Indianapolis race car engines of the early 1970s. The 180-degree design made the engines look like an enormous octopus engulfing the rear of the car. The system was totally efficient but hardly practical for RVs.

So what we get with a proper set of "restricted" headers for use on specific RV engines is a more uniform flow of exhaust gases at low rpm, with improved air/fuel intake flow, plus the scavenging effect at higher rpm for improvement in maximum power. Restricted headers for RV use have tube sizes and collector cone sizes that are suitable for the type of use involved—a good deal of moderate-rpm operation with only occasional bursts to 4000 rpm. If nonrestricted racing-oriented headers are used in an RV situation, low-end torque and fuel economy will suffer.

All this may sound fine, but the comparative effect of headers is dependent upon the design of the engine in question. Many RV owners fall victim to the exaggerated performance and fuel economy claims applied generally to all headers by the manufacturers, when actually the benefits vary widely from engine to engine.

The equalizer pipe is a pipe that joins the exhaust pipes ahead of the mufflers. The only function is to reduce exhaust noise. The 40-inch glasspack mufflers are not noisy when the equalizer is used, and they provide for the correct exhaust flow.

Stock dual exhaust systems used with the Chevy 454 are quite sufficient. In those cases where a single 2½-inch exhaust system is used, it will suffice un-less substantially more power is needed. In the case of Ford 460s, if the single muffler has one inlet and one outlet, it's OK. If it has one inlet and two outlets, it's rather restrictive and dual exhausts would be advised.

Dual exhausts must always be used when headers are installed, or the advantages of the headers would be reduced. Also, good air flow through the air cleaner is needed. If the engine's air intake is restricted, an improvement in exhaust flow capability will not be fully utilized. The same applies to carburetion: a 2-barrel carburetor will restrict engine intake during full throttle operation at rpm exceeding about 3000. Below that, a 4-barrel carburetor normally would be operating as a 2-barrel (vacuum operates secondary venturi).

Some Worse Than Others

Despite the intake restriction of a 2-barrel carburetor, proper exhaust headers will help certain engines more substantially than others. The reason is design of the exhaust manifolds. When the stock cast iron exhaust manifolds are particularly restrictive, headers really make a difference, regardless of carburetion. Such engines are the Ford 360 and 390 and the Dodge 360. Headers improve power with the 2-barrel carburetor, and more so with a proper 4-barrel. Fuel economy usually remains about the same. These three engines tend to burn valves due to excessive combustion chamber heat and improper carburetor calibration, so the combination of proper carburetor re-tuning and installation of headers plus dual exhausts can do dramatic things for engine durability. When valve work is done, it's critical that proper clearances are met and the valve surfaces are machined properly. If that is not the case, the tuning and exhaust improvements may still permit valve problems, but for different reasons. See Chapter 14 on proper valve work.

When installing headers, if the work is performed at a shop it's important to watch what's being done. As described previously, most shops figure bigger is better. They may use headers with excessively large tube size. Maximum size for RVs should be 1⅞ inches. It's important that the collector cones at the header outlet *not* be larger than 2½ inches and should taper to accept the 2-inch exhaust pipe.

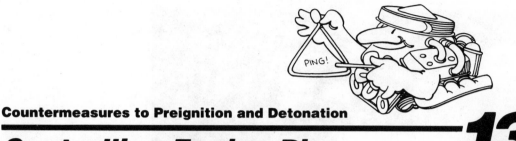

Controlling Engine Ping

13

Preignition (ping) is a widely misunderstood subject and yet one of the most important phenomena associated with the internal combustion engine. Extensive studies and numerous research papers have been published dealing with combustion chamber design, compression, turbulence, heat dissipation, flame propagation and fuel control to suppress the problem and increase efficiency. Although these studies have enabled the more efficient utilization of fuel, we have found ourselves at a point where emission requirements and poor quality fuels have increased the tendency for preignition to occur, particularly in RVs.

Combustion chamber carbon deposits are the primary cause of preignition. Preignition may be silent or it may become manifest in a variety of engine noises ranging from light pings to violent explosions. Its occurrence is the result of changes in engine operational conditions such as towing heavy loads or rapid acceleration. Such conditions cause higher pressures and temperatures to develop during compression, or create an increase in the concentration of oxygen available to support combustion of carbonaceous material.

A quick review of the combustion procedure will help us understand this subject:

The piston moves downward in the cylinder during the intake cycle, creating a partial vacuum that is relieved by the atmospheric pressure charging through the carburetor, bringing fuel mixed with the air through the intake valve. The valve closes and the piston

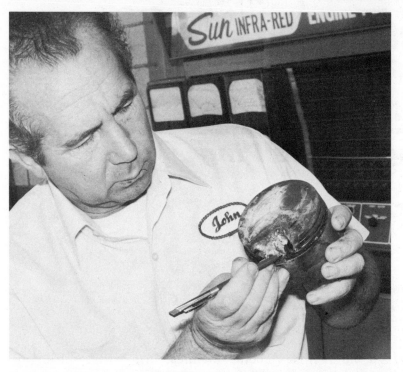

Engine preignition or detonation (ping) can cause severe damage, such as holes burned in pistons, if allowed to occur unchecked.

moves up the cylinder, compressing the air-fuel mixture. Just before reaching the top of its travel, at a precise and determined position designated by engine speed and load, the spark plug fires and the compressed mixture begins to burn evenly across the combustion chamber.

After the piston reaches the top of its travel, the burning rate and compression of the unburned fuel create a tremendous pressure rise and accelerate the burning rate, producing a controlled explosion. This results in a force against the piston downward and a rotation of the crankshaft, producing torque. The burned mixture is exhausted, the combustion chamber is cooled, and the cycle begins again.

Preignition is a term associated with ignition from an internal source ahead of the firing of the spark plug. Preheated combustion chamber deposits, under certain conditions, can become hot enough to ignite the fuel-air mixture prior to ignition by the spark plug. Early ignition results in abnormally high rates of pressure rise in the cylinder, which are often accompanied by a loud noise and which, if severe enough, can cause actual destruction of engine parts.

NORMAL COMBUSTION

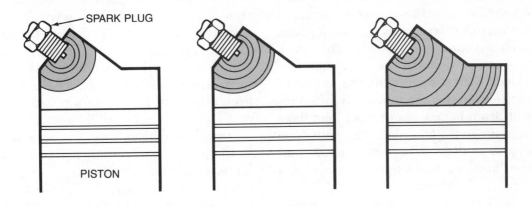

KNOCKING

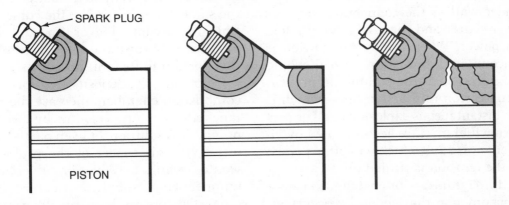

When proper combustion occurs, spark plug ignites fuel/air mix and flame front proceeds across combustion chamber. Ping occurs when spontaneous combustion occurs in another part of the chamber and two flame fronts meet. Or initial spark occurs other than from spark plug.

Four Categories

There are four categories of abnormal combustion that we will briefly cover in their progression.

The first is referred to as *silent preignition*. Silent preignition is an increase in the normal rate of pressure change which occurs before ignition by the spark plug and which is not accompanied by an unusual engine noise. It can normally be detected only by a slight loss in power due to the presence of a flame in the combustion chamber be-

155

fore the firing of the spark plug. Tests on silent preignition have shown that an engine operating under a sustained load actually will run at constant speed even without any power to the spark plugs. The deposits have actually replaced the spark plug as the source of ignition. In these instances, ignition results from hot surfaces rather than flake deposits in the chamber. This causes no damage unless it becomes erratic and continues at low engine speeds preventing shutdown.

Second, there's *steady preignition* with noise—which is very much like silent preignition. However, at this point high frequency gas vibrations occur. The piston skirt is slammed against the cylinder wall as the connecting rod goes over center and there is a definite loss in power. When steady preignition is encountered, reduction in load should be introduced immediately to prevent progression into *detonation*—which is an instantaneous explosion of all or part of the fuel mixture accompanied by violent noise and which will often persist if the ignition is turned off.

Auto ignition —or past ignition—is a phenomenon that generally occurs after or during severe preignition. It can produce instantaneous reactions and represent the most violent form of abnormal combustion. The condition is caused most often from the flaking characteristics of carbon deposits. The flakes, which are broken loose during disturbed combustion, become hot enough to glow; once in this state, they may serve as an ignition source either while still attached to the combustion chamber wall or while floating about in the combustion space. Tests have shown the deposits which have flaked appearances to be most effective in producing preignition, while deposits which are relatively smooth and uniform are much less prone to induce preignition. In fact, wild pings do not occur in the absence of flaking.

Deposit particles that are detached from the walls and remain in the engine for one or more cycles are at higher temperatures because they are in more intimate contact with the hot gases and are not cooled appreciably by heat losses to the combustion chamber walls. Since detached particles move with the gas stream, they remain in contact with the same small portion of the combustible mixture for a longer time and can more readily raise the temperature of this portion to its ignition point.

Unfortunately, deposits that form in combustion chambers increase the octane requirements of engines by several numbers. A solution, or even partial solution, to this aspect of the problem would permit a reduction in octane number of fuels supplied for current engines. Or conversely, it would permit an increase in compression ratios or leaner mixtures producing impressive increases in performance and efficiency.

An Old Problem

These problems of combustion chamber deposits, although more prevalent in today's conditions, are by no means

Carbon deposits increase fuel octane requirements of engines. Deposits do occur in engines burning lead-free fuel.

new ones. Orelup and Lee, prominent researchers in 1925, stated: "Carbon in an engine is like scale in a boiler. It is one of the best heat insulators." The temperature of fuel burning in a heat-insulated cylinder soon rises above its critical temperature and thereupon breaks down and is made manifest by knocking and detonating. In 1936, Livingstone, Greese, and another team of researchers predicted, "It may be that soon we will realize the importance of carbon deposits in offering one of the main obstacles which stand between us and the advantages of high compression engines."

Considerable progress has been made and greater advances may be anticipated. It is an established fact that the problem of increasing the efficiency of gasoline engines without requiring fuels of higher anti-knock quality is one that today challenges the ingenuity of technicians. It is accepted that the efficiency during which heat energy of fuel is best converted into work is fundamentally dependent upon compression. Unfortunately, hands are tied by the refinery. Unleaded high-octane fuels are available today for aircraft but they are expensive. However, high fuel cost could be offset by a return to the compression ratios which we had through 1970. Many of the emission devices we have today could be modified as the fuel would be more efficiently used—although the present catalytic convertors could not be used.

What can you do about your problem now? Being able to recognize the occurrence of preignition is a step in the right direction. Every octane number that can be saved by any means is significant. Operational temperature of the engine helps. Install a 180-degree thermostat in place of the 195-degree thermostat now common in most engines. This will help cool the fuel-air charge. If your exhaust system is equipped with a catalytic convertor, buy the best grade of fuel available. Unleaded is rated from 87 through 91 octane. If your system is not convertor equipped, dual exhausts are helpful in almost every case. Precise tuning procedures producing proper control of fuel mixtures in each power stage and correct spark timing curves throughout the operational range of the engine are most important. When preignition occurs, ease up and try to prevent it. Allow the carbon deposits to settle down and become smooth and stable; preignition creates flaking and worsens the problem. Carbon removers poured through the carburetor while the engine is running are of some temporary help. The most effective countermeasure is use of an effective water injection system.

Towing is another problem. The catalytic convertor engines limit the fuel that can be used. Without precise tuning and the help of a variable pressure water injection system, ping may be very difficult to eliminate. When choosing a tow vehicle, look for a noncatalytic convertor-equipped vehicle that will accept modification allowing a greater flexibility in operation. Specific modifications tailored to your particular application—such as precision tuning, improved exhaust systems, increased breathing, the injection system—all these options when properly selected will assure improved performance and efficiency.

Proper Valve Work

14

Although premature valve problems were not unknown in the 1960s, when high-octane fuels were in common use, they were considerably less prevalent than in the 1970s, after the advent of more extensive emission control systems, reduced octane and lead-free gasoline.

Metallurgy has improved greatly to withstand increased combustion chamber temperatures. But valve problems still occur regularly due to incorrect carburetion and spark advance calibration—combined with more restrictive exhaust systems and increased tendency toward detonation and pre-ignition (ping).

Carburetion and ignition problems can be corrected; unfortunately many of the corrections are not completed in time, and damage already has been done. Extreme heat will initiate burning of the edges of the exhaust valve heads. Subsequent fatigue and warpage will create leakage at the seats, which shortly destroys the combustion seal. Detonation or preignition occurring while the valves are not fully seated destroys the stem-to-guide clearance by rattling or vibrating the valve stem in the guide. Premature valve jobs are common for these reasons. It's often necessary to grind valves with mileage as low as 15,000 on the odometer, with no other contributing factors such as excessive carbon deposits or valve seal oil leakage.

Most RV owners may not feel inclined to get intimately involved in the mechanics of a valve repair job. But the frequency of inadequate work is significant, so it's beneficial to know how to

John Geraghty sets a cylinder head in place on a Chevrolet 350 block following valve work.

high degree of expertise. Such work is best left to the professional mechanic, but there are specific steps and not all professional mechanics cover all the bases. Factory valve job quality leaves a lot to be desired and valve leakage can occur even with new vehicles. Consequently, low mileage on the odometer does not automatically preclude valve leakage.

Choosing a Shop

Before becoming involved in valve work, locate a machine shop or repair facility that is clean in appearance, with relatively new equipment. Older equipment becomes worn and will not hold tolerances. Discuss the work. If the mechanic is knowledgeable with the following steps and is willing to take the

recognize good procedures associated with quality work. Also, it's helpful to know the underlying causes—improper carburetion and ignition—that create the problem.

Leaky valves immediately and directly affect fuel economy and performance. With escalating fuel costs it's critical to have any RV engine in the best possible condition, for maximum efficiency.

Repair of valve and valve guide damage is a complex operation. It's not suggested here that you take it on, because it requires expensive equipment and a

Excessive valve guide clearance causes many problems. Here, mechanic hand-checks movement of valve in guide. A gauge is used to measure movement accurately. Valve stem and valve guide diameter are also measured.

Valve guide oil seals are critical on many engines, to prevent oil leakage. Here guide is machined for installation of special Teflon spring-loaded seal. Stock seal is retained to seal upper spring retainer area. Teflon seal protects stem-to-guide contact area. Close-up of seal shows inner spring and white Teflon surface.

time to proceed accordingly, you should receive good quality work.

Sharp surfaces of the combustion chamber must be removed with emery paper. Any sharp edges around the chambers will remain red hot and cause preignition. It's an innocuous step but a very important one that is often not performed.

Valve seat width should be $1/16$-inch for intake valves and $3/32$-inch for exhaust valves. It's important to machine the area immediately above and below the valve seats, to control width of the seat. Otherwise it might not be uniform. One side might be proper width and the other twice as thick.

The valve seat must be machined to

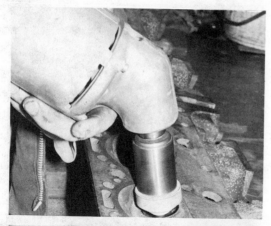

In most valve jobs, only the actual valve seat is resurfaced to 45 degrees. Special grindstone is used. However, proper seat width in position can be controlled only by machining surfaces above and below the seat. Cutter is used to create a 70-degree angle below the seat and a different stone is used for 15-degree angle on top of the seat.

a 45-degree angle. Immediately above that angle, the surface should be machined to 15 degrees, and immediately below it should be 70 degrees. These operations insure uniformity and help keep a narrow section of the valve seat from burning under heavy engine load if the seat is not uniform.

Valve stem clearance should never exceed the factory minimum. If stems are worn in excess of .005-inch, the valve should be discarded. The guides should never be knurled to account for more than .002-inch clearance. Knurling is a term that refers to use of a tool inside the guide to create a circular ridge that reduces guide-to-stem clearance. Some shops will knurl for as much as .004-inch but this is not recommended, because generally the wear pattern will be egg-shaped and the knurling process will not hold up. In a short period the clearance will be worse than before. This is a common reason for oil consumption problems in overhauled engines.

Valve, ready for grinding on machine, should not be thinner than ¹⁄₁₆ to ³⁄₆₄-inch because the edge will remain red hot and cause preignition. Aft-facing outer edge should not be thinner than ¹⁄₁₆-inch for intake and ³⁄₆₄-inch for exhaust.

The valve spring is checked for proper factory recommended tension at assembled length and at maximum lift.

Valve face angles should be 44 degrees. Seat contact should be in the center of the face. In other words, if the valve seat is slightly too small or too large for the valve size, the valve face will not be centered on the seat. This is corrected while grinding the seat and positioning it with the 15- and 70-degree angles.

Edge of the valve head should be a minimum of ¹⁄₁₆-inch for intake and ³⁄₆₄-inch for exhaust. Thin valves will have short life as the ³⁄₆₄-inch edge of the head becomes wafer-thin and almost

sharp. Again, any sharp edges can cause preignition. In an effort to hold total cost down, a mechanic sometimes will reinstall valves that should have been replaced.

Regarding valve springs, refer to factory specifications. Check installed height. Put the retainer and keepers in position on the valve, with the valve seated in the head. Measure distance between the cylinder head and the

Valve stems must be checked for wear. Maximum acceptable is .0005-inch below the original diameter.

spring retainer. This height should be the same as the factory valve spring installed height recommendation. If it is more, then correct by using a spacer under the spring. It's better to have the spring under slightly more rather than less recommended tension.

Always lubricate the valve stems during assembly with STP or engine assembly lube. Lubricate seals and valve stem ends before assembly. Use guide seal protective covers to prevent damage to seals during assembly. Check clearance between the top of the guide and retainer for minimum clearance of .006-inch to prevent seal damage. Use Pioneer brand Teflon spring-loaded seals in situations where chronic oil consumption is a problem. These seals require machining of the valve guides for installation. Most good shops will have the necessary cutting tool.

With proper attention to detail, a valve job should practically eliminate leakage of combustion gases during the critical periods of compression and ignition; substantially improved engine efficiency should result.

In other chapters we discussed progressive forms of preignition, improper spark timing procedures, incorrect gearing, reduction of octane of the fuel we're offered these days and excessively high operational temperatures which can create engine damage.

Unfortunately the internal combustion engine doesn't have the ability to heal itself. Once damage is done, it will remain. The rate of progression of failure of the component can only be controlled through corrected timing procedures, more efficient intake and exhaust systems, and better understanding of operational theory.

Importance of Carburetion

Carburetion is one of the major contributors to internal damage. Very lean air/fuel ratios are used and very high engine temperatures are employed to allow such lean mixtures to be maintained. This has created an increased tendency for all forms of preignition, especially inaudible (silent) preignition. To help guard against this, the timing has been retarded, which in turn causes even higher combustion temperatures. It's a vicious cycle. Efficiency is reduced, engine life is shortened, and performance is less than adequate. The RV owner is particularly affected because RVs do require performance in excess of that needed for normal passenger car transportation.

In the carburetor, the cruise air/fuel mixtures generally are kept very lean to obtain as much fuel economy as possible, but without inducing surge. But the point at which enrichment of air/fuel ratios occurs often must be corrected. The work required of the RV engine creates conditions of sustained loading at nearly full throttle. At this point, fuel mixtures become critical. If we relate this to a manifold vacuum gauge, we can understand it better, and also appreciate the role of the vacuum gauge in allowing maximum mileage.

During idle conditions in neutral, vacuum readings will be 18 to 20 inches. At this point the engine is creating a negative pressure in the manifold, or partial vacuum. The carburetor throttle is nearly closed and atmospheric pressure has no way to rush into the manifold to fill the manifold and cylinders. At full throttle, the partial vacuum is reduced to nearly 0 inches as, at this point, the restriction at the carburetor is removed and atmospheric pressure is nearly filling the cylinders. As the combustion chamber fills more effectively, the volumetric efficiency of the engine improves.

When the automatic transmission is slipped into gear, the vacuum gauge indicates about 15 inches. The reduction at this point is due to additional load on the engine with the same throttle position. As the load increases, the readings decrease. If the work load is the same and the engine rpm is increased, vacuum readings will increase with rpm.

While cruising down a level highway at 55 mph, 12 to 15 inches of vacuum might be normal for a lightly loaded vehicle. During these conditions a lean mixture is desired. As the vehicle approaches a hill, the additional power required will cause the driver to increase the throttle. Consequently, the load on the engine increases. Vacuum will decrease relative to engine size, gearing and load.

Enrichment of the air/fuel mixture is needed between 8½ and 6½ inches of vacuum. This is accomplished either through the opening of an enrichment diaphragm in the carburetor or a change in the main metering orifice size relative to position of metering rods. This is referred to as the primary power enrichment system. If this enrichment does not occur, preignition will occur. Initially it will be inaudible, producing a flat, nonresponsive power curve. It might progress to audible preignition, then to severe audible preignition, which results in engine damage, particularly to valves.

Late Power System

In many cases the primary power system fails to engage until the vacuum has dropped to 4 inches, or maybe as low as 2 inches. In some cases, this will result in improved mileage, but hesitation, lag, flat spots in acceleration, and surging may occur. The inherent damage created by detonation or preignition while maintaining a load (for example, at 5 inches vacuum) without fuel enrichment can break pistons and rings, rattle valves in their guides, etc. Opening the primary power system properly

Severe valve and valve-seat damage can be caused by a variety of problems, including engine ping and improper valve repair work.

at 6½ to 7 inches will assure maximum efficiency. When necessary to drop into the primary power system, performance can be increased without damage. Use of a vacuum gauge as a load meter will control your driving habits. You should find it possible to move away from stops without engaging the power system. On many hills that you are climbing at 6 inches or thereabouts, slightly releasing the accelerator pedal to put you at 7 inches will reduce fuel consumption about 26 percent. The vacuum gauge can tell you where that 26 percent dividing line is.

Ignition timing is an important aspect of performance and efficiency; it is totally dependent on clean combustion chambers, proper fuel mixtures, operational temperature, and a correct selection of spark plug heat range.

Timing is generally thought of as the initial setting of the distributor relative to top dead center position of the piston. But timing must change throughout the entire operational curve of the engine according to engine rpm and load, as the volumetric efficiency of the engine changes. Burning rate of the compressed gases will change, and the spark timing is critical to the position of the piston so that maximum downward pressure can be exerted against the piston. If timing is early, preignition will occur. If it is late, power is lost and increased operational temperatures result because fuel still in the combustion stage is exhausted.

All these factors affect valve life. And valve condition in turn affects whether or not the proper settings can be maintained. For instance, oil consumption through leaky valve guides creates excessive carbon deposits which retain heat and cause preignition. Thus, the engine cannot tolerate the proper amount of spark advance for best fuel economy and mileage. Remove the carbon, correct the oiling problem, repair any damage to valves, and the engine will return to its peak efficiency (assuming no other damage).

The internal combustion engine by design is not very efficient in its use of fuel. When it must operate with additional handicaps such as improper fuel and spark calibrations and leaking valves, it isn't any wonder that fuel appetite increases. As always, prevention is much less costly than cure.

Changing the Cam

15

The camshaft is the heart of an engine. Consequently, it's understandable that vehicle manufacturers as well as aftermarket specialty companies have devoted a great deal of experimentation to camshaft design.

Camshaft theory is the most misunderstood of all internal combustion engine functions, presenting an elusive mystery to both the layman and the general mechanic. In the past, specialty cam makers concentrated on racing, but the gasoline crisis of the 1970s brought realization to many of them that the average motorist—particularly the RV owner—would spend sizable sums of money on products purported to increase mileage and/or performance.

Cam advertisements directed at the general motoring public usually offer both. Unfortunately, the RV owner often finds a cam replacement project costly and disappointing. Reasons are fairly simple but before they can be explained, it's necessary to have a basic understanding of engine operating principles relating to the camshaft.

You might refer back to Chapter 1 for a refresher on how an engine works.

It is generally believed that valves open and close at TDC (top dead center) and BDC (bottom dead center). For example, one might assume that the intake valve opens as the piston begins its downward travel on the induction stroke. However, this could only be possible if gases were weightless and their flow could be started or stopped instantly. They are governed by laws of inertia that also govern solids. It takes time to get them moving. Once moving, it takes time to get them stopped.

Replacement of the cam involves a substantial amount of work, so the vehicle owner should be quite sure the benefits will justify the cost; they usually don't. Here, cam is being removed from Ford 460 V-8.

The Challenge: Inertia

The greatest challenge in camshaft design involves inertia. The ability of the piston to fill the cylinder is totally related to the partial vacuum created by the piston as it moves downward. Atmospheric pressure (14.7 pounds per square inch, maximum) is the only available force to move the fuel and air into the cylinder in response to existence of the partial vacuum. It doesn't happen instantly. At normal cruise speeds, the intake cycle occurs about 80 times per second, which should give you an idea of the problem.

To increase cylinder filling (volumetric efficiency), the intake valve is open longer than one complete downward stroke (180 degrees of crankshaft rotation). In camshaft design terminology, this is known as *increased duration* (length of time the valve is open).

Opening the intake valve before top dead center may seem illogical in that it would appear to interfere with flow of expanded, heated gases out of the exhaust valve during the exhaust stroke (immediately prior to the intake stroke). It would seem that the exhaust pressures would force the intake charge backward. In fact, this can happen at

Effectiveness of Camshaft Modification Relative to Available Torque

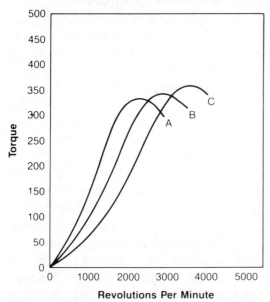

Graph illustrates the approximate sacrifice that often is necessary with replacement cams that supposedly offer improved mileage and power. Stock cam is represented by curve A. Curve B represents a conservative RV cam grind with more lift, 10 degrees increase in duration and 10 degrees earlier exhaust valve opening. Curve C represents an RV grind with about 20 degrees more duration, more lift and 20 degrees earlier exhaust valve opening. Torque is improved, but the torque curve has been moved up the rpm scale.

low engine rpm and results in the rough idle associated with radical cam designs in racing engines. However, as engine rpm increases, velocity of the exhaust gases moving through the exhaust port *scavenges* the intake flow, actually inititating the intake flow. In other words, the inertia of the gases moving through the exhaust port does not instantly change direction when the intake valve opens. Were it not for in-

ertia, the exhaust gases would indeed flow through the intake valve. (When both valves are open simultaneously, it's called *overlap*.) Scavenging occurs only to a limited degree in RV engines, where the prime goal is low-rpm power, because overlap is very limited.

Next, imagine that the piston has traveled its full distance downward on the intake stroke. Should the valve close as the piston moves into the next upward (compression) stroke? Not necessarily. Allowing the intake valve to remain open for as much as 60 degrees of upward piston movement begins compression of the air/fuel mixture while air and fuel still are moving through the intake valve. That may not seem possible, but remember inertia. The gases are moving downward in the intake stroke. Suddenly, the piston changes direction. Static compression occurs immediately above the piston but, much higher up in the cylinder, fuel and air are still moving in.

Timing of the exhaust valve differs from that of the intake valve because the exhaust situation is not dependent on atmospheric pressure. However, it is influenced by the efficiency of the intake cycle.

The exhaust valve opens 40 to 80 degrees before the bottom of the power stroke. That means it also is open more than the assumed 180-degree rotation of the crankshaft. Why open the exhaust valve before the power stroke is completed? The piston has absorbed the power from combustion before it reaches the bottom of the stroke. By opening the exhaust valve early, release of exhaust gases starts prior to upward movement of the piston during the exhaust stroke.

Late Opening and Closing

Due to inertia, it is not possible to instantly open or close valves. Late opening or closing allows the valve to be fully open during the most desirable time of piston travel. Additional valve lift is desirable. However, camshaft wear must be considered. To achieve additional lift or more rapid valve opening and closing, special alloy metals must be used in higher quality rocker arm assemblies with stiffer valve springs. They are costly.

It should be evident at this point that modification of the camshaft must be very conservative in RV situations. Increased duration and overlap can result in loss of low-speed torque in a trade-off for power gains at high rpm. Most RV owners seek the opposite—a trade of high-rpm power for more low-rpm torque. The cam may be advertised as an improver of low-rpm torque when actually it does the opposite. Most cam makers are too race-oriented to accept the fact that RV owners want to pull heavy loads at low engine rpm . . . *really* low rpm in the cam makers' frame of reference.

If you find it difficult to climb a specific hill in high gear at 35 mph with the stock camshaft, increasing duration and overlap could make it even harder to climb the same hill in high gear. However, the hill could become easier to climb in second gear when engine rpm is higher. So the first item of consideration in choosing a replacement camshaft is engine rpm at cruise speeds.

With RVs, cruise speeds only occasionally exceed 55 mph, for obvious reasons. To determine if a cam change could be beneficial, check the rpm at which your engine is rated by its manufacturer for maximum torque. This information is available in engine manuals and in reference manuals at libraries, or in company literature. Determine the engine rpm at which your vehicle cruises at 55 mph. The engine speed at cruise should be 5 to 10 percent below the maximum torque rpm for overall efficiency. If your vehicle is heavy, use 5 percent.

Example: You own a 1975 Chevrolet with a 454 engine, rated at 350 lb.-ft torque at 2400 rpm. Let's say your vehicle cruises at 55 mph at 2200 rpm. You have an ideal combination and a cam change would be of little or no benefit. Your use situation happens to coincide with Chevrolet's cam shaft design for that engine. You would lose mileage as well as performance with a cam change. If cruise rpm were in excess of 2400, a cam change might be considered.

The Correct Choice

How do you choose the correct cam? Request specifications from the manufacturer of the camshaft(s) you are considering. Specifically, ask them the point at which the engine will develop peak torque with their camshaft. Compare that with the torque peak of your stock engine. Ask them if the camshaft will affect idle smoothness and reduce

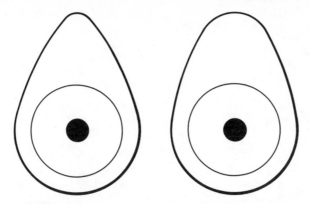

Cam profile at left does not reduce idle vacuum. Nor does it reduce low-rpm torque. The more aggressive racing-oriented profile at right reduces low-rpm torque. Illustrations are exaggerated for clarity.

manifold vacuum readings at idle. A replacement cam for an RV should not reduce idle vacuum readings or create idle roughness. If it does, you didn't get an RV cam. You got a race-oriented cam that possibly has been modified a bit and re-labeled "RV" or "low-end torque."

The important fact to realize here is that a cam change has considerably less chance of success in an RV than it does in hot-rodding or racing. This is not to say that no specialty cams are suitable. Some are, but you *must* do some homework to find out which ones (if any) apply to your specific engine/ axle combination and the way you usually drive.

If a salesman does not have the printed information you need, write to the camshaft manufacturer. *Get it in writing.* Word of mouth is not good enough, because this is an expensive modification which can actually reduce usable power as well as mileage if not performed properly.

The Timing Chain

16

Most engines used in RV service use a chain and two gears, allowing the crankshaft to drive the cam. A small sprocket on the crankshaft drives a chain which rotates a larger sprocket attached to the cam. All this happens behind the front engine cover, which is just behind and below the water pump.

The timing chain never has been much of a point of concern to the RV owner, partly because it's hidden from view but also because few mechanics appreciate the effect of improper cam timing on performance and fuel economy, or how rapidly the timing chain (cam chain) wears in many engines. Wear of the timing chain is one of the primary reasons an engine with 40,000 to 70,000 miles on the odometer may be "tired," even though a compression check shows that everything is in order. Primary reasons for a "tired" engine are:

- Loss of compression, due to valve leakage and/or worn piston rings. Results are hard starting (especially cold), rough idle (burned valves) and excessive blow-by (flow of gases into the crankcase from the combustion chambers) due to leaking rings, and loss of mileage and power.
- Timing chain wear. Results are poor responsiveness to throttle, need for excessive spark advance settings, reduction in mileage and power.
- Restricted spark advance due to gummed or rusted components in the

mechanical advance system of the distributor. Results are hesitation, surging, flat spots in acceleration, fuel load-up at idle, poor mileage and performance.

- Improper fuel vaporization due to gum or varnish in carburetor restricting choke and throttle valve operation. The results are loss of mileage, sluggish performance when cold, hesitation.
- Improper fuel vaporization due to intake manifold heat crossover clogged with carbon. Results are dramatic power loss above half-throttle, rpm limited while operating under load.
- Improper exhaust flow due to inoperative (rusted) exhaust heat riser valve (not used in all vehicles) or restricted muffler or exhaust pipe. Results are dramatic power loss above half-throttle, and rpm limited while operating under load.

Checking Chain Slack

Logical time to change the timing chain is when the engine is torn down for a valve job, although wear on the chain may call for earlier replacement. Here's how to find out:

Remove the distributor cap and use a long-handled wrench to slowly turn the engine. Turn in clockwise direction until the initial spark timing mark is at top dead center. Use a piece of tape or other material to form a precise reference point between the distributor body and the rotor. Have an assistant closely watch the reference point on the

The timing chain is the weak link in most RV engines. As it wears, cam timing is retarded. Cam gears with nylon teeth usually wear more rapidly and should be replaced by metal gears.

distributor and rotor. Turn the engine in the *opposite* direction very slowly. The assistant should tell you precisely when the rotor begins to move and you should stop turning the engine. Note the position of the timing mark on the scale. The difference between your previous position (top dead center) and the new position indicates the amount of timing chain slack, in degrees. If it's more than 9 degrees, it's worthwhile to change the chain and top gear. If slack is 15 degrees or more, the timing gear and chain are worn to the point where you can expect slippage of the chain, which normally will throw the engine out of time enough that the vehicle must be towed in and repaired.

The distributor is driven by the cam, so the timing chain not only affects cam timing, it affects the distributor. Since distributor position is adjustable, timing chain wear doesn't permanently retard spark timing. But cam timing is affected.

The engine can be turned using a socket wrench on the crankshaft pulley bolt. Or, if the spark plugs have been removed, the engine may be rotated merely by turning the alternator with a wrench on the pulley bolt. Logical time to check the chain slack is when replacing plugs, and it's logical when replacing plugs to check cylinder compression and to check spark advance systems (as was described in Chapter 4).

Most motor companies use cam gears with nylon teeth, to reduce chain noise. Nylon teeth are subject to more rapid wear than are steel teeth, and the nylon-tooth gears should be replaced by steel gears. It's difficult to figure why the factories went that route in the first place since cam gear/chain noise is a very small factor in the overall noise picture.

Double-row chain retards wear rate, but top as well as bottom gears must be changed. Above, double-row is at left, stock chain at right.

Try to use a chain that will last longer than the factory part. The steel gear will increase chain life considerably. The Cloyes double-row chain will double chain life. However, it is expensive. Check local performance shops, as double-row chains are used widely in racing. Obviously, a change to a double-row chain is more involved, since the sprocket on the crankshaft must also be changed, requiring a puller. The cam sprocket is merely unbolted from the cam.

High Wear Rates

Some engines will show substantial timing chain wear within 20,000 miles. The Ford 460 is one such engine, and the Dodge 360 is close behind. It's not uncommon with the Dodge 360 and the Ford 460 that timing chains grow so slack within 40,000 miles the chain slips on the bottom sprocket. If one's luck is good, this will merely shut the engine down. If it's bad, one or more valves could be bent. (Incorrect cam timing could have a valve open at top of piston stroke.) Whether or not it's possible to bend a valve in this manner varies with engine design.

Most of us are interested in preventive maintenance and mechanical changes that will forestall expensive breakdowns on the road. Periodic checks on timing chain wear (initially at 20,000 miles and every 10,000 miles thereafter if the chain is not changed) will help prevent such incidents.

Troubleshooting an Automatic Choke

17

If you can remember the days when all motor vehicles were equipped with manual chokes, you might recall the chokes as being a pain in the neck. The frequent adjustment necessary during engine warm-up can be rather tiresome in a vehicle used every day.

On the other hand, if you're having problems with erratic operation of an automatic choke—especially in high altitude—you might yearn for the good old days of manual chokes. Many RV owners whose automatic chokes malfunction on a chronic basis have converted to manual chokes. Kits for doing so are available at most auto parts stores. Holley kits are good, while many others are mediocre.

If improper performance of an automatic choke merely created inconvenience, it would not be such a prob-

lem. Unfortunately, a faulty automatic choke can cause poor fuel economy, spark plug fouling, backfiring and stalling, which can be dangerous. Also, a variety of engine performance problems are mistakenly attributed to improper choke operation.

Let's clear away the smoke, explain how an automatic choke is supposed to operate, and see how to determine if an engine malfunction is caused by the choke or by something else.

How It Works

The automatic choke affects the engine just like the manual choke—a valve on top of the carburetor partially restricts air intake while the engine is cold. This restriction creates a partial vacuum in-

Chokes with adjustable settings (such as this one on Rochester Quadrajet) may be changed for varying operating conditions and to correct cold-start problems. Other Quadrajet carbs have heat-stove choke linkage not as easily adjustable.

Inside the choke housing is a bi-metal spring. When subjected to heat from the engine or from a 12-volt source, the spring unwinds, opening the choke. Rate of unwind should follow the engine warm-up rate.

side the carburetor venturi, where the fuel distribution nozzles are located; that partial vacuum raises fuel flow above normal.

An engine relies on ingestion of properly vaporized fuel for proper combustion. Vaporization of the fuel occurs inside the intake manifold where the fuel is heated. When the engine is cold, fuel vaporization is poor—too poor (usually) to support proper engine operation. To make up for this lack of proper fuel vaporization, more fuel must be added. The choke does this.

An automatic choke system is supposed to open the choke valve on top of the carburetor gradually, as the engine warms up. As miles accumulate on the engine, the choke mechanism may

become gummed and sticky from road grime and the residue that remains from evaporation of fuel that may have leaked onto the linkage.

Several components are subject to restricted operation due to accumulation of dirt and grime. The choke valve at the top of the carburetor usually is controlled by a rod connected to a device which reacts to engine heat. (Late-model vehicles use electrical heating methods in many cases.) Usually it's a bi-metal coil. As more heat is applied to the coil, it expands and grows longer. Thus, the tip of the coil moves. The tip is connected to the choke actuation rod. When the coil grows longer through heat expansion and unwinds, it moves the choke actuation rod, which in turn changes position of the valve on top of the carburetor.

Late-model Quadrajet carburetor used on GM vehicles has choke pull-off diaphragm. Choke is closed when engine is cranking but diaphragm opens it slightly when engine starts. Amount of pull-off can be adjusted with screw above choke housing. Choke spring can be adjusted as well.

Choke adjustment on Motorcraft 4300-series carburetors (used on Ford 460) is similar to that of many other engines. Choke spring housing can be rotated as indicated for rich or lean settings. Tube leading into housing applies exhaust heat to spring.

Design of the steel coil, together with how much heat is applied to it, controls the gradual change in choke setting and how well the setting follows engine temperature rise. Most automotive manufacturers do this properly, but in many instances the choke comes off (opens) too early. Or it doesn't open early enough, even when it is not gummed up. Late-model vehicles are required to open the choke almost immediately, to meet EPA requirements, and in many cases an electric (12-volt) assist is used with the bi-metal thermostat coil. Choke pull-off diaphragms have become common. More engines are prone to run well for about the first half-mile, and then very poorly (too lean) until almost fully warmed up, due to improper choke performance.

Diagnosing Problems

Here's how to diagnose basic choke-related problems:

Problem: Engine loads up (runs rich) during cold starts but runs well after engine warm-up.

Cause: Choke comes off only partially, or not at all. Engine with considerable miles on odometer may have plugged heat riser passage in intake manifold, and/or gummed choke linkage. Check for free movement of linkage and choke pull-off diaphragm (if so equipped). If none of these problems exist, choke setting may be too rich.

Problem: Engine backfires, coughs, sputters and often dies during or shortly after cold starts, but runs well after engine comes up to operating temperature.

Cause: Choke linkage may be binding due to dirt or grime, preventing the choke from closing. Check for free movement of linkage. Check setting. If too lean, adjust. While idling engine, check choke automatic control to see how rapidly it comes off (opens) due to thermostatic action.

Problem: Choke comes off only partially and may not open fully. Linkage is clean.

Cause: Air horn may be binding the choke valve. File choke butterfly or deflect the air horn by using a flat-nosed punch and light hammer as necessary to permit free movement of valve.

Choke adjustments vary from one carburetor to the next. Some appear nonadjustable, such as the mechanical linkage of many Quadrajet carburetors on GM vehicles. However, that system can be adjusted by bending the linkage rod to make it longer or shorter. The bending should not restrict its free movement through the carburetor air horn. Others have an obvious adjustment method, using arrows to indicate proper rotation for rich or lean adjustment. Unfortunately, it's not possible to include exact and full adjustment procedures on all chokes here. Suffice it to say, purchase of a shop manual (available through the vehicle dealership) is the proper way to solve problems. The choke should be adjusted at the alti-

tude in which the vehicle is operated, and at the average air temperature. It's desirable to set the choke as lean as possible to avoid excessive fuel consumption, but not so lean that drivability problems occur. If the adjustment on the choke thermostat requires a position more than three marks away from "normal," it indicates that either the mechanism is rusted or dirty or the bi-metal spring has lost its tension and should be replaced.

Before attempting to adjust any choke, refer to the shop manual and set everything to standard positions. Be sure not only that the choke adjustment is proper but that the fast-idle and all other adjustments also meet the specs listed in the book. After adjustments meet the factory specs, make modifications only on a cold engine, and only one at a time.

Some carburetors are equipped with choke diaphragms which may also cause problems. The choke diaphragm "dashpot" is vacuum-controlled and is connected to the choke linkage. While the engine is cranking, there is no vacuum and the diaphragm does not affect choke linkage. When the engine starts, vacuum is applied and the diaphragm partially opens the choke. An inoperative diaphragm will cause over-rich operation immediately after a cold start. You can check operation by using the following procedure after the engine has sat overnight without use:

1. Press the accelerator pedal to the floor and release it. Start the engine in a normal manner. Allow it to idle for about 20 seconds, or until it will idle without dying. Turn off the key.

2. Remove the air cleaner lid and observe the choke valve. It should be closed or nearly closed. Have an assistant start the engine *without touching the accelerator pedal* while you watch the diaphragm linkage and position of the choke valve. Immediately on starting, the diaphragm lever should pull in, slightly opening the choke valve. If it pulls in, but not far enough to open the choke valve, adjust the position to factory specs. If the diaphragm does not move, use mouth suction to see if vacuum leaks through it. If so, the diaphragm is ruptured and the dashpot should be replaced.

This situation is fairly common, and makes RV owners wonder if the choke is at fault:

Problem: Engine runs well until it is fully up to operating temperature. Then it lags, stumbles and occasionally backfires.

Cause: Worn or improperly adjusted accelerator pump, or primary jets in the carburetor are too small and the engine is running too lean in the cruise system. The lean condition is corrected by the choke, while it is in operation. Solution is recalibration of the carburetor with one of the tuning kits described elsewhere in this book.

Another Common Situation:

Problem: Engine runs well immediately after a cold start, but begins to run rich shortly afterward. It runs rich until full engine warm-up, at which time it begins to run normally.

Cause: Choke setting is proper. First check: pull off diaphragm. If okay, check the thermostat coil or other heat-sensing device for dirty or oily condition. If the choke has a heat conduit from the exhaust manifold (a steel tube connecting the choke thermostat with the exhaust manifold), check connections and check the tube for obstruction, as the choke thermostat is not subjected to enough heat. Exhaust gases cross over the engine through a passageway in the center of the intake manifold. These gases provide heat for the choke thermostat as well as heat for the interior floor of the intake manifold, which aids fuel vaporization. The passageway tends to become clogged with carbon on some engines—particularly Dodge 318s and 360s—and this not only prevents the choke from coming off completely, it reduces fuel vaporization. The result can be a substantial reduction in fuel economy. After the engine is fully up to operational temperature, check the choke to see that it's fully open. If not, feel the choke thermostat coil. It should be uncomfortable to touch. Make sure choke linkage is free. Carbon blockage of the heat crossover passage is a possibility if the engine has at least 25,000 miles. Carbon blockage is dealt with in Chapter 29 on the Dodge 360.

Engine Overhaul

18

With prices of new vehicles having gone out of sight, more RV owners are considering keeping vehicles longer, even though they are getting a bit rough around the edges—and balky, at times. Before deciding whether to trade your vehicle, consider the points in Chapter 6—the pros and cons of used versus new vehicles. Possibly a new vehicle makes sense. If not, an older vehicle usually can be put into very good condition at considerably less expense than the cost of a new one, if the body is in good shape. If the body is rusted and corroded beyond repair, the vehicle probably should be sold or junked.

Engine overhaul is the most apparent and significant move in keeping a used vehicle. Next comes transmission overhaul. However, don't automatically assume either is needed. Check their condition first. Just because a vehicle has 70,000 to 80,000 miles on it doesn't mean it's due for overhaul, although it well may be.

Transmissions can last as long as 200,000 miles if maintained properly and if the oil is cooled properly. Condition of an engine will vary with maintenance, type of use, and its original quality. Some engines have been known to go 125,000 to 150,000 miles before overhaul, while others seem to need it by about 80,000 miles—or earlier, if maintenance has not been proper or if use has been severe. Severe use doesn't necessarily mean RV travel. In many cases, RV travel is less harmful than around-town commuting. During short trips, especially in cold weather, engine oil does not have time to come up to

Engine overhaul offers opportunity to correct deficiencies in the original design, for improvement of mileage and performance.

normal temperature (at least 180 degrees) so it can dissipate pollutants such as water and unburned fuel. Water gets into the crankcase through expansion and contraction of engine parts and air, during temperature changes. The engine breathes in air when it cools down and expels air when it warms up. The air it takes in contains moisture, which settles on the interior surfaces and gets into the oil when the engine is restarted.

If short-distance around-town driving is the worst possible use, long oil-change intervals add to the problems. When water and fuel combine with engine oil, acids form and they attack bearings. Contaminants in the oil form sludge that builds up in an engine. When an engine has progressed to this point, it's a good bet that wear has been

fairly rapid. Sludge may be noticed on top of cylinder heads and in the valley between cylinder heads (under the intake manifold). The moral of the story is need for proper maintenance—especially in short-distance driving in cold weather.

Checking Engine Condition

Many engines grow "tired" at around 50,000 miles, even though the usual tests show no physical signs of accelerated wear. For example, cylinder compression may still be good, but the engine has less power, uses more fuel and is more prone to ping. When all cylinders are within 10 percent of each other, compression can be regarded as good. When one cylinder (or more) differs substantially, a valve job may be in order. Or, piston rings may be worn, although piston ring wear usually will result in all cylinders showing lower compression than called for in manufacturers' shop manuals. Or, the valves as well as piston rings may be in poor condition. Good shops can perform cylinder leak-down tests to evaluate condition of piston rings more accurately. A compression test is more simple and will indicate piston ring condition if oil is added to each cylinder as part of the test procedure.

Compression Test Procedure

• Remove all spark plugs and identify them by cylinder number where they were used. Prop the throttle open and measure compression by cranking the engine with the compression gauge in each cylinder. Record the readings indicating which cylinder was tested.

- Go through the procedure again, but inject two or three squirts of oil from a pressure oil can into each cylinder. (First spin the engine with the starter to distribute the oil throughout the cylinder).
- If compression improves substantially during the second test (with oil in cylinders), ring wear is indicated. If it does not—and if compression readings are low—valve leakage is indicated.

Another method of checking for ring wear or valve leakage is to bring the piston to top dead center on the firing stroke. Insert an air pressure fitting into the spark plug hole and apply 30 to 50 pounds of air pressure into the cylinder. The air will pass either into the oil pan, which can be heard through the oil fill tube, or through the intake or exhaust valve, which can be determined by listening at the carburetor and exhaust pipes (throttle open). This is a more precise method but will require the appropriate spark plug adaptor valve and an air compressor. More sophisticated equipment will indicate percentage of pressure loss, but it's best to have a good shop perform this work.

A valve job usually will put new life into an engine that has lost most of its spunk. But all too often the work is not performed properly—especially with regard to valve guide clearances and oil seals. The engine may use oil immediately after an overhaul, and the problem is explained away with the old adage that a valve job often will make an engine use oil if the rings are the least bit worn. It's true, when there is considerable ring wear. But if the compression check with oil in the cylinders indicates rings are good, chances are quite good that a valve job is all that may be needed to put the engine into good shape. If oil consumption occurs after a valve job on an engine that did not show ring wear during a compression test, odds are that the mechanic did not do the valves properly— too much valve stem-to-guide clearance exists. See Chapter 14 on proper valve work.

If a valve job seems OK for a while but the engine starts to use oil in a few thousand miles, there is a good chance the shop knurled the guides rather than replacing them, when replacement was called for. Knurling is described in Chapter 14. In all too many cases, an engine may go 50,000 to 70,000 miles before needing a valve job, but the valves are bad again in only 20,000 miles. The answer in many cases is fairly obvious.

When a valve job appears needed and the rings appear good, the time is opportune to really bring the engine back to life. With the heads already removed for valve work, it's foolish not to replace the timing chain and cam gear at the same time, if the engine has at least 30,000 miles. See Chapter 16 for timing chain information. Also, inspect the cam and lifters if the engine has more than 50,000 miles on the odometer. Often, cam wear occurs by that point and it's not difficult to justify replacement. Timing chain wear is severe on most V-

Selection of an inappropriate cam is the downfall of many overhaul projects. Unless you're certain that choice of a specialty cam is correct, stick with the stock cam. Here, cam is fitted into Ford 351W engine.

8 engines. The few mechanics who try to talk customers into such work, with 50,000 miles or less on the odometer, often are accused of hustling. But in fact they're doing the customer a favor. At least, they should be permitted to check the timing chain for slack, with the method described in Chapter 16. If piston rings appear worn enough to justify a full overhaul, the cam and chain plus valve work are always included in the job.

When overhaul appears needed, a reliable shop usually decides on components to be used. But the vehicle owner should participate in the decision on selection of some parts—specifically piston rings. The reason is that all too

many shops make the wrong decision, even though they have the customer's best interests in mind. While the shop is responsible to correct any problems an improper selection may create, the vehicle owner must put up with considerable inconvenience and hassle.

Well-meaning shops may use chrome rings, for example, thinking they'll wear longer. They will. But if they don't seat to the cylinder walls—which is fairly common—the engine will use copious amounts of oil. Then there is no fix but to tear the engine down, replace the rings, hone the cylinders and try again. If the replacement rings are chrome as well, the same thing could happen again.

Choice of piston rings is critical. An incorrect choice may result in failure of rings to seat, causing high oil consumption.

Choosing Piston Rings

Any sign of excessive oil consumption or smoke from the tail pipe is immediately attributed to piston rings when rings may not be at fault. The mechanic diagnoses the problem and a considerable amount of money is spent, but the problem may persist or may be only partially corrected. In some cases, the original oil consumption habits return in a short time.

In most cases, excessive oil consumption is not directly related to piston ring failure. In fact, 90 percent of all premature ring failure is related to improper installation and break-in procedures or to other component failures contributing to loss of ring seal or irreversible damage.

The more common cause of excessive oil consumption is related to leakage through the intake system. While the engine is operated during part throttle and especially when descending grades, a considerable differential in pressure exists between the intake system and atmospheric pressure. The lower pressure found in the intake system is known as vacuum (partial vacuum) and is measured in inches of mercury. This lower pressure is caused by downward movement of the piston during the intake cycle. When the throttle is closed or partly closed, a partial vacuum is created in the cylinder. Actually, pressure is greater outside the cylinder than inside and the pressure (15 pounds per square inch) attempts to force its way into the cylinder (low pressure area) by any means possible. The weak points are seals—intake manifold gaskets and valve guide seals.

Intake manifold gaskets, which seal the manifold to the cylinder head and block (lifter valley), often leak from improper preparation and sealing or neglect in retorquing bolts after the break-in period. A leak at this point will allow oil to pass from the lifter valley through the intake ports and into the combustion chamber. In its advanced state this condition is diagnosed by loss of idle vacuum or rough idle. If cranking compression is uniform from one cylinder to the next, and all tuning specifications are within acceptable limits, it would be logical to assume a gasket leak is the cause of oil consumption. Intake manifold bolts are loose in most engines. Check them and torque to specifications in shop manuals. The recommended tightening procedure is from the center out, alternating from side to side. Use of a spray lubricant such as WD-40 along the gasket edge will generally indicate seepage while engine speed is being changed rapidly.

Valve Guide Leakage

Second point of oil leakage due to the pressure differences described earlier is through intake valve guides. Exhaust valve guides also are a problem but seldom are a major consideration in oil consumption. Factory-installed valve seals in many engines are less than adequate, and premature failure of the seals, plus excessive clearance between the valve stem and guide, will allow the oil which lubricates the valve train to enter the engine. If a relatively new engine has this problem, external replacement of the valve guide seals is worth a try. Often, improved designs are available. To change seals, valve springs must be removed and the valves thus must be kept from dropping into the cylinders. Compressed air can be administered through the spark plug port to keep valves in place.

If mileage is approaching 30,000 or

if uneven compression exists, installation of full-floating Pioneer brand Teflon seals is recommended. They require machining of the guides. A good examination of valve stem and guide wear should be done at this time and if necessary, new guides should be installed. The common practice of knurling guides should not be used if guide wear goes .001-inch beyond factory specifications.

Oil entering the intake system has an adverse effect on piston rings and over a prolonged period creates varnish on the cylinder walls, causing rings to lose their seal. This varnish deposit appears as a brown polished surface on cylinder walls. If the engine has less than 40,000 miles and cylinder taper is less than .004-inch, it's possible to correct the problem and avoid an overhaul. Move the piston to the bottom of its travel and use a very fine emery paper with a light honing oil, rotated horizontally in the cylinder until this coating is removed. Wipe the surface clean and coat generously with 20-40 motor oil and the rings should reseal.

Oil entering combustion chambers through the intake system can be determined in a road test. With an assistant driving your vehicle, observe the tail pipes. If excessive smoke is obvious during sustained hard throttle application as in climbing a grade, this indicates bad rings. If the smoke diminishes as the climb is continued, it doesn't indicate rings; oil buildup simply is burning out of the engine and exhaust system. After decelerating down a long grade and upon applying hard throttle, if a considerable amount of smoke is expelled, this indicates oil leakage through the intake system. After stopping the engine for 15 minutes, restart and if smoke is observed, it indicates oil passage through valve guides.

Washing down of cylinder walls is a common cause of premature ring failure. Over-rich fuel mixtures from incorrect carburetor jetting or carburetor malfunctions can wash the oil film from cylinder walls, destroying the seal. When this condition is prolonged, cylinder taper in excess of .012-inch can occur in just 25,000 miles, whereas cylinder taper may be only .002-inch in 80,000 miles in an engine that has not suffered the problem.

It's a common fallacy that water injection also causes wash-down of cylinder walls. Water is not a solvent for oil, as is gasoline, and when injected in proper amounts it is quickly vaporized, reducing or eliminating preignition or detonation (ping) after which it is blown out the exhaust.

If it is determined that rings are to be replaced either in a total rebuild with a new bore, or just a re-ring job, it is important that you are familiar with what is available and the various materials used relative to your vehicle situation, so the proper choice of piston rings can be made even though your mechanic will do the work.

Many materials are used to make piston rings. They include combinations of cast, ductile and high-strength iron and steel in a variety of designs. Facings or coatings of lapped chrome, moly plus lubrite and bluing are used to enhance seating, improve scuff resistance and wear characteristics.

We prefer nodular iron for RV situations where higher strength is required. The composition of nodular iron produces two to three times the strength of gray iron and is ductile rather than brittle (will bend rather than break). This is because the graphite in nodular iron is spherical rather than in the form of random flakes, as in gray iron. This graphite distributed throughout the iron provides self-lubrication which reduces friction and helps prevent scuffing during the critical break-in period.

Chrome Rings

Chrome-faced rings were developed during World War II to combat abrasive wear. The hardness of the chrome made them resistant to abrasives while at the same time it minimized cylinder wear. Chromium has a much higher melting temperature than cast iron. This makes the chrome-plated rings more resistant to scuffing because they are better able to withstand marginal lubrication. Chrome rings usually are preseated to cylinder walls at the factory by lapping (minute grooves in the face of the ring) to ensure faster break-in. However, it always has been a problem to seat chrome rings after an overhaul and we don't use them for that reason.

Moly piston rings have all the advantages of chrome. The characteristics of molybdenum are more impressive than chrome. It melts at 4750 degrees F while

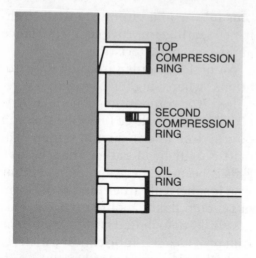

TOP
COMPRESSION
RING

SECOND
COMPRESSION
RING

OIL
RING

Modern engines are fitted with three piston rings that seal compression and keep oil out of combustion chambers.

chrome melts at 3212. This increases scuff resistance. Surface of a moly ring is porous. About 15 percent of it consists of small voids which retain oil, reducing frictional loss. The moly plating on the ring ranges from .004 to .008-inch. This particular ring, we feel, produces the surest seating combined with extended service.

In selecting rings, stay with a recognized manufacturer. Having decided on the material to use, follow the actual recommended combination of oil rings for your application as they are designed to function together.

In the case of a re-ring, wear should not exceed .010-inch cylinder taper and .004-inch out of round. We feel anything above this point will not be cost-effective. Ring life is limited when cylinder taper is more than .010-inch. The engine should be re-bored.

If it is determined that a re-ring will be the plan, a ridge should be carefully

removed at the top of the cylinder. The finish should blend smoothly. This will allow the pistons to be removed without damage to ring lands and also assure that the new rings will not contact the previous wear ridge, causing ring damage.

A cylinder hone must be used to both remove the glaze and help true the cylinder walls. A honing stone of 220 grit should be used with a honing oil. In cases of re-bore the same hone should be used and in each cylinder should be operated to produce a uniform cross hatch angle of 22 to 32 degrees from horizontal. It is imperative that all honing residue be removed from cylinders. Washing with solvent is not adequate. Washing with soap and water and a stiff brush is necessary. Abrasive materials from honing are found in nearly all ring jobs either due to ignorance or carelessness. Immediately coat cylinder walls with oil to prevent rusting.

Rings must be checked for fit relative to the cylinder walls and piston. A shop manual for the vehicle in question details how to do it. Even though the ring container indicates the specific size, rings must be placed into the cylinder bore to check for end gap. When you are checking end gap on a fresh bore, the ring may be placed in the top of the cylinder. In a re-ring it must be placed at the bottom where less wear has occurred. Stay as near minimum clearance as possible.

Rings should be checked for proper ring groove fit. If a re-ring is being done, not only must the pistons be checked for conformity but also the ring grooves must be thoroughly cleaned with a ring groove cleaner and the ring lands should be examined for damage. Maximum clearance between the ring and ring land should be .005-inch.

All compression rings are marked to indicate top side. They are designed to remove excess oil from cylinder walls and if installed upside down they will force oil into the combustion chamber. Care should be used not to expand or twist the rings or permanent distortion will occur. A proper ring expander should be used; this is especially true with moly rings. All parts should be saturated with oil before installation.

To fit piston rings, check the piston ring groove depth by sliding a ring into the groove. The depth of the groove must be deeper than the ring width. Place the ring into the cylinder. Invert the pistons and shove the ring down into the cylinder about two inches and check end gap. Gap should be between .015-inch and .025-inch on compression rings. Oil rings will seal properly up to .050-inch maximum.

When installing rings try not to spread the rings. Rotate or walk the rings onto the pistons. Staggering the gaps is important. The compression ring gaps should be 180 degrees from each other in line with the piston wrist pin. The oil ring rails and spacer should be 45 degrees from each other and should begin 45 degrees from the front indicator on the piston—to 135 degrees, then 225 degrees, then 315 degrees.

Proper Break-In

Break-in should consist of using nondetergent oil for at least 500 miles and a maximum of 1500. This is subject to controversy, but the nondetergent oil offers less friction-reducing ability and the rings will seal more quickly and more effectively. After seating use a detergent 20W-50 SF rated oil.

Prolonged gentle operation of the engine during break-in will often cause the cylinder walls to glaze, preventing adequate oil control. Harsh operation may cause localized over-heating, resulting in scuffing. Use this procedure: Upon initial start, avoid prolonged slow idle. Run the engine at a fast idle until normal operational temperature is reached. Make sure initial timing is correct. Drive at normal speeds, not to exceed 55 mph. Accelerate from 25 to 55 at about two-thirds throttle, at least 12 times. Avoid downshifting for additional speed reduction on downhill grades. Continue variation in speeds for the first 100 miles of operation. Refrain from towing during the initial 1500 miles.

Proper selection of piston rings and proper break-in are critical to ensure that rings seat. With regular oil changes and proper carburetor jetting to avoid cylinder wash-down, piston rings can do their rather amazing multi-faceted job quite well for thousands of miles.

As for other aspects of engine overhaul, the RV owner must make several more important choices. (The rest is up to the mechanic and his expertise and experience.) The RV owner must determine if he wants to stay with the stock engine compression, or increase it. This can be done by using replacement pistons with higher crowns or modification of deck height. If the engine must be bored to oversize, new pistons must be purchased anyway. The additional performance provided by slightly higher compression can be enjoyed without additional expense for internal engine components.

However, increased compression does raise an engine's fuel octane requirements. As we all know, fuel quality is not very good. It's usually possible to raise compression to about 9 to 1 and still burn regular fuel by using an effective water injection system to reduce the engine's fuel octane requirements. Pistons with higher crowns are fitted to the engine just as the stock pistons were used. Be sure the mechanic has chosen pistons accurately, so that you don't end up with 10 to 1 compression. Get it in writing on the work order.

An engine consistently operated above 5000 feet can handle about 10 to 1 compression, although that compression ratio can present problems if the vehicle is ever driven at low altitude. With water injection and premium fuel (or regular fuel and one of the more effective fuel octane-improving additives) short-duration low-altitude driving can be done without incurring engine damage due to ping.

Engines operated solely on propane will handle about 10.5 to 1 compression, and this makes up for most of the power and mileage reduction caused by the fuel's lower heat content than gasoline. Propane enters the engine as a gas, so vaporization is total in contrast with gasoline. But the lower heat content still is a disadvantage.

Deck Height

Deck height should be checked, regardless of what compression is used. Deck height is the distance between the top of the block and the top of the piston at the top of its stroke. In many cases it's more on one side than the other, and engine efficiency suffers. The high side should be milled more so deck height is identical on both sides. This increases compression, but usually the increase is slight if deck height is merely being evened up.

When deck height is excessive, as it is in some cases, a worthwhile increase in compression can be gained by reducing deck height more than the amount necessary just to even it up. The Dodge 440 is the prime example of this, since deck height is .187-inch. The Chevrolet 454, by comparison, has a mere .025-inch deck height. When deck height of the Dodge 440 is reduced to .060-inch, compression is increased to about 8.5 to 1. Stock compression of post-1970 440s is about 7.8 to 1, regardless of how it's listed in factory literature. When that deck height change is combined with a change to pistons with higher crowns, compression can be boosted to about 9 to 1, which is the maximum for low altitude, using regular fuel and an effective water injection system to prevent ping. With the deck height modification alone, power and mileage are improved noticeably and piston cooling is improved, which dampens the engine's tendency to ping. Rear-wheel horsepower gain with the deck height reduction and piston change is about 18 percent, and mileage usually improves 5 percent to 10 percent, depending on load and driving conditions.

When making substantial deck height reduction by milling the block, the end result should always be uniform—same deck height on both sides. For example, it may be necessary to take .040-inch off one side of the block and .025-inch off the other, to produce the desired deck height. Why not cut it down more? The manifold hold-down bolts won't line up properly. With the deck height reduction described here it's usually necessary to drill the manifold bolt holes larger. Most engines can benefit from deck height reduction. Here's how.

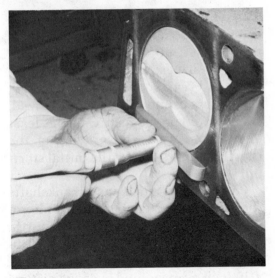

Deck height (top of piston to top of block) should be checked and correct if one side of V-8 engine is different from the other. Reduction of deck height is a method of increasing compression.

Deck Height Reduction

Using a dial indicator, bring the number one piston to absolute top dead center. Check deck height (distance from top of piston to top of block). Number six will also be at TDC at this point. Check it also, and record the numbers. Rotate the engine until deck height of all cylinders is recorded. Differential between cylinders should not exceed .005-inch. If it's greater, the higher pistons should be machined down. Differential from side to side should be corrected by milling the block.

To raise compression, as much as .040-inch can be removed from the block and heads, but it is important that deck height be not less that .010. For example, if deck height is .025-inch, .015-inch can be removed from the block

and .025-inch from the heads, producing the desired .040-inch total reduction. Up to .045-inch can be removed without encountering problems in seating the intake manifold to the heads, but a .005-inch margin should be retained for later head surfacing which could become necessary. Always remove the same amount of material from both heads, regardless of the deck machining variances. In most engines, the material removed from the block results in about twice the benefit as the same amount of material removed from the heads. This is due not only to improved cooling of the pistons but also to the fact that the amount of increase in compression is about double–i.e., .015-inch removed from the block is twice as good as .015-inch removed from the heads.

In other areas of engine overhaul, choice and setup of bearings usually is properly left up to the shop manager. When bearings, crankshafts, pistons, rods and cams are being handled, cleanliness cannot be overemphasized. If engine components are in the least dirty, rapid wear and graying of the bearings occurs during the initial start-up.

Components such as crankshafts should be subjected to standard micro-polishing and resurfacing procedures. If any cylinders have more than .010-inch taper, the block should be re-bored .030-inch oversize, and oversize pistons should be fitted.

When oversize pistons are required, pistons with higher compression usu-ally can be selected at little or no ad-ditional cost—if the engine and the owner's use situation permit using higher than normal compression. Deck height modification may be the only procedure called for under the circum-stances, to create only modest com-pression increase.

However, increased compression does raise an engine's fuel octane require-ments. As we all know, fuel quality is not very good. It's usually possible to raise compression to about 9 to 1 and still burn regular fuel by using an ef-fective water injection system to re-duce the engine's fuel octane re-quirements. Pistons with higher crowns are fitted to the engine just as the stock pistons were used.

Diminishing Lead Content of Gasoline

19

During the past several years RV owners have grown accustomed to living from one crisis to another. If it's not fuel availability, it's fuel price. Or both.

The latest development, fortunately, isn't a crisis. But it's a point of serious concern among many RV owners concerned with fuel quality—added to the price spiral problem, of course. Specifically, it appears to many motorists that leaded gasoline is disappearing. If so, what can owners of pre-1971 vehicles do to combat the adverse effects of unleaded gasoline on engine valves and valve seats? (Beginning in 1971, vehicle manufacturers made design changes to accommodate introduction of unleaded fuels.)

In view of how the cost of new tow vehicles, vans and motorhomes has in-

creased during the past few years, sizable numbers of RV owners are electing not to trade up, choosing instead to renovate the old rig that is almost part of the family. Does disappearance of lead in gasoline reduce desirability of owning an older vehicle? By itself, no. But there are extenuating circumstances that we'll examine here.

Why is lead used in fuel? Tetraethyl lead is used as an octane improver and as a lubricant for valve faces, seats and stems. For decades it has been the least expensive way to boost octane. But in the early 1970s, with the advent of catalytic convertors, lead had to go because it would coat the insides of convertors, gradually restricting exhaust flow. As insurance against valve problems, motor companies began using better quality (harder) steel in

Lead content has diminished greatly since the 1960s but leaded regular is expected to be available for many more years.

valves, and they began induction-hardening the valve seats in cylinder heads. (Induction-hardening is a heat-treatment process that results in more hardness in the valve seat area than elsewhere in the cylinder head.)

Aids Lubrication

The specific role of lead in operation of valves is to aid lubrication of the valve stem. But it also produces a microscopic coating which separates the valve from the valve seat. This prevents something known as valve seat recession. It occurs when the valve and the valve seat are extremely hot. The valve comes to rest momentarily on the seat and, due to the heat, the valve becomes welded to the seat at microscopic points. Thus, the seat gradually is eroded. Also, heat has an eroding effect on the valve itself and the valve as well as the seat may deteriorate.

However, in these extreme cases, absence of lead usually is merely a minor factor. Much worse than absence of lead is the presence of preignition (ping). Ping causes rapid wearing of valves, valve seats and even valve stems and guides because the shock of ping rattles the valve in the guide. This disturbs the valve guide oil seals and introduces a different problem—oil consumption.

Use of unleaded gasoline in pre-1971 RVs is not a serious problem, providing it is not a steady diet. Use of leaded gasoline—either regular or premium—at every third or fourth tank filling usually is sufficient to prevent problems that might be caused by absence of lead. The engineers suggested that unleaded fuel is no problem even as a steady diet in a vehicle used for light duty, but that leaded fuel should be used continually or, if that's not possible, alternately with unleaded fuel in RVs that are subject to severe operating conditions.

Very small amounts of lead are needed to provide the necessary valve protection. Tetraethyl lead is not available as a do-it-yourself additive because of its highly poisonous nature and the inability of the consumer to be sure he is using proper proportions and proper mixing.

Shops that can perform cylinder head work are able to machine recesses into cylinder heads. Hardened valve seats are then pressed into them. It's an expensive procedure, though, and sometimes the pressed-in valve seats come loose. While leaded fuel is still available, it's an unnecessary process.

Availability to Continue

Availability of leaded regular fuel is expected to continue on a widespread basis for an indefinite period, and premium leaded fuel should be available on a very limited basis for several more years. Of course, premium unleaded is widely available.

Difficulty in finding premium leaded fuel has caused quite a bit of concern among owners of pre-1971 high-compression engines. Most light truck and motorhome engines had compression ratios in the area of 8.5 to 1 in the late 1960s but passenger car engines ranged from 9 to 1 up to 11.5 to 1.

Although engines will vary in their octane requirements, our experience indicates it's not realistic to expect an engine with compression higher than 9 to 1 to serve well, due more to low fuel octane than to absence of lead. RV usage creates more heat during uphill travel than does typical street and highway use. For engines lower than 9 to 1 compression, combination of an effective water injection system with leaded regular (or a blend of leaded regular and unleaded premium) has proven effective. Blending usually is inconvenient, especially in a busy service station, so the obvious solution is leaded or unleaded regular along with effective water injection, which reduces octane requirements by controlling combustion and heat. Great numbers of engines, including many late-models, are inclined to ping, so the applicability of effective water injection is widespread.

Water injectors vary widely in effectiveness, quality and warranty coverage. Comparative shopping is in order before a purchase is made. Many systems called "injectors" are not injectors. Rather, they're metering devices that employ engine vacuum to draw water into the engine. Engine vacuum drops as the throttle is opened. Consequently, there is no vacuum to operate these water metering devices under full throttle—when the engine needs the water most.

Vapor injection systems don't inject water. Engine vacuum draws air through a water container, and small amounts of humidified air are drawn into the engine. We have not found these effective in controlling ping.

An effective water injection system has a water pump plus a control system that varies the amount of water injected, according to engine load. Less water is needed at light throttle than at heavy throttle. Check warranty coverage because it may be less than adequate.

Many different engines and gasoline types have been discussed here and it may be helpful at this point to recap the fuel requirements:
- Pre-1971 *low compression* engines need leaded fuel if available, and leaded premium or a water injector if they will not run without ping on leaded regular. If leaded fuel is not available, unleaded regular or premium can be used, as necessary to prevent ping. Revert to leaded fuel when possible.

Fuel Requirements for Engines in RV (Heavy-Duty) Use

	Leaded Regular	Unleaded Regular	Leaded Premium	Unleaded Premium
Pre-1971 Low Compression Engines	Yes [1]	O.I.U.	Yes	O.I.U.
Pre-1971 High Compression Engines	Yes [2,4]	No	Yes	O.I.U.
Post-1971 Engines	Yes [3]	Yes	Yes [3,4]	Yes [4]

O.I.U.—Only if unavoidable

[1] Use leaded regular only if engine will operate on that fuel without ping. Water injector may be used in place of higher-grade fuel.

[2] With compression ratios of 10 to 1 or less. More than 10 to 1 not usually suitable for RV situations.

[3] May be used if vehicle does not have catalytic convertor.

[4] Premium grades necessary only if engine pings on regular grades. Or water injector may be used.

- Pre-1971 *high compression* engines with ratios exceeding 10 to 1 need leaded premium (alternate with unleaded premium if necessary) plus a water injector. Engines with ratios less than 10 to 1 can use leaded regular (alternate with unleaded regular if necessary) plus a water injector.
- Engines built after 1971 (low compression) may use leaded or unleaded fuels, with octane ratings high enough to prevent ping. Lower octane fuels may be used if water injection is employed to prevent ping.

With only a couple of exceptions, engines built in 1971 and later are designed for use of low-lead or unleaded fuel, whether they are in cars, trucks or motorhomes. Unfortunately, not all vehicles for which regular grades of fuel are recommended will run on regular without ping. Even if regular is recommended in the owner's manual, higher octane fuel must be used (or water injection) if the engine pings on regular.

In summary, it appears that the RV owner has little to fear from the gradually diminishing lead content of gasoline, unless compression is in excess of 9 to 1. With proper precautions against engine ping, and by using at least some leaded fuel, accelerated wear of valves and valve seats can be avoided. That may be the only good fuel-related news we've heard in several years.

Engine Reprogramming

20

*T*heory behind an engine tuning kit involves precise, individual calibration of the various systems based on hundreds of tests made on a chassis dynamometer. That's a system of rollers connected to a turbine, on which the vehicle can be operated at various engine loads, simulating road conditions and enabling the dyno operator to record horsepower, along with other items such as emission of carbon monoxide (CO), hydrocarbons (HC), and performance of the ignition system. Air/fuel ratios are derived from the CO and HC readings. When carburetion and ignition changes are made, the effects can be read in horsepower, air/fuel ratios and combustion efficiency.

John Geraghty tests many engines to come up with a tuning kit, partly because factory calibration varies but also because the same engine in a given year may have several different carburetor numbers. A different carburetor number signifies that at least one of the metering systems inside the carburetor has been changed. Consequently, a tuning kit for an engine with a certain carb number won't work for an engine of the same year with a different number. GM, Ford and Chrysler Corporation use different numbering systems, but the intent is the same—to indicate changes in fuel metering.

Geraghty tests an engine to find out if it's too lean or too rich in each of the individual fuel metering systems, except the idle circuit. In a 2-barrel carb, the systems are cruise and power enrichment. In a 4-barrel, it is cruise, primary power enrichment, and secondary power. Any combination of errors may

Road conditions can be simulated on a chassis dynamometer. Vehicle wheels turn rollers and varying resistance can be applied. Horsepower, air/fuel ratios and emissions are monitored.

occur. The cruise system may be too lean and one of the power systems too rich. Or, the cruise may be OK and one of the power systems too lean. Most commonly, cruise is too lean and the power systems are too rich.

Correcting the cruise system is a simple matter. One can drill main jets .002-inch larger and (in most cases) this will solve the problem. However, the metering systems "stack up" on each other. Fuel flow in the cruise system is combined with one or more of the power systems when they are actuated (the first one comes in at 6½ to 7 inches manifold vacuum), so enrichment of the cruise system adds more fuel to the total picture. If one or more of the power systems is too rich, merely enlarging primary metering jets to solve a cruise-system problem will make the fuel mix-

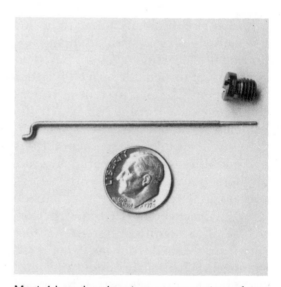

Most 4-barrel carburetors use a system of metering rods and jets to control fuel flow rates. Metering rod is suspended in jet at a specific position during cruise conditions. As throttle increases, reducing manifold vacuum below 6.5 inches, vacuum piston raises tapered rod, permitting more fuel to flow through jet.

Distributor spark advance characteristics can be modified based on test results with machine such as this. Or more fundamental testing can be done with distributor in engine.

tures under heavy throttle very rich, wasting fuel. For good results, each of the fuel metering systems must be corrected with respect to its relationship to total fuel flow to the engine.

Ideally, correction of the system can be accomplished while keeping the engine within the spirit of emissions laws, since the laws don't actually require that an engine be so lean it will hardly run. The laws just dictate the end result: tailpipe emissions.

Spark Timing—Juggling Act

Distributing tuning is something of a juggling act. Manufacturers try to set up spark advance curves that will keep the engine from pinging, even under severe use, on the fuels currently available. Unfortunately, fuel quality has dropped substantially in recent years and the factory tuning in many cases

will cause an engine to detonate (ping). The tuning kits are designed to correct that where possible. But ideally the tuning kits are most effective when a good automotive water injection system is used because water injection controls combustion, allowing more aggressive spark advance calibration, which in turn allows the engine to do its work more efficiently with less throttle.

Many vehicle owners mistakenly believe distributor calibration cannot be changed if the engine has electronic ignition. In fact, the systems that control spark advance are the same as those used with the old breaker-points ignitions. A system of centrifugal weights working against spring tension is used for mechanical advance; vacuum diaphragm is used for vacuum advance.

To determine the most efficient ignition advance curve, the spark re-

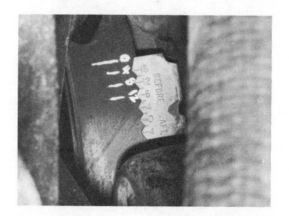

Automatic advance can be checked with timing light, as engine rpm increases. In this case, standard degree scale is too short and scale extension is painted on crankshaft pulley. Zero on flywheel is the timing mark. Shown here is a total of 20 degrees of advance.

quirements for maximum power are determined first. The mechanical advance system in the distributor is locked into a stationary position, vacuum advance is disconnected, and the engine is operated under full throttle on the dyno. At rpm increments of 500, horsepower is checked and the spark timing is adjusted for maximum power output. Degrees of advance are noted. After the runs are completed, a graph is drawn indicating the desirable full-throttle spark advance throughout the operational range (usually from 1500 to 4500 rpm) and changes for the mechanical spark advance system are then designed. Usually, a combination of different springs is all that is needed.

Computerized Testing

Tests to determine best possible fuel economy under light load are conducted, and modifications to vacuum advance are designed. A sophisticated computerized analyzer uses comparative memories to evaluate changes from one test to the next. The dyno operator is able to simulate road conditions by changing the amount of resistance the dyno rollers offer to the vehicle's drive wheels. Thus, the resistance can precisely control engine rpm even though throttle may be continually wide open. In part-throttle tests the adjustability

of the dyno is used similarly. For example, it's easy to see what effect operating at 7 and then at 6 inches manifold vacuum has on air/fuel ratios. At 7 inches power enrichment system of the carburetor is not operating. At 6, it is. The dyno holds engine rpm steady while the slight throttle change is made; the effect on air/fuel ratios is displayed on meters that record exhaust emissions.

The decision to market a tuning kit is based on the number of different vehicles with the same carburetor number that can be tested on the dyno, creating a large cross-section of information. When sufficient numbers of vehicles cannot be found with a particular carburetor number, a do-it-yourself tuning kit is not offered for an engine with that carb number, although Geraghty can individually tune the vehicle by testing it on the dyno. The need for this cross-section of information is why do-it-yourself kits are not offered for all engines with all carburetor numbers. (Other omissions in the tuning kit availability list are dictated merely by low demand.)

After the optimum fuel ratios and spark timing are obtained for all operational loads and speeds, proper selection of spark plug heat range is made. Thus, all conditions are met, and maximum performance as well as efficiency can be obtained.

Tuning the Chevrolet 350 V-8

21

In 1955 Chevrolet introduced the first sophisticated short-stroke V-8 engine, the 265 cubic inch V-8. It was put down by mechanics as structurally weak. They said the stamped steel valve rockers on pressed individual studs would never work.

Of course, the statements were unfounded and the 265 was the first of many Chevrolet small-block engines. It greatly influenced the design of larger engines.

In 1957 the 283 V-8 was introduced, using the same 3-inch stroke with an increase in bore from the 3¾ inches of the 265 engine, to 3⅞ inches. This proved to be one of the more flexible small-block engines and was used in a wide range of applications.

In 1963 the stroke was increased to 3¼ inches, creating the 327-cubic-inch engine, mainly for low-rpm torque. This became a very popular engine although it was not used in light truck service until 1966.

In 1968 the truck applications totally changed. The 283 was dropped as well as the 327. The 307 was introduced with the bore size of the 265 (3⅞ inches) and the stroke of the 327 (to 3¼ inches). Intent was improved mileage and low-speed torque, while a new large-block 396 was introduced for heavy service. The 396 used a 4.094 bore and 3.76 stroke, incorporating many of the features of the small-block engines. It proved equally popular. A 396-cubic-inch version was used only in medium-duty trucks and the famous 427 used in racing applications was introduced. The 427 used the stroke of the 396 engine, with a 4.250-inch bore.

Throttle response of Chevrolet 350 engines in trailer-towing vehicles such as this Blazer (test vehicle for results described here) can be improved considerably.

In 1971 a 402-cubic-inch engine replaced the 396. The same stroke was used, with a 4.126-inch bore. The 427 was replaced by the now popular 454, which became the only large-block engine offered after 1972.

In small-block engines, the 350-cubic-inch engine replaced the 327 in 1969. The 350 had a 4-inch bore and 3.48-inch stroke and became the Chevrolet light- and medium-duty backbone engine. It has proven to be the best all-around V-8 engine produced.

In 1975 the 400 small-block engine was introduced in light trucks, with 4.125-inch bore and 3.750-inch stroke. It changed the character of the 350 from

an engine capable of high-rpm flexibility to a low-speed torquer. It filled a necessary gap in truck service between the 350 and the 454.

In 1977 the 305 V-8 appeared. It was very similar to the previous 307 and has proven capable of providing increased mileage with sufficient low-speed torque.

Although the Chevrolet 350 consistently has been one of the best small-block engines in RV service, its performance can be improved noticeably. An increase in fuel economy is possible.

A 350-equipped Blazer towing a 24-foot trailer for gross combined weight of 9200 pounds proved that it is possible to improve performance as well as fuel economy without major internal engine work.

We have always known that the 350 comes on really strong with better carburetion, better manifolding, improved exhaust flow and precise tuning. But lately Geraghty has been having even better results because he has concentrated on exceptionally precise tuning of the carburetor and distributor to take best possible advantage of the improved manifolding and exhaust flow.

What are the stock 350 engine's problems? Step-by-step results provide the answers.

- *Dual Exhausts.* First step in the modification program was installation of a dual exhaust system utilizing low-restriction 40-inch glasspack mufflers. With the Ford 390, the gain from this step was nominal. With the 350 Chevy, it is substantial. With no other changes than installation of dual exhausts, using 2-inch pipe and a 2-inch crossover, throttle response was noticeably improved. Top-end power came up as well.

Whereas in previous tests with other engines much fuel economy improvement from dual exhausts alone had not been noted, in this instance .3-mpg was picked up with the modification. Two-inch pipe rather than larger pipe is specified because it's important for low-end torque and for fuel economy not to have a wide-open system with the largest pipe possible. The 2-inch pipe is the

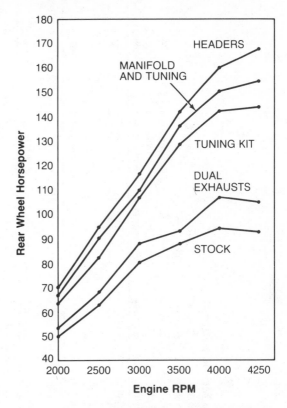

Graph indicates full-throttle horsepower as recorded on a chassis dynamometer with Chevrolet 350 engine in stock condition and in various stages of modification.

same diameter as the 2-inch core of the mufflers. The proper exhaust system—not necessarily a totally unrestricted one—is an important initial step for the 350 engine.

- *Carburetor and Distributor Tuning.* Precise tuning was the key to getting the fuel economy improvement in addition to the performance. The Geraghty MPG-Performance Products carburetor/distributor tuning kit was installed immediately following the

Test Results of Chevrolet/GMC 350 V-8 with Modifications

	Test 1 0–60 mph Acceleration	Test 2 40–60 mph Acceleration	Test 3 Manifold Vacuum on 45 mph Hill Climb	Test 4 Manifold Vacuum on Level Highway	Test 5 Fuel Economy w/Trailer 50/50% Hills and Flat Highway	Test 6 Fuel Economy w/Trailer on Flat Highway	Test 7 Solo Fuel Economy on Flat Highway
Stock Engine	32.5 sec	21.5 sec	4.5 in	13 in	7.2 mpg	8.4 mpg	11.2 mpg
Dual Exhausts w/40-inch Mufflers	29 sec	18 sec	6 in	13.5 in	7.5 mpg	8.6 mpg	11.3 mpg
Carburetor/ Distributor Tuning Kit	25 sec	14 sec	8.5 in	14 in	8.3 mpg	9.3 mpg	12.0 mpg
Carburetor Re-tuning and Edelbrock Streetmaster Manifold	24.5 sec	14 sec	8.5 in	14 in	8.9 mpg	9.6 mpg	12.4 mpg
Carburetor Re-tuning and Eagle Exhaust Headers	24 sec	13 sec	9 in	14 in	8.4 mpg	9.3 mpg	11.7 mpg

Tests conducted at 65–70 degrees F. ambient temperature, 800–1200 feet altitude, not affected by wind. Test 3: throttle adjusted by driver to maintain 45 mph in second gear on 5% grade; manifold vacuum recorded at top of grade. Fuel economy results 5, 6 and 7 were each the average of two to four tests run with fuel in precise amounts fed to carburetor from separate container. Standard Quadrajet carburetor used in all tests, but modified at various stages.

Removal of Quadrajet carburetor's air horn exposes fuel bowl area where main jets and primary metering rods are located.

Tuning kit usually calls for jet change to create more ideal air/fuel ratios.

Primary metering rods and vacuum piston that control their position are lifted out.

dual exhausts project. Later, after the manifold and headers installations, modifications of the original kit were used to take best advantage of the improved efficiency of the manifold and the headers.

The tuning kit recalibrates the carburetor and distributor for best efficiency in view of how the vehicle is used—the load being towed, terrain, altitude, etc.

Tuning kit results vary somewhat between different engine brands and sizes. The kit proved quite worthwhile on the 350, in terms of enabling the vehicle to do its work with less throttle. Climbing those hills with less throttle is the name of the game in RV situations. Efficiency improvement is how it's done. Carburetor air/fuel ratios and the distributor advance curve are corrected to be as close to ideal as possible.

The kit includes a booklet with detailed instructions and photos for installation of the recalibration parts and for specific spark advance settings. Tools required for installation are a timing light, some sort of tachometer and normal hand tools. Combining the

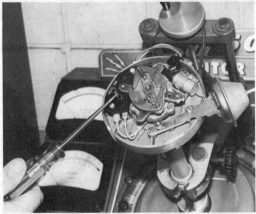

Prior to 1976, distributors were equipped with breaker-points system but automatic spark advance system, using weights, was not changed substantially in later vehicles. After 1976 the High Energy Ignition system has been used. System of weights and springs still is used to control automatic spark advance.

kit installation with a dual exhaust system produces a really substantial gain, at a relatively low cost.

Carburetor and Intake Manifold

An option must be taken here, since the stock Quadrajet 4-barrel carburetor on the 350 is serviceable, and offers slightly better fuel economy than a properly tuned replacement Holley. The Holley, on a replacement aluminum intake manifold, offers better throttle response and low-rpm power. The Holley must be jetted properly for the engine and how it's equipped, and for the vehicle use situation. The difference during our tests appeared to be .25- to .5-mpg under cruise conditions. The Holley has larger primary venturi than does the stock carburetor.

Float Correction

The Quadrajet has several problems that should be corrected if it is to be retained. The float should be replaced if the carb is more than two years old, as the float tends to soak up fuel, raising fuel level in the bowl and causing fuel percolation when the engine is shut down. When replacing the float, set fuel level $1/32$-inch lower than stock. For external cooling, recesses at the bottom of the fuel bowl should be filled in with epoxy glue. The soft plugs used to partially fill those recesses tend to leak.

The test engine we used was equipped at the factory with the Quadrajet 4-barrel carburetor, but other 350s in different vehicles are equipped with 2-barrel carburetors. A change from a stock 2-barrel setup to the Edelbrock Performer manifold and the proper Holley model (jetted accurately for the owner's driving situation) produces much more dramatic comparative power gains than are shown here.

Exhaust Headers

The 350 Chevy engine is one that responds well to exhaust headers of the proper design, although headers are not a fuel economy device. They're for performance. Headers must have small tubing compared to racing oriented headers and the cones attached to the collectors should be about 2 inches in diameter. Cone sizes must be 2 or not larger than 2¼ inches, or low-end torque will be sacrificed. Slight reduction in throttle response was noticed upon picking up the vehicle at a local muffler shop where the work was done. They had cut the cones larger. Most muffler shops figure "bigger is better" and will go for the largest possible pipe and cone sizes. The proper size cones were later installed and a difference in low-end torque could be felt.

Initially, we ran the vehicle without carburetor changes to determine the effect of the headers. Mixtures were lean in the interest of best possible fuel economy. Headers do lean out fuel mixtures; this was demonstrated by the fact that we lost power as well as mileage during initial tests. Manifold vacuum dropped substantially, as the engine required more throttle to get over hills with the excessively lean mixtures.

Then the carburetor was rejetted to compensate for effect of the headers and the performance potential of the headers was realized. Carburetor tuning for good power with the headers resulted in a fuel economy drop from the previous status of the engine, but again the goal was power. If the goal is purely fuel economy, retention of the stock exhaust manifolds would be in order with this engine.

The test vehicle was equipped with AIR (air injection reactor) which was retained. Although carburetion was changed several times during our test procedure to accommodate each individual step, only one carburetor reprogramming step is necessary in an actual owner situation, based on how much of the equipment tested here will be installed at the same time.

Results during our tests won't necessarily conform precisely to yours, but you can improve fuel economy by employing some of the techniques, such as driving with a manifold vacuum gauge. The fuel enrichment system of the stock Rochester Quadrajet carburetor begins to open at 6½ inches vacuum. The replacement Holley carburetors usually are fitted with 6½-inch power valves. Thus, by driving so vacuum readings are above those levels (when possible), fuel economy can be improved. When readings are below those levels, fuel mixtures are enriched considerably.

Incidentally, all of our tests were conducted with the air cleaner lid inverted, for 360-degree air intake. The small snorkel size on the stock air cleaner of this engine is restrictive. We have found it to impair fuel economy as well as performance.

It's possible to take the Chevrolet 350 even farther by raising compression with special pistons. This usually must accompany boring of the cylinders and a complete overhaul, but is highly effective, especially in high altitudes where power losses due to lower atmospheric pressure can make RV travel difficult. With flat-top pistons that raise compression to about 9.2 to 1, regular fuel may be used if water injection is employed. However, the bolt-on conversion is highly effective and does not require internal engine modifications.

With our test Chevy Blazer, performance of the stock engine was quite marginal for towing the 24-foot Argosy in the mountains. Following our test modifications, it was a very strong performer, which could make the difference between keeping the vehicle and trading for a larger engine—not to mention the fuel economy improvement.

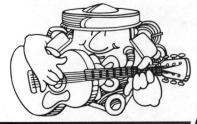

The Chevy 454 V-8: Split RV Personality

22

The Chevrolet 454 V-8 has something of a split personality. While it is one of the most popular engines in RV service because of its power, it also is one of the most maligned, due to its habit in the 1970s of using large amounts of oil. It isn't renowned for its miserliness with fuel, although it has good company with the Ford 460.

With the disappearance of the Dodge 440 from the RV scene in 1979, and with Ford having limited availability of the 460 during the past several years, the Chevrolet 454 understandably has turned up in a large number of RVs.

Lately, the 454 engine's power output has dropped in light-duty vehicles due to more restrictive tuning and use of catalytic convertors in single exhaust systems on vehicles with gross vehicle weight ratings lower than 8500 pounds.

Of course, those restrictions are avoided in motorhome chassis that are in higher weight categories. Still, it is possible to make all 454s run better with a minimum of expense and to solve a variety of problems the engine presented in the 1970s—all in the interest of holding the cost of RV travel to a minimum.

Before we get into specifics on fuel economy, performance and correction of mechanical problems, some historical insight may be interesting.

Origins of the 454

During Detroit's scramble for superiority in the horsepower race during the 1960s, a rumor leaked out that Chevrolet had developed an engine of 427 cubic inches that would be ideal for the

Distributor is lifted out of a Chevrolet 454 in a motorhome. Same basic engine is used in pickup trucks and Suburbans.

NASCAR racing circuit. It was said to be capable of producing more than one horsepower per cubic inch displacement with only a single 4-barrel carburetor. The rumor indicated that horsepower would be more than 500; that stopped everyone in their tracks. Of course, it proved factual when the 427 was introduced for racing. The engine was not made available for street use at that time but in 1965 two versions of the engine—forerunners of today's 454—were released. The engines were of 396 cid, one a moderate high-performance engine suitable for the street and the other a normal passenger car engine. Compression ratios were 11 to 1 and 10.25 to 1, respectively.

Although the basic engine blocks were the same, the two 396 engines differed greatly not only in camshaft design and compression ratio, but also in cylinder head design, intake manifolding and carburetion. Instead of the large rectangular free-flowing port design of the 427, an oval-port head with smaller valves was used to increase low-rpm air/fuel velocity. The aluminum high-performance intake manifold of the 427 was replaced with a lower profile cast iron manifold designed to retain more heat and increase fuel economy. The 785-cfm carburetor was replaced with a unit that had smaller primary venturi, to increase low-rpm response. The reduced horsepower created by these changes allowed the factory to go from 4-bolt main bearing structure, flame-hardened steel crankshaft and heavy-duty connecting rods of the high performance engine to 2-bolt mains and less strength in other components, for reduced production cost. Still, the 396 engines were very strong by usual standards on the street at that time.

The passenger car version proved to be an excellent engine, despite the difference between its 325 hp and the 375 hp of the high-performance version. When related to everyday driving, the 415 lb.-ft. of torque at 4000 rpm of the high-performance version didn't compare favorably with the 410 lb-ft. of torque at 3200 rpm offered by the passenger car engine. Low-speed throttle response was better with the passenger car engine.

The 427 was released in 1966 and proved successful, although the 396 engines were retained due to their overwhelming acceptance.

In 1970 the 454 version of this original 427 engine was introduced. The additional displacement not only kept Chevrolet up in the horsepower race but also allowed eventual reduction in compression and taming of camshaft timing without losing too much power. However, the changes caused quite a transformation in the character of the engine. No longer did it respond immediately to almost any modification. Popular modifications proved marginal at best. In many cases they produced negative results. And to this day, costly changes such as addition of exhaust headers, special cams and use of replacement carburetors and manifolds produce marginal results on the 454, if any change is noticeble at all.

With addition of the 454 to light trucks and Suburbans in 1973, that engine became much better known among RV owners because trailer-towing with light trucks and Suburbans increased. At about this time, some inherent problems that previously were not widely known came to the surface.

Oil Consumption

The most pronounced of these problems was oil consumption due to inadequate oil seals on the valve guides. In the 454 and other Chevrolet engines, valve train components receive a heavy flow of oil, overcoming the ability of the stock seals to keep manifold vacuum from sucking oil through the valve guides. As a result, many engines would use large amounts of oil even when new. Others would go along for a few thousand miles with moderate but tolerable oil consumption (around 1000 miles per quart) and then suddenly drop to 500 miles per quart or less, and start fouling spark plugs. The factory's official attitude was that 500 miles per quart was acceptable.

The 454 owner's woes were compounded by the fact that many shops that did valve jobs on 454 cylinder heads didn't pay proper attention to clearances between valve guides and stems. A 454 that went into the shop for work to correct oil consumption often came out just as bad, with the owner quite a few hundred dollars poorer. Too many shops use knurling as a method to reduce clearance between valve guide and stem, even when the clearance is too large for knurling to be effective. If valve stem to guide clearance is in excess of .004-inch, TRW bronze valve guide inserts should be installed.

Chevrolet's umbrella-type valve seal, Part No. 460527 is reasonably effective and is used on the 454 engine. Less effective O-ring seals are used on the small-block 400 and 350 engines. The 454 has $3/8$-inch valve stems and the small-block engines have $11/32$-inch stems, so the 454 seals won't fit. However, stock 460 Ford valve seals will work on the small-block Chevies.

When the 454 uses oil due to oil seal leakage, the umbrella seals can be replaced without removing the cylinder heads. If the vehicle uses oil from this problem, it is noticeable during deceleration, such as when descending a long mountain grade. At the bottom, when power is applied, blue-white exhaust smoke will appear. An engine that has worn piston rings will produce exhaust smoke under acceleration while climbing a grade and it may produce smoke on a downhill as well, if the valve guides and seals also are worn.

Here's how the umbrella seals are replaced (or how they can be added to a small-block engine not already equipped):

1) Remove spark plugs and valve covers.

2) Rotate the crankshaft until both valves on one cylinder are closed.

3) Apply air pressure to the cylinder through a spark plug adaptor (available at tool supply stores) to hold valves in place.

4) Remove valve string retainer and valve spring with the necessary tool.

5) Replace seal.

The Chevrolet seals are not as good as the full-floating spring-loaded Teflon seals. Installation of the Teflon seals (Pioneer brand) requires removal of the heads and machining of the valve guides. When this is done, the Chevrolet seals can be used on top of the Teflon seals.

When heads are off, the rocker arm assemblies should be examined for any signs of wear at the contact areas. In particular the point where the rocker arm contacts the push rod (rocker arm socket) and the tip of the push rod should be examined for wear. Both push rod ends should be checked for wear. Motor oil should be used on contact areas before reassembly.

The rocker arm assembly is the last system to receive oil. Many drivers start a cold engine, race the motor a bit and pull away. This is hard on rocker arms. The motor should be started without higher rpm than necessary (fast idle) and it should be allowed to fast-idle for about 30 seconds before the vehicle is driven. A rule of thumb in the old days was to watch the oil pressure gauge rise and reach its normal position, count to 10 and go.

Proper Valve Adjustment

The valve adjustment procedure prescribed by the factory for the 454 also leaves much to be desired. The adjustment calls for more tightening of the rocker am adjustment nuts than we believe is necessary. The normal procedure calls for loosening the nuts until tappet noise can be heard, then tightening the nuts one full turn. We have found 1/4-turn quite sufficient. One full turn tends to promote "valve float" when the hydraulic lifters "pump up" at high rpm, and reduce valve life. Valve float means that the valves do not fully close. You can imagine what that does to performance. The 1/4-turn adjustment should be performed on any 454, whether new or used, and it will help high-rpm performance.

The 454 had yet another strange symptom until the early 1970s. After starting, a considerable amount of erratic valve clatter could occur, and the solution was elusive. After warm-up, the problem would disappear. Cause was air getting into the lubrication system

Air trapped in oil galleys can be relieved by drilling holes in oil galley plugs, located immediately above camshaft on front of engine block.

through the oil intake. The air would pass through valve lifters and reduce lubrication. Solution was to drill a .032-inch hole in each oil galley plug on either side of the cam—on the face of the engine right behind the cam sprocket. Chevrolet started doing this at the factory in late 1974.

While the 454 does not respond well to replacement carburetors, intake manifolds or headers, it does respond to precise carburetor and distributor tuning changes. The carburetor often is far from correct in air/fuel mixtures. The cruise system usually is overly lean, creating rather flat response to throttle in the medium to light-throttle range. More specifically, this is the range about seven inches on a manifold vacuum gauge. If you don't have such a gauge, it is one of the best additions you can make. Then, air/fuel mixtures are usually overly rich in the primary power system, which comes into play as throttle application is increased and as vacuum readings drop below seven inches. These two systems operate in the primary side (primary venturi) of the 4-barrel Rochester Quadrajet carburetor used as standard on the 454 for all the years it has been produced. The carburetor has been improved somewhat during the years but the basic design has not been changed. It is not a bad choice if tuned properly.

The fuel metering system in the secondary venturi also may be rather rich. Most RV owners assume the secondaries come into action anytime heavy or full throttle is applied. In fact, they don't open until about 2600-2800 rpm, even under full throttle. The secondaries are vacuum-controlled to open when the engine's demands exceed the capability of the primary venturi.

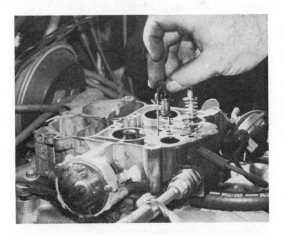

Primary metering rods are attached to a vacuum piston that moves up and down in response to throttle position. Main jets are in bottom of carburetor directly below.

Secondary metering rods are lifted when the secondary air valve opens, responding to the engine's demand (under heavy throttle) for more air and fuel.

Metering of the fuel is controlled by metering rods that hang inside jets. When heavy throttle is applied, first the primary metering rods are raised, enlarging the size of the opening in the jet through which fuel can pass. Then the secondary rods lift and permit more fuel enrichment to occur only when the secondary venturi are brought into action by even heavier throttle.

Spark Advance Characteristics

The progression of spark advance likewise leaves something to be desired, primarily because factories must try to tune engines so they won't "ping" under the most severe driving conditions and while using the cheapest fuel. Spark ad-

vance can be increased, if it is done properly, and it can be particularly aggressive if proper water injection is used to lower the engine's fuel octane requirements (prevent ping).

When correction of spark advance and air/fuel ratios are combined, the results can be very substantial. We commonly record 20-percent increases in horsepower at the 4000 rpm level (peak horsepower) and 10 percent in the 2600 to 2800 rpm range.

Problems with Rust

Many owners of 454 engines join owners of many other GM engines using the High Energy Ignition (HEI) system in being subjected regularly to a problem caused by rust in the distributor. The advance mechanism controlled by the distributor weights is supposed to move back and forth freely on the distributor shaft. However, rust forms at the top of the shaft and the automatic advance mechanism sticks. This causes loss of performance, loss of mileage, overheating and hard starting. But it is easily checked simply by holding a timing light on the crankshaft pulley timing marks while raising and lowering engine rpm. The timing mark should move up and down the scale, illustrating that the mechanical advance system responds to engine rpm. If timing doesn't change, the mechanism is stuck and can be corrected by disassembling the distributor and cleaning the distributor shaft. Relubricate with light grease.

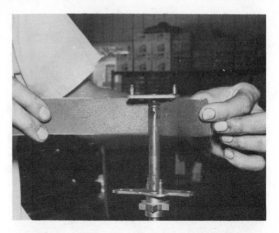

Common cause of performance and starting problems with all GM V-8 engines using HEI ignition is binding of spark advance mechanism. Distributor shaft is shown extended out of housing, with mechanical advance plate halfway down shaft. It normally operates at top, where binding occurs. Clean with emery paper and re-lubricate with WD-40 or other light oil.

Fuel Overflow

The Quadrajet carburetor shares a defect with several other carburetors, notably the Carter ThermoQuad used on many Dodge engines. Plastic fuel bowl floats will gradually soak up small amounts of fuel. This causes the float to ride lower in the fuel and raise fuel level. The higher fuel level enriches mixtures, reducing mileage and causing the engine to stall. Performance also is reduced and the engine is liable to be flooded by fuel percolation out of the carburetor into the engine after shutdown. Attempts to restart the engine are futile until the fuel has had time to vaporize and/or leak past the piston rings into the crankcase. The solution

is to change the float about every two years and set fuel float level $1/32$-inch lower than the factory specification. Fuel floats are available from dealership parts counters.

Distributor Rotors

The HEI system usually does a good job. But one weak point is the distributor rotor and it is weak only because GM originally recommended wide spark plug gaps. The connection between spark plug gaps and distributor rotors may seem remote, but here's how it works. A higher voltage level is required to ionize (create a spark) across a gap of .060-inch than across a .042-

GM's High Energy Ignition system has the ignition coil in the distributor cap (arrow). Rotor should be checked about every two years for electrical leakage of the type shown here. Hole was burned through rotor (arrow) by electrical charge going to ground on distributor shaft.

inch gap. GM originally recommended .060-inch when the HEI system was introduced. The problem is that the high voltage constantly seeks a place to go to ground. While it is zapping around inside the distributor, it goes right through the plastic rotor. Carbon tracings can be seen on the underside when this happens. The result is that the spark may intermittently ground on the distributor shaft, causing erratic misfire and erratic starting. The engine may suddenly quit, and restart later as if nothing had happened. Rotors should be replaced about every two years. Spark plugs should be gapped to .042. Electrical connections to the distributor should be cleaned, roughed with emery paper and coated with silicone dialectric compound.

Hot Start Problems

During the 1970s many Chevrolet engines, including the 454, would fail to start and the solution was elusive. The problem would occur after a considerable amount of driving. The owner might pull into a service station, fill the tank and try to restart but nothing would happen—not a sound from the starter. This would continue for 20 to 30 minutes and finally the starter would work normally.

The problem is insufficient voltage to the starter solenoid. The wire to the solenoid passes through the ignition system and voltage drop occurs. More power is required to activate the starter solenoid with a hot engine. The solution is to:

1) Remove the wire from the "S" terminal on the solenoid,

2) Run a No. 10 wire from the battery through a 20-amp circuit breaker to a relay rated for at least 20 amps,

3) Run more No. 10 wire from the other side of the relay to the "S" terminal on the starter solenoid,

4) Connect the original wire removed from the "S" terminal to the terminal that triggers the relay. The relay body should be grounded.

The result is reduction in voltage drop and the problem usually is solved.

In extreme cases, use of a Chevrolet heavy-duty starter solenoid may be in order, as well as a Chevrolet heat shield. While involved in this kind of work, remove all battery cables, clean them and coat with silicone dialectric compound or petroleum jelly.

For situations where the starter turns the engine over, but slowly and often hanging, first check to make sure the mechanical spark advance in the distributor is not stuck. This creates excessive initial spark advance and spark plugs fire so early they tend to stop upward piston movement on the compression stroke.

Next, check starter current draw. Ideal is about 180 amps. Draw should not be more than about 280. Possibly the battery has deteriorated to the point where it will not produce the necessary amount of cranking amperage.

Modifications for the 454

For many years, manufacturers of exhaust headers, performance carburetors and intake manifolds have described fantastic mileage and performance gains possible with their products on a variety of engines including the 454. The products do help many engines, but *not* the 454. Headers do not noticeably improve power in the rpm ranges usual with RVs, and they will usually cut mileage a bit. However, dual exhausts are needed and pipe size should be 2-inch minimum, 2.25-inch maximum.

Many RV owners are enticed to change the cam to one of the aftermarket cams that supposedly will boost low rpm torque. Unfortunately, the opposite usually occurs. Even when a genuinely effective replacement cam is found, cost of its installation is not justified unless the engine is torn down for overhaul. Even then, the choice of cam must be absolutely certain, or it's better to use the stock cam.

The only replacement intake manifold that makes any difference at all on the 454 is the Edelbrock Performer and the difference is not sufficient to justify the cost.

Modifications During Overhaul

One modification really makes the 454 come on strong but it is cost-effective only when overhaul is needed. When reboring is needed, pistons must be replaced anyway so use of special pistons at this point adds nothing to the cost. By using TRW Part Number L2399F pistons, compression can be raised to about 9 to 1. The engine still will run well on regular leaded gasoline if an effective water injector is used to reduce fuel octane requirements and the horsepower increase over stock is about 40 percent. Fuel economy usually is improved as well, since the engine will pull or haul the same amount of weight with less throttle.

When overhauling, it is important to check deck height (distance from top of piston to top of block, at top of piston stroke), as this can vary from one side of the block to the other. Compression will be imbalanced if deck height is not uniform. Deck height can be reduced to .010-inch but not more than .040-inch should be removed from the block.

With the lineup of problems described here, the reader may feel sufficiently warned to stay away from the 454. However, that is not our intention, because the engine basically is a good design for RV service since it has the performance potential to move substantial amounts of weight without accelerated wear. It is a *strong* engine when tuned properly. Since none of the problems are insurmountable, the 454 is a good choice for RV service if the owner has bought the vehicle at a price that allows him to make the appropriate corrections—or for the owner who has decided to repair a 454 rather than buying an expensive new vehicle.

Testing a Tuning Kit for the 454

One might assume that the Chevrolet 454 could pull or haul just about anything, if the axle ratio is proper. Indeed, the 454 used in late-model recreational vehicles is strong, as any engine expected to propel upwards of 18,000 pounds must be. However, few RVs weighing over 10,000 pounds can be classified as over-powered for mountain travel. Improvement in throttle response and overall performance always is welcome with any engine, if the price isn't too high (purchase price of whatever it is that improves performance, plus a possible fuel economy penalty).

Geraghty has offered an engine tuning kit for the past several years that offers a performance increase, usually

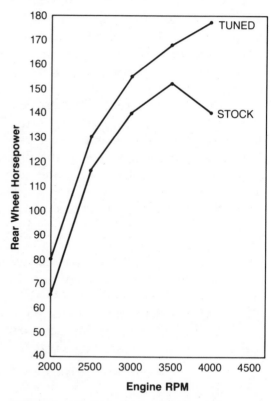

The 454 responds well to more aggressive tuning, particularly in the rpm range between 3500 and 4000.

Performance and Fuel Economy Tests of Chevrolet 454

	Fuel Economy	Accleration 0–60 mph	Accleration 40–60 mpg	Manifold Vacuum, Flat-Highway Cruise
Stock Engine	8.12 mpg	24.2 sec	14.1 sec	11 in
Geraghty Tuning Kit Installed	8.20 mpg	23.0 sec	13.5 sec	11.5 in

Test vehicle, 1978 Chevrolet C-30 crew-cab towing 25-foot trailer for gross combined weight of 12,800 pounds. Axle ratio 4.1 to 1, tires 7.50–16. Ambient conditions 60–70° F. Test conducted at 800–1200 feet elevation. Fuel economy tests on 50/50% flat highway, low hills.

without a fuel economy penalty, for $32.95. When we consider that it's possible to add a lot of equipment such as replacement carburetors, manifolds and headers, to the tune of $1000 or better, $32.95 sounds more realistic. Replacement equipment does work on some engines, but not the 454, as many RV owners have discovered the hard way.

No two engines are precisely alike and a tuning kit like Geraghty's won't work precisely the same on all engines. But with the ones we've tried, including 454s in motorhomes and pickup trucks, the noticeable improvement in throttle response is worth the kit price alone. A bonus is the ability to climb mountain grades with less throttle. A further bonus—fuel economy improvement—occurs when installation of the kit corrects a mechanical deficiency such as an inoperative mechanical spark advance system. The 454 and all other GM engines are subject to a binding condition between the mechanical advance unit and the distributor shaft. The vehicle owner is able to detect such problems while modifying spark advance sys-

tems according to instructions in the tuning kit.

Content of the tuning kit usually consists of carburetor primary metering jets, primary and secondary metering rods, a pair of distributor springs and detailed instructions on how to install the parts and test for proper results. Basic tools, plus a timing light and tachometer are needed.

Kit instructions call for replacement of the two stock distributor springs with

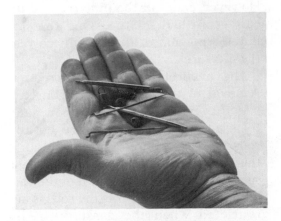

Performance and fuel economy of an engine are controlled by metering rods and jets in carburetor and return springs on spark advance system in distributor. Geraghty tuning kit includes parts for recalibration.

Distributor springs are replaced with tuning kit springs to create more aggressive spark advance curve.

kit springs that permit slightly more aggressive spark advance curve. This is beneficial with many 454s that are not over-sensitive to fuel quality. If the engine already pings, this modification certainly won't help that situation. However, cause of the ping may be incorrect air/fuel mixtures and the carburetor portion of the kit will correct the mixtures.

The carburetor modifications require removal of the top of the carburetor, which is possible with common hand tools, and a change in primary jets and rods. (Some carburetors do not require this step.) Care should be taken to make sure the up-down movement of the vacuum piston that controls the rods is not restricted when the gasket is re-installed. Also check to make sure that the fuel pickup tubes for the secondary venturi have not dropped out, as they often do. This creates an excessive

lean condition under heavy throttle when the secondaries come into action.

If the vehicle is more than two years old, the plastic fuel float should be replaced and float level should be re-set 1/32-inch below the factory specification. The kit does not include the float or the specification, which are available from Chevrolet dealers.

Effect of the replacement jets and metering rods on air/fuel ratios will vary depending on the carburetor. Each variance in carburetor number means a variance in fuel metering. The carburetor number is stamped vertically on the carburetor body, just aft of the throttle lever. The kits are marketed according to carburetor number and selection of parts is based on Geraghty's more than 30 years of dyno testing. In one carburetor, an excessively lean cruise metering system may be fattened up a bit while the primary and secondary power systems (power enrichment) may be leaned out. In another, the cruise and primary power systems may be left alone while the secondary enrichment system is leaned out.

If correction of fuel metering systems does not correct a pre-existing ping problem, use of water injection is a valid way to reduce the engine's fuel octane requirements and avoid the only other alternative—reduction of spark advance, which cuts power and mileage. Reduction of spark advance also tends to raise engine temperatures under heavy load.

The effect on the 454 engine of the tuning kit is increase in horsepower of

While carburetor is disassembled, check for missing pickup tubes that draw fuel for the secondary venturi. Here, one is missing.

Soft plugs in bottom of Quadrajet carburetor body often leak, allowing fuel to drain into engine and causing hard starting. Epoxy glue can be used to stop leakage.

about 20 percent, at 4000 rpm. That is a substantial difference, although it doesn't necessarily mean a 20-percent increase in performance. The effect on performance varies with weight of the vehicle. But it is quite noticeable in the seat-of-the-pants feel of engine performance and in the motorhome's willingness to climb mountain grades. Another grade-climbing aid is improvement of air flow to the air cleaner. Early-model air cleaners with 1½-inch air inlets serve as partial chokes while the engine is under heavy throttle. Merely reversing the air cleaner lid, for 360-degree air intake, can make a dramatic difference, although it does increase noise. Late-model air cleaners were equipped with much larger air inlets.

Fuel economy under typical low-altitude cruise conditions with our test motorhome was not changed appreciably, so the benefit of the kit in this case is purely in performance. As a performance-improver, it was well worthwhile.

Q & A on Chevrolet

23

For more than 10 years, readers of *Trailer Life* and *MotorHome* magazines have been able to present inquiries about technical problems to the editors. The following selection of those questions and the replies to them deals with problems that occur frequently.

Chevrolet/General Motors Q & A

Erratic 350

My engine is a Chevrolet 350 in a pickup truck and it seems to be very erratic in operation. Some times it will ping and is often hard to start. After several trips to the dealer they have finally diagnosed the problem as a loose timing chain, as the timing seems not to stay where they put it. The engine has only 18,000 miles, so I am reluctant to believe this will cure the problem. Could there be another reason?

B. Thompson
Omaha, Nebraska

This problem relates to all GM engines equipped with the HEI ignition system. The problem seems to occur around 20,000-mile intervals. Problems include erratic operation and gas mileage, inconsistent low speed operation, pinging and surging. All are indicative of inconsistent spark advance characteristics in the distributor. The mechanical spark advance system does not move through the advance curve smoothly, and it often does not return to the retracted position.

Correction is not difficult. The distributor must be removed and disassembled. Remove the cap and mark the positions of the rotor and the distributor housing so the distributor can be re-installed exactly the same way. Disassembly is accomplished by driving out the drift pin that retains the distributor gear. Slip the gear from the shaft. The shaft can then be removed from the housing. Check the shaft end play. A maximum of .007-inch and minimum of .004-inch is ideal. If excessive end play exists, variations in timing will occur. Shim washers are available: Chevrolet Part Number 1927529.

At the top of the shaft there is a horseshoe clip and washers that retain the reluctor (cam assembly). You will find the problem by removing the clip and sliding the reluctor assembly off the shaft. Rust forms and causes the reluctor assembly to bind on the shaft. Thoroughly clean and polish the shaft with crocus cloth or fine emery cloth. Before assembly, use a thin coating of heavy grease on the shaft where the rust occurred. Also, remove the advance weights and springs and clean and lubricate them with a light machine oil. Once all this is accomplished, the shaft should last for another 20,000 miles.

Even though the rotor appears good, in many cases close inspection after removal will show electrical leakage to ground from under the rotor through the body to the center cap connector. When replacing the rotor, slightly bend the metal cap connector upward to assure contact with the distributor cap.

Also check all connector plugs. It's good practice not only to be sure they are firmly in place but also to take each one apart and inspect for corrosion. If you see a greasy substance on the contacts, don't remove it unless you have some electrical silicone with which to replace it. This grease assures proper contact. The special grease can be obtained from your local dealer or from a parts house. Be sure it is the type without metal particles.

On Target

Thanks for your advice on the rotor with electrical leakage. For years this was my problem with the 1975 Sportvan G20. No one could pick it up on scopes. Made an appointment with a mechanic to have the rotor changed. There was an electrical leakage in the spot on the rotor where you said it would be. The van seems to run fine now. Thanks again!

Melvin M. Starbard
Lake Odessa, Michigan

Erratic Idle

My Chevy 400 engine has erratic idle and I have not been able to solve it with tuning or adjustment of the idle mixture screws. Am I overlooking something?

Bob Branowski
Chicago, Illinois

Chevrolet/GMC engines sometimes have erratic rough idle, surging at high *speed and at light throttle and valve lifter noise. It's usually traced to the way valves are adjusted at the factory.*

The factory method is certainly quicker and easier, but is not always the best. Here's a more effective method:

After the engine reaches normal operational temperature, remove one valve cover. With the engine at idle, back the adjusting nut of each lifter off until it produces an audible clicking noise. Retighten slowly until the noise subsides. Then tighten an eighth-to quarter-turn farther. Replace the valve cover and repeat the procedure on the other side. If any of the adjustment nuts turn freely (they're locking nuts), replace them.

Overfilled?

I have a 1979 Chevy 454 trailering special pulling a 22-foot Holiday that weights about 6000 pounds. I have had some transmission trouble. On a recent trip the rig appeared to lose some trans oil, so I added about half a quart. Next time I checked it, I was surprised to see it overfilled.

I took it to a GM dealer where they checked the pan bolts and tightened them. They checked fluid level and it was overfilled, so the mechanics drew out about half a pint. They checked again and the fluid level was low, so they added almost all the half pint. I then drove several miles up the road and back, checked again and it was overfilled.

I have heard there is some sort of check valve in the torque convertor that should control the level of oil between the trans and convertor. Could that be the problem? Could overfilling cause a foaming action? It seems that I cannot get an accurate check on trans fluid when I check it.

Roger Corbet
St. Joseph, Missouri

There is a variation in oil level from hot to cold when checking the trans. However, this does not appear to be your problem.

In the valve body there is a valve designed to close as pressure in the torque convertor drops. This valve prevents oil from draining back into the trans pan. It is a simple valve that does not have a history of failure. If the valve body becomes loose from the transmission case, or is not properly torqued, leakage can occur and this would cause your problem—or a faulty valve.

Overfilling can indeed cause foaming, which in turn can cause overheating of the oil. Under these conditions some of the oil may be pushed out the dip stick tube.

Black Smoke

I have a 1977 Chevrolet Suburban with a 454 engine. It tows my 4200 pound trailer. The vehicle has been very versatile for our type of travel.

One problem has been impossible to solve though I have tried mechanics all over the country. Originally the problem was diagnosed as vapor lock and an electric fuel pump was installed and fuel lines were insulated and rerouted;

this made no difference. The Chevrolet dealer in Flagstaff, Arizona, diagnosed the problem as fuel percolation in the carburetor and installed an insulator under the carb and lowered the fuel level $1/32$-inch. This made no noticeable difference, either.

I have isolated the problem to a particular condition which can be duplicated on a continual uphill climb. Altitude makes it worse. At about $1/2$ to $2/3$ throttle the engine begins to miss and black smoke comes out the tailpipe. Finally, it becomes so bad the engine will stall momentarily. I can prevent it if, when the problem first appears, I drop to a lower gear and floor the throttle until it clears up. Otherwise I must reduce throttle and put the trans in neutal to clear it up.

D. R. Rogers
Phoenix, Arizona

The problem is related to the Quadrajet carburetor, which is standard on all 454s. It has relatively small primary venturi (primary "barrels"), which is an advantageous feature. However, when throttle is heavy enough that secondary venturi begin to open, the air/fuel mixture must be slightly overrich to prevent bogging and hesitation. This is controlled by the primary metering rods and jets. As the throttle is increased, the manifold vacuum drops, allowing the metering rods to lift upward in the jets. The rods are tapered; as they lift, their smaller diameter reduces the restriction in the jet and enriches the mixture.

In your case the taper apparently is severe, creating an overly rich mixture.

The tuning kits described in this book include jets and rods designed to prevent this problem. Factory tuning does not relate specifically enough to sustained loads during uphill climbs with RVs. In light-load conditions, the troublesome point usually is passed rather quickly and many owners don't find it a problem.

Hard Starting

Some time ago you printed an item on hard starting caused by something wrong with the carburetor. It was relative to the Carter ThermoQuad carburetor used on Dodge vehicles. I have a GM and wonder if that applies to me. My engine is difficult to start when it is hot. I have to crank it for quite a while and it acts flooded. I have checked the choke and it's open.

Bob Lamerouex
San Francisco, California

Progressive carburetor float failure is a problem with the ThermoQuad as well as with the Rochester Quadrajet used by GM. This progressive failure is caused by fuel saturation of the plastic float in the fuel bowl.

The condition is indicated by a gradual reduction in mileage, stalling after abrupt starts and hard starting of a hot engine. At 25,000 to 30,000 miles (or intervals of about $2^{1/2}$ years) these floats should be replaced. When installing the new float, lower the float level setting $1/32$-inch below the factory setting.

Inspection of the original float will not indicate an obvious difference.

Generally the weight difference caused by soaking of the fuel into the plastic will be very small and hard to detect.

Oil Loss

My automatic transmission in my 1975 Chevy truck is giving me a problem that the dealer has always claimed is normal. I have the Turbo-Hydra-matic 400. Under hard use it has always forced fluid from the dipstick tube onto the exhaust manifold causing smoke and—in one case—a minor fire. It was suggested that I replace the dipstick with a newer one to attain a better seal. A trans oil cooler was installed, as the temperature was blamed. I have spoken to several Chevrolet owners with this trans and found they have similar problems. If you have any suggestions other than running the trans one pint low, which helps, I would appreciate it.

W. P. Cook
Phoenix, Arizona

Relief of pressure in the transmission by pushing oil from the fill tube has been a common problem with your trans for years. Running up to a half-pint low does help. However, it produces a marginal safety situation on an abrupt turn. The fill tube is sealed at the case by an O-ring. Remove the fill tube and drill a couple of quarter-inch holes in the tube about 90 degrees apart directly below the O-ring. This allows the bottom of the tube to relieve pressure. Coat the O-ring with grease before reinstallation and be sure all metal burrs and metal from drilling are

washed away. The tube extends down into the casing; the holes, in effect, raise the oil pickup level of the tube so the oil has to be higher before it is forced out.

Check your oil level with the trans fully up to operational temperature while towing your trailer (if you use a trailer). Adjust the oil level just slightly below the full mark with the oil up to temp. If the level is adjusted to the full mark without the oil fully up to temp, expansion from increased temperature causes the oil to expand and an overfill condition results.

Oil Pressure

I have towed all over the United States, Canada and Mexico with passenger cars using heavy-duty suspensions and trailering packages, I believe I am a trailer-wise traveler. I now have a 1977 Cadillac that has given us a fit. First, the performance was bad. I followed your advice, much against Cadillac's recommendations, and changed the axle ratio. I installed a transmission cooler as I normally do and followed you tuning recommendations.

It now performs well. The problem remaining is loss of oil pressure after driving for a long distance and shutting off the engine. It takes a long time to get oil pressure. I installed a pressure gauge to double-check. The agency claims it is due to the lower rear axle and due to towing as my oil gets thin. I use Mobil 1. I tried going to 20-50 oil with no change. According to my oil temperature gauge, 280 degrees is the highest temperature. I cannot believe it is relative to oil temperature or thinning, since this is normal for other tow vehicles.

Bill Lautan
Fort Lauderdale, Florida

Your oil pump is losing its prime or sucking air from a poor connection. Some of the late GM engines, especially Cadillac, have had a problem with the metal oil pump gasket. A compressed asbestos gasket is available through your dealer.

Elusive Problem

I have a 1973 Chevrolet 454 that has required replacement of two rear main bearings and finally a new crankshaft. The main thrust bearing wears out. I have an automatic transmission and there shouldn't be any pressure on the thrust bearing, as there would be when depressing the clutch with a manual transmission. The last two times I have carefully checked the crankshaft end play and it has been well within specifications. I just checked the bearing surface since replacing the crankshaft and it is showing excessive wear already. It is beyond me and I have been a mechanic for seven years. None of my friends have any more suggestions.

Bob Meridian
Dallas, Texas

The torque convertor under extreme stress can balloon or expand and take a set, eliminating the thrust clearance it must maintain with the crankshaft. In other words, the torque convertor pulls the crankshaft toward the rear of the engine, forcing the crankshaft to exert excessive pressure on the bearing designed to keep it from moving longitudinally in the engine.

The internal clearance in the torque convertor can be checked with a dial indicator.

Another method of checking can be used while the crankshaft and convertor are mounted. Take a large brass hammer and after removing the crankshaft belt pulley, hit the vibration damper on the center, driving it toward the rear of the engine. Place a dial indicator on the crank nut and pry the vibration damper forward. If there is clearance at the thrust bearing, it will register on the indicator. If not, you have a problem with a ballooned convertor.

High Idle

I have a F-250 Ford, 1979 model, which I use to tow a fifth-wheel trailer. Traveling down mountain grades is a problem because the engine refuses to drop to a normal idle speed. It remains high for an extended period of time, creating even greater strain on the brakes. I have been told this is normal. After driving cars for 40 years, I find this hard to accept. Must I change carburetors, or what? This can be a dangerous condition. This also occurs when not towing.

William Marcus
Phoenix, Arizona

Many later-model Ford and GM engines have this characteristic; you're quite correct that it can be dangerous. The danger occurs mainly when the device that causes high idle is not properly adjusted. Purpose for the high idle is to control emissions. The throttle is prevented from returning fully to idle position during periods when the vehicle is coasting.

On Fords the high idle is created by the decel throttle modulator. On your carburetor it is located on the right front of the lower portion of the carb. It is best described as a metal diaphragm. An adjusting nut allows the effect of this device on idle speed to be changed. This device also reduces fuel economy, since it applies light throttle even when you're going downhill.

On GM vehicles a dual valve called TRC (throttle return control) is the culprit. It is made up of two valves. The primary accelerator valve is on the right side and controls movement of a slave valve known as the throttle lever actuator. The valve is adjustable.

Head Start

My 1975 Chevy (350 engine) is very erratic in starting. It starts most of the time. Then every once in a while it turns over OK while cranking, but doesn't start. Sometimes it will quit while driving, and I have to be towed in. The local dealer cannot locate the problem.

Alan Richardson
Seattle, Washington

All GM cars and trucks with the high energy ignition system can produce this problem, that usually is caused by an improperly installed ignition feed (pink wire) at the distributor cap. Check this connection by pulling on the wire. If the pink wire and terminal pull out of the connector easily, bend the tang on the back of the terminal and bend the blades in the cap slightly outward to make a better connection that won't come loose.

Cold-Morning Stumble

My Chevy 350 engine with Quadrajet carburetor has had a problem since new; no one seems able to solve it. After the choke comes off in the morning, but while the engine is not up to operating temperature, there is a very annoying hesitation or stumble just off idle. A garage installed larger jets that helped somewhat but my mileage dropped about 2 mpg. I have been told to replace the carburetor as it is faulty.

Ron Campbell
Holland, Michigan

The problem is associated with all Quadrajet carburetors on late-model engines, related to an excessively lean mixture. When opening the throttle, the accelerator pump does not initially produce enough enrichment to overcome the lean mixture.

There are three corrections you can make, and they should help. The carburetor flange bolts should be securely tightened. The two front bolts help hold the carburetor together; when not tight, they will allow an internal vacuum leak, exaggerating the problem. Next, check the response of the accelerator pump. With the engine not running, look into the primary venturi. By slowly opening the throttle, fuel should be ejected from the pump nozzles. If it takes rapid movement of the throttle to produce fuel through the nozzles, the accelerator pump should be replaced. Finally, idle mix control screws should be opened until the idle falls off and then turned back in just enough to raise the idle to maximum. This should eliminate the stumble. Never increase jet size to eliminate a problem such as this. A change of metering rods would be an appropriate last step if all else fails, but the rod change shouldn't be necessary

Vibration

There is vibration in the drivetrain of my 1981 three-quarter-ton Chevy Suburban with 454 engine. It is noticeable when I'm accelerating fairly fast from a stop and again at about 30 mph. It dies out at about 45 mph. The dealer and factory rep have been unable to pinpoint the problem.

All tires have been checked for roundness and have been balanced several times; front brake rotors and bearings were replaced; the driveshaft was removed and checked for straightness and replaced. The vibration remains the same even with the motor shut off and coasting at 35 mph.

Glenn Zeller
Yuba City, California

It's somewhat more common for your problem to occur in vehicles with two-piece driveshafts than with a one-piece shaft, but it can happen either way. Under acceleration, the rear axle wraps the springs slightly, changing the angle at which the driveshaft meets the differential. This sometimes can set up oscillation. Also, limited slip rear axles can cause the problem if the clutches in the limited slip are chattering.

Since your problem continues even while coasting, you might recheck the tires. A good wheel balance man could check for roundness of the tires and trueness of the wheels.

Valve Noise

I have a 1974 Chevrolet with the 454-cid engine that has had a considerable amount of valve lifter noise since new. I have decided to drill a .032-inch hole in the front oil galley plugs behind the timing chain cover. I also thought it might be a good idea to clean the lifters while I'm at it, and would appreciate some suggestions.

Steve Calagher
Portland, Oregon

Drilling the oil galley plugs will allow trapped air to escape, stablizing the valve lifter operation, and the practice is viable on all 1973 to 1975 454-cid Chevy engines. Most later engines have this modification already made at the factory.

Foaming oil can cause similar problems. Check the dip stick after hard running to see if foam exists. This is generally caused by incorrect oil level or water in the oil. If water is suspected, let the engine sit for about eight hours, open the oil pan drain plug slightly and let oil begin to trickle into a pan. If water precedes the oil, the leak must be found and repaired. If no water appears, the oil pump pickup could be loose and sucking air. It is advisable to braze the pickup to the pump body to prevent this. Obviously, when adding oil to this engine, don't overfill.

Servicing the hydraulic lifters is quite simple. Closely check plunger and body clearance. It is quite common for the plunger to stick. Crocus cloth may be used to remove any burrs. Wash the entire unit in acetone, and check the ball valve for excessive wear.

Thousands of valve lifters are replaced during overhaul jobs when most needn't be. The mechanic would rather replace the lifter than spend the time cleaning it. In an engine overhaul being performed by the vehicle owner when time is not a problem, wash the parts. The main reason for lifter problems is varnish. A clean lifter that does not have any worn parts will operate just as well as a new one. It's important to inspect the bottom of the lifter to see if it has been worn slightly concave from the action of the cam. Such a lifter should be replaced.

After reassembly, Chevrolet engines require adjustment of the valve lifters. The best method is to set the adjustment at zero lash initially. After starting the engine, back off each valve adjustment until noise is heard. Tighten until noise disappears. Then tighten 1/4

to 1/8 turn more. Repeat after the engine warms up.

Contamination

Recently our Suburban with 454 engine began to run roughly; the mechanic disassembled the carburetor to find out why. He found debris in the carburetor that apparently had gone through the filter that is built into the carburetor. The filter appeared to be damaged. We installed a different fuel filter on the inlet line to the carburetor and eliminated that one. Other readers who have had fuel problems with GM engines might take a look at the condition of that small built-in filter.

Richard Keys
Seattle, Washington

It's a good idea to check that filter periodically, as it may become clogged with debris if contaminated fuel is present. This can cause fuel starvation resembling vapor lock. Aside from that, when replacing that filter on all GM Quadrajet carburetors, use only the original GM part.

Several aftermarket filters, especially with the roll-over check valve, tend to disintegrate, allowing debris into the fuel bowl. This can not only affect fuel metering, but also may keep the fuel inlet valve from closing, thereby causing flooding. Note the position of the GM filter when installing it. The flat side should face the carburetor (concave side facing the fuel flow).

Spark Timing

My 1979 GMC truck is equipped with the 454 engine, and it cannot be timed at the factory setting. It just will not run. The dealer says the timing mark is in the wrong location. The timing tab that is generally located on the front engine cover is on the left side of the oil pan. If I try to set the engine as the manual states, it will not run at all. Should I have the timing tab changed so the indication is in the normal place as Chevrolet suggests? There must be a logical answer to this.

Dave Bonte
Salt Lake City, Utah

The 1980 Chevrolet 454 and a few 350 and 400 engines are equipped this way. We found it on 1979 models only twice. This was purposely done by the factory to help set timing, due to use of various accessories that block the view. The engine must be timed by connecting the timing light to No. 5 or No. 8 cylinder, while lying under the vehicle with the timing light pointed up at the vibration damper.

Won't Start

My 1977 Olds engine stops for no apparent reason. It doesn't make any difference whether it is hot or cold, and it starts in the morning without a problem. The dealer replaced the ignition module, but the problem still exists.

Bob Walters
Portland, Oregon

This problem occurs with many GM vehicles, and in some cases it can be traced to a defective module. In others, it's a black (ground) wire broken where it attaches to the distributor module terminal. The break is caused when the wire is crimped. Or, it could be excessive paint on either the tan or black wire terminals at the distributor connection.

Knock

I have a late 1976, 454 engine with 8500 miles on it. At about 3000 miles a noise developed in the engine. I immediately took it to the agency where it was purchased; after two days they told me to keep driving and see if it would improve. I have been back twice. The noise, which is a knocking sound, persists. If anything, it has become more noticeable when cold. I can almost eliminate the noise by grounding one particular spark plug.

Tom Warren
Boulder Nevada

If the noise diminishes with increased temperature, and if it can be changed by grounding of spark plugs at low idle, it generally is a piston. There have been factory bulletins for all late-model 454 engines regarding this problem. A replacement factory piston is available with a different skirt design. Ask your dealer service manager to check his factory bulletins for this information. The unfortunate attitude taken by many dealers—that if you leave it alone it will go away—doesn't generally apply to cars and trucks. They don't usually get well by themselves.

Move Up

A note on all GMC and Chevrolet engines with Quadrajet carburetors: There have been numerous complaints about rough idle on 1973 through 1976 engines. The rough idle is associated with a vacuum leak originating at the carburetor base gasket. The gasket is made of solid phenolic plastic with a thin gasket on each side. The gasket parts separate, creating a vacuum leak. There is a better gasket available, Part No. 35431D, which will eliminate the problem. When installing the new gasket, tighten the carburetor retaining bolts (which extend through the carburetor body) tighter than you think necessary; insufficient tightening also causes a vacuum leakage problem with the Quadrajet.

350 Chevy Choke

Everyone in town has tried to adjust the choke on my 1976 350 Chevy engine, but the engine still hesitates and stalls, bogs down and such until it gets warm. The choke is definitely working. My mechanic has put in richer jets and now my mileage has gone down the tubes.

Jim Bollar
Portland, Maine

All 350 and 400 V-8 engines of 1976 and before can develop this problem, but it can usually be corrected with a newer choke coil that was phased into production in January 1976: Part No. 460110. We have found this to be the answer in most cases. Also, check that your accelerator pump is producing adequate fuel into the carburetor venturi when operating normally.

Hard Start

I have a 1974 Chevy 350 that takes a long time to start after it sits a few days. Much pumping of the accelerator pedal and grinding on the starter is required, but it starts fine thereafter. The mechanic has checked the choke, and says it is working properly. The carburetor is 4-barrel.

Richard Johnson
Portland, Oregon

It could be either or both of two problems, both relating to the carburetor. In the bottom of the bowl, your Quadrajet carburetor has soft plugs that may leak. This allows the fuel to drain out of the bowl when the vehicle sits for a considerable length of time. Or, the accelerator pump may be faulty. This is the small pump inside the carburetor which produces two streams of fuel into the venturi to prime the engine. If the pump is faulty, the fuel it produces each time the throttle is opened and closed may be insignificant. Some Quadrajet carburetors may have both of these problems.

To check, allow the vehicle to sit for

a period of time long enough to create the problem. Remove the air cleaner. Do not start the engine. Hold the choke plate so it won't snap shut when you move the throttle. Open and close the throttle a few times while looking down the venturi (engine not running).

You should see two strong streams of fuel with each stroke of the throttle. If you don't, the fuel pump may be faulty, or there may be no fuel in the bowl if it has leaked out through the plugs. The top of the carburetor must be removed to determine if the bowl is empty. If it is, the carburetor body can be detached from the throttle plate, and epoxy cement can be used to seal the plugs.

Racing Oriented

I have a 1974 Sportscoach 25-footer with a 1973 Chevrolet 454 engine, series 30 chassis, load limit 11,500 pounds. It has a 4-barrel Rochester carburetor.

I took the unit down to a shop here that deals in racing cars. The mechanic put lighter springs in the distributor, and disconnected the vacuum advance unit. The carburetor had No. 73 jets in it, and the mechanic put in either 71 or 70. The motor runs a little rough after first starting, but after warming up, it has been running fine. The smog equipment has been removed.

Last year we made a trip from Lincoln to Dallas and then out to Orange, Calif., and back—round-trip 4000 miles. We averaged 6½ mpg. Will your kit do me any good?

Carl DeVany
Lincoln, Nebraska

It should, because the modifications you describe work on race cars, but not on motorhomes. Removal of the smog equipment does not in itself produce great gains in either performance or mileage.

Disconnecting the vacuum advance diaphragm will reduce mileage, not improve it. Leaning the main jets is entirely wrong on your engine, for power or mileage, because your particular carburetor is already lean in the primary power system.

Oil Leak

I have a Chevy Blazer with 350 engine that has had a continual oil leak in the front of the engine since it was overhauled six months ago. First it appeared to be the oil pan. We found two different front pan seals were available due to a change in oil pan design. I fixed that, but a smaller leak in the front remained. We have replaced the fuel pump and gaskets twice and the cam chain cover, but the problem remains. It will not leak sitting still; it must be run on the road before it leaks.

Robert Venton
Klamath Falls, Oregon

The early 283 V-8 Chevy engines mounted from the front of the engine rather than on the side, and these mounting pads have been retained on later engines. There are four 4-inch mounting holes in front. In some cases these have leaked, especially after boiling the engine in a hot tank and removing paint that had previously sealed the holes. The upper one next to the fuel pump location is the most common offender as there is no oil pressure at this point, and splash in the crankcase plus slight pressure inside the crankcase are needed to create the leakage. Use of sealer on four short ⅛-inch bolts will solve the problem.

454 Pushrods

My 1978 Chevy with 454 engine does not suffer the common problem of oil seepage through the valve guides. It did suffer from erratic valve lifter noise. I removed the timing chain cover and drilled a .035-inch hole into each oil galley plug to relieve air trapped in the oil galleys. Then I adjusted the valves between ⅛- and ¼-turn down from zero lash. All is now well with the exception of some early morning clatter immediately after starting.

One other problem has plagued this engine since new. Either the end of the pushrod wears out, or the rocker arm fails and the pushrod protrudes through the rocker arm. I have found it necessary to carry spare pushrods and rocker arms on trips. It doesn't happen often, but when it does there is very little warning. The dealership has assured me the oil supply is adequate.

James Ryan
San Antonio, Texas

On many engines of several brands, including yours, the valve train receives oil last. The 454 and all the small-block engines (such as the 400 and 350 Chevrolet) are equipped with individual rocker arms. There is no rocker arm shaft to retain oil after engine shutdown, as is the case with some other engines. The pushrods are hollow and the oil is forced up the pushrods to the rocker arms, direct from the valve lifter. When the engine is idling, you can see the oil coming out of a hole in the back side of the rocker arm where the pushrod contacts the rocker arm.

When the engine is shut down, the oil drains down. Thus there is a short lag before it gets back up the pushrod, even though your oil pressure gauge may already show a full pressure reading. For this reason, it is good when starting these engines to allow them to run at idle for at least 30 seconds, before driving away. Or, if you don't have the patience for that, drive away slowly and allow the transmission to upshift as quickly as possible. Never race the engine immediately after starting. Without proper lubrication, the rocker arm pushrod socket, and the end of the pushrod, will gall. Once that starts, it will wear through the rocker arm, as in your case. When doing valve work, reassemble the rocker arms and pushrods with lubricant.

Tuning the Ford 460

24

The V-8 engine has been something of a trademark with Ford since the flat-head 221-cubic-inch V-8 was introduced in 1932. Ford's V-8 engines were the subject of ridicule and were subjected to old wives' tales with respect to uneven cylinder wear relative to cylinder angle. Ford's simple design, relatively good overall weight, compact valve assemblies and multiple cylinder head bolts allowed extensive modification for improved performance and mileage. Ford kept the 221 through 1953, with modifications along the way. Then it went from 221 to 239 cubic inches.

In 1954 Ford was the first to introduce an overhead valve V-8 engine; Chevrolet did so the following year. The engine was a somewhat cumbersome small-displacement V-8; Ford tried to

be competitive by changing from 239 to 272 cubic inches, and then to 292 and (finally) to 312 cubic inches. They even had a centrifugal supercharger in 1957 on the Thunderbird.

The 352 V-8 was the popular light-truck engine from 1958 through 1967. It was the forerunner of the even more popular 360 and 390 V-8 engines.

In 1961 the 390 began to appear in passenger cars but was not used in trucks until 1968—along with the 360. The two engines share the same block and most of the other components are identical. Bore and stroke are different, which means different connecting rods and crankshaft. Currently, any 352 or 360 can be converted to a 390 merely by changing the connecting rods and crankshaft.

The 360 and 390 responded very well

to aftermarket modifications and produced excellent power and efficiency. However, Ford did little to take advantage of this until 1975 when the 4-barrel carburetor became standard on 390 truck engines.

In 1963 Ford reacted to the popularity of General Motors' small-block short-stroke engines and introduced an even shorter stroke 260-cubic-inch engine in cars. It had a 3.800 bore and 2.87-inch stroke. In 1964 the bore was increased to 4 inches, producing 289 cubic inches. This 289 became famous in racing with the Cobra sports cars and factory-sponsored modified production race classes. In 1968 the stroke was increased to 3 inches. This constituted the introduction of Ford's popular 302 engine, which has been used continually since for truck light-duty and car applications.

In 1969 Ford produced the 351W (Windsor) engine, based on the 302 with 4-inch bore and 3½-inch stroke. After satisfactory passenger car applications, they began to use this engine in trucks; it also became popular in vans.

In 1977 the 351M and 400M (Modified) engines were developed for truck applications. They were not based on the 351W, and although Ford claimed the M engines to be better suited for truck applications, this has never been the case. However, the 400M allowed more flexibility in application. And although both engines responded reasonably well to aftermarket modifications, they were never on a par with their GM counterparts.

Ford's big motor in passenger cars since 1966 has been the 460. In 1968 a

lighter version of the 460 was produced, which in 1973 found its way into the truck line. Thought of as nonresponsive and as a fuel hog, with only minor modifications the 460 has proven to be one of the most reliable and trouble-free of the big engines, well-suited to RV use.

Ford 460 V-8

You would think that a 460 engine, hitched to the correct axle ratio, would be large enough to pull or haul just about any RV ever made.

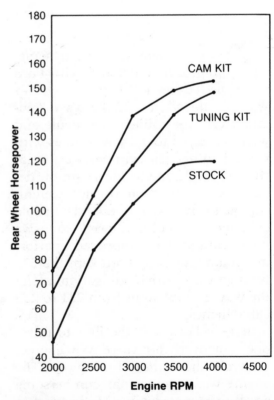

Graph illustrates rear-wheel horsepower with 460 in stock condition, and with modifications.

Geraghty Tuning and Cam Timing Kits

	Fuel Economy	0–60 mph Acceleration	40–60 mpg Acceleration
Stock	7.53 mpg	19.5 sec	10 sec
Tuning Kit Installed	7.59 mpg	18.5 sec	9.5 sec
Cam Timing Kit Installed	7.57 mpg	18.0 sec	9.5 sec

Test conducted at 800-1000 feet elevation, 55 mpg, 50/50% flat highway and low hills. Cruise control used to eliminate effect of driver inconsistency. Fuel in precisely measured amounts pumped direct to carburetor from separate container (vehicle fuel tank not used). Each fuel economy figure an average of three test runs. Margin of error in fuel economy runs approximately 1/10 mpg; fuel economy results were within the margin of error. Acceleration times do not portray improvement in part-throttle response.

Indeed, the Ford 460 does pull well at the top end—at high rpm under heavy throttle. But, as many owners have found, it can be quite soggy at modest rpm, under part throttle. It seems that a very heavy foot is required before the engine will act like it wants to make an honest effort. This varies somewhat from one engine to the next, but with many 460s there is a flat spot in the power curve between 1500 and 2500 rpm. It's most noticeable when pulling away from a stop sign.

Performance and fuel economy expert Geraghty has spent a good deal of effort in singling out the causes for this problem and in developing curves. He has come up with two that are fairly inexpensive and make a dramatic difference in throttle response with this engine.

They did, at least, with our test vehicle, a 1976 Ford E-250 van equipped with the 460 engine and 3.73 axle ratio. That should be a strong combination for towing heavy trailers such as the 5500-pound coach we used during this test. But our 460 had a big lag in response in the part-throttle range at low rpm. And Geraghty's corrections possibly were even more dramatic than would have been the case with a 460 that runs a little better in those ranges. Although solid improvement seems possible with any 460, including late models with catalytic convertors. Convertors do limit performance under heavy throttle and they make the engine more prone to ping, causing more heat retention in the combustion chambers.

Throttle Response Lacking

When moving away from a stop sign with our test vehicle, our use of about half the accelerator pedal travel would hardly produce enough acceleration to even get moving. Three-fourths of the pedal would produce more activity under the engine housing, but it required

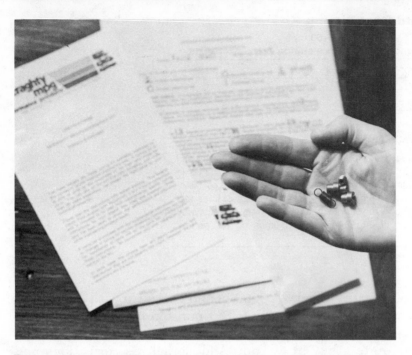

Tuning kit parts include primary jets, drilled plugs for secondary fuel passages,, replacement distributor spring and recalibration instructions.

almost full throttle to produce good acceleration. Throttle response, in short, was practically nil. By having to lead-foot the accelerator pedal when pulling away from stops or when climbing even slight grades, we managed to use quite a bit of gas because we were into the power enrichment system of the carburetor much of the time. A 4-barrel carburetor has three different mixture systems for varying engine loads. The cruise system obviously is used during light-throttle operation. When the pedal goes down farther and manifold vacuum is reduced, the primary power system enriches the mixture about 27 percent compared to cruise mixtures.

And when the secondary venturi opens, the mixture is enriched even more.

Obviously, we can conserve gasoline by staying with the cruise mixture—by keeping manifold vacuum above 6½ inches. With an engine that lacks low-end torque, this is practically impossible when a heavy load is being towed or hauled.

Correction of this problem consists of two separate modifications (the tuning kit, and cam timing correction), either of which can be performed without the other, although they work hand in hand. We tested them separately.

First, the tuning kit. It alone made a substantial improvement in throttle response and low-end torque. In stock condition, the vehicle required second gear to climb one particular hill on our test course at 45 mph, with the trailer. Following the kit installation, the vehicle would climb the same hill in third gear. Heavier throttle was required, but it did climb the hill at the same speed. In second gear we had 4 inches of manifold vacuum during the climb in stock condition, In third gear vacuum was 2½ inches.

We used our routine test procedure on the first runs with the stock engine and consequently had to follow the same procedure throughout. Actually, the test procedure should have been modified at the outset to illustrate the effect realized on fuel economy by getting the carburetor out of the primary power range. Climbing the grade in third gear rather than second, as a result of the tuning kit installation, illustrates the effect of the kit on performance. But had we remained in second gear, we probably would have climbed the hill with manifold vacuum at 6½ inches or better, thus putting the carburetor into the cruise range and improving fuel economy.

As you can see in the chart shown on a previous page, the fuel economy improvement we recorded was small enough to be within our margin of error, which is about ¹⁄₁₀-mpg. Those figures should be valid for moderate driving conditions, but the kit should pay off better in fuel economy improvement during mountain or hill-country travel when heavier throttle normally is needed.

Distributor, in front of engine, is easy to reach but automatic spark advance system is under advance plate (being held above distributor). Note springs attached to posts, restraining advance weights.

Any fuel economy improvement at all seems quite a bargain in view of what the kit did for throttle response in the low rpm ranges.

The tuning kit provides for correction of distributor spark advance and for carburetor calibration to more efficient settings. Manufacturing tolerances are substantial. Also, vehicles must be factory-tuned for such a wide variety of uses and possible abuses that horsepower gains can be made consistently by precise tuning corrections.

Kit installation with the 460 can be accomplished without removal of the distributor from the engine if the owner plans to check distributor internal advance and vacuum advance himself. This is possible with a conventional timing light and a tachometer, by following kit instructions. Otherwise, the distributor is removed and then taken to a garage equipped with a distributor-calibration machine for a checkup which takes only a few minutes. The instructions are very specific on spark timing adjustment.

Carburetor Modifications

Modification of the carburetor requires removal of the top. Primary jets are changed. With some carburetors, the fuel metering system for the secondary power system is restricted (leaned out) by installation of special screws provided in the kit. Shallow threads are created in the orifices with a ¼ x 28 tap; the hollow screws are inserted with an Allen wrench and glued into place with epoxy. Size of the opening in the screw restricts the fuel metered to the

Jets in bottom of fuel bowl are changed to correct air/fuel ratios.

secondary venturi of the carburetor, depending on how "fat" the secondaries have been found to be on the engine in question.

This modification should not only help fuel economy during full-throttle hill climbs. It should also help performance in the mountains, where lower atmospheric pressures enrich the already fat mixture and cause the engine to bog due to overloading of the combustion chambers with fuel. Again, this modification is called for only in kits for specific carburetors.

The kit installation on a van takes more time than on a pickup or car, due to less working room above the carburetor, but it's not difficult for the do-it-yourselfer who has previously had the lid off his carburetor for one reason or another.

The 0-60 and 40-60 mph acceleration times listed in the accompanying table don't really tell how satisfying it is to pull away from a stop sign without hav-

Air horn is removed from Motorcraft 4-barrel carburetor, bringing fuel floats with it. Floats should be changed every two years, as they tend to absorb fuel.

Some carburetors have overly rich secondary jetting. To correct this, kit calls for installation of drilled plugs in the fuel flow orifices. Tap is used to thread the orifices.

L-shaped plastic retainer must be in place to retain primary metering rods, prior to carburetor reassembly.

feels so much better. But employment of a vacuum gauge to utilize the additional throttle response and stay out of the power enrichment system should enable the 460 owner to make some significant gains. Even if no gain is recorded, the added performance seems well worthwhile.

Cam Timing Correction

To eliminate noise, the stock cam gear has nylon teeth. Since 1973 the cam is factory-retarded 8½ degrees. Geraghty can furnish an offset bushing to correct this or an early 429 or pre-73 crank gear can be used. The gear will advance the cam 15 degrees, which slightly affects mileage. Wear of the chain by 20,000 miles is sufficient for replacement. A new steel top gear should be purchased

ing to stick your entire leg in the carburetor, because they are full-throttle runs. Part-throttle response is much improved.

Fuel economy results in mostly flat-highway driving will vary. Some drivers record no fuel economy gain, and others see a modest gain—possibly of around 5 percent. It's difficult not to react to the improved throttle response with a heavier foot because the engine

Cam timing of the Ford 460 is retarded approximately 8 degrees and correction improves performance.

Eccentric bushing is used to advance the cam gear. When replacing gear, use one with steel teeth.

to replace the one with nylon teeth. A pin hole in the gear determines the gear's position on the cam. The pin hole is drilled larger, the offset bushing is inserted in the hole (in proper position) and the gear is bolted into place on the cam with the pin inserted through the offset bushing. The result is an 8-degree advance of cam timing, which brings it up to the best setting for performance and fuel economy.

When installing the steel gear, be sure to check for camshaft end play. This can be done by placing the camshaft retaining plate over the new gear and measuring the depth differential. This will be obvious when examining the relationship between gear and cam. A minimum of .004-inch end play must exist. If it is less, another gear must be obtained or the gear must be machined.

The camshaft retaining plate has two milled slots on either side. These lubrication slots do not extend across the plate. On the lower side of the plate (toward the crankshaft, when assembled) file the slot across the remaining portion of the plate. This will increase oil flow to the chain and help increase life.

Before you install the steel gear, the camshaft thrust plate located directly behind the gear should be removed. If you have a micrometer, measure the thickness of the thrust plate and the depth of the relief in the gear into which the plate fits. The plate should be at least .003-inch thinner than the relief, to allow end clearance with the camshaft. If no micrometer is available, the plate can be laid in place in the gear and a straight-edge can be used to assure some clearance is present.

When the clearance is not sufficient,

If a micrometer is not available, use a straight-edge to make sure clearance exists.

Retainer plate is used to hold cam in place and a minimum of .003-inch cam end play must exist. Use micrometer to measure thickness of retainer plate.

too much pressure is exerted and the camshaft snout (protrusion at the end of the shaft) may break off. This can, in turn, produce other serious damage in the engine. For some reason, apparently no factory bulletins have been issued on this problem.

Correction of the thrust plate problem along with correction of the gear position with the offset bushing will improve engine durability while also improving performance and mileage.

Results Impressive

In terms of horsepower, the combined results of the tuning kit and cam timing are impressive, to put it mildly. During hill climbs at 45 to 50 mph in second gear with a 3.73 axle ratio, engine rpm will be in the 3500 rpm range. And in

that range the two alterations produced a 26 percent horsepower gain, as recorded at the rear wheels on Geraghty's chassis dynamometer. Just how dramatic that gain will seem, from a seat-of-the-pants standpoint, will depend to some degree on the weight involved, since higher vehicle weights tend to reduce the impact. Improvement with our heavy van and the 5500-pound trailer was substantial.

Engine durability should be improved as well. The spark plugs (which apparently had been in the engine for at least 5000 to 7000 miles) were fried and some had begun to misfire—the result of higher than desirable combustion chamber temperatures.

Following neither the tuning kit installation nor the cam timing did we encounter detonation (ping) on name-brand leaded regular fuel—although this may occur in warmer weather, with air-conditioning in use, and higher grade fuel may then be required. This varies from one engine to the next. In all cases, regular can be used above 4000-foot elevation.

Geraghty receives many inquiries about special equipment items for the 460, and he offers comments that many 460 owners may find surprising. What he says is that most of the items popularly recommended do very little good. Thus they are not cost-effective.

Exhaust headers improve mid-range and high-rpm performance but not mileage. Also, headers for the 460 are quite expensive to install. Conversion to dual exhausts is recommended when the stock single exhaust has a muffler with two inlets and one outlet. If the muffler has one inlet and one outlet, it can be retained; benefits of the dual exhaust conversion are not as great. When converting to dual exhausts, pipe size can be 2 or 2½ inches. With smaller engines, such as the Ford 351, 360, 390 and 400, pipe size should be 2 inches. In a dual exhaust conversion, a crossover tube between the head pipes is recommended to reduce sound level if straight mufflers are used. Forty-inch glasspack mufflers are recommended. The mufflers are relatively quiet when used with the crossover tube and are considerably less restrictive than the two-pass and three-pass mufflers (exhaust flow changing direction two or three times).

Replacement of the stock carburetor or intake manifold is not cost-effective. Tuning of the stock carburetor to correct air/fuel ratios provides maximum efficiency that can be accomplished with conventional carburetion.

Modifications for Ford 352, 360 and 390 V-8s

25

While it takes a secondary role to fuel economy, engine performance still is important to RV owners who enjoy the ability to travel at realistic speeds without having to ride the accelerator pedal heavily, and to climb mountain grades without lagging to a snail's pace.

Most of us are looking for ways to boost power if we can do it without sacrificing fuel economy. While it does take more fuel to produce power, the key to making significant power gains without reducing average fuel economy is improved *efficiency*. Engine designs vary widely, dramatic efficiency improvements are possible with specific models.

Ford 360 and 390 V-8 Engines

Three perfect cases in point are the Ford 352, 360 and 390 engines, which were highly popular in pickup trucks in the 1970s and late 1960s. The three engines are almost identical in design, with the 390 getting its additional cubic inch displacement from longer piston stroke and larger bore. Modifications which apply to one apply equally as well to the others, with only minor changes. The 352 was last produced in 1967; the 360 and 390 were discontinued by Ford in the 1977 model year and were replaced by 351 and 400 engines with different block designs.

Although it's a good workhorse, the 360/390 design has some serious limitations. First, the 2-barrel carburetor limits the engine's ability to ingest air and fuel. Then, the exhaust manifolds are very shallow and are not well contoured to the flow of gases exiting the combustion chambers. The result is that the engine is partially plugged at both ends. To improve carburetion is not totally effective unless the exhaust also is improved. Exhaust improvements alone, including use of exhaust headers, are not very effective due to the engine's inability to "breathe" at the top end. Thus, the 360 and 390 are prime candidates for bolt-on improvements. Performance results can be outstanding, with proper choice of equipment and proper tuning.

To test effectiveness of a complete bolt-on carburetion and exhaust conversion, we performed a step-by-step test on a Ford 390 engine in a 1973 Ford pickup towing a 6500-pound fifth-wheel trailer. Gross combined weight was 12,000 pounds. Axle ratio was 3.73 to 1. Needless to say, with that much weight the 390 had its work cut out for it. In stock condition, throttle response and acceleration were dismal. The 44½-second time for 0 to 60 mph acceleration listed in the accompanying performance chart is better than that of some other rigs, which can't even reach 60 mph going downhill. But it reflects soggy performance compared to engines with better factory-installed carburetion and exhaust design.

Horsepower Gains

The success of the project is quite obvious in the horsepower comparison shown in the accompanying graph. As indicated, rear wheel horsepower at 4000 rpm went from 89 with the engine in stock condition to 153 after the modifications, or an increase of 71 percent. At 4500 rpm the increase was an incredible 92 percent! Most RV owners see 4500 rpm only occasionaly. This is

roughly the rpm at which the transmission automatically up-shifts from low to second or second to high after having been kicked down with the accelerator pedal. But the performance is very usable when you really need it. In the area where most of us climb mountain grades—in second gear at 3000 to 3500 rpm—the rear wheel horsepower gain ranges from 42 to 58 percent. Those are highly practical, usable horsepower gains. How dramatically they affect uphill speeds will vary with gross weight. With lighter weights than ours, better acceleration times, vacuum

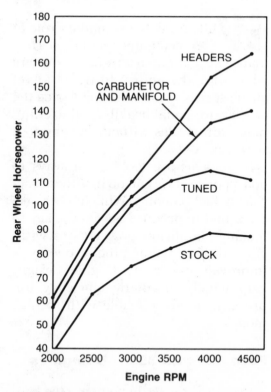

Graph illustrates horsepower gains possible with three-step modification program for 352, 360 and 390 Ford engines.

Test Results of Ford 390 V-8 with Modifications

	Test 1 0–60 mph Accleration	Test 2 40–60 mph Accleration	Test 3 Manifold Vacuum in 45 mph Hill Climb	Test 4 Top Speed in Full-throttle Hill Climb	Test 5 Fuel Economy w/Trailer, 50/50% Hills/ Flat Highway	Test 6 Fuel Economy w/Trailer, Flat Highway	Test 7 Fuel Economy w/o Trailer Flat Highway
Stock Engine	44.5 sec	18.5 sec	4 in	47 mph	6.6 mpg	7.5 mpg	10.7 mpg
Carburetor/ Distributor Tuning Kit & Dual Exhausts	37.5 sec	18.5 sec	6 in	50 mpg	6.8 mpg	7.6 mpg	10.8 mpg
Holley 4-barrel Carburetor, Edelbrock Manifold	33 sec	15 sec	4.5 in	52 mph	6.7 mpg	7.5 mpg	10.7 mpg
Headers, 40-inch Glasspack Mufflers	28 sec	14.5 sec	6.5 in	59 mph	6.9 mpg	7.6 mpg	10.8 mpg

Tests conducted at 60–65 degrees F. ambient temperature, 800–1200 feet altitude, not affected by wind. Tests 1 and 2: Conducted on flat highway. Test 3: Accelerator adjusted by driver (cruise control deactivated) to produce 45 mph uphill speed in second gear; manifold vacuum reading recorded at top of climb with grade approximately 4–5%. Test 4: Full throttle applied in second gear at bottom of 4–5% grade; speed recorded at top. Tests 5, 6, 7: Each result is the average of three test runs with fuel in precise amounts fed to carburetor from separate container. Cruise control used to minimize driving inconsistencies.

251

readings and maximum uphill speeds would have occurred.

In short, the conversion made a willing engine out of this 390 at low to moderate rpm and a real beast at high rpm—when previously it wanted to lie down and go to sleep at stop signs and fall on its face during uphill climbs with the trailer in tow.

The project encompassed three stages:

• Geraghty carburetor/distributor tuning kit plus dual exhausts.
• Distributor tuning plus conversion to Holley 4-barrel carburetor and an aluminum intake manifold.
• Exhaust headers and 40-inch glasspack mufflers with crossover tube between the head pipes.

It's a step-by-step modification program designed so maximum results can be obtained from each step and so the vehicle owner can stop anywhere along the way, as opposed to haphazard modifications which may not be effective due to omission of necessary steps.

The seat-of-the-pants feel for any horsepower gain is affected by how much weight is being hauled or towed. Consequently, a power gain of almost 100 percent really makes a racehorse of an unladen vehicle. With 6500 pounds tagging along behind, the results are obvious but much less dramatic. The additional performance pays off not only in periods when full-throttle, top-end power is required but also in enabling the vehicle to move the weight with less throttle during more moderate conditions.

Here's a description of the modifications and how they worked:

Step-by-step Modifications

Stage 1: Tuning Kit and Dual Exhausts

The Geraghty tuning kit consists of recalibration parts and instructions for carburetor and distributor. By calibrating specifically for the way the engine is used, improvement in efficiency is achieved. With the test engine, the tuning kit made a very worthwhile difference and enabled us to climb the grades on our test course with less throttle, which meant slightly improved fuel economy. The kit significantly reduced acceleration times. For its cost, it's the most effective modification available on the 360 and 390 engines—and on others as well. Instructions have been updated and installation is fairly simple for the do-it-

Motorcraft 2-barrel used on 352, 360 and 390 Ford engines is easy to work on; jets are easily accessible.

Some carburetors have excessively lean power enrichment circuits. This is corrected by removing power valve and drilling fuel orifices larger.

yourselfer who performs his own maintenance and minor tune-ups. Common tools plus a timing light and tachometer (or dwell-tachometer) are needed.

Addition of dual exhausts was for engine longevity more than for performance or mileage. A substantial number of 352, 360 and 390 owners encounter burned valves at relatively low mileage—and they encounter this problem repeatedly, with valve jobs required every 30,000 or 40,000 miles. The causes are incorrect air/fuel ratios in one or both of the main metering systems of the stock carburetor, combined with the restrictive single exhaust system which causes too much retention of combustion chamber heat. Headers are required to fully correct the exhaust heat situation. But just the addition of dual exhausts, retaining the stock exhaust manifolds, along with the tuning changes usually are sufficient to prevent further valve damage. In the horsepower gain shown for the tuning kit plus dual exhausts, the exhausts account for about 2 hp.

Stage 2: Replacement Carburetor

Equipment used in this step included a Holley 600 cfm 4-barrel carburetor, four-barrel intake manifold and the Geraghty distributor tuning kit. Distributor tuning accounted for much of the gain shown in Stage 1 and should be included with any engine modification program. In our opinion, a wrong carburetor or manifold choice can lead to loss of fuel economy and performance. The list of carburetors which Holley builds is long; there are dozens in the 500 to 600 cfm range alone. Geraghty recommends different carburetor sizes and models according to how he evaluates the vehicle use. Most of the sizes recommended are in the 500 to 600 cfm range; the cfm rating is cubic feet per minute of air volume. The carburetor metering systems are modified for the air/fuel ratios required, according to information the owner provides on operating conditions and loads. The tuning changes can make significant performance and fuel economy differences.

The Holley 600 cfm chosen for this engine offers good throttle response and good high-rpm performance. It's equipped with an electric choke. A manual choke conversion kit is available. The carburetor is simple to work on and the replacement parts are widely available.

Ford's stock cast-iron intake manifold used with 4-barrel Holley carburetors on pickup truck 390s of 1975 and later will work fine in a conversion of an earlier 2-barrel setup to 4-barrel. Or an aftermarket aluminum intake man-

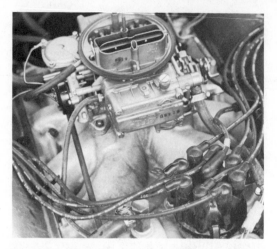

The 390 with tuned 600 cfm Holley 4-barrel carburetor, installed on a replacement 4-barrel aluminum intake manifold. Stock Ford cast-iron 4-barrel manifold, available in wrecking yards, may also be used.

Difference between stock 2-barrel and replacement 4-barrel Holley carburetors is evident.

ifold may be used, although it usually creates little or no improvement over the stock cast-iron model.

In a conversion from 2-barrel to 4-barrel carburetor, fuel economy does not necessarily decline. The 4-barrel is believed by some motorists to cause lower fuel economy, but the opposite actually can occur. The results are up to the owner. The 4-barrel will permit the lead-foot driver to reduce mileage. But a careful driver will stay out of the secondaries except when really necessary and he may even be able to improve mileage because the 4-barrel can more precisely tailor fuel mixtures to varying road conditions than can the 2-barrel. The 4-barrel acts as a 2-barrel most of the time. The secondary venturi are vacuum-actuated (automatic) and do not open, even with full throttle, until 2500 to 3000 engine rpm.

As evidence of the fact that these improvements work hand in hand, we actually lost a little throttle response (part-throttle low-rpm performance) with installation of the carburetor and manifold, compared to Stage 1. The Holley has smaller primary venturi than the venturi of the stock 2-barrel and it apparently needs a free-flowing exhaust for best efficiency. Top-end performance was improved with Stage 2, but not dramatically. It was our impression in this particular case that the 360/390 owner considering the replacement carb and manifold should figure in the headers as well, or he won't be taking sufficient advantage of the carb/manifold purchase.

Stage 3: Headers and Mufflers

The accompanying horsepower chart and the performance chart tell the story well on the effect of headers . . . too well, in fact. The headers enable the carburetor and manifold to develop their full potential and thus the headers get some credit which should be shared. Not only was horsepower increased

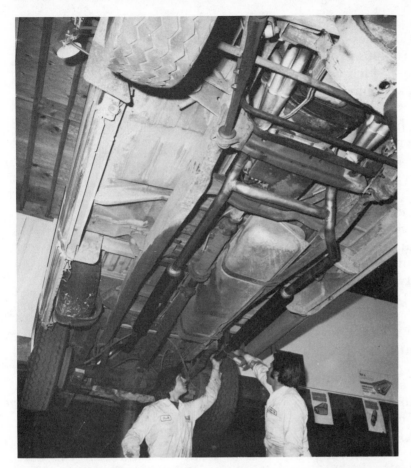

The 352, 360 and 390 all need dual exhausts and have restrictive exhaust manifolds, which makes them prime candidates for exhaust headers. Exhaust pipe size should be 2-inch.

substantially, low-end throttle response improved noticeably and the total package now arrived at those really fantastic horsepower gains mentioned earlier.

A complete new exhaust system was installed along with the headers. It consisted of 2-inch pipe, 40-inch glasspack mufflers and a crossover tube between the head pipes, sole purpose for which is noise reduction. Exhaust systems are almost a work of art in muffler shops equipped with hydraulic pipe benders. The boys at the local muffler shop can bend pipe to almost any configuration and, as can be seen in the photos, they detoured the Ford frame-mounted auxiliary tank and ran the second pipe to the rear through the wheel house area, leaving plenty of room for use of tire chains with the 9.50-16.5 tires.

The 40-inch glasspacks are non-restrictive yet they are a far cry, noise-wise, from 30-inch glasspacks or Corvair turbo mufflers. The 40s produced an exhaust sound level which was not audible inside the truck cab under usual driving conditions.

Geraghty sticks with Holley on most engines. His recommendations vary for reasons that are not obvious. "Generally" he says, "carburetors are recommended according to cubic-inch displacement of the engine, which is totally incorrect. The carburetor has no way of knowing what size the engine is. The carburetor only produces fuel relative to the velocity of air traveling through its venturi. Different engines in the same cubic-inch size will be completely different in volumetric efficiency (breathing) and will require different carburetors."

Carburetor tuning should be different for engines with stock exhausts from those with headers because headers cause leaner mixtures, which might result in burned valves.

Installation Problems

The header installation in past years has been a real challenge to the backyard mechanic because of header interference with the starter. But Geraghty markets a set of headers with one separable head pipe, so the starter needn't be removed for installation or removal of the headers.

The carburetor and manifold installation was routine on this engine. Everything fit perfectly except for a

Stock exhaust manifolds from 390 create high combustion chamber temperatures during sustained engine load and headers help.

short piece of gasket that had to be trimmed to clear a bracket at the forward edge of the manifold. In some cases, throttle linkage must be extended and reshaped using metal stock available in hardware stores. Care should be taken in using a good gasket adhesive to hold gaskets in place while the manifold is being positioned, to prevent oil and coolant leaks. Installation instructions are included with all the equipment, including the tuning kits. But the owner might also get a Ford shop manual if he's unfamiliar with the manifold replacement procedure—either that or some help from a more knowledgeable friend.

The gasket situation is rather important with the 352, 360 and 390 engines. Problems with a carb/manifold replacement situation are few, but when they do occur, the cause usually is a leaking intake manifold gasket or carb base gasket. A letter featured in Chapter 27 deals with this problem in more detail, and is included there rather than here since the practices should be used on other engines as well.

Geraghty preaches quite a bit on one particular theme: Bolt-on improvements such as those described here work well on some engines, while they have little or no effect on others. Every day we hear from someone who has installed equipment which does very little good on a particular engine.

Four or five modifications are popularly suggested by most speed shops as highly effective on almost all engines, and worth tremendous fuel economy gains. If you believe everything you hear, headers alone will get you 3 to 5 mpg. As you can see in this test, there aren't any fuel economy miracles with this equipment, although the test engine had very lean carburetion and was heading for burned valves. In fattening it up just enough to avoid such problems, Geraghty tuned out the modest fuel economy gain which sometimes is possible.

Modifying the Ford 351 and 400 V-8s

26

With availability of the Ford 460 V-8 engine limited to only a few models in recent years, and availability of the 400 V-8 also limited, emphasis has been heavy on the 351. Even if this engine performed well for its size, it would still be marginal for heavier trailers and motorhomes. And in fact, the 351 does not perform well for its size, as can be seen when comparing its horsepower (149 in 1981) to that of the popular Chevrolet 350 (160 hp in 1981).

Part of the reason for the difference is the fact that the Chevy 350 is equipped at the factory with a 4-barrel carburetor; Ford uses only 2-barrel carburetors on 302, 351 and 400 engines. Only on the Ford 460 is a 4-barrel used. The 351 is a descendant of the 302, as indicated in previous pages.

Ford produced two versions of the 351

engine. The Windsor version had the engine water outlet connected to the top front of the intake manifold, and the Modified version had it connected to the water pump. The M version has been used in trucks and vans and the W version has been used in vans. 1981 and later vans have the 351M (except California).

Despite the fact that the M version was shown as producing higher horsepower and wider torque range in Ford specifications, it had the reputation for less performance. Here's the way Ford listed the two engines in light truck specs for 1978 in all states except California. Figures vary a bit from year to year. But we're listing 1978 because that's the year of manufacture of the truck used for the tests that are described here.

- 351M: 163 hp @ 3800 rpm; 267 lb.-ft. torque @ 2200 rpm
- 351W: 147 hp @ 3400 rpm; 276 lb.-ft. torque @ 1800 rpm

The 351M was supposed to be a more responsive engine but on the road it hasn't turned out that way. Few 351s, hopefully, would be tuned quite as lean as our test vehicle, but considerable improvement is possible in all of them. Our test vehicle was not equipped with a catalytic convertor. Later models that are so equipped have even less horsepower.

For 1982, the specs for the 351M engine are 144 hp @ 3200 rpm and 269 lb.-ft. torque at 1200 rpm for the light-duty engine (catalytic convertor) and 157 hp @ 3400, 271 lb.-ft. torque at 2400 for heavy duty emissions (no catalytic convertor, permitted by gross vehicle weight rating above 8300 pounds). Notice the rather tame peak rpm figures for horsepower. This is caused by 2-barrel carburetion and cam characteristics and means the engine has very little "punch" when the driver downshifts and pulls out to pass another vehicle—very little top end, compared to the Chevrolet engines which get peak horsepower at 3800 to 4400 rpm, depending on the year.

Performance expert Geraghty uses the same approach on the Ford 351 and 400 that he applies to the other engines, but with different equipment and tuning. The 400 is identical to the 351 except for bore and stroke.

Results with the 351 project were quite successful in view of the 67 per-cent full-throttle horsepower increase recorded at 4250 rpm, 53 percent at 4000 rpm, 42 percent at 3500 rpm and 27 percent increase at 3000 rpm. The horsepower improvement is more dramatic in the higher rpm ranges, which most RV owners will see only when passing other vehicles. But the changes made to this engine did improve throttle response in the low-rpm partial-throttle areas and this is significant during everyday driving.

Dual exhausts with 40-inch glass-pack mufflers were installed first. That's

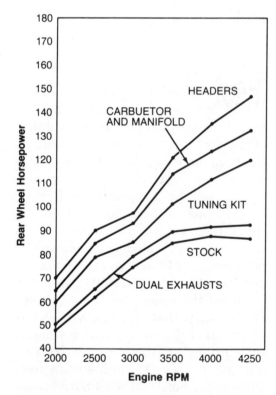

Graph illustrates rear-wheel horsepower improvement resulting from four-stage program of modifications on Ford 351. Similar results occur with the Ford 400 engine.

Test Results of Ford 351W V-8 with Modifications

	Test 1	Test 2	Test 3	Test 4	Test 5	Test 6
	0–60 mph Accleration	40–60 mph Accleration	Manifold Vacuum on level Highway	Top Speed, Hill Climb	Fuel Mileage w/Trailer	Fuel Mileage
Stock Engine	27 sec	19 sec	8 in	45 mph	8.5 mpg	10 mpg
Dual Exhausts with 40-inch Mufflers	27 sec	19 sec	8–9 in	46 mph	8.5 mpg	10 mpg
Carburetor/ Distributor Tuning Kit	25 sec	17.5 sec	9–9.5 in	48 mph	8.7 mpg	10 mpg
4-barrel Carburetor and Manifold	23 sec	16.5 sec	10 in	52 mph	8.9 mpg	10.2 mpg
Exhaust Headers	22.5 sec	15.5 sec	10 in	53 mph	8.4 mpg	9.8 mpg

Tests were performed with 17-foot trailer weighing 3500 pounds, loaded. Top speed hill climb test was on 5% grade, full throttle high year (4-speed manual transmission). Fuel economy tests performed on test course with 50/50% flat highway and low hills, using accurately measured amounts of fuel pumped to the carburetor from a separate container.

because this engine, with a stock single exhaust system (no catalytic convertor) needs better exhaust flow for improved maximum horsepower output and to help reduce combustion chamber temperatures which affect valve life and fuel octane requirements. The effect on fuel octane requirements is usually marginal but we have noticed, in some cases, that dual exhausts will reduce the tendency of an engine to ping on regular gas. Our test engine was not sensitive to octane; we used low-lead regular gasoline of medium quality throughout the test.

The test vehicle, a flat-bed F-350, was unusual because most trailerists don't tow with such vehicles. However, the engine is the same as in a conventional pickup truck. Dual exhausts were routed side by side and brought out ahead of the rear wheels. A crossover pipe between the headpipes was used for control of sound, which was slightly higher than stock but not enough to be audible in the cab under usual highway conditions. In other types of vehicles, use of conventional tail pipes which exit behind the rear wheels would further reduce sound. The side-by-side routing permitted by the small outside diameter of these mufflers avoids conflicts with the frame-mounted fuel tank.

Correcting Acceleration Lag

Next came tuning kit installation and correction of the big lag in acceleration under heavy throttle. The stock 2-barrel carburetor has three metering sys-

Distributor on Ford 351 engines is similar or identical to those used on other Ford V-8s. Vacuum advance is being removed.

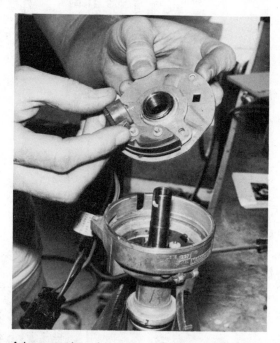

Advance plate is removed and automatic advance system is accessible for modification.

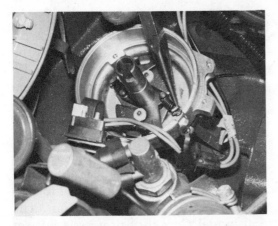

With advance plate off, springs and weights are exposed.

Correction of main-jet sizing improves throttle response and may improve mileage.

tems: idle, cruise and power. When on the road, the cruise and power enrichment systems control air/fuel mixtures. In stock condition there were no obvious problems with lag or surge in the cruise system. But upon opening the throttle about two-thirds of the way (3 to 4 inches manifold vacuum) the engine would almost quit pulling due to

excessively lean calibration of the power enrichment system. Letting up on the throttle to bring vacuum up to 5 to 6 inches actually would improve acceleration. The effect of this lean condition was obvious: the spark plugs, which had been in the engine only 5000 miles, were fried. The center electrodes on two of the plugs had been eroded halfway down to the porcelain. With that kind of heat on the plugs, the engine would have been subject to premature valve wear. A valve job would have been likely at 20,000 to 25,000 miles. The modifications described here will prevent premature valve wear and need for such repairs.

Not all 351s and 400s are calibrated this poorly. It demonstrates that factory carburetor and distributor calibration does vary, which is natural for an assembly-line product. But the variance should not be so severe as to make vehicle practically inoperable.

The Geraghty carburetor/distributor tuning kit provides for recalibration of distributor and carburetor for more efficient operation. The results are shown in the accompanying table and graph.

The kit corrects the lag and stumble problems and improves top-end power as well, although the top end still is limited by the 2-barrel carburetor.

Installation of the kit on the Ford 2-barrel carburetor is quite simple, requiring only removal of the top of the carb and replacement of the jets with others provided in the kit. Some kits require modification of the power enrichment system, but this isn't difficult. Most of the power system modifications are made in 4-barrel carburetors.

The Ford distributor, located in the front of the engine, is easy to reach and the kit tuning procedures can be performed without removing the distributor if the engine spark timing scale can be seen. Use a timing light to check effects of the distributor modifications on the engine timing scale.

The carburetor change is based on the fact that the 4-barrel uses three metering systems while under way, whereas the 2-barrel uses only two. Three metering systems can be programmed more precisely for accurate air/fuel ratios under widely varying load conditions. In the 2-barrel, air/fuel ratio compromises must be made. The additional volume capacity of the 4-barrel also raises full-throttle horsepower in the rpm ranges where the secondary venturi are open (3000 rpm or above). The primary venturi of the 4-barrel are slightly smaller than the venturi of the 2-barrel and air/fuel velocity is improved. All three of the metering systems of the replacement 4-barrel carburetor must be calibrated for the engine, the load being hauled or towed, and other such factors.

Unfortunately, all these advantages don't add up to large fuel economy gains. But any fuel economy gain at all is significant when accompanied by a large performance increase.

Carburetor Choice

The carburetor used here is a 600 cfm Holley with vacuum-operated secondary venturi. Geraghty specifies 600 cfm models for some engines and 550 or 500 cfm models for others, depending on engine efficiency and on emissions requirements. He insists the size of the carburetor should be determined by how much air/fuel volume the engine will draw rather than by engine size alone, because two different engine designs of the same displacement may be quite different in efficiency. In fact, he would have preferred a 550 cfm model on the 351 M engine were it not for the EGR (exhaust gas recirculation). The 550 model Geraghty prefers is not set up with the vacuum port to operate the EGR valve, whereas the 600 cfm model is. The test engine was equipped also with AIR (air injection reactor). These smog control systems remained intact throughout the test.

In installation of the manifold and carburetor, the tricky aspect is gaskets. The only gaskets available for this engine are all metal, as opposed to a combination metal-paper gasket or an all paper gasket. The paper permits compression and a better seal. We had no leak problems, but during manifold installation it's important to use a good gasket sealer, such as Felpro silicone, between manifold and gasket. Manifold bolts should be tightened evenly with a torque wrench to 25 pounds, and retightened after a couple of days.

All linkages that normally connect to the stock 2-barrel carburetor were attached to the replacement 4-barrel carb in like manner. The air cleaner fits the 4-barrel carburetor, although we discovered during the tests it produces restriction that noticeably affects performance under heavy throttle. We detoured this situation temporarily by using a taller air filter inside the same housing. This raised the air cleaner lid off the housing by about a half-inch, for 360-degree air intake.

Headers are a borderline situation on the 351M. On the dyno, the horsepower gain was of 5 to 7 percent, depending on engine rpm. We lost ½ mpg with our test 351M engine. But it's usually possible with the 351W engine to pick up about the same amount of horsepower without losing mileage, due to differences in the way the two engines respond. The loss of mileage with our test engine was due to the fact that carburetor re-jetting was required to compensate for the effect of the headers on air/fuel ratios. Headers normally cause the ratios to become slightly leaner. Without re-jetting, this can reduce throttle response or cause lag in partial-throttle operation.

The correct headers are of the restricted RV-type with small tubing size and 2¼-inch collector cones. Larger tubing size and cones will cause a loss in low-rpm torque.

Headers are worthwhile only if the axle ratio is 3.70 or numerically higher and only if the vehicle is used to tow or haul heavy loads such as an RV.

There is good clearance around the 351M engine in pickup trucks and vans. Ford uses the AIR system, with air injected into the heads through the exhaust manifolds. The headers must accommodate this system to be legal.

Headers should be the last move with either version of the 351. Horsepower gain shown on the chassis dynamometer at full throttle indicates a 5 percent to 7 percent gain in the 2500 to 3500 rpm range, but this is not readily noticeable during typical driving. The payoff comes in passing situations in which the transmission kickdown is used for maximum acceleration and the engine is allowed to wind out to the shift point, around 4000 or 4200 rpm. It's easy to feel the difference here, but that may not be enough to justify use of headers on this engine or on the 351W.

Horsepower at the rear wheels with the 351W (the engine used in vans) will average from 6 percent to 10 percent higher than the 351M. Why? Head design. Despite the fact that Ford's factory engine dyno horsepower figures show the M version stronger, we have found the W version stronger in chassis dyno tests.

Even though 351M is not a particularly strong engine due to head design, substantial improvement can be made with the right sequence of modifications. At the beginning of the test, performance was so flat the test vehicle, with a 4.1 to 1 axle ratio, was a sorry performer even for the 17-foot 3500-pound trailer we towed. By most definitions it would have been classified inadequate. In a great number of vans, the 351 is coupled with a rather high axle ratio, such as 3.25 to 1, and this compounds the problems. At the end of the project the test engine was a much more willing performer and the towing situation was more than adequate for the test trailer and would have been adequate for gross trailer weight up to about 5000 pounds.

Modifications described here will work on Ford 302, 351M, 351W and 400M engines, with minor changes.

Questions & Answers, Ford Motor Co.

27

For more than 10 years, Readers of *Trailer Life* and *MotorHome* magazines have been able to present inquiries about technical problems to the editors. The following selection of those questions and the replies to them deals with problems that occur frequently.

Questions and Answers on Ford V-8 Engines

Gasket Leak

My 460 engine has developed a rough idle problem for no apparent reason. The engine has been running fine for several years.

Several mechanics have checked it out and found nothing. I feel this is a vacuum problem because the cruise control has been operating a little differently and the engine seems to respond to throttle differently.

G. M. Masters
San Jose, California

It's a leak in the gasket between the intake manifold and the cylinder head. Replace the gasket, using a good sealant. The problem is rather common in the 460.

460 Mileage

I have a 1978 Ford F-350 with a 460 engine. I use it for general transportation plus trailer-towing of our fifthwheeler. It had always been fairly consistent in mileage until three months ago, when the mileage dropped to about six mpg from eight to nine.

The engine has 28,000 miles and checks out perfectly in compression. The timing chain was replaced last year along with Geraghty's prescribed change in position of the timing gear. I have had the tuning checked as well as the carburetor floats and fuel level. I would appreciate your suggestions.

Steven Gledden
Knoxville, Tennessee

The metering rods in your carburetor are operated by movement of a piston that is controlled by manifold vacuum. The cylinder into which the piston fits is controlled by manifold vacuum and the piston is sealed to the cylinder by an O-ring. If the O-ring becomes worn or damaged, the piston will remain in the enrichment mode, causing dramatic reduction in mileage. This O-ring is often left out during carburetor overhaul or other work. In some cases it is not identified in parts diagrams provided with overhaul kits. While the carburetor is disassembled, clean the piston and polish it lightly with crocus cloth to make sure it moves freely up and down in the cylinder, and make sure the O-ring is in place.

Electronic Ignition

Since I bought my 1975 Ford truck for towing my fifth-wheel trailer it has left me stranded three times due to the solid state ignition. It generally warns me by stopping and then restarting right away. But the last time when I was in Mexico it just quit. Lucky for me I had read a previous item about this

problem in a GM vehicle and had carried an extra control unit with me which got us home. I am thinking seriously about going to the old standard breaker points distributor.

R. W. Thompson
Phoenix, Ariz.

Unfortunately this has been a problem with most factory units. However, there are more desirable systems than the old standby and these are still being improved. I would suggest you install the 1977 module. The early module has a 3-wire 4-connector design. The later module has two wires and four connectors. One of the early circuits has been incorporated into the later unit eliminating the blue wire. This is a more dependable unit.

351 Starting Problem

In the recent rains here my 1976 Ford van with 351 engine decided to revolt and refuse to start. This is a problem which does not always happen, at least not regularly enough for someone to pin down the problem. Sometimes the starter just spins. Sometimes it refuses to engage. I have had the starter drive checked and it seems normal. I have checked the battery and cables and the neutral safety switch on the shift lever.

Robert Parker
San Rafael, Calif.

That condition often is the result of water having splashed on the armature shaft of the starter through improper sealing between the cylinder block and the rear cover plate or around the inspection cover.

Remove the starter, inspect the drive assembly and armature shaft for signs of wear. Use emery paper to clean rust from the shaft and lubricate with light grease. Pick up some Felpro sealer and use it in the area where the block joins the rear cover plate and to seal the inspection cover. This is a common problem with many engines.

Valve Guides

I have a 1973 Ford 390 engine in a truck that is used to tow a fifth-wheel trailer. After 52,000 miles I had a valve job performed locally by an excellent mechanic. Special bronze valve guides were used and Teflon-type valve seals were installed. On three occasions since this work was done I have bent push rods. The last time one cylinder head was removed and another valve guide was replaced. The mechanic said it had galled from lack of oil, possibly too tight a fit. I have become concerned about traveling very far from home.

Martin Schmidt
Sacramento, California

The bronze guides work well if installed properly. It is important, however, to make sure valve stem-to-guide clearance is not below the factory recommendation (refer to auto repair manual). Many of the 360 and 390 engines are marginal on lubrication to the rocker arm assemblies due to a restriction caused by the rocker assembly

hold-down bolt that occupies part of the space in the oil supply channel. Remove the rocker assembly, locate the oil supply port in the cylinder head. Disassemble the rocker assembly and drill the rocker stand that lines up with the oil supply hole to $^{15}/_{32}$-inch. This will increase oil flow.

When disassembling the rocker system keep all parts in order. Wash and lubricate as you reassemble. STP oil additive serves as an excellent lubricant for this purpose.

460 Start Problem

After following your recommendations with my Ford 460 it is performing well and the mileage, although not the greatest, is acceptable. I still have one problem. This engine does not seem to start as easily when cold as it should and after starting, it is extremely cold-blooded. The local dealer has adjusted the choke several times with no help. They increased the size of the carburetor jets you sent, which helped the cold-start problem but destroyed the mileage. I had them reinstall your jets.

Once the engine warms up it runs just fine.

Bob Magee
Seattle, Washington.

Ford offers an alteration kit which should solve your problem. Part No. 07PZ-90544-A is adaptable to most 1975 and 1976 460 carburetors. This kit will provide a positive choke closure and provide additional enrichment during engine cranking. You might have your *dealer order this kit and install it. When installing the new unit, make sure the keyed end of the new choke rod is not installed on the auto kickdown lever from which the old one was removed. The instructions with the kit should be followed precisely by a competent mechanic who will take the time to do it properly.*

460 Choke Problem

My Ford van with 460 engine is used as a tow vehicle. I have a problem with the choke operation. Sometimes the choke works and sometimes it doesn't seem to come on at all. I have had it adjusted several times and it doesn't seem to help. It seems to be a good carburetor but if necessary I will buy a different one—whatever you prescribe, as I am tired of this hassle.

W. S. Walters
Shreveport, La.

Often there is interference between the choke plate and the air horn and it causes this problem.

Remove the air cleaner, move the choke plate to open position and look for scrape marks on the inside of the air horn wall. Check plate travel. Move the plate from side to side and check for free travel. There should be a minimum of .006-inch on a fully open choke.

400 Valve Problem

I have a 1972 Ford LTD wagon with the factory trailering package, 3.25 to 1 axle ratio and 400 V-8 engine. It has a single exhaust system. Total weight of the tow vehicle plus 28-foot trailer is 10,000 pounds with no load.

I have had two valve jobs and the third one is due. One of the valve failures occurred when I was doing no trailer towing.

I burn regular leaded gas. The valve failures seem due to a soft paste-like buildup in the intake manifold and valve chambers. I have normal wear on the valve guides, no valve warpage. One exhaust valve has been burned so far. I may get 6000 to 12,000 between valve jobs. I have also found some valve seal failure on tear-down. One mechanic said the problem is inherent in the design of the Windsor 400 engine due to a problem which allows raw gas to enter the intake manifold.

I would like to convert to a 4-barrel carburetor and adapt the valves to accept spring-loaded Teflon valve guide seals. Also I plan to convert to a dual exhaust system. Would these modifications correct my problem?

Eldon Jones
Wardensville, W. Va.

They would, Eldon, providing the carburetor is modified properly for the correct air/fuel ratios. That's where your problem lies with the current setup, although it is compounded by poor manifold design which results in uneven fuel distribution.

I doubt the soft paste has anything to do with it. It's normal for gum, varnishes and other by-products of the gas-

oline to build up in some volume on the undersides and stem of the intake valves. This normally will not cause problems. It's more severe in stop-and-go driving and when poor-quality gasoline is used.

Use of dual exhausts will cut down on combustion chamber heat. The right replacement aluminum 4-barrel intake manifold will solve the fuel distribution problem and the properly tuned 4-barrel carburetor will be more efficient with those two improvements in place. Or, if you decide to retain your stock setup, the manifold still is not ideal but by correcting air/fuel ratios in the stock 2-barrel carburetor you should be able to eliminate or at least curtail the problem (with dual exhausts installed).

Throwing Belts

My 460 Ford consistently throws alternator belts and the dealer has not been able to solve the problem. Apparently it's unusual, as my friends with 460s don't have this problem.

Jack Mitchell
Miami, Florida

The problem is not pulley alignment, which is the general opinion when this situation occurs. There is a mistake in some aftermarket parts books which indicates a 7/16-inch belt is needed when actually the requirement is for a 3/8-inch belt. The 7/16-inch belt will not fit into the pulley grooves properly and consequently it jumps off.

Which Carburetor?

I have purchased a 600 cfm Holley carburetor but it does not fit my engine—a 1972 Ford 390. At least, the linkages to the throttle and transmission kickdown won't work. It is a Holley No. 6619 4-barrel carburetor. Also, I have a friend who has installed a 500 cfm 2-barrel carb on his stock intake manifold on his 360 Ford engine. It does not run right and his mileage has dropped. How can he correct that carburetor so it will run properly?

R. W. Cooper
Ft. Myers, Fla.

Your carburetor is not the right model for your engine. You might peddle it to someone who can use it and start again. A 600 cfm Holley 4-barrel is suitable for your engine, but there are many different 600 cfm carburetors. Not only is it critical to select the right one so linkages will fit, it's also critical to have the air/fuel ratios proper for the engine and the way the vehicle is used.

Your friend might start again, too. The throttle bores on that 2-barrel are so large that velocity is poor and fuel mixtures will be erratic. He should either go back to his stock 2-barrel or install the proper 4-barrel carburetor, modified properly for his engine and his situation.

Gasket Leakage

Recently I replaced the intake manifold on my Ford 390 with an Edelbrock unit and ever since then I have not been able to get the engine to idle properly. I don't know if the problem is in the carburetor or manifold.

Dennis Richards
Portland, Oregon

Intake manifold gasket leaks are a major problem not only after replacing a stock manifold with one of the aluminum designs but in standard engines as well, when the bolts have not been torqued properly.

Rough idle, increased oil consumption, exhaust smoke especially at starting, and decreased fuel economy are all related to this problem.

When replacing intake manifold gaskets, all the metal surfaces must be scraped absolutely clean. Any sealer that remains despite scraping must be removed with emery paper.

For installation of a manifold, two types of sealer must be obtained: Permatex Hi-Tac and a good automotive silicone gasket sealer.

The Hi-Tac should be generously placed on the cylinder head surfaces and adjoining areas. The underside of the gaskets must also be coated. After the sealer becomes tacky, the gaskets can be pressed into position and the sealer will hold them to the cylinder heads. Coat the upper surfaces of the gaskets with the same sealer. Allow to set for about 10 minutes. Coat all corners and circle all port areas with Form-A-Gasket or silicone sealer and immediately place the intake manifold in position. With aluminum manifolds, it's helpful to use washers under the bolt heads. The washers should not be larger

than the bolt head. These are hard to find in conventional metal but are available in stainless steel. Immediately start all bolts and tighten progressively in a cross pattern, starting from the center and working outward. Torque to factory specifications and retorque at 500 miles, when the engine is cold.

Don't forget to use sealer (silicone is a good choice) on the gasket between carb and manifold. Vacuum leaks frequently occur there and cause rough idle.

Elusive "Ping"

I am a retired auto mechanic and shop owner but have one problem which has baffled me. I have a Ford F350 which I use to tow a 7000-pound fifth-wheel trailer. I have installed the Geraghty tuning kit, dual exhausts and timing gear correction in this 460 engine. The increase in power and efficiency is great and we now have no problems with any hill.

However, there has been a pinging sound for some time at partial throttle. I tried upgrading the fuel which seemed to help. Retarding the ignition accomplished about the same results, with a loss of performance. I purchased a water injector and found that the engine would accept an additional three degrees initial spark advance, which increased power. But the ping at light throttle remains. This noise has come on gradually. I'm sure it's ping. I tried removing the vacuum advance line to the distributor, which seemed to help some. The vacuum advance is within your specifications. Any suggestions will be appreciated. We're totally pleased with the results of the modifications but this remaining problem doesn't seem consistent with our other results.

F. Bowman
San Diego, California

The 1975 to '77 460 engine produced a ping-type knock at partial throttle especially at 1200 to 1700 rpm. Check this by putting the transmission in drive with your foot on the brake, windows rolled up and listen for the noise while increasing engine rpm slowly to 1700. Then slowly return speed back to idle, listening for a recurring cyclic thump or ping. This is incorrect main bearing clearance. Verify the clearance with Plastigage on the lower bearings. Be sure the crankshaft is held upward against the block to assure proper readings before number one bearing cup bolts are torqued.

Carburetor Whistle

I have a 351 V-8 in a 1978 Ford van used to tow our camping trailer. I have not been able to get rid of a whistle coming from the carburetor under certain throttle conditions.

I have overhauled the carburetor, adjusted it, finally replaced it and the whistle continues. It is very much like an old 4-barrel I used to have on my last vehicle.

William Winters
Flagstaff, Arizona

There are specific 2-barrel carburetors on both the 351 and 400 Ford engines which have this tendency. On your carburetor there is an identification tag. See if your number is among the following:

351 V-8	400 V-8
D8AE 9510-TA	*D8OE 9510-CA*
D8AE 9510-UA	*D8OE 9510-HA*
D8AE 9510-ADA	
D8AE 9510-AEA	

If one of those is yours, go to your Ford parts counter and order Part No. D5VZ-9D597-AA power valve rod and N383191S expansion plug, plus a new standard carb base gasket. When you have the parts, remove the carburetor and turn it upside down. There is a small expansion plug in the bottom of the base (like the one you bought) directly at the end of the EGR tube. Remove it, slide the rod into the hole, replace the expansion plug and install the new base gasket.

Oil Fix

I have a 1978 Ford van with a 460 engine which burns one quart of oil every 1100 miles—and that's without towing a trailer. The Ford garage can't find anything wrong. I now have 12,000 miles on it and have had this problem since the day I took delivery.

William Pellicia
Los Angeles, California

The 460 engine supplies a generous amount of oil to the rocker arm assem-

blies; because of this, it has a tendency to pass excessive oil through both the intake and exhaust valve guides. However, this engine is not a chronic oil user as some others. The cure for the 460 is considerably simpler compared to other engines. Most mechanics are familiar with pressurization of the combustion chamber with air, supplied through a special adaptor in the spark plug hole. This method allows the valve spring assembly to be removed with the cylinder head in place. The stock valve seal boot works as well as anything.

Before installing the boot, coat the top of the valve stem and inside of the seal with Lubriplate or similar light grease to prevent damage during installation. Average oil consumption on 460 engines seems to be about one quart per 1500 miles. If it remains above one quart per 1000 miles, don't be concerned. Excessively high oil consumption—one quart per 500 miles—when accompanied by erratic rough idle is generally an indication of an intake manifold gasket leak, which is fairly common on the 460 engine. The cure for this is to remove the intake manifold, clean the surfaces and use emery paper to remove even the slightest residue. Use a good gasket sealer such as Gasket Cinch or Hi-Track to secure the gaskets in place.

Wheel Bearings

I have a 1976 Ford F-250 truck with 351 engine. I had my brakes replaced after 38,000 miles of trouble-free driving and ever since that time I have had a continued problem with grabbing of one brake or the other, rear wheel bearing failures, and grease seals breaking. I had the entire brake job redone but the problems still persist.

Dan Reynolds
Atlanta, Georgia

Your problems can be traced to replacement of one or more of the original wheel bearings. This probably was done with the first brake job.

Many Fords have a tapered roller bearing which must be replaced with the original Ford part. Aftermarket replacements are available to fit this application but they are of other design, with straight- or ball-type. When these are interchanged, problems such as you describe can occur.

In addition, load-carrying capacity is affected. At full gross weight loading of the vehicle, bearing failure is virtually assured.

Timing Cover Problem

I have a 460 Ford engine which continues to blow front timing cover seals. The crankshaft seems to be true. I have checked the run-out with a dial indicator. There appears to be no groove worn on the dampener. I'm at a loss for the reason. No excessive crankcase pressure is evident.

Bill Fellows
Glendon Beach, Oregon

It sounds as though you have covered the more typical problems associated with timing cover/crankshaft seal leaks. However, the crank seal is dependent upon how well the cover is centered on the crankshaft. To assure alignment of the cover after removal, install a new seal and put the cover gasket in place with no bolts. Install the crank pulley to support the timing cover. Align the cover against the block. Drill a hole in each side between the cover bolt holes with a No. 21 drill. Go into the block about 1/4-inch. Thread the holes in the block with a 10/32 tap. Install the cover with 10/32 screws in those holes. This will center the cover. Attempt to install the standard retaining bolts. If they do not line up, it may be necessary to slightly enlarge the holes in the cover.

Oil Pressure

I have three Ford products with the same problem. The first one is a 1973 Grand Torino wagon with a 351 engine. The other two are pickups, one a 1966 F-250 with 352 engine and an F-100 with 360 engine.

All three are in good shape; they run and start well. But when I start them, after they've been sitting all night, the oil light stays on longer than I think it should. The old F-250 rattles a little if I start it quick.

I have tried different oil filters with the check valves. Some of them stop the trouble for a while, but within 500 miles the trouble is back. They all have good oil pressure after starting. I use STP in the crankcase.

Phil Carlisle
Clay, Kentucky

It is normal for the oil system to drain partially overnight and it may take several seconds with some engines to attain operational pressure. When starting, prevent excessive engine rpm. If the oil light remains on for more than 5 to 7 seconds, installation of an oil pressure gauge is wise to double-check the light system. If the pressure does not come up, check the oil pump pickup assembly in the engine pan for an air leak, and check the pump gears and case for wear.

Big Six

I have been towing a 5300-pound trailer with a three-quarter-ton Ford with 360 engine, 3.73 axle ratio. Since gasoline is becoming more expensive, I have talked to an experienced trailerist who advises that the Ford big six (300 cubic inch) engine is best for towing the above rig. What is your opinion about using a truck with this six?

Reason for this change is that the 360 uses excessive oil, which is going from the crankcase into the cooling system. A mechanic told me this defect is common in the 360 engine and he quoted from some mechanical magazine about how it's caused by some bolt on the end of the camshaft that allows engine oil to leak into the cooling system. To repair this requires dismantling the entire engine.

My engine gets 11 mpg running free and 10 mpg towing. All 6-cylinder engines I have used had 4-speed manual transmissions. Why is that?

Charles Spears
Cassville, Montana

Oil consumption problems are not the general rule with the 360 and I definitely would not recommend that you trade for that reason. The 300 six is too small for your trailer weight. You would lose fuel economy as well as performance by having to run this engine too hard while pulling the trailer. You might be able to improve fuel economy modestly while not towing, but towing performance would be unacceptable. The reason the 4-speed normally is used with this engine is to give a lower first gear for uphill starts with a heavy load. The six has good mid-range torque but it is not as good a trailer-towing performer as your 360 in stock condition. It will not hold a candle to a 360 engine properly converted to 4-barrel carburetion and to proper exhaust flow.

Your oil leakage problem probably occurs between the block and the head. A passage that channels oil to the rocker arms goes between the block and the head and is sealed by the head gasket. A head gasket change should solve the problem. If the engine has a sufficient number of miles, have the valves ground at the same time.

As long as the manifold must be removed for this work, it would be worthwhile to make the conversion to the proper 4-barrel carburetor and manifold at this time.

If you retain the stock manifold and stock 2-barrel carburetor, check the underside of the stock cast iron manifold while it is removed. A metal plate is secured to the underside of the manifold with rivets. Make sure none of the rivets have fallen out. If one has fallen

out, it could cause oil consumption by leaking oil into the intake manifold. This would have nothing to do with your oil leakage into the cooling system.

Valve Failure

I have a 1973 Ford 390 engine in an F-250. After 52,000 miles of dependable service this engine was given a valve job. Dual exhausts were installed, plus headers and a 4-barrel carburetor. The power increase was dramatic. However, since this time I have broken two valves. The second time required replacing a piston due to the head of the valve being trapped between the cylinder head and piston. This time all valves were magnafluxed. The mechanic blames it on the headers, claiming the valves are cooling too quickly, causing the metal to fail. I find this hard to believe, as so many people are using them.

Wayne Nicholson
Omaha, Nebraska

The idea of headers causing your problem is ridiculous.

Valve breakage is not a common problem. But as you know, it is very serious. Valve breakage can be separated into two classifications: impact failure and fatigue failure. If you observe the faulty valve, the impact failure fans out from a starting point in a crow's foot pattern, generally leaving a small portion of the surface smooth opposite the starting point. The fatigue failure progresses from the starting point in the form of crescents.

Impact breakage is a result of the piston striking the valve head in the open position. On a new engine this can be associated with a tight valve guide, improper lubrication during assembly, or inadequate oil flow through the rocker assembly. The valve sticks in the open position and the piston hits it at the top of the stroke.

Fatigue breakage generally results from an abnormal condition that causes repeated bending or flexing of the valve stem. In 360 and 390 Fords this can be caused by interference in the valve train due either to improper positioning of the intake manifold or, with replacement manifolds, the area through which the push rod extends through the intake manifold. It does not allow adequate clearance and this exerts pressure on the rocker arm that bends the valve stem during operation. Check push rods for clearance in this area. The correct installation procedure of intake manifolds on this engine calls for intalling the distributor before installing the manifold bolts. This will properly center the manifold.

Hard Starting

I have a 1975 Ford three-quarter-ton truck with 460 engine that is used as a tow vehicle but also for around-town use. When the weather grows colder, it becomes very hard to start. The choke seems to perform properly and I have checked the accelerator pump operation. It seems adequate. There are few repair shops in my area that are really well equipped and no solution seems apparent.

Bill Matthews
Lake Havasu, Arizona

There is a choke alteration kit. Part No. is D7PZ-90544-A, which will work in 1975 and 1976 engines. It's neccessary only in very cold climates.

Additionally, during high ambient temperatures, there is a restrictor available for the carburetor bowl vent hose which will help. It's Part No. D7PZ-9A521-B, supplied by your local Ford dealer. To install this restrictor, disconnect the external vent hose from the vent tube on the carburetor air horn and insert it into the hose. Reconnect to the carburetor.

A note on 1977 and 1978 Fords: Many dealers are recommending the installation of a high-flow PCV valve to improve mileage. It is being recommended after the warranty period has expired. Don't install this valve unless your engine has excessive crankcase pressure, as it leans the fuel mixture to the point that internal damage can occur.

If your 1977 or 1978 Ford 302, 351 or 400 engine hesitates during initial acceleration, it can be corrected easily by installing a small cover cap on the external piston of the accelerator pump. The 1977 engines use cap No. D7A7-6935-A. The 1978 engines use cap No. D8ZZ-9635-A. These caps remove any slack in the linkage and also partially pre-load the pump diaphragm, for better pump performance. The caps are easily installed; disconnect the lever rod, slip the cap in place, and reconnect the rod.

Throttle Problem

I have a 1976 Ford with the 400 engine and have an erratic throttle problem. Sometimes the throttle becomes very hard to push. I have taken the carburetor off and inspected it, lubed the linkage and still have the problem. The carburetor is a 2150 series 2-barrel.

Bob Whiteman
Las Vegas, Nevada

This is caused by a binding condition between the high speed bleed metering rod yoke lift rod and the high speed bleed cam located between the throttle plates in the carburetor. It can be corrected by replacing the cam assembly with Ford Part No. D7A-9A965-A.

Finding the Timing Mark

I have a Ford van with the 351 engine. Recently I tried to check my timing. I cannot find the timing mark. I made a trip into the agency and they can't seem to find it. They told me that vans sometimes do not have the timing indicator.

D. G. Milhouse
Frederick, Maryland

The only instances in which the marks were not usable or were missing were with early 1970 302 engines in vans. Incorrect vibration dampers were used and did not line up properly with the stationary marks used for timing.

On your engine the marks are relo-cated and require sighting between the water pump and front engine cover, over the edge of the power steering bracket.

Air-conditioner Vibration

An add-on air-conditioning unit was installed in my Ford van with 302 engine. Ever since, it has vibrated terribly. I have taken it back several times and they have replaced the crank pulleys but have not corrected the problem. On my insistence they even ran it without the air-conditioner pulleys and the vibration was still there. They claim internal problems either in the engine or trans. I find this hard to believe unless they damaged the crakshaft in some way.

Ed Johnson
Northridge, California

The add-on AC units very often create a vibration; in some cases it's severe enough to be felt throughout the vehicle. The cause generally is in the mounting of the compressor. The mounts place the compressor away from the engine and are not solid enough. They make a harmonic vibration which in short order will break the mounting bolts and fatigue the mounts.

I would suggest you bypass the dealer and go directly to the manufacturer. They are familiar with this problem and generally can solve it. If not, shop the wrecking yards for a factory set-up.

Fuel Quality

I have been shopping around for a late 1960 or early 1970s vehicle and am specifically interested in a Ford wagon with a 429 engine, as available locally from a private party. It's a 1969 model. I don't know what the compression ratio is, but it's probably rather high. I would tow a 5500-pound trailer with the car.

Power is excellent—far better than late models. However I have heard that there are ping problems with some of these engines, even when using premium fuel. Is that true and if so what can be done about it?

Raymond Mitchell
Atlanta, Georgia

It's true that some grades of premium fuel don't have sufficiently high octane to prevent preignition (ping) on some of those 429s and 460s with compression ratios higher than 10 to one. Ford has issued a special set of head gaskets to correct this problem, but they're rather hard to find. Sometimes you'll find a Ford parts man who can't even locate them in his book. The part number is C8SZ6051A.

When installing these gaskets (after valves are ground), use a large-diameter grinding stone. Using the same pilot shaft used to grind the valve seats, cut away the area behind the valves that extends beyond the gasket line. To determine this line, position the gasket on the head so it won't move and scribe around the gasket line, indicating that portion of the head that will be ground away. It allows better cooling of that area of the combustion chamber and helps further to prevent preignition.

Low Compression

I traded in a 1970 Ford van with 302 engine on a 1975 van with the same engine. The old one would run circles around the new one. Needless to say, I'm desperate to get this engine to run better. Any suggestions?

R. S. Foland
Jonesboro, Arkansas

Your major problem is compression. We have actually measured the ratio of late-model 302s and have found them consistently at 7.8 to 1 compression. The culprit is the piston. It has a very large relief in the top. The early piston, which is available only through Ford (Part No. C90Z6108U), combined with milling of the block and head surfaces, will produce 9.3 to 1 compression. The deck height should be checked with the new pistons (top of piston to top of block). Generally it's from .030-inch to .035. This should be corrected to zero difference, or no more than .005. Additional material should be removed, for a total of .050-inch. The material not removed from the top of the block should come off the heads. A 4-barrel intake manifold and properly modified Holley 4-barrel carburetor, plus a tuning kit, headers and dual exhausts, will have you running circles around your old van. A good water injector will be needed to permit use of regular fuel.

The manifold, carb, dual exhausts and headers along with the tuning kit will produce a considerable increase without the piston change, if you don't want to get that involved.

Modifying the Dodge 440

28

Before getting into modifications to the 440 and modifications to the Dodge 360 and 318 (in the next chapter), a historical perspective on all Chrysler V-8s may be in order. The 318 V-8, from its introduction in the late 1950s, has been an exceptionally versatile engine, and all of the Chrysler Corporation divisions have used it to good advantage. The 318 came out with a 3.91-inch bore and 3.31-inch stroke, and has been used in everything from cars to motorhomes. The only major change came in 1966, when a more efficient cylinder head design was incorporated, improving the operational curve and efficiency. This head design was to be used in other Chrysler Corporation engines.

In 1965 a 273-cubic-inch engine was introduced for light service. Its limited usefulness brought about the popular high-performance 340 passenger car engine. The increase to 4.04-inch bore in that engine, and a long list of performance options, proved to be stiff competition for Ford and GM.

During development of the 340, a 383 engine with 4.25-inch bore and 3.38-inch stroke (which had been used in passenger cars since 1959) was introduced into the truck line in 1967. The 383 was widely used in three-quarter-ton truck applications until 1971, when a 400-cubic-inch engine took its place. The 400 used a 4.342-inch bore and a 3.325-inch stroke; other than an increase in displacement, it never presented any great improvement over the 383. It was dropped in 1978. The 413, which had appeared in Chrysler's more prestigious passenger cars since 1959 and in heavy-service vehicles since 1970, used a 4.190 bore and 3.75-inch stroke and produced excellent performance and efficiency; it became the mainstay of Chrysler's heavy service line until 1973 when the 440 was introduced into the truck and heavy-service line. The 440 had been used in passenger cars since 1966 to compete in the displacement war between Detroit's big three. With reduction in fuel octane beginning to take effect in the early 1970s, the high compression of the 440 passenger car engines had to be reduced. Octane levels fell even lower than expected and Chrysler's financial picture grew rather soft. A decision was made to short-cut the cost of designing new cylinder heads to increase combustion area, which was the proper way to do it. Instead, they dropped the pistons lower in the cylinders, reducing efficiency of the engine. But even with this inherent problem, the engine was widely used in motorhomes, pickup trucks and vans during the 1970s. Introduction of effective water injection systems has permitted the best possible tuning of the 440 to gain maximum performance and efficiency.

Back on the small-block scene, the 340 engine was modified in 1971 to a 360-cubic-inch engine, using a 4-inch bore and 3.58-inch stroke. The 360 has appeared in passenger cars as well as pickup trucks, vans and mini-motorhome chassis and has received well-deserved recognition. It responds well to aftermarket modifications and is a very flexible engine, producing excellent performance and reliability. The 360 is equal to or better than any other small-block engine and it outperforms the Ford 351 and 400 engines.

Modifying the 440

The Dodge 440 V-8 engine, although discontinued, still seems like an old friend—or foe, if the engine has proved troublesome. The last 440 was built for motorhomes and vans in 1979, which now seems like a long time ago.

Dodge built thousands of trucks, vans and motorhome chassis equipped with the 440; it's safe to say that the engine will be with us in great numbers for many years. The 440 can be a fairly good workhorse, but several problems have plagued it. They deserve consideration by someone who intends to live with this engine for several more years. By understanding the problems, it's easier to diagnose them if they occur, rather than relying on a local mechanic in an on-the-road situation.

Before we get into specific mechanical problems and the solutions, let's have a bit more 440 background.

During the late 1950s and throughout the 1960s a horsepower and displacement war was forced on Detroit manufacturers by the performance-minded consumer. Ford was producing a 460-cubic-inch engine for the Lincoln; General Motors had several 450-plus engines in testing for Chevrolet, Olds, Buick and Pontiac and word had slipped out on a 472-cubic-inch Cadillac engine to be released in 1968.

Chrysler's largest engine was a 413,

already smaller than many competitive engines. It was a proven, reliable motor but was already stretched to meet stiffening competition. Rather than be left in the dust, Chrysler decided to increase the design displacement of the 413 to 440 cubic inches. The 440 was the same physical size, had the same bearing area and retained the 3.750-inch stroke of the 413. But a much larger bore was used; it went from 4.1875 to 4.3200 inches. Cooling was improved and this combination held promise of adding the performance of a larger displacement engine without the cost, testing and delays associated with an all-new engine design.

The initial 440 was released in the 1966 Imperial and was rated at 350 hp at 4400 rpm, with 480-lb.-ft. torque at 2800 rpm. It boasted 10.1 to 1 compression and demanded 96-octane fuel. This edged out the competition.

In 1967, the 375-hp version of the 440 was added to the line and proved to be the most versatile of all 440 engines. Undoubtedly it was the best engine for RV use at that time, although it was not specifically marketed that way. It was advertised as the high-performance police interceptor option. The Holley carburetor was replaced with with a larger, improved Carter model; dual exhausts were standard; and an increase in camshaft timing was used. This bumped the maximum torque rpm up 400 lb.-ft., produced a more flexible operational range and also reduced the tendency toward preignition (ping) under sustained loads. Higher axle ratios began to appear, taking advantage of the high torque output of these engines, and mileage improved.

However, fuel octane levels began to drop in the early 1970s and rumors of further reductions, along with stricter EPA regulations, forced a reduction in compression in 1971. The 350-hp version was reduced to 335 hp and 460-lb.-ft. torque at 3200 rpm (very optimistic). The 375-hp engine dropped to 370 at 4600 rpm.

Compression Reduced

In 1972, two things happened which totally confused everyone. The compression was further reduced on both engines to 8.2 to 1, due to low octane fuel and EPA regulations, and the original method of determining factory-rated horsepower then came under investigation. It was determined that ratings directly associated with the engine as equipped for use in the vehicle should be used. Previously, the factory specially prepared a test engine to specifications, less all accessories and equipped with a special exhaust system. The engine was spark-timed to maximum power and was running under controlled conditions. These figures were inflated, based on power output of routine production engines. The figures were listed as *gross* horsepower and torque. The new testing methods produced figures on *net* horsepower and torque. The net figures were much more realistic. The confusion occurred because many motorists believed that the sudden drop in horsepower and torque figures was due to the effect of emission controls. Certainly, some loss can be attributed to the controls, but not such a large one.

The new net ratings were 225 hp at 4400 rpm with 345 lb.-ft. torque at 3200 rpm and 245 hp at 4400 rpm and 360 lb.-ft torque at 3600 rpm. This was a dramatic and shocking change for the consumer and greatly affected the market—although realistically the factory ratings had been around 25 percent high, not due to exaggeration but due to the types of engines tested and the methods of testing.

The 413 engine was used in motorhome chassis until 1973 when the 440 came into the picture. Until 1977, various combinations of the 8.2 to 1-compression 440 were used in cars, light trucks and motorhome chassis. The differences between motorhome engines and the car/light truck 440s had to do with durability rather than performance. The heavy-duty 440 engine was known as the 440-3.

In 1977 the 7.8 to 1 engine was introduced. This represented one of the few mistakes in engine design Chrysler had made to this point. Rather than redesign the combustion chambers and cast new cylinder heads with increased area to reduce compression and properly control combustion, Chrysler chose instead to merely drop the piston farther down in the cylinder, so the top of the piston only moved to .187-inch from the top of the block at the top of piston stroke. They had previously used this method of reducing compression, but to a lesser degree (not as much reduc-

tion in piston height), with marginal results. So it was difficult to see any reason for the 440 blunder except cost.

The result was loss in combustion chamber efficiency and a dramatic loss in cooling of the piston. There was a tendency of the combustion chamber to collect abnormal amounts of carbon. Shorter camshaft timing was necessary due to loss of compression; the cam timing made the problems worse, in addition to increasing the tendency toward preignition (ping). Quite often, the ping is inaudible in motorhome engines due to combustion chamber design, fan noise and road noise. Loss of power and a flattening sensation during periods of sustained engine load have been the only indications that something is amiss.

The 440 had thus gone from one of the strongest, most efficient large-displacement engines to possibly the weakest, despite its use in motorhomes weighing up to 15,000 pounds. The situation understandably has prompted a lot of motorhomers to do a lot of work on their engines. Unfortunately, many of the highly touted power improvers and gas-saving miracles don't work very well, if at all.

Now that you know the basic problems of the late-model 440, it should help you understand the specific problem areas and solutions. To some degree, the fact of the piston's being too far down in the cylinder can be corrected with major internal modifications. But let's get into external changes first, since you may not yet be ready for engine overhaul or major work.

Performance and Fuel Economy Tests of Dodge 440 V-8

	0–60 mph Acceleration	40–60 mph Acceleration	Fuel Economy
Stock Engine	23 sec	12.5 sec	7.4 mpg
Geraghty Tuning Kit Installed	21 sec	11.5 sec	7.5 mpg

Tests conducted at 800 feet elevation, 50–55 mph, 70° F. ambient temperature. Cruise control used to limit effect of driver inconsistencies. Fuel economy figures each are the average of three test runs using separate container for accurately measured fuel pumped directly to carburetor. Test course consisted of 75% flat highway, 25% hills.

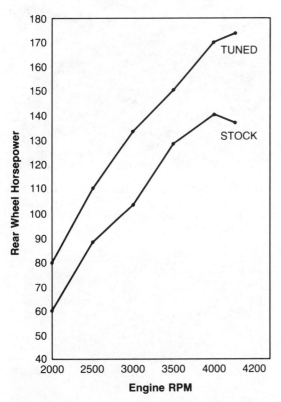

Graph demonstrates effect of carburetor/distributor tuning on rear-wheel horsepower of Dodge 440.

Carburetion

Most 440s were equipped with the Carter ThermoQuad carburetors. They're fairly good performers when jetting is correct, but nagging problems do occur with fuel floats. Made of plastic, they gradually absorb fuel. This makes the floats ride lower in the fuel bowls and raises fuel level, causing hot-start problems. After the engine is turned off, fuel percolates from the carburetor into the engine, flooding it. This can create fuel odor in a motorhome. The fix: Replace floats about every two years and set fuel level $\frac{1}{32}$-inch lower than the factory specification.

Dodge calibrated many 440s quite lean, which creates lag, stumble, hesitation and backfiring when accelerating. The problem was a combination of excessively lean fuel mixtures in the cruise range and late actuation of the power-enrichment system. Merely drilling the main jets larger will solve the part-throttle lag and stumble problem but usually will cut mileage. Without correction of the power enrichment system, main jets must be drilled excessively large. This, in turn, creates an over-rich condition and dramatic power loss when operating at heavy throttle in high altitude. When main jets are enlarged, secondary jets normally should be reduced in size. The rich mixtures are compounded by air-cleaner restriction. The result can be a 440 that won't run at all under heavy throttle in high altitude.

When work is done on the Carter ThermoQuad, the plastic fuel bowl should be checked for cracks around the main jets. The cracks can be repaired with epoxy cement. Also, inspect neoprene O-rings used to seal fuel transfer passages for the secondary metering system. The O-rings may crack and the effect is the same as having excessively large, secondary jets. The O-rings fit between the top of the carb (air horn) and the body. The main discharge nozzles are cast into the air horn and an O-ring on each side seals the passage between air horn and body.

The Dodge 440 is noted for a few engine tuning problems that can create annoying drivability problems—most notably its tendency to lag or stumble when accelerating away from a stoplight. The problem is severe with some 440s and nonexistent in others—which illustrates the fact that no two engines are precisely the same. The engine also tends to backfire occasionally, signaling excessively lean fuel mixtures; the power curve may be quite flat until the accelerator is given quite a kick and the secondary venturi of the carburetor open, enriching fuel mixtures.

Carter Thermoquad used on Dodge 440 and on late-model 360 engines is the only one with external mechanism for control of primary metering rods. Metering-rod actuation often is late; spring tension can be corrected.

Fuel bowl is plastic and often cracks when jets are screwed in too tightly at the factory. Cracks can be repaired with epoxy cement.

Plastic fuel bowl is lifted away from throttle body.

Secondary jets may be excessively large and new jets reduce fuel consumption.

Plastic fuel floats in the Thermoquad (arrow) are the worst to saturate with fuel, raising fuel level and causing flooding after shutdown of hot engine.

During reassembly make sure O-ring seals are in bottom of wells (arrow) or improper carburetion will result.

This and other performance problems with the 440 can be corrected rather easily with the Geraghty engine tuning kit, which has found reasonably good success in the past several years.

The premise of the tuning kit is custom calibration of an engine according to load and driving situation, rather than on a mass production basis. Geraghty has tested thousands of 440s in various uses over the years and says he can provide proper parts and specifications for more accurate and realistic tuning that permits best possible performance and fuel economy.

The tuning kit is designed for installation by the competent do-it-yourself mechanic. It includes the necessary jets, metering rods and a power piston spring for the carburetor. Also included are springs that change the distributor spark advance curve, new specifications for initial spark advance and vacuum spark advance, and specific spark plug recommendations.

The installation involves common hand tools and is not difficult for someone who has previously performed distributor and carburetor work, but it would require some help for someone who has not. Full instructions are provided and are fairly easy to follow if you're familiar with the equipment. The top of the ThermoQuad carburetor is removed and new jets are installed.

With some engines, only the secondary jets are replaced, while with others the primary jets are replaced as well. The fuel bowl floats should be replaced if the engine is more than two years old. The floats are not included in the kit but are available from Dodge dealers.

Distributor Tuning

Distributor tuning can be accomplished without removing the distributor from the motorhome if access is no problem. But it's wise to check access to the spark timing marks on the front vibration damper. If the marks can't be seen easily, it's best to remove the distributor and take it to a shop equipped with a distributor tuning machine for calibration to the specs listed in the kit.

Disassembly of the distributor is fairly simple; the only change in parts involves replacement of the stock distributor springs with the kit springs. The tricky part is recalibration of the vacuum advance unit, which involves bending the actuation arm to limit vacuum advance. The instructions describe it fairly well, but there is no way to do it with precision. If the results are a little different than the instructions describe, disassembly and rebending are necessary.

If the engine is one of those that lags during acceleration, the effect of this tuning kit can be dramatic. The engine will pull willingly with only moderate throttle, rather than chugging and protesting until almost full throttle is ap-

Reluctor is pried off distributor, which can be recalibrated without removal from engine.

plied. With an engine that already runs smoothly, the results are less dramatic, but noticeable. Performance is improved in all throttle ranges and high-altitude performance is particularly improved if the tuning kit installation is combined with improvement of airflow to the carburetor. Further improvement is possible with the proper exhaust headers and dual exhausts.

If you drive with a vacuum gauge, it's possible to check operation of the primary power piston while driving. Simply remove the air cleaner lid and have an assistant watch for up/down motion of the piston during changes in throttle position. Ideally, the piston should begin to move upward at 6.5 inches manifold vacuum, but in stock condition it often doesn't move until about 2 to 4 inches. The spring included in the kit corrects that problem. Effect of the spring can be checked the same way. There is danger, however, if the engine has a tendency to backfire. That can be startling and it's wise to keep a fire extinguisher handy, although usually there is only a momentary flash.

Horsepower increases along with engine rpm and peaks at about 26 percent improvement at maximum rpm (4200). In normal driving we hit that rpm only when attempting to pass. But the power increase at 3500 rpm is substantial, and most hill climbs in lower gears are made with engine rpm between 3000 and 3500. The horsepower figures were recorded at the rear wheels on a chassis dynamometer and do not relate to engine horsepower figures published by motor companies.

Of course, 26 percent sounds like a lot, but how it *feels* depends on the weight of the vehicle. A 26 percent improvement will feel a lot better in a pickup truck than in a motorhome, but it does help get a motorhome over the hills and it makes the vehicle more fun to drive. Engine durability should be improved, as excessively lean air/fuel ratios tend to cause detonation (ping), which can burn valves and cause other damage.

Fuel Economy Results

Fuel economy results will vary. In tests comparing stock 440s with those that have been tuned, fuel economy either remained about the same or improved slightly. The improvement in a 28-foot motorhome for this test was 0.1-mpg— an insignificant change—on level highway at 55 mph. More substantial improvement has been reported by readers who have installed this kit and fuel economy reduction has been reported as well—although that should not occur unless the driver gets rather aggressive with the accelerator pedal due to the improved responsiveness of the engine.

The kit undoubtedly will not work in all cases but quite a large number of 440s were improperly tuned at the factory (excessively lean) and the kit appears quite capable of turning those stumblers into willing performers. At the price, it's much less risky than a cam change or some other expensive move that often returns no benefit.

Geraghty emphasizes use of a good water injector along with the tuning kit, because the injector controls combustion chamber temperatures and allows leaner mixtures with maximum spark advance settings that otherwise would not be possible without inducing preignition (ping). A free catalog lists tuning kits and a water injector, plus other mileage and performance improvers.

Air Cleaner Restriction

Shortly before Dodge stopped production of the 440 motorhome engine, a duel-inlet air cleaner was announced to improve airflow to the carburetor under heavy throttle. The engine was fed through a standard inlet during light and medium throttle, and a second inlet opened only under heavy throttle. Although information on the air cleaner was included with the press announcement for 1979, the air cleaner apparently never went into production.

A do-it-yourself method of improving airflow is inexpensive and is an excellent alteration for any 440 and many other engines as well. Use an appropriate length of 5/16-inch fuel line to make a spacer the same diameter as the air filter. Arrange the fuel line in a circle and join it with a piece of 5/16-inch copper tubing. Place the circle of fuel line under the air filter, so it serves as a shim. Put the filter in place and replace the lid, tightening the nut securely. This will partially flatten the fuel line and create a good seal but will leave a gap of about 1/4-inch between the air cleaner lid and body, permitting 360-degree air intake.

Exhaust System

The single exhaust system on the 440 motorhome chassis is large diameter and reasonably efficient. However, a conversion to dual exhausts usually offers a noticeable power increase under heavy throttle and a slight mileage increase. When combined with a proper set of exhaust headers, performance at midrange and high rpm is substantially improved. Many owners of the larger, heavier motorhomes complain of inadequate power and the solution

lies in a combination of the items mentioned here: Carburetor/distributor tuning, improved air intake, dual exhausts and headers.

However, caution should be exercised in the decision to install headers. They improve performance at midrange and high rpm, but engine compartment temperature is increased beyond the already high levels, creating problems with spark plug cables and valve cover gaskets. Headers should be used only for extremely heavy service in which performance still is lacking despite the improvements already described here. The 440 will burn out most thin-wall headers. Good results are possible with the heavy-wall Gemini headers.

Engine Compartment Heat

Use of headers increases engine compartment temperature, but the Dodge 440 has some problems in that area even in stock configuration. Due to the aforementioned factory carburetor tuning, air/fuel ratios may be quite lean down to heavy throttle. Although designed to automatically enrich fuel mixtures at 6.5 inches manifold vacuum, the power-enrichment system of the ThermoQuad carburetor often is late; this causes a rise in combustion temperatures and becomes critical under sustained load. The heat cooks spark plug cables and boots as well as valve cover gaskets. The gaskets begin to leak oil onto hot exhaust manifolds; the result is an unpleasant burned oil smell inside the motorhome. A replacement high-temperature gasket set is available under Dodge Part No. 4095787. Good results are achieved with high-temperature silicone spark plug cables and silicone spark plug boots.

The Cam

Many motorhomers looking for improved power are talked into replacing the cam with one of the specialty aftermarket cams designed for improved mileage and power. Save your bucks for something else and stick with the stock cam. The specialty cams usually advertise an improvement in low-rpm torque but, in fact, most of them raise the torque curve, reducing low-end response. In most cases their effect on mileage is negligible and even if there is a noticeable effect, it is more than canceled out by the cost of the cam and new lifters, plus labor.

If the engine has more than about 40,000 miles, it's a good bet that the timing chain has suffered some wear. This makes the chain longer and retards cam timing. It is particularly a problem on the 360 engine, but not quite as bad on the 440. Chapter 16 details how to check timing chain wear.

You should also check compression. If it varies more than 15 percent from one cylinder to the next, a valve job is justified. The combination of a valve job and timing chain replacement can put new life into an engine that still has good piston rings and bearings.

Although the design problems of the 440 can't be totally solved during overhaul, they can be substantially reduced. The problem of the piston at TDC being too far below the top of the block can be reduced by changing to pistons with slightly higher crowns and milling the block a bit lower. Stock deck height (distance from top of piston to top of block) on the late-model 440 is .187 inch. By changing pistons and shaving a bit off the block, the deck height can be reduced to .060 inch. Compression is raised to 9 to 1, which still permits use of U.S. regular gasoline when a good water-injection system is used. It does not permit use of Mexican regular. The engine runs much better; the piston is cooled better and there is considerably less carbon formation. The only other way to solve the problem is by redesigning cylinder heads, which is hardly practical.

Also, proper attention must be paid to valve-guide clearances, and to valve-guide oil seals.

In most other areas of the overhaul procedure, just use stock parts. Balancing, head porting and polishing aren't cost-effective—the engine isn't usually operated at high enough rpm for the benefits to show up. During overhaul, many shops like to use fancy chrome moly rings because they may last longer. They may. But they also may not seat to the cylinders. We all know what happens when rings don't seat; oil consumption is a serious problem.

A motorhome 440 V-8, overhauled and modified as described here, is quite different from the way it came out of the factory. Its efficiency is greatly improved and, with water injection, it makes the best of the poor grades of gasoline we are offered these days at very high prices. Short of turbocharging, it is the best way to improve performance of the 440. Turbocharging improves power but we have not found it cost-effective at $2500 or more. A worn engine still must be put into good condition for decent efficiency, whether a turbocharger is used or not, and it makes economic sense to get full benefit from an engine overhaul by correcting deficiencies.

Modifying Dodge 360 and 318 V-8s

29

Dodge 360 and 318 engines have built fairly good reputations despite the fact that factory tuning has created drivability and reliability problems during the mid-1970s. Problems still persist, although not to the degree which occurred in the mid-1970s, when some engines were tuned so lean they would lag, stumble and backfire when pulling away from a stop. This was a more prevalent problem in the 360 than the 318.

The two engines do respond to similar aftermarket modifications for improved performance and fuel economy (hence their inclusion in the same chapter). But they are of different origin; parts such as cylinder heads, crankshaft, etc., are not interchangeable.

Through the years, both engines have been available mainly with 2-barrel carburetors, but in recent years 4-barrel Carter ThermoQuads were used. The ThermoQuad need not be changed, but the various systems are calibrated incorrectly.

If it were human, the 360 2-barrel engine would have a case of asthma, similar to the situation with the Ford 352, 360 and 390 engines. All the engines have similar problems, but the stock cast-iron exhaust manifolds of the Ford are a bit more restrictive than those of the Dodge, and those of the 360 are more restrictive than the 318.

In both cases the manifolds cause too much retention of combustion chamber heat. This not only restricts performance, it also leads to prematurely burned valves when carburetor air/fuel ratios are too lean or close to it, as they usually are.

Dodge truck equipped with 360 V-8 is prepared for dyno run.

and one that has been modified with all the items described in this chapter. That horsepower table reflects full throttle power. Figures for the 318 are slightly lower, but the power curve is similar. Throttle response in the part-throttle range also is substantially improved, which greatly improves the pleasure of driving. It takes less throttle to move away from a stop or to accelerate to cruising speeds.

Although the engine will use more fuel under heavy throttle, conservative driving will limit heavy throttle use to the minimum necessary. Fuel economy

With the 360, the stock 2-barrel carburetor by its nature limits maximum performance; under heavy throttle it does not feed the engine as much air/fuel mixture as it is capable of ingesting. The carburetor simply isn't large enough. The 318 also responds well to conversion to 4-barrel carburetion. However, the modification is cost-effective only when numerically high axle ratios are used. A properly tuned 550 cfm carburetor should be used. However, for the full potential of a larger carburetor to be realized, exhaust flow must be improved. Restriction at either end will limit performance capability. The 318 and 360 have rather tame spark advance characteristics.

Correcting those factors produces quite a substantial performance increase. At the top end it's a whopping 80 percent at 4000 rpm. The accompanying horsepower graph shows this in the comparison between a stock 360

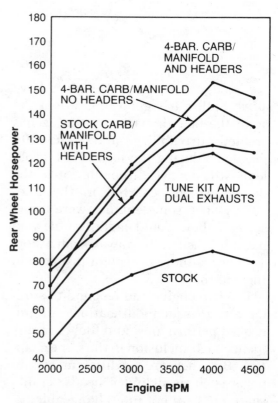

Graph shows rear-wheel horsepower at full throttle with Dodge 360 in various stages of modification.

Test Results of Dodge 360 V-8 with Modifications

	0–60 mph Acceleration	40–60 mph Acceleration	Top Speed Hill Climb	Fuel Economy on 50/50% Hills and Flat Highway
Stock Engine	22 sec	14 sec	57 mph	8.7 mpg
Dual Exhausts with 40-inch Mufflers	21.5 sec	13.5 sec	57.5 mph	8.7 mpg
Carburetor/ Distributor Tuning Kit	19 sec	12 sec	60 mph	8.9 mpg
Special 4-barrel Carburetor and Intake Manifold	18.5 sec	11.5 sec	62 mpg	8.9 mpg
Exhaust Headers	17 sec	10 sec	65 mph	8.8 mpg

Tested on approximately 6% uphill grade, second gear, full throttle. Tests conducted in 60–65 degree ambient temperature, 800–1100 feet elevation. Fuel economy tests conducted with fuel in precise amounts fed to carburetor from separate container. Test motorhome weight (22-foot length), 10,100 lbs.

should increase with an improvement in throttle response if conservative driving practices are used. But correction of air/fuel ratios for improved valve life in this test case compensated for any improvement that might otherwise have occurred.

Following is a description of the Dodge 318 and 360 modification program as developed by John Geraghty.

Step-by-step Modifications

Step 1: Retuning, Dual Exhausts

Carburetor/distributor retuning and dual exhausts constitutes a combination that yields substantial gains. Dual exhausts alone account for a small portion of the total horsepower yield, but not enough alone to justify the cost of a custom dual exhaust system. However, dual exhausts are necessary to allow the engine to take advantage of other improvements, and to improve valve life. The 360 retains a lot of combustion chamber heat (the 318 not as much). Combined with excessively lean carburetion, the excessive heat can, in many cases, add up to a premature valve job.

The custom dual exhaust system described here is fitted to a Dodge half-ton pickup truck equipped with the 360 engine. Most muffler shops figure bigger is better and they normally use the largest pipe size they can handle. But Geraghty specifies that the proper dual

Tuning kit for 360 includes proper jets, distributor spring, instructions on how to reprogram engine.

The 360 with 2-barrel carburetor is one of many engines calibrated excessively lean, causing stumbling and backfiring. Use of correct jets solves the problem.

exhaust system for RV use (and other non-racing uses) should provide some restriction; he specifically recommends 2-inch exhaust and tail pipe diameter and 40-inch mufflers with 2-inch cores. The 40-inch mufflers are straight-through design; when used in a dual exhaust system with a crossover pipe between the head pipes, they are not noisy. Other mufflers, including 30-inch straight mufflers and the so-called turbo mufflers, are more noisy.

The tuning kit is worthwhile on many RV engines and it did a particularly good performance job on the 360.

The kit consists of only a few small parts. As described in the instructions, the primary ingredient is many years of knowledge in tuning engines of this type, including a great deal of work on RVs in the past 10 years. That knowledge enables Geraghty to come up with

the proper specifications. The kit recalibrates the carburetor and distributor for maximum efficiency. Why is this necessary? Because factory tuning is a compromise and must take into account an extremely wide variance in vehicle usage, fuel quality and loading situations. The kit literature calls for specific information on vehicle type, weight, operating conditions, altitude, etc., and all the factors are taken into account. Only a distributor tuning kit is used on the 318, because the selection of stock carburetors has been so varied over the years, and also because factory tuning is usually more realistic than with the 360.

In the case of the Dodge 360, the kit installation is fairly simple—especially if the owner is able to clearly view the

Automatic advance springs are accessible after removing reluctor and advance plate.

timing scale on the front of the engine (it's often a problem on vans and mini motorhomes). Use of a timing light is necessary to check calibration of the distributor after the prescribed modifications are made. If the timing scale cannot be seen adequately (as in a van or mini motorhome), the distributor must be removed and taken to a garage equipped with a distributor tuning machine for checking calibration. Step-by-step instructions detail the procedure. A modification of the vacuum advance unit is called for and this can require some experimentation, as it requires slight bending of a certain section of the housing to limit vacuum advance to the prescribed number of degrees. The modification is performed and the distributor is re-assembled and checked. If the proper number of degrees is not achieved, a further adjustment is necessary. Viewing the timing scale was no problem on the test truck.

The carburetor portion of the kit requires removal of the top of the carburetor and use of kit jets in place of the stock jets. It's a fairly simple procedure with the stock 2-barrel Holley carburetor used on this engine.

The kit instructions are easy to follow for the reasonably competent backyard mechanic. However, someone who has never looked inside a distributor or carburetor should enlist the aid of a more knowledgeable friend.

The combination of dual exhausts and the tuning kit produced a substantial performance improvement, as can be seen in the performance/mileage table and in the horsepower graph on preceding pages. The fuel economy improvement was slight in this case, due to correction of air/fuel ratios to prevent premature valve wear.

The 318 and 360 are very responsive to distributor recalibration. Also, they are ideally suited to use of a good water injector, because water bridges the gap between cruise fuel mixtures and enrichment for full throttle operation. The 360 should never be operated under sustained load above about 220 degrees coolant temperature. The combustion chambers provide excellent turbulence and efficiency but cooling of the chambers is not adequate when temperature is that high. Detonation (ping) will be introduced, shortening engine life.

Step 2: Carb-Manifold Change

Specially tuned 4-barrel Holley, aluminum intake manifold. The Carter ThermoQuad used on late-model 360s

The 360, equipped with 4-barrel conversion, exhaust headers and re-programmed distributor, has greatly improved throttle response.

is not ideal for that engine but works well enough that a change is not realistic. The ThermoQuad can be recalibrated for improved efficiency.

The Holley 2-barrel used on 360s works fairly well if jetted properly, but a conversion to a properly tuned 4-barrel Holley is worthwhile if the vehicle's axle ratio is 3.7 to 1 or numerically higher. Axles numerically lower than 3.7 limit rpm and reduce the effectiveness of the carburetor. It still works well, but cost-effectiveness becomes questionable. Only when operating in second gear or passing do the secondaries of the carburetor become effective.

Choice of equipment is critical here. Just any 4-barrel carburetor mounted on any manifold will not necessarily improve performance or mileage, as was demonstrated during our tests. A replacement 4-barrel carburetor must be specifically tuned in all three metering systems for the engine on which it's used and for the load and driving situation.

Velocity is critical in a carburetor choice. If the carb is too large, velocity of air moving through the venturis suffers. If it's too small, air/fuel intake is restricted. Generally, the way the carburetors are recommended is according to engine cubic-inch displacement of the engine, which is totally incorrect. The carburetor has no way of knowing what size the engine is. The carburetor only produces fuel relative to the velocity of air traveling through its venturi. Different engines in the same cubic-inch displacement will be completely different in volumetric efficiency and will require different carburetors.

For the same reasons, the carburetor jetting is not suitable for a variety of engines. To just pull one out of the box and slap it on invites either restricted performance or lower fuel economy than can be achieved.

Installation of an aluminum intake manifold is fairly simple, with proper attention paid to gaskets. Clean the surfaces, use silicone on the manifold and Gasket Cinch or High Tack on the head surfaces. Tighten evenly; in two weeks retighten when the engine is cold.

The only custom modification occurs after the carburetor is bolted into place. Throttle linkage is modified according to instructions, which include photos. A low-profile air cleaner is needed for vans and mini-motorhomes.

It's important to understand the operation of this carburetor lest you expect miracles. It is not a miracle on this engine—or any other—but on the 360 it will produce worthwhile performance gains when accompanied by the installation of exhaust headers (the next step). The gain produced by the carburetor/manifold installation alone may not be cost-effective; the owner looking for an effective setup should consider the carburetor, manifold and headers together. The Holley has vacuum-operated secondary venturi that do not open until engine demand requires additional flow, always above 3000 rpm at full throttle. The carbure-

tor functions as a 2-barrel until that point. Without headers, the carb/manifold installation did not produce an obvious improvement in throttle response or low-end torque. The primary venturi of the 4-barrel carb are slightly smaller than the venturi of the 2-barrel.

Improved Breathing

When headers are used, the breathing ability of the engine is improved and the full potential of the 4-barrel carburetor is realized. By driving conservatively, average fuel economy needn't suffer. The carburetor will allow more fuel to be used under heavy throttle, but this should constitute only a very small portion of total driving time.

As the horsepower graph indicates, exhaust headers on an engine with the stock carburetor and manifold (carburetor and distributor tuned with the aforementioned kit) do produce a respectable gain, especially around 2000 rpm when the stock 2-barrel carb has an advantage over the 4-barrel due to its larger venturi. The primary venturi of the 4-barrel are smaller than the venturi of the 2-barrel and in actual road tests the 4-barrel does not pull away from the 2-barrel until about 3000 rpm, when the secondaries open. There is a difference here between what the chassis dynamometer "sees" in rear-wheel horsepower and the feel of what actually happens on the road. What it boils down to is that the combination of the carburetor/distributor tuning kit, dual exhausts and exhaust headers is

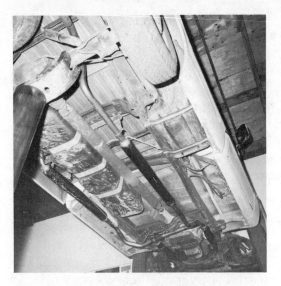

One exhaust may have to be routed outside frame member, for good separation from fuel tank.

Exhaust headers, with crossover tube, improve performance and reduce tendency of the 360 to ping on low-grade fuel.

worthwhile on the Dodge 318 and 360 when maximum power is desired.

Step 3: Exhaust Headers

Exhaust headers. In the previous step we discussed some of the benefits of headers on this engine. Headers must be of the restricted type, with small tubing size and with collector cones not larger than 2¼ inches. Again, bigger is not better. Larger tubing and collector cone sizes reduce low-end torque.

Slightly more engine noise is heard after the header installation because some exhaust noise resonates through the walls of the steel tubing. But soon it begins to sound normal. With the combination of the exhaust headers with the dual exhaust system and 40-inch mufflers, you can actually feel and hear the difference. No longer does the system sound hissy and feel restricted. Combustion chamber heat is reduced and valve life is improved.

Chrysler Corporation, Questions & Answers

30

For more than 10 years, Readers of Trailer Life and Motorhome magazines have been able to present inquiries about technical problems to the editors. The following selection of those questions and the replies to them deals with problems that occur frequently.

Chrysler Corporation, Q & A

Stranded

The ignition system in my motorhome with Dodge 440 has left me stranded several times, requiring a new ignition coil. I now carry a spare. In Mexico recently I came across a fellow Good Sam Club member with a 360 Dodge; he was stranded with the same problem. Fortunately, I had the extra coil and bailed him out, but I sweated all the way back to the border, wondering if mine would go out. Is a better coil available?

Robert Patterson
Tucson, Arizona

All Chrysler products have ballast resistors in the primary electrical system. Purpose is to reduce voltage in the wire leading to the coil (positive). The ballastor resistor is in the engine compartment. You should always carry a spare, but in a pinch you can just bypass it, if it goes out and the coil is still good. It is easily identifiable and when you purchase one from the dealer you will recognize it if you've examined what's under your engine cover.

The coil appears to fail due to the loss of adequate primary voltage from the ballast resistor. But in fact, it still may be OK. Installation of a new coil solves the problem for a while because the new coil usually has lower resistance. However, with reduced available voltage through a faulty ballast resistor, voltage to the spark plugs will be reduced and an indication of coil failure will appear again shortly.

Hesitation

I have a 1979 Dodge van with the 440 engine. During the last six months I have experienced a problem with hesitation during light acceleration. So far the problem has baffled everyone. I finally gave up on the local dealer and sent for Geraghty's tuning kit, which improved it substantially and added to power as well. But I still have some hesitation and it is worse when the engine is cold. However, the choke seems to be set properly. I have replaced the carb float and set float level and have checked for vacuum leaks. Once the engine picks up rpm, it's no problem— the hesitation occurs just at low rpm.

Gene Thompson
Dallas, Texas

You're on the right track but you probably have missed a vacuum leak. The ThermoQuad carburetor, which is used on your 440 and on many 360s, is famous for leaking vacuum at the carburetor base gasket. With the engine hot and idling, squirt some WD-40 around the base of the carburetor. This will cause a change in engine rpm if there is a vacuum leak that allows the WD-40 to be drawn into the engine. Replace the gasket and use a thin layer of gasket sealer. If a leak is not detected in this area, disconnect each vacuum line, one at a time, and plug the vacuum port until the culprit is located.

Burned Gaskets

I have had continual problems with burning of valve cover gaskets on my Dodge 440. When the gasket gets burned, oil leaks out onto the hot exhaust manifold and creates a lot of smoke.

J. L. Kennedy
Richmond, Virginia

Special heat-resistant gaskets are available from your Dodge dealer under Part No. 4095787. When installing the gaskets, make sure the valve cover surfaces that contact the gasket are straight. Often, cinching the bolts too tightly will bend the valve cover at the bolt holes. This may cause leakage even with temperature-resistant gaskets because the valve cover pressure on the gasket is not uniform. Straighten the valve cover by positioning it on a flat surface (such as the head of a vice) and pounding bent surfaces straight with a hammer.

Motorhome Steering

My Dodge chassis motorhome has a front shimmy problem. Originally it was thought to be brakes because the vibration occurred after the brakes were applied. The rotors have been ground and double-checked. There doesn't seem to be any excess play in the steering.

Robert La Sage
Flagstaff, Arizona

Some motorhome makers have repositioned the steering brackets and control box and they sometimes come loose. The best way to correct this situation is to find a competent alignment shop (one not so eager to sell shocks for this type of complaint) and have them increase caster of the front wheels to the factory recommended maximum, plus one-half to one degree positive. Then install a steering damper of the type used on four-wheel-drive vehicles.

Engine Knock

My motorhome with the Dodge 440 engine has produced a strange knocking sound ever since it was new. It's a 1979 model. The sound occurs during very light throttle operation, as I come up off the throttle or during very light sustained throttle. At first I thought it was ping, even though that didn't make too much sense, because ping usually occurs at heavier throttle. Use of premium gasoline doesn't have any effect.

My Dodge dealer says it isn't important, don't worry about it. Should I?

A.F. McDonald
Tucson, Arizona

Some 440s have a problem with wrist pins. If you're not familiar with engine components, that's the pin used to connect the piston with the connecting rod. In some 440s, the pin is loose when it should be retained in one position by being pressed into the rod. The looseness creates a rapping sound under light throttle. Beyond that, it can move laterally and score the cylinder wall, which will cause serious problems, such as oil consumption and loss of compression due to leakage past the piston rings.

To check for the problem, set initial spark timing about 4 to 5 degrees behind the factory-recommended setting. Drive the vehicle. If the problem persists, it's probably a wrist pin. A mechanic who is experienced in finding this problem can find it by running the engine about 1500 rpm (vehicle not moving) and grounding out each spark plug one by one while listening for the sound.

Cam Timing

I have a Dodge-powered motorhome, a 28-footer powered by the 440 engine. Ever since the day I bought it, it has been the deadest thing on six wheels. On any hill everyone passes me. My brother has a 24-foot unit with the 360 engine with Geraghty's equipment, and he tows a trailer loaded with motorcycles and leaves me in the dust. I have installed dual exhausts, the tuning kit and have rechecked everything, but there is very little improvement no matter what I do.

It is impossible to climb higher than 8000 feet; I have had to be towed. Several mechanics have looked at the engine and checked the transmission and they just shake their heads. The engine doesn't seem to miss or run out of fuel. I have driven other identical motorhomes and they run much, much better. We're desperate for solution.

Bob McDillim
Prescott, Arizona

In 1977 through early 1979 motorhomes, the camshaft timing may be retarded in a few cases. The timing marks on the camshaft and crankshaft sprockets are not aligned properly. I would suggest you check this as there is no other logical reason why your motorhome is so sick, in view of what you've done with it.

The usual method of checking it is to begin by removing the valve cover on number one cylinder bank, rotating the engine to exact top dead center position on the firing stroke, and carefully measuring the valve spring heights of both the No. 1 intake and exhaust valves. Write those measurements down.

Then, rotate the engine one full revolution to top dead center and measure the spring lengths again. At this point the engine is in the overlap position (both valves open) and the spring heights will shorten. If the cam is on center, the difference between the seated or original measurements will be the same on both intake and exhaust springs. If the spring of the exhaust valve shows a height less than the intake valve, the cam is retarded and would produce the loss of power you describe. Remove the front engine cover and correct the cam position. Reset ignition timing.

ThermoQuad Carburetor Corrections

I have a Dodge 440 engine in a motorhome and am having problems with hard starting after the engine sits for a while, having been shut off while fully warmed up. It seems like the engine floods.

G.J. McPherson
Sacramento, California

Failure to recognize the cause of carburetor problem leads many vehicle owners to replace the carburetor with one of another brand, which in many cases cannot supply the flexibility of operation that the ThermoQuad provides.

A common complaint is surging or lag in acceleration. These have nothing to do with the basic design of the carburetor. Rather they're due to the way the motor company orders them calibrated.

However, flooding, over-rich mixtures, stumbling, flat and non-responsive power are often caused by inherent problems.

The carburetor float is made from a nitrophil plastic which, after some time, can become saturated with fuel, causing a progressive failure in control of fuel level in the bowl. Although the difference in weight of a partially saturated float and the weight of a new one is hard to detect, rough idle after abrupt stops and stalling on hard turns are indicators of this problem. Replacement of the float every two years would be in order even if the problems don't seem apparent. An immediate replacement would be indicated if they are.

Over-rich mixtures, smoke at idle, reduced mileage and black tail pipe condition can be traced directly to failure of an O-ring seal located in the float bowl which contacts the base of the primary venturi cluster, sealing the idle tube pick-up. A separate O-ring is on each side of the primary venturi. The O-ring becomes compressed or deteriorates, or in some cases it's misplaced during carburetor work. The O-rings are hard to find outside of a complete carburetor overhaul kit from your Dodge or Chrysler dealer. The kit will show location of parts, and you might invest in a shop manual for further clarification of how this carburetor operates.

Erratic operation, hesitation, reduced power and flat acceleration also can be traced to shrinkage of the air cleaner-to-carburetor air horn gasket. This narrow, large-diameter gasket often shrinks, loses its shape and comes in contact with the primary metering rods, stopping their travel. This causes erratic fuel mixtures, depending on the position in which the rods are held. Elimination of this gasket will not cause any problems.

One additional item which greatly enhances performance (especially at high altitudes) is to open up the air cleaner for additional flow.

Don't give up your ThermoQuad. It's a good carburetor and can be easily corrected to operate as it was designed to operate.

Bearing Knock

In my '75 Dodge with 440 engine there is an engine noise which the dealer can only help by relieving tension on the belt that drives the air-conditioning compressor. They claim this is accepted practice and won't hurt anything. Am I headed for problems?

Hollis Nichols
Salt Lake City, Utah

There is a slight bearing knock due to the load from the belt on the crankshaft front main bearing, and it is common with several Dodge engines including the 440. The knock usually is most evident at idle or at high rpm.

440 Miss

Since new, my motorhome with 440 engine has had a problem with erratic missing only on acceleration or on hills. I have replaced spark plugs; that helps but doesn't seem to cure the problem totally. I read that preignition can cause this. However, I have not detected any ping noise. I have had the engine scoped and no cause has been determined. I am certain it is not running out of fuel. The distributor cap looks perfect.

Robert Burns
San Raphael, California

The Dodge 440 engine in motorhomes has a problem with secondary ignition wires (spark plug wires) due to excessive heat and due to the way they are installed. It's especially true of wires to Nos. 1, 3 and 5 cylinders. There are brackets which retain the wires and they are generally bent out of shape. (The wires are installed as though the factory is trying to save a nickel or two on length of each wire.) They are so short they almost contact the exhaust manifolds. Use a high-temperature Teflon/silicone solid-core secondary wire with silicone spark plug boots with enough length to ensure adequate clearance from the exhaust system.

Belt Problem

My 1970 motorhome on a Dodge chassis has an alternator belt problem. I cannot keep an alternator belt on the engine more than 1000 miles. Sometimes it will go anywhere from 250 up to 1000 miles. Pulleys are in line and smooth. Have had three new regulators besides the original. Also overhauled the alternator.

The power steering belt is the original and has 55,000 miles on it; it's still good as new.

Some time ago I decided to move the power steering belt back to the alternator and get a long Gates belt to go on all four pulleys. The long belt went into shreds at 1150 miles on the same pulleys where the other belt had lasted 55,000 miles, except that now the alternator was added to it.

I have talked to several dealer service managers and they have no solution.

H.A. McWilliams
St. Petersburg, Florida

Your complaint is most prevalent in motorhomes and usually is due to the increased load on the alternator from vehicle and coach appliances and from battery charging. In most cases, the drive belt does not contact enough surface area on the alternator pulley and the belt will slip. Once the belt becomes glazed, this problem progresses rapidly. In some cases a longer belt can be used to increase contact, with the alternator adjusted to take up the slack. If this is not possible, addition of an idler pulley is required. The idler pulley and bracket can be purchased through your local Dodge parts counter. The idler pulley normally is used in conjunction with an air-conditioner. It might require some simple adaptation for placement, but should solve the problem.

Blowing Oil

My problem has to do with a 413 V-8 engine in a 1971 Dodge chassis in a 25-foot motorhome. It has 57,000 miles and for the past 6000 miles has been blowing oil into the air breather on the carburetor. The PCV system is clear and the manifold vacuum is proper. There is no appreciable loss of oil from the crankcase but oil continues to collect in the breather pan and continues to saturate the air filter. The shops I have had the unit to simply don't know, or they say "ring job."

Will Harrison
Ocala, Florida

You might check to make sure your PCV hose is not collapsing, which would restrict or at least inhibit its ability to pull gases from the crankcase. If that's not the case, there may be pressure in the crankcase caused by a broken compression ring on one of the pistons.

Head Change

My motorhome is powered by the Dodge 318 engine. It has 60,000 miles and I am told it's due for a valve job. The mechanic has recommended that at the same time I change the heads to those from the Dodge 340 engine, saying it will give me more power and better mileage. Also, he says I should use the 340 intake manifold and a new Carter 4-barrel carburetor. But nobody will assure me that this will improve performance and gas mileage.

R. F. McCord
Chicago, Illinois

The 340 heads are not a good alteration for the 318 engine. You can remove .040-inch from your stock heads. However the 340 intake manifold will work on your engine. The Carter 9501 is adaptable, although better results are possible with a Holley of the proper cfm. rating, jetted properly for the situation. The carburetor and manifold plus proper distributor tuning and dual exhausts will produce additional performance—roughly 42 percent—and possibly a modest fuel economy increase, although this will depend on how you drive.

More Lifter Noise

I have a 360 Dodge engine and have had continual noise from valve lifters, whether the engine is hot or cold. I have

changed the oil religiously and my local mechanic has tried bleeding the lifters down. Two lifters have been replaced. But nothing seems to work. What can I do?

Richard Maxwell
Reseda, California

Chrysler Corporation had two suppliers of hydraulic lifters: Eaton and Stanadyne. Eaton lifters used prior to July 1, 1976—which can be identified by a conical push rod seat rather than a spherical seat—must be replaced. This will correct your problem.

Backfire Problem

I have a Fan Cruiser mini motorhome with the Dodge 360-cubic-inch engine. I have trouble with it backfiring. I can be cruising on the Interstate and all at once it will backfire five or six times. Then it will quit backfiring and maybe not do it again for 100 miles or so.

I have replaced the electronic ignition control unit, spark plugs and wires and coil, and checked the vacuum advance. I have replaced the ballast resistor, checked the timing and checked the gap on the pickup unit in the distributor. I did not replace the pickup unit or the reluctor. I have not received any effective help from any mechanics. They tell me it should be OK.

Raymond McCombs
Charleston Heights, South Carolina

Excessively lean air/fuel mixtures and late engagement of the primary power system in the carburetor create ex-

treme heat in the combustion chambers. This causes preignition and reduction of engine life. The backfiring is the result of premature combustion while an intake valve is open. Most engines are very lean but not lean enough to cause chronic problems such as you have. Correction of air/fuel ratios will solve the problem.

440 Bowl Problem

I have a motorhome with Dodge 440 engine and, thanks to Geraghty's recomendations, the hesitation and lag are gone. But I have had a carburetor problem which is getting rather expensive. The plastic carburetor float bowl has cracked three times. Nothing seems warped and I installed the last one very carefully.

John Letmar
Las Cruces, New Mexico

When you are installing the bowl cover on the Carter ThermoQuad carburetor used on these engines, it is important that the float lever pins be correctly positioned and centered in the supports. Otherwise they will be caught between the gasket surface and the bowl and then the bowl will be cracked as the bowl cover screws are tightened.

Motorhome Overheating

My mini motorhome built on the Dodge chassis has had a consistent overheating problem. Any time we get into hot weather or climb hills—even when it is only warm weather—temperature goes to the top of the gauge.

We've changed the fan, thermostat and have added a coolant recovery system, with no results. What can we do?

B.J. Barnow
Dallas, Texas

Overheating in your motorhome (and in 440s as well) is due in many cases to an undersized radiator core. Install a 180-degree thermostat and you'll probably see very normal temperatures on level roads in cool weather. A hill climb probably will continue to give you the heating problem. The problem affects engine life and should be corrected.

The factory heavy-duty radiator, although furnishing excellent frontal area, only has two rows of cores; this is not adequate. Installing the 4-core radiator produces good results. It's available from Dodge parts counters. Overheating is one of the major contributors to premature valve work, especially in the 360 engine. Lean fuel mixtures, restricted exhausts and design of the intake manifold also contribute. Dual exhausts and proper tuning will improve engine life and enhance performance and efficiency.

Manifold design is responsible for premature failure of valves in the No. 4 cylinder. However, after correction of overheating, tuning and exhaust restriction, the manifold flow becomes less important. Replacement of the manifold with an aftermarket unit is not required unless additional perfor-

mance is also desired, since the cost is a factor.

Low Oil Pressure

I have a 1978 Dodge van with 360 engine. Since it was new it has had low oil pressure. The low speed and idle pressure appears to be normal. However, as I speed up the pressure drops. The oil pump has been replaced and recently all bearings were checked. I know this is not right. Everyone says it's OK, but my feeling is that there must be a galley plug or something missing that doesn't affect idle.

Phil Hoover
San Luis Obispo, California

There is an oil line plug in the feed line which runs from No. 5 bearing to the oil pressure sending unit.

Remove the oil pressure sending unit. Insert a ⅓-inch diameter length of wire into the oil galley. It should travel 7½ to 7⁄₁₆ inches from the machined surface of the block until it contacts the oil line plug. If the plug is too high, use a flat dowel drift to reposition it. If it is too low, drain the oil, remove the oil pan and the No. 5 main bearing cap and reposition the plug from below. This problem also exists on the 318 engine.

Electrical Leakage

I have an electrical problem with my 1976 Chrysler. If the car is parked over the weekend, the battery becomes low. I have had the battery checked and the garage claims it's perfect. They hook up all their equipment and tell me there is no excessive drain. Is there a method I can use to determine the reason for this problem?

R.J. Phillips
Philadelphia, Pennsylvania

One way to check for current leakage is to connect an ammeter, which reads in tenths of an amp, in series with the negative battery cable.

If a low-reading ammeter is not available, disconnect the positive cable from the battery and connect a 12-volt test light with a 1-candlepower or smaller bulb. Connect it between the cable and the battery; if the lamp does not light, there is not enough current drain to be concerned with. Make sure the electrical clock is wound so it doesn't draw current. You "wind" an electrical clock by tapping the positive cable against the battery post a few times. The on-off switching of the power stores energy in the clock.

If the lamp is on, the problem is outside the battery and can only be located through a process of elimination. Remove fuses one at a time with the test light in place to help narrow down the possibilities.

Keep in mind that a discharge of .1 amp will drain a good battery totally in about three weeks—1-amp discharge every 2½ days.

318 Performance

I have a 1978 Dodge van with 318 engine, automatic transmission. It seems to work fairly well except when

I hook onto our trailer, which is only 16 feet and lightweight. The van literally falls on its face and shudders, pings and almost quits running. I can't understand how such a relatively light trailer can make such a drastic difference in operation. I have towed the same trailer for years and it has never made such a change in other vehicles I have owned. I know it cannot be timed farther ahead because it pings now.

R.W. Hensley
Tulsa, Oklahoma

The vibration and detonation (ping) you describe is common with 1978 Chrysler products, especially when under load. The automatic transmission's torque convertor locks up early in an attempt to improve gas mileage. When this happens, the engine is under low rpm and heavy load, so it starts to ping and lose power. The torque convertor lockup device subsequently doesn't know what to do and it repeatedly locks and unlocks, creating the shudder. Most of these lockup torque convertors are used on cars but we've found some on vans. They don't tend to work out too well, especially if the axle ratio is high, because the engine won't pull well when the trans upshifts, the lockup goes into action and engine rpm drops.

To correct this, it's necessary to get the serial number from the transmission. Your local Dodge dealer should be aware of a change which is referred to as correction of the lockup spring and convertor package. It's a relatively simple correction and will allow the trans-mission to function more like a conventional transmission.

Oil Leak

My Dodge 318 engine has 21,000 miles on it and has developed an oil leak which I cannot correct. It started when I changed the oil and filter. After running for a short while, the filter will leak. I have taken it to three different gas stations, and each time their mechanics have replaced the filter. The last time, a mechanic checked the block with an indicator to make sure everything was in line. But it still leaks.

Cliff Krasner
Miami, Florida

The problem is not due to your filter change and is not relative to just the 318 engine. In fact, it is most common in some of the older Ford engines. The oil pump has a pressure control relief valve which prevents excessive pressures from developing in the system. This valve can stick either open or shut and will cause a loss of pressure control. If pressure is excessive, the filter seal will give up. Remove the oil pump, take out the valve and clean it with a fine sandpaper or emery cloth until it moves freely in its well; reassemble.

Surging

I have a 1979 Dodge 1-ton van with the 360 engine which is equipped with a 4-barrel standard-production manifold and ThermoQuad 9246S carburetor. The van has been back to the dealer twice in the last three months to correct surging at highway speeds. I use this vehicle daily in my business and it is hard to give it up to take it in for service, especially when they give it back with no improvement of the problem. If you have any suggestions, I would appreciate them.

Sam Bates
Miami, Florida

The ThermoQuad 9246S carburetor has been replaced with a ThermoQuad 9250S, Chrysler Part No. 4095978. The surging at highway cruise conditions is caused by lean air/fuel ratios in the cruise fuel metering system. In other words, primary jets in the original carburetor were too small. Jets provided in the tuning kit described in chapter 28 will solve this problem.

Fire Damage, O-Rings

Recently during disassembly of my Carter ThermoQuad carburetor I discovered what appeared to be fire or heat damage on the underside. The engine does not seem to backfire that much and, even so, I have not heard that an occasional backfire can burn the plastic body that badly.

R.T. Rasmussen
Camden, Arkansas

The ThermoQuad carburetor used on Dodge 440 engines and on some Dodge 360 engines has a problem with failure of the float bowl due to internal fire damage. Extremely rough running and refusal to accept throttle are indications of a damaged float bowl. That's the black plastic section in the center of the carburetor.

The area generally affected is recognizable inside the secondary throttle bores. With the air cleaner removed and the engine not running, hold the throttle at full open. A flashlight directed to the secondary or rear barrels will show a burned or heavily charred area in the vicinity of the base of the carburetor bowl body, if the carb has this problem.

In most cases, a mechanic will recommend a new carburetor. In fact a replacement float bowl is available and comes with necessary gaskets. It's very reasonable in price. There are two neoprene O-rings, each approximately the diameter of a pencil, which seal the secondary metering system of the air horn assembly to the body. They fit into the base of the rear section of the bowl. Quite often these are missing and must be replaced. It's not hard to recognize their function or position when you're aware of the necessity.

The replacement or repair of the bowl will not cure the problem caused by preignition (engine ping), which is uncontrolled combustion. It is not uncommon for the 440 engine used in RVs to have extreme preignition but produce no tell-tale sound. Inaudible preignition is consistent with the inability of the late-model 440 combustion chamber to cool properly while climbing high grades with sustained heavy loads. This is caused by the fact that piston height was reduced to decrease the compression ratio. Combustion chambers retain heat, preigniting the air/fuel mixtures while some of the intake valves are open, causing a violent backfire through the intake manifold and into the base of the carburetor.

Dual exhausts and correction of spark timing will help. Use of a quality water injector will eliminate the problem.

Another ThermoQuad problem is extreme loss of low-speed throttle response on the 440 and 360 engines with ThermoQuad carburetors.

If the secondary governor butterfly located in the air horn stays open or partially open, it will destroy low-speed response due to the loss of air velocity through the primary venturi. Part of the air that should be going through the primaries is leaking past the butterfly in the secondary side. This is corrected by spraying the governor butterfly with a suitable cleaner and checking the external linkage to the vacuum control diaphragm to be sure it works freely.

Questions and Answers— All Brands

31

For more than 10 years, Readers of Trailer Life and Motorhome magazines have been able to present inquiries about technical problems to the editors. The following selection of those questions and the replies to them deals with problems that occur frequently.

Questions & Answers—General

Spare Parts

We are traveling to Mexico and need a list of certain items to take when traveling into areas where engine parts may be hard to find. I have a 1978 Ford 460 and would like to have that list. Also, which fuel should I use while I'm in Mexico?

Jack Mitchell
Lompoc, California

The question of what to take can produce some varied answers, depending on how well prepared you want to be. The ultimate would be to take an extra truck. But that might not be too practical, so let's limit the list to bare necessities—items that are good to have in the U.S. as well as in Mexico.

If you have more than 20,000 miles on the odometer or two years of use, install new belts and take the old ones as spares. Check all hoses and carry an upper and lower radiator hose.

If you intend to travel in excess of 1000 miles, an extra set of spark plugs would be handy in case you use fuel that is marginal in quality and you fry a set of plugs. The installation of a fuel filter that has a trap (sediment bowl) will help prevent contamination in the fuel from reaching the carburetor.

On late model Ford, GM and Chrysler products with high-energy ignitions, spare ignition parts may come in very handy. An amplifier module is a prime item for Ford products. Be sure it is a Ford factory replacement for your particular engine and application. The units are not always interchangeable, as suggested by some aftermarket rebuilders and manufacturers. GM generally requires only a spare rotor because the rotors tend to burn through from voltage leaks. Weak point in the Chyrsler system is the ballast resistor.

If you have a standard distributor—the old style with points and condensor—a condensor should be carried. Next time you change the points, keep the old set as spare.

Another item to take along is a plastic hot water bottle with about five feet of hose adaptable to your carburetor fuel line. Don't laugh—this has saved many stranded motorists since the days of the Model A. If a fuel pump should fail, you can hang the water bottle from your antenna, fill it with fuel and attach the line to the carburetor. Then proceed to the closest repair facility, refilling the bottle as needed by siphoning from the fuel tank. Check to make sure you can siphon from the fuel tank, as some have such long fill necks that it's difficult to get the siphon tube into the fuel.

Fuel in Mexico is acceptable if you use unleaded regular. The leaded regular is only about 80 octane and can destroy a good engine due to preignition (ping). A good water injector is strongly suggested for traveling in Mexico. This will allow you to use a mix of one-half leaded regular and one-half unleaded regular. Keep your tank half-full in an area that may have only the 80-octane regular. That way, you'll at least have a 50/50 mixture.

Belts Won't Last

I have a 29-foot motorhome with the Dodge 440 engine and have a problem that five different garages have not been able to correct. About every 3000 to 5000 miles I lose the power steering, alternator and air-conditioning belts. They fly off. I have tried retightening them periodically and this doesn't seem to produce any positive results.

Bob Stevenson
Phoenix, Arizona

The problem is common with many engines, but not generally to such a severe extent. There is misalignment of the pulleys. In most cases it is the power steering. The misalignment not only wears the belt prematurely, but also quick changes in engine rpm will cause the belt to jump off the pulley, taking the other belts along.

Find a local mechanic who will take the time to space and modify the power steering and air-conditioning brackets until perfect alignment is accomplished. The best way to check this is with a straight-edge, not eye-balling the situation. Also check for matching pulley groove sizes; combinations of $\frac{3}{8}$-inch and $\frac{1}{2}$-inch pulleys sometimes are found on the same belt train. The air-conditioning idler pulleys should be checked for bearing wear, especially with add-on air-conditioners or with Ford products.

Transmission Failure

The transmission in my tow car has gone out twice, even though the car has only 20,000 miles. I have two coolers on it and am sure the trans is not overheated; I wonder if it will happen again.

Robert Streand
Dallas, Texas

Many transmission failures are related to overheating and in many cases repeated failures are related to poor circulation of transmission fluid. Multiple coolers sometimes are installed in conjunction with the stock cooler inside the radiator to overcome a heating problem when, in fact, a restriction in the system has been the culprit.

A transmission should be serviced at intervals not exceeding 20,000 miles and should be checked before each trip to be sure the oil is at proper level. You should also examine the oil to see if it has a burned appearance and smell it to check for an odor that indicates overheating. The cooling system should be checked often for leakage and chafing of cooler lines against sharp edges.

If a restriction in flow of fluid is suspected, the vehicle should be brought up to operating temperature by driving several miles. The return cooler line should be removed and connected to a hose leading to a container. With the engine at normal idle in neutral, a quart of oil should accumulate in the container in about 20 seconds. If not, locate the restriction, which may be a collapsed line or plugged cooler. If it is in a cooler, it can generally be back-flushed with a hand pump using mineral spirits, followed by use of low air pressure. Then flush the system with trans oil. Don't forget to replace that quart of oil lost during the test.

Regarding auxiliary oil coolers, only one single cooler should be used because two in line will create flow restriction. The original cooler integral in the radiator should be retained in the system.

One other note: When checking transmission oil level, it should be at 150 degrees or higher (too hot to touch) or you must compensate for expansion of the oil. When the oil is cool, it should be slightly below the add mark or expansion will push it over the full mark when up to temperature.

If you'd like to install a temperature gauge for a closer check on transmission oil, it's important to do it right. Many gauge makers indicate that the temperature sensor can be mounted in one of the lines leading to or from the cooler, by using a tee fitting. That's true, but the readings provided by the sensor in that position do not properly relate the recommended temperature ranges. The sensor should be in the pan.

The proper method for installation is to remove the pan. Locate an area in which the sensor will not encounter clearance problems inside or outside the pan and drill the proper size hole. Silver-solder the threaded fitting in the pan. Do not braze the fitting as the heat required to do this may cause surface cracks that can spread, causing leaks.

A good operating range for trans oil (reading in the pan) is 180 to 220 de-

grees. Temperature should not exceed 250 degrees even under the most severe conditions.

AMC Performance

My Jeep Wagoneer seems to have lost power since it was new. I have only 30,000 miles on the odometer. Tuning has been checked by two competent garages and they say everything meets specifications. I can appreciate how performance can be improved by carburetor and distributor re-tuning such as you have described previously, but I can't see why the engine would be worse now than when new, with only a modest amount of driving.

R. W. Silizonoff
San Diego, California

The AMC 304, 360 and 401 engines have had a problem with premature timing chain wear, occurring by about 20,000 miles; it affects low-speed performance. One solution is to install the roller double-row Cloyes timing chain and gear kit, which is expensive. AMC has these parts available under these part numbers:

Chain: 3234433
Cam Sprocket: 3234234
Crankshaft Sprocket: 3234235

The new timing chain has different deflection characteristics and will increase durability. All three items must be installed at the same time.

Engine Damage

We have a 1977 Ford LTD with a 400 cid engine and a Class III towing package, which is used to pull our 25-foot trailer. On a trip to Colorado in September we experienced an engine failure that required replacing the engine. The engine dropped No. 5 exhaust valve, which cracked the block in No. 2 cylinder, damaged No. 5 and No. 2 pistons and put a hole in the left-hand head above No. 5 cylinder. The car was 13½ months old with 17,000 miles. We have the following questions:

1. Do you know similar problems?

2. Is there a history of engine overheating problems with the Ford 400 cid engine? At Monarch Pass the car failed to move the trailer at approximately 10,000 feet altitude (engine stalled). The engine hot light did not come on until after the engine stalled. After a Ford garage changed the initial timing to 13½ degrees BTDC, the car developed adequate power, although we had to stop one time going over Monarch Pass because the hot light came on. We did not overheat returning across the Continental Divide with the rebuilt engine. The engine failure occurred two days after crossing Monarch Pass.

3. Both the original and replacement engines have excessive gas ping at low throttle. Can anything be done to correct this condition?

Max E. Siegrist
Los Angeles, California

The Ford 400 doesn't have a history of problems such as yours. But problems do occur with that engine and any other that is allowed to ping (preignition) when towing a trailer. Your engine failure was caused by preignition (ping).

The same thing may happen to your second engine if you don't solve the preignition problem. Unfortunately, many engines won't run on the grades of lead-free fuel available today, even at the factory-recommended initial spark advance settings.

Best solution to the problem is use of a good water injector.

Oil Consumption

I have a Ford F-250 with a 460 engine that uses oil excessively. I have had several people look at it and have had several answers. Is there any method to determine where the oil goes? It disappears at a rate of one quart per 300 miles but I can't see any smoke at the tail pipe, and I have no serious leaks.

Cliff Roberts
Sacramento, California

There are several ways of checking for oil loss. The simplest method is to have someone drive the vehicle while you follow closely in another vehicle. Find a hill that will require sustained power application for the climb. While the vehicle is climbing, if there is exhaust smoke that increases or remains constant, leakage is past the rings. If it reduces as you proceed up the hill, this points to intake valve oil seals. Decelerate down the hill. After reaching the

bottom, resume power and watch for excessive smoke. This verifies the oil leakage past valve guide seals.

Often it's difficult to see this smoke accurately through a rearview mirror, especially if you have dual exhausts and can watch only one side. But by driving behind your vehicle, you can watch both sides closely.

Changing Oil

There is so much contradictory information regarding changing engine oil that I would appreciate some straight information, including your feelings for or against the friction-reducing oils and additives.

George Kendall
Sacramento, California

This all started with auto manufacturers trying to promote low maintenance by advertising 6000-mile oil change intervals and it has progressed into the 25,000-mile claims of some oil companies.

However, in many of the advertisements, the small print recommends this only if the vehicle is driven within a certain time period. If the vehicle is used in town a lot where oil temperatures frequently are not allowed to reach at least 180 degrees, the oil should regularly be changed every 2000 miles. Regardless of who makes the oil or whether it costs $10 a quart, it will become contaminated under this type of use. The contamination is from unburned fuel and from condensation in the crankcase. When the oil does not become hot enough to vaporize the contaminants, they become concentrated in the oil and it loses some of its lubricating properties. Also, acids form and they go to work on bearings.

Higher operational temperatures (such as in sustained cruising on a long trip) do not produce nearly as much of this type of contamination, so 6000-mile oil change intervals can be allowed, assuming the engine does not run excessively high oil temperatures that would tend to cause a higher-than-normal oxidation rate of the oil.

The new friction-reducing oils theoretically should produce some subtle advantages in efficiency and mileage, but the evidence is not usually sufficient to support the cost difference.

Exhaust Efficiency

I have a 1978 Chevrolet Suburban with a Quadrajet carburetor. I'm seriously considering the tuning kit and Vari-Flow water injector, but before I make any changes I would like some questions answered.

I tow a heavy trailer and believe that if the exhaust catalytic convertor fell off and dual exhausts appeared, it would help; the 1973 Suburban I previously owned had duals and was a lot better in performance. A friend of mine installed a Holley Economaster carburetor on his 454 and increased mileage. What is your opinion of that change?

Robert McWhirter
El Paso, Texas

Dual exhausts are a definite advantage on the 454. The catalytic convertor is a hindrance on any tow vehicle, but removal is illegal. If it should fall off, be sure to pick it up so it can be reinstalled, at least when the vehicle is sold, as it cannot be reregistered without it. Also, convertors are expensive.

The Holley Economaster is not a good choice on a vehicle that is used to tow or haul quite a bit of weight. Holley doesn't even recommend that carburetor for that kind of use. The primary power system generally does not enrich the fuel mixtures until the manifold vacuum drops to 2 to 4 inches. In an RV, the enrichment for part-throttle operation should take place no later than 6 inches manifold vacuum. If the vehicle is used in sustained load (such as pulling in hills) without proper enrichment, extreme combustion chamber temperatures could result, damaging the engine and shortening life expectancy. This does not compensate for the small fuel savings the carburetor might provide by delaying the enrichment function. Keep your Quadrajet and correct the air/fuel ratios.

Mileage Improvers

I have recently read several articles and ads for various methods of improving mileage through addition of accessories. One dealt with preheating the gasoline and another with changing its chemical structure. I don't claim to be an engineer, but some of the claims don't seem to hold water. What is your opinion about some of the mileage improvers advertised these days?

D. E. Cartwright
Salt Lake City, Utah

The first thing to remember is that two and two still equal four, and you can't fool Mother Nature. Once you realize there is no magic involved, the rest becomes simple.

Application of logical theory, physics and testing produce specific results— good or bad.

The fuel preheating theory is one of the more popular approaches at present, although it is hardly new. Spacers heated by engine coolant were standard under Ford carburetors for years. Heating intake manifolds through exhaust circulation is standard. Thermostats in the cooling systems to accelerate engine warm-up are all based on the accepted fact that a cold liquid will not vaporize as well as a warm one. It would seem logical that preheating the fuel before it enters the carburetor would result in greater vaporization, resulting in improved mixing with air and increased efficiency. However, several factors complicate the picture in application.

During winter months, especially in colder climates, the preheating results in greater efficiency, especially at idle and lower engine speeds when velocity of fuel through the carburetor is low and mixing of fuel and air is not ideal. As outside air temperature increases, the picture changes. When the temperature of fuel reaches 120 degrees F, an increase in reed pressure or expansion of the gasoline takes place, increasing the supply line pressure. This introduces the tendency for vapor lock and percolation of the fuel in the fuel bowl; this often forces fuel through the main discharge nozzles, enriching fuel mixtures and resulting in stalling and hard starting due to flooding after engine-shutdown.

Some of the preheat units also claim to ionize or reverse the oxidation of gasoline, increasing its stability. Gasoline, when stored, continually oxidizes, gradually losing its stability. Anyone who claims the ability to reverse this process should also be able to turn lead into gold.

In cold climates, consider obtaining a heavy-wall aluminum tube about 12 to 16 inches long. Install fittings in each end to accept the fuel line. Secure the tube between the valve cover and the intake manifold. Attach the fuel pump supply line to one end and extend a line to the carburetor from the other. (Make sure the tube is clean and free of metal shavings.) Neoprene fuel line can be used to make the connections, but make certain the lines are free of sharp edges and make sure the neoprene is clear of areas that could burn it. As summer approaches, return the fuel line to its original status.

Control of engine operational temperature during cold weather also can increase efficiency. If you don't consider it too much trouble, use a 195-degree thermostat in winter and a 180 in summer.

Universal Joints

Universal joints have been giving me a problem with the 1972 Chevy half-ton that I use for everyday transportation plus towing my 22-foot trailer. The truck has 96,000 miles and does a good job, especially after installing the Geraghty tuneup kit.

The problem: Earlier when I would pull the driveshaft down to lube the universal joints, because they didn't have external grease fittings, I usually would find one joint which was marginal. Then I installed joints that had grease fittings. They seem to wear more than the standard joints. What would you suggest?

A. J. Richardson
Los Angeles, California

The replacement universal joints with grease fittings are best. However, care must be taken to use only a hand-operated lube gun, as pressure lube guns will blow out the seals and cut the life of the joints.

Also, check driveshaft angle at the transmission and differential. The relative angles should be about the same. Spring shims are available to correct the differential angle if necessary. This will create longer universal joint life.

Radio Interference

I have a radio interference problem with a 1978 Chrysler 440 engine. The interference started after the last tuneup. All connectors have been checked. The distributor cap and rotor appear to be OK. Spark plugs and wires are new and the wires are resistance-type. An extra engine ground connection has been installed. Everyone has exhausted their ideas but the noise remains and is directly related to engine rpm. Have you encountered this problem?

Dean Mansfield
San Diego, California

This problem often occurs when additional radio equipment has been installed. The best approach is to be sure the items you have checked are not at fault, despite your inspection. A silicone electrical connection lubricant is available under several brand names at dealers or electrical shops. Echlin is one of the more popular. Put a very light coat only on the distributor cap connectors and a heavy coat on the tip of the rotor. This will ensure adequate contact and also eliminate the ionization of the wider gap between the rotor tip and the contacts inside the cap. This should eliminate the problem.

Auxiliary Fuel Tank Problem

I have added two fuel tanks to my Chevrolet pickup truck for better fuel capacity while towing my trailer.

This modification has presented several problems. The engine is equipped with a fuel return system on the fuel pump. When operating on one of the auxiliary fuel tanks, fuel is returned to the main tank through the fuel return system, causing the main tank to overflow into the tank venting system. I corrected this by blocking the fuel return line. My local dealer installed the tanks legally, hooking them to the closed venting system. During operation on auxiliary tanks, flooding of the venting cannister takes place and the dealer cannot correct this. He has suggested I individually vent each tank.

Steve Wilson
Houston, Texas

The fuel return line is intended to help prevent vapor lock by keeping the fuel moving through the supply line, reducing the fuel temperature. You might return it to operation. You might install a tee fitting in the engine fuel pump supply line and attach the return line to this tee. It will maintain circulation of fuel in the forward section of the vehicle without affecting the auxiliary tanks.

Gasohol

My Winnebago motorhome is powered by a Dodge 440 engine and I have periodically been using gasohol. Recently, during a meeting of our RV club, a speaker representing an oil company said gasohol would cause the engine to run leaner and hotter and is not desirable. What is your attitude toward use of gasohol in RVs?

William Sperry
Buffalo, New York

Due to the composition of gasohol, an engine running on it will operate somewhat leaner than with gasoline. Engine operational temperature should not be

affected and the gasohol will not reduce engine life.

I recommend use of gasohol at least one tank each six months, or the addition of about 5 percent alcohol per volume, to remove condensation from the fuel system. You might continue your use of the fuel as it has many advantages over straight gasoline and no undesirable effects serious enough to be of concern.

Oil Choice

I recently bought a 1980 truck with low mileage and plan to tow my trailer with it. I ran my last truck for 75,000 miles without any problems, so you can see I like to maintain vehicles properly.

I have been talking to several people about oil for late model engines. Some say use 10-40, others say straight 30 weight. My neighbor suggests non-detergent and the dealer says detergent. I would appreciate your recommendations. I live where it gets cold in winter and would like to know more about oil ratings.

Robert McIntyre
Salt Lake City, Utah

You should use detergent oil, unless you're breaking in an engine after an overhaul. In that situation, use of nondetergent oil for the first thousand miles will aid in break-in and seating of piston rings. If an engine has been operated for many thousands of miles on nondetergent oil, a change to detergent oil must be closely monitored because the detergent oil will clean the sludge accumulation and require frequent changes of filter and oil to prevent clogging of the lubrication system. I suspect that very few engines are operated on nondetergent oil any more, and the chance that you have one is very small.

Detergent oil is prerequisite for hydraulic valve lifters and the micro-finished bearing surfaces.

Motor oil viscosity is measured hot and cold. Cold is established at zero degrees F, hot at 210 degrees F. Oils tested at zero are assigned the letter W. An oil described as 10W-30 for example has a viscosity of 10 at zero degrees F and 30 at 210 degrees F. The Society of Automotive Engineers (SAE) viscosity ratings include 5W, 10W, 20W, 20, 30, 40 and 50. These ratings can be combined in a single oil that is identified as 10W-30, 10W-40 or 20W-50. These are multigrade oils.

The single most important criteria is oil with the highest API rating. Until 1981 it was the SE rating, which was replaced by SF.

Oil Consumption

A few months ago I installed a water injector in my 1968 Dodge pickup with a 318-cid engine. I am quite pleased with the performance of the pickup pulling my 18-foot trailer.

There is an unexpected added benefit I thought you might like to know about. After driving 2000 miles, I had used only a pint of oil! Normally I would have used three to five quarts under the same conditions (mountains and head winds).

At first I was a little concerned that water was getting into the oil, but actually at 1000 miles, the oil was cleaner than it had been at 100 miles.

There has to be an explanation for this phenomenon. Could it be that a cooler, cleaner engine would use that much less oil?

Stanley A. Jones
Salem, Oregon

There is a valid explanation and it has to do with something you apparently didn't know was going on in your engine. Engine ping always occurs at inaudible levels before you can hear it over engine and road noise. You apparently had inaudible ping and this may explain the reduction in oil consumption.

Engine ping is out-of-control combustion that creates a great deal of shock during the compression stroke of the piston. This shock can actually rattle the valves in the guides, destroying their ability to seal out oil. Also, it can reduce the oil-sealing ability of the piston rings. When ping is eliminated through use of a water injector or by any other means, oil consumption may be reduced if it is abnormally high solely due to the ping problem. Of course, an engine may use oil for several reasons that have nothing to do with ping. Elimination of ping in those cases will not reduce oil consumption. However, elimination of ping always is of benefit to the engine because ping can cause severe damage. Mild cases merely burn the valves; severe cases can break piston rings and even burn holes in the tops of pistons.

Cruise Control Benefits

I have been thinking of adding cruise control to my motorhome but wonder if it will affect gas mileage one way or the other.

Ben Mitchell
Memphis, Tennessee

Cruise control definitely is an asset in a RV since it relieves driver tedium and maintains a prescribed speed. It certainly makes driving more enjoyable. In flat, noncongested highway travel it does an excellent job. On hills, it does not compensate for road conditions like the driver can. It does not plan for an upcoming hill or take advantage of a downgrade. Application of throttle may be erratic and improper.

In other words, better fuel economy can be had in mountainous terrain if the driver controls the throttle, especially if a manifold vacuum gauge is used. Stay above 6½ inches on the gauge when possible, as this is where most carburetors enrich the fuel mixture.

All cruise control units should be checked periodically for internal vacuum leaks. If the vehicle sustains a 13-inch reading on a vacuum gauge during cruising on level roads at 55 mph, and vacuum drops when the cruise control is engaged while still maintaining 55 mph, this indicates an internal vacuum leak. If you have even a minor vacuum loss it will bring the fuel-enrichment system in earlier and affect fuel economy. Loss of power at high altitude may also occur.

Brake Improver

I have a 1972 motorhome that has been very enjoyable except for one thing. During travel on prolonged downgrades in the West, we encounter brake fade even when using lower gears. We have installed the factory modification to the brake booster and are using the highest grade brake linings available, which has helped. But the problem still exists.

We have found it necessary in many cases to pull off the road and allow the brakes to cool. The brake pedal actually becomes spongy during this situation, as though air was in the system. I know this has been checked thoroughly. In discussion with owners of motorhomes of other makes, I have found that this problem exists in varying degrees throughout the industry. I would appreciate your suggestions.

Donald Abramson
Flagstaff, Arizona

Many motorhomers have encountered brake fade in varying degrees, dependent on brake-system design, type of driving and vehicle weight. It can be a hair-raising experience. You were wise to stop as you did.

Considerable energy is required to accelerate and maintain speed with a motorhome and this energy is heat. Heat must be absorbed through braking to slow the vehicle. This process is referred to as transforming kinetic motion into heat. This transfer of energy not only can overcome the braking surface area but has an adverse effect on brake fluid.

Various brake fluids are available with different ratings and boiling points. Disc brakes require a special brake fluid with a higher boiling point than do drum brakes, because disc brake systems apply more heat to the brake cylinder containing the fluid.

As boiling point of conventional brake fluid was raised, it became increasingly susceptible to contamination by water through hygroscopicity, which means the fluid absorbs water through the rubber components of the brake system and through condensation in the master cylinder. As operational temperatures increase, the water is transformed into vapor and becomes compressible, which produces a spongy brake pedal. Not only should brake systems be checked periodically for seepage of fluid and surface wear, but also the fluid should be thoroughly flushed by pressure bleeding about every two to three years of normal use. The highest grades of fluid should be used.

Recently, synthetic brake fluids with higher boiling points were introduced. They have a much higher resistance to water contamination. One such fluid contains silicone, which not only has the above qualities but also retains its stability over a greater time span. The fluid reduces hydraulic system corrosion. It was developed by Dow Corning and is compatible with conventional fluids, so it's not critical to get the brake system perfectly clean of conventional fluid before using the new fluid. The product is available through Cartel Products, 3133 Madison SE, Grand Rapids, Michigan 49508. It's helpful in any motorhome brake system.

Vehicle Storage

I have a 1976 Ford LTD station wagon with only 13,000 miles on it, about half of them pulling my 27-foot Holiday Rambler (1976). This car is completely equipped with factory-installed Trailer Package, 460 4-barrel, air shocks, extended-range fuel tank and everything needed to pull beautifully. And it does.

My problem is that it is not a practical car for going to the grocery store about a mile and a half away, and I don't believe it is good to use this type of car for short hauls.

I doubt if the future will allow such cars to be produced, so I want to store it and save it for pulling only. That way I won't have to buy a truck or van in the future.

What I want to know is a proper procedure for storing. I need such questions answered as: Do I disconnect the battery? Do I fill the gas tank to the top? Do I reconnect and run it every few months?

T.M. Broadston
La Habra, California

Several maintenance operations will ensure protection during storage.

Engine oil should be replaced, unless it is less than 30 days old, and the filter. This prevents the possibility of acid etching the bearings. When oil remains in an engine for long periods of time, contamination from water creates certain kinds of acids that attack metal.

Engine coolant should be checked for proper concentration, and should be replaced if it's more than 18 months old. If a coolant change is needed, the cool-

ing system should be flushed with fresh water before the new coolant is added, in a 50/50 percent solution with water.

All water supply systems should be drained and purged, and a nontoxic RV antifreeze should be used.

The engine should receive upper cylinder lubrication before finally shutting down. There are several makes, such as Marvel Mystery oil, on the market. The first step is to be sure that the engine is at normal operating temperature. Remove every other spark plug wire in the firing order—or the two inside (center) wires on one side and the two outside wires (on each end) on the other (V-8 engine). Ground the spark plug wires by placing them against an engine metal part. Start the engine, and at a fast idle, pour the upper cylinder lubricant into the side of the carburetor (primary venturi) which has less effect on idle speed. Replace the wires. Re-start the engine and let it run until smooth, then remove the remaining four wires and repeat. With this method, the oil enters the cylinders while those plugs are not firing and it coats the cylinder walls, valve stems, and piston rings better than is the case when the plugs are firing.

The tires should be brought to maximum factory recommended pressure (as stamped on the side of the tire), to help protect the sidewall and carcass. Tires as well as rubber door moldings and seals should receive a light coat of a product such as Armorall.

Batteries should be disconnected, checked for electrolyte level and periodically placed on a trickle charger to maintain their state of charge. Never cover the battery; that could prevent it from venting.

The confusion on fuel tanks stems from a procedure used with aircraft. Filling the tanks in storage prevents condensation from developing and contaminating the fuel. Fuel tanks on RVs and automobiles have expansion areas and it's usually not possible to fill them totally. Therefore, condensation still occurs. Gasoline also has a deterioration problem in storage and becomes unstable after a long period, but it's usually not a problem during one winter. Deterioration is more rapid in hot weather than in cold.

Don't fill gasoline tanks. Instead, add about 5 percent alcohol to the fuel while the unit is still being driven on trips. This will remove any water that might be present because alcohol absorbs water. The same procedure should be used upon refilling the tanks when the vehicle is taken out of storage. Any water that has collected will be absorbed by the alcohol and carried through for combustion; it might form pockets without the alcohol. Either methyl or ethyl alcohol can be used.

Place the vehicle on jack stands to prevent premature failure of tire sidewalls. They are more prone to develop checking, or hairline cracks, when under load and highly inflated. If not under load, inflation can be reduced. Tires should also be protected from sunlight. Placing the vehicle on jack stands may not be practical in some cases, but it's a good move when possible.

It is a good practice before restarting the engine in the spring to slowly tap the starter until about a dozen revolutions have occurred. This allows the engine's valve mechanism to function and oil to flow to the bearings. I am not a believer in starting the engine once a week or once a month during storage. If it is properly prepared for storage and if batteries are kept charged, this isn't necessary.

Air-Conditioner Compressors

The 1978 440 Dodge engine in my motorhome has 42,000 miles and I have replaced two air-conditioner compressors and am ready for number three when the weather warms up enough to prompt me to get it done. They start getting noisy. I have carefully checked alignment and everything seems OK.

John Byrnes
Pomona, California

Chrysler Corporation air-conditioner compressors are generally noisy and will continue to operate that way. Don't be concerned about the noise, but be sure belt tension is not excessive. This is harder on compressors than anything else.

Ford products suffer from idler pulley failures when belts are overtightened. Such conditions can reduce their life by as much as 70 percent.

General Motors sometimes requires additional bracing of the compressor on the engine to remove harmonic vibrations set up by the compressor moving. This problem exists also on most aftermarket installations and can be solved by bracing. In other words, most compressor failures are caused by excessive belt tension.

Brakes

My 1974 International truck has served very well to tow my trailer, with very little maintenance. It could stand more power but at the present time I have a problem with my brakes. I have a pulsating brake pedal. I have had all the lining checked and the drums turned. And again there is the same problem. My mechanic thinks it is in the power brake unit but this is hard to believe.

Bob Hinsler
Cedar Rapids, Iowa

The most common cause of your complaint would be out-of-round drums or lateral runout of disc brake rotors. But eliminating the possibility of these causes, as you have, would point to a bent rear axle shaft.

Air-conditioner Hoses

My problem is the continual necessity of replacing air-conditioner hoses on my 1976 Chevy three-quarter-ton truck. Not only are they expensive but also they always time their demise to coincide with the hottest, loneliest part of the country. Are there better hoses?

Jay McAllister
Rialto, California

Most GM vehicles have what is called an Inland-type AC hose coupling. These can be easily repaired, rather than replaced. Most failures are where the hose meets the fittings, due to vibration and deflection.

If the original hose is not in a bind and has an easy curvature, the end can be cut with a sharp knife, keeping it square. Buy a replacement fitting, lubricate it with refrigeration oil and force-feed it into the hose with a rotation motion. Position clamps, tighten to 40 inch-pounds, secure hoses with nylon tie straps to minimize movement and to add support and your troubles should be over. If the standard hose is not long enough to prevent crimping, long lengths are available.

Heat Riser Role

I recently installed a 4-barrel carburetor and manifold on my 1972 390 Ford engine. A friend who is an avid automotive enthusiast and has owned several modified cars suggested I should have blocked off the heat riser passages before installing the manifold. I have read several articles on modifications by Geraghty and this has never been suggested. I would appreciate your comments.

Robert Howard
Tucson, Arizona

If you were building a race car and high-rpm power was your goal, your friend's suggestion would be valid. Keeping the intake manifold cool reduces expansion of the incoming fuel/air charge and increases volumetric ef-

ficiency. In other words, a greater amount of fuel and air can enter the cylinders during each intake cycle, resulting in increased power.

Unfortunately, this requires a richer mixture, reducing mileage and necessitating a longer warm-up period, with decreased engine life. The aluminum intake manifold offsets absence of the heat crossover because of its more uniform heat distribution. But don't block the passages of a stock manifold in situations where low-speed torque is important in recreational vehicles.

Rich Choke

I am using a Holley replacement carburetor and twice it has broken the fast idle cam that controls idle speed while the choke is on. Without the fast idle cam, the engine has a tendency to load up with rich mixture and die if I don't keep on the throttle. My local parts store wants to sell me the complete choke assembly, which is rather expensive. I only need the small fast idle cam. Must I buy the whole assembly just to get this small part?

Leo Blackburn
Atlanta, Georgia

Holley replacement carburetors have a tendency to do this. The usual opinion is that the fast idle cam was damaged during installation or shipment, whereas in fact, the cam may break when a violent backfire occurs. Backfire is caused by using too much throttle with a cold engine; it is not good for *other parts of the carburetor, such as the power valve, either. Without the fast idle cam the engine runs rich to the point where it may foul spark plugs. The part number for the fast idle cam is 41R-498A-AT.*

International Manifold Swap

I have an International/Traveler with 345 V-8 engine which needs help. I know a special 4-barrel carburetor is recommended for this engine, and a distributor tuning kit, but how do I obtain an intake manifold for this? I ordered one from International, but it will not accept the Holley carburetor.

Stephen Johnston
Rupert, Idaho

The manifold you ordered from IH apparently was incorrect. The part number you need is 151539R31. It is an earlier manifold and will provide the proper bolt pattern for the Holley.

Generator Starting

I retired last year and bought a 29-foot motorhome which has been a great experience for us. We have covered the entire western U.S. and plan to tackle Canada next year. Fortunately, problems have been few. I have followed your recommendations to the letter and am getting about 8½ mpg overall and use one quart of oil in 1500 miles. I am contemplating installing the intake manifold, possibly before our next trip, as the dual exhausts and tuning kit produced good results.

I have one problem which defies solution. I have a 6½-kw Onan generator which often is hard to start at altitudes above 5000 feet. Sometimes it totally refuses to start. It has been thoroughly checked, adjusted, new spark plugs installed and the problem persists.

William Murry
Portland, Oregon

Before attempting to start the unit, make sure all accessories are turned off because the initial load increases this problem. As in all internal combustion engines, altitude does affect fuel/air mixture. At altitude the mixture can be over-rich and the engine will not start immediately. Go to the generator compartment, open the choke and push the start button located on the engine. Hold the choke open for a short time until the engine is running well.

If you plan to stay at high altitudes for some time, adjust the choke to a leaner setting. Test that setting after you return to a lower altitude to see if it produces a starting problem. If it doesn't, leave it that way. If it does, return it to the original setting. Mark the factory-original setting before you make any adjustments.

Oil Changes

I have read several recommendations from oil companies, especially the manufacturers of synthetics, regarding extended oil changes. I have a 1973 Chevrolet Suburban with 454 engine that tows a 25-foot trailer about 25 percent of the time. I generally change oil every 3000 to 4000 miles. Should I make a change?

Max Edelmann
Grand Rapids, Michigan

During continual use such as during an extended trip when oil temperatures remain high, contamination is low and the oil can remain in the engine for up to about 6000 miles unless it is suspected that oil temperature is exceptionally high, which causes oxidation. During normal around-town use I would suggest 3000-mile oil and filter changes. Oil manufactureres who recommend extended change intervals beyond 6000 miles do so to justify the cost of their products.

Brake Lockup

The rear brakes on my 1976 Chevrolet wagon usually lock up in a panic stop. This increases the stopping distances and makes the situation dangerous. I have had the brakes checked professionally and they cannot seem to correct the problem. Two mechanics, one from Chevrolet, claim it is in the design. I have driven other station wagons and have not found this to be true. I have gone over the entire system and found no damaged steel lines. The system was bled under pressure. The rear shoes have been replaced. Still the problem persists.

Stanton Jackson
Atlanta, Georgia

The problem probably is in the proportioning valve. When line pressures to the rear wheels are more than 50 percent of total brake line pressure, this problem will exist. Have a new valve professionally installed and the system professionally bled. The valve can be tested with a high-pressure gauge. The exact proportion will vary from one valve to the next, depending on how it's designed, according to the brake system requirements of the particular vehicle.

Running On

I bought a new 1980 tow vehicle—a Ford with a 400 engine—and lately it has tended to run-on on diesel. Nothing the mechanics have done for it has helped. Sometimes it will diesel for 30 seconds or more, and clatter and sound like it's coming apart. They tell me nothing can be done about it. That's hard to believe.

R. W. Samuelson
Dallas, Texas

With reduction of gasoline octane, dieseling (the engine's tendency to continue running erratically after the engine is off) is prevalent.
Actually, the problem is not directly associated with reduction of octane, but that does exaggerate the condition. Dieseling, or running-on, is caused by retention of heat in the combustion chambers, due to either excessive carbon deposits or the presence of oil. At low engine speeds the turbulence in the

combustion chambers is reduced; therefore, cooling of the intake flow is drastically reduced, allowing the hot carbon deposits to ignite the fuel mixture. This happens in a varying number of cylinders, hence the very erratic behavior of the engine.

Reduction of idle speed and shutting the engine off while the transmission (automatic) is in gear will help. The cure is reduction of carbon deposits through use of an effective water injection system.

Starter Problems

My GM vehicle with 350 engine will not crank properly at certain times. I wonder if you have any advice.

Jack Mitchell
Sylmar, California

Although starter problems are among the most easily corrected automotive deficiencies, the starter is a very misunderstood piece of equipment. The number of starter problems seems to be on the rise; however, the starter often is blamed for deficiencies elsewhere in the system.

The most common cause of starter problems is relative to the supply of electrical current. The battery should be checked thoroughly to be sure its capacity is adequate. All RVs should be equipped with at least 80-amp-hour batteries. All cable connections should be cleaned and sanded—not only the battery terminals but also the cable ends. Use baking soda and water to clean; afterward apply a light grease.

If the battery is more than 10 feet from the starter, the largest cables should be used to reduce the resistance. Using the chassis frame as a ground connection is OK if connections to the frame are free of paint and are cleaned as indicated above. The same size cable must be used for positive as well as negative connections if a cable is used for the negative rather than the frame. If the frame is used, proper cable size is necessary from the battery to the frame and from the frame to the starter. These connections will adequately tie the chassis, engine and battery into a solid common ground connection. That will eliminate excessive resistance during peak amperage draw periods, and will ensure good life for components such as the starter and starter solenoid.

After making sure connections are proper, the starter should be checked for amperage draw. Specifications for this test vary considerably; 250 amps or less are acceptable. Draw of 280 amps is marginal. Anything exceeding 290 amps requires replacement of the starter.

If the starter draw is excessive before replacement, there are some additional checks which should be made, especially if the problem occurs mainly when the engine is hot.

Check initial spark timing. If it appears to be advanced excessively, rather than retarding the timing you should remove the distributor cap and apply light pressure against the rotor to determine if the automatic advance mechanism is returning to the rest position. In other words, lightly turn the rotor counterclockwise, which will bring it to the "rest" position if it is sticking in an advanced position. This is a common problem, especially with GM engines and with some Fords. It forces the engine to crank against too much intial spark advance; when combustion occurs, it is prone to kick the pistons back the other way. If this problem exists, remove the distributor, disassemble it and clean the advance mechanism and inner shafts. Use crocus cloth on the inner shafts and lubricate with a light oil such as WD-40.

Another indication of starter deficiency caused by combustion problems is the tendency of an engine to run on or "diesel," after the key is turned off. This is caused by excessive carbon in the combustion chambers. The carbon retains heat and ignites the fuel/air mixture early in the compression stroke, which attempts to reverse rotation of the engine. This is even more prevalent when restarting a hot engine, as there has been considerable heat soak time (heat saturation) of the chambers. During starting, turbulence in the combustion chambers is very low and does not produce adequate cooling. Therefore, the preignition, in effect, prevents the starter from rotating the engine. Cooling the combustion chambers and removing the carbon is a good move, accomplished through use of an effective water injection system.

Excessive operational temperatures, especially in RVs, can result also in a heat soak problem relative to the starter assembly, increasing resistance. GM has made available a remote solenoid kit to overcome this problem. Custom heat shields are sometimes required. In this case, the starter solenoid gets hot and the solenoid movement is somewhat restricted by expansion of the solenoid and increased friction. The wiring which triggers the solenoid is routed through the ignition system and voltage drop occurs. Consequently, when the engine is hot, the operator may turn the key but there will be no sound— nothing happening. The starter is not bad; there is inadequate voltage to move the solenoid and spin the starter.

When the starter is at fault, we would suggest use of a factory-original rebuilt starter assembly. It should be checked for amperage draw immediately after installation. Many of the aftermarket starter rebuilding shops use armatures which have been reduced in diameter so starter effectiveness is marginal.

Power Valve Problem

I have a Holley carburetor. About every month the power enrichment valve ruptures and causes my mileage to drop terribly. It smokes at idle and becomes hard to start when hot. My mechanic has replaced the valve so many times it is a joke. He has put in 10.5, 8.5 and 6.5 valves, which don't help. He says a dual stage power valve is available. What should I do?

Jason Burrows
New Orleans, Louisiana

The power valve problem is associated with Holley carburetors but it only ruptures when there is extensive violent backfiring through the carburetor. The power valve is designed to enrich fuel mixtures during the medium-to-heavy throttle operation. The numbers 10.5. 8.5 and 6.5 are designated measurements of manifold vacuum. At these points on a vacuum gauge the power valve becomes operational.

The valve, when operational, enriches fuel mixtures about 27 percent. Selection of the proper valve is very important, expecially to an RV owner, and is directly related to mileage and performance. The dual stage power valve should only be used when ideal fuel ratios are produced in all ranges of operation and this can only be accomplished with extensive testing of the carburetor and calibration for the engine on which it's used.

The problem you have is created through violent backfiring during warm-up or from an internal carburetor vacuum leak. Often, the metering block attached to the carburetor body will become warped. This can be checked with a straight-edge. A vacuum leak occurs at this point and the power valve will operate prematurely, producing the same problem as a ruptured unit. Often the use of double gaskets between the metering block and the body will solve this problem.

Install the 6.5 power valve and double gaskets. Tighten the four retaining bolts to hold the float bowl and metering block evenly and securely. Retighten after a couple of days. Adjust the choke so the engine does not backfire following a cold start. The only other reason it would backfire under power (open throttle) is improper jetting.

Transmission Overhaul

At what mileage should I overhaul my automatic transmission? The answers I have received from transmission shops have varied from "now" to "anything over 50,000 miles is borrowed time." We have 74,000 miles on ours and worry every time we leave town.

Dale Robinson
Lake Tahoe, Nevada

An automatic transmission, properly maintained, has no limit on its ability to function. Proper operational temperatures and regular maintenance can extend life indefinitely.

Braking Problems

I have a Ford three-quarter-ton with front drum brakes and cannot keep brakes on this vehicle. I qualify as a cautious driver with no panic stops. I keep burning the brakes. The local shop says hard spots get in the brake drums and the lining becomes glazed. They suggest metallic linings or a disc brake conversion. My original brakes lasted 40,000 miles under the same conditions but now I can't get anything to last. What would you suggest?

Bruce McDonald
Seattle, Washington

Unfortunately, your letter has left several questions unanswered, such as gross weight and whether you travel mostly flat or mountainous terrain. However, we'll try to cover most of the possibilities.

If you are easy on brakes, as you say, the general problem is associated with the preparation of your brakes when new linings are installed. It is most important to properly arc grind the brake shoes to fit each drum. In doing this the toe and heel of the shoe will have additional clearance of about .005-inch, ensuring full contact of the shoe and preventing the problem with hot spots, which you describe. If this is not done, only the heel and toe will be applied under light use. That will generate sufficient heat to create brake fade and glazing in those areas.

If full contact is shown on the shoe and if your gross weight is above about 8500 pounds or so, or if you live in hilly country which requires continual braking, a metallic-type lining will prevent brake fade. However, this lining is not suggested for light use as the efficiency is not comparable to normal linings under that kind of use.

Proper installation and break-in of the metallic linings is critical.

Changing to disc brakes is expensive and has some drawbacks—such as increased drag and control of braking proportion between front and rear.

Pull a wheel and look at the lining. Inspect the surface for total contact and it will be obvious what parts are in contact. If there is any doubt, sand the lining with coarse emery cloth. Take some carbon paper and rub the shoes until a blue tint is on the surface. Replace the brake drum and drive a couple of miles with several normal brake applications. Reinspect the surface. The blue tint of the carbon paper will tell you if the entire shoe does not contact the

drum. If it doesn't, find a new brake shop and ask them to do it right.

Oil Coolers

My trailer is heavy and I have been thinking of installing an engine oil cooler, in addition to a trans oil cooler, on my truck with the Chevy 454 engine. Are these recommended?

John McDonald
Richmond, Virginia

Installation of an oil cooler to control engine oil temperature is only necessary in unusual cases. Often more harm is done than good. Temperatures of 180 to 220 degrees F. are ideal; 260 is roughly the maximum and should not be a continuous operating temperature. Often when the cooler is installed, the minimum temperature is not attained and the oil does not reach adequate temperature vaporization for separation of moisture and fuel byproducts from the oil. This allows the accumulation of sludge and fuel byproducts which attack bearings and shorten engine life. If you believe that a cooler might be needed, install a 180-degree engine water thermostat and install an engine oil temperature gauge. Check the actual oil temperature.

To determine whether there is a need for a trans/cooler, the water thermostat should be a 180-degree one and a temperature gauge should be installed, with the sensor in the transmission pan; 190 to 220 F can be considered normal operating temperature, with 250 degrees F the maximum for short periods such as in climbing mountain grades. If that temperature, or higher, is sustained for a prolonged time, the transmission oil should be changed.

Winter Shifts

The C-6 transmission in my Ford pickup truck doesn't want to shift during really cold weather. Or if it does shift, it is erratic. The transmission has been checked by a local transmission rebuilder but there is no change.

Leon Dunaway
Miami, Florida

This occurs with several transmissions and is not particularly a Ford problem. It's generally associated with presence of water in the vacuum modulator assembly. Replace the assembly and check all vacuum lines for tight fit.

Wrong Transmission Oil?

A matter which has been puzzling me concerns the type of transmission fluid which should be used in automatic transmissions.

Ford transmissions specify the use of type A fluid whereas Chrysler and GM transmissions specify Dextron II.

Service stations say it is very important that the correct fluid be used. Transmission shops say that type A must be used in Ford transmissions but that either type may be used in Chrysler and GM. Their explanation is that Ford transmissions run hotter and therefore require the heavier type A90

grade. They say the Chrysler and GM transmissions run cooler and can use either 90 or 80 grade. They also say that use of 90 grade in Chrysler or GM transmissions might result in blown seals, but that they have never heard of this occurring.

John Wesley
Kissimmee, Florida

No problems have been reported with the interchange of these transmission oils. The Ford A fluid will withstand greater temperatures and can be used in all transmissions when heavy service is encountered. The viscosity difference is actually very small and the chance of blowing a seal due to higher pressure when cold is very slight.

IH Fix

My International truck has been virtually trouble-free. However, it needs a lot of help in the power department. There doesn't seem to be any equipment available for increased performance. I installed dual exhausts, which did help, and had a dyno-tuneup locally, which unfortunately did very little other than increase my fuel bills.

Gene Anderson
Boston, Massachusetts

You forgot to mention the size of your engine, or the weight you're towing or hauling, but you probably have the 345 engine if power is substantially lacking. It's true that availability of special equipment for the IH engine is limited.

The dual exhaust system was a good move and works well in all Internationals. There is a lot to be accomplished through proper tuning; it is unfortunate that you have experienced less than satisfactory results. An increase in rear wheel horsepower in excess of 20 percent usually is possible without sacrificing mileage. A chassis dynamometer (dyno) is only a tool and not a magic wand. Unfortunately, most people do not realize this and blame the dyno, rather than the tuning changes made by its operator, for the poor results. Precision tuning involves not only precise control of fuel mixtures, timing, spark plug selection and engine temperature control; these functions must also be correct for the specific engine and the specific way it is used.

Loss of Power

About a year ago I noticed a definite loss of power with my 1975 International Travelall. I noticed the loss on a particular grade that I have been pulling since the truck was new. The power loss has become more noticeable and lately after the engine is warm there is no top-end power. Even the vacuum gauge at idle seems to read lower. I have had it tuned. The timing chain has been checked and both head gaskets were replaced, with very little change. I have been to two independent garages and one dealer. I would estimate my loss in power to be at least 20 percent.

Bob Mandequik
Tulsa, Oklahoma

Your problem undoubtedly is associated with an exhaust restriction. Check the heat riser. Be sure it's not frozen shut. Inspect the exhaust and tail pipes to see if they have been crushed. Then inspect the muffler. If a baffle has come loose, it will block the system and greatly reduce flow of exhaust. This problem can occur with many different engines. This explanation may sound too simple, after all that you've been through, but this may be your answer.

Dragging Brakes

I have a Dodge mini motorhome and the front brakes drag. I noticed this when the vehicle was jacked up off the ground for tire work. It was very hard for me to rotate the wheel by hand.

I am sure this reduces mileage. Is there any solution?

John C. Richardson
Memphis, Tennessee

Your problem is among several general complaints about disc brakes in certain vehicles. The drag problem seems more prevalent in Chrysler products.

An elastomeric multi-polymer compound called EMP is available at many parts houses and most large brake shops. It will attach the brake pad to the brake piston and reduce or eliminate the problem. It should be spread liberally on the backs of the outboard pads on both sides, being certain to cover the entire surface evenly. Apply one half-inch wide strip to the back of each inboard pad. Allow to set about 10 minutes and install while the material is tacky. This compound is designed to form a noise absorbing water-resistant, high-temperature membrane that dampens vibration noise and reduces drag.

When having disc brake work done, it's important that the rotors be trued. Do not remove any more material than necessary. Adjust wheel bearing preload and chamfer the edges of the brake pads.

Backfiring

I am having problems with my 1972 truck with 307 engine and would appreciate some help. Normally the truck runs fine. However, as soon as I put my 5400-pound 24-foot Shasta trailer on a hill and climb, the truck starts backfiring and I lose all power. But when I'm on flat road it is fine. I have replaced the plugs, points, condensor, rotor, distributor cap, spark plug wires, PCV valve, gas filter, air filter, coil, and coil wire and I have set the swell and timed it properly. By the way, the truck pulled the trailer fine during the spring and summer.

Wayne Moreau
Attleboro, Massachusetts

It sounds as though you have covered most of the bases. You might install a fuel pressure gauge in the main supply line near the carburetor and make sure you are not running out of fuel due to a weak fuel pump and/or restriction in the fuel line. A minimum of 4 pounds pressure should exist even under hill-climbing conditions to make sure the carburetor bowl is filled properly.

If you find the supply adequate, re-check the fuel filter in the carburetor inlet. Then try reducing the timing about 3 degrees if the problem still exists and you're certain the spark plugs are in good condition. The problem might be associated with a combustion chamber problem such as excessive carbon caused by oil consumption.

Radio Interference

I have engine noise in my FM radio and have taken this problem to several radio shops and my local Ford dealer. They installed new resistor-type spark plug wires and resistor plugs. The noise continues.

R. B. Johnson
Seattle, Washington

The answer quite often is found in the distributor rotor. Insufficient contact pressure between the rotor spring and the distributor carbon button will cause this noise if free height of the rotor spring is less than .280-inch. If it is less than that measurement, replace the rotor. Do not bend the spring to increase height.

Valve Noise

I have a 1970 Ford 390 engine with 2-barrel carburetor. It has always had valve noise that comes and goes at times. I have had the car at three different garages, all good. They did a valve job at 42,000 miles. No one can tell me why this is. It seems to make no difference whether the car is cold or warm, idling or pulling. I use 10-30 or 10-40 Quaker State oil and also STP. I change the oil and filter at about 2500 miles. Also I pull an 18-foot trailer and need to use half and half regular and premium gas to keep from pinging. I get about 13½ mpg with just the car and about 10 mpg pulling the trailer. I seldom hear noise above 40 mph.

Russell McCloney
Osceola, Iowa

If noise comes and goes, it is in most cases a marginal lifter—one which does not hold oil pressure as well as the others. Valve springs can also create a similar noise. To pinpoint which valve is causing the noise, remove the valve cover and push on each rocker arm with a wooden hammer handle until it changes the sound. Then, with the engine idling, push hard on the top of the noisy rocker arm until the lifter has collapsed (leaked down). Release it. You'll hear quite a bit of noise, but as the lifter pumps back up the noise should reduce or disappear. You have flushed the lifter. If you no longer hear the noise, fine, you're in. If it reappears in about 30 seconds or a minute, the lifter has leaked back down to its original status and probably will continue to be noisy. Dirty oil can cause this. Change oil more often and continue to use the STP. If all fails, the lifter will have to be replaced. Check the rocker arms and shaft for wear.

Late Cam

Recently I had a ring, valve and bearing job done on my 1968 Dodge 383 engine. A new timing chain was installed. Is there some way to check valve timing without removing the chain cover?

Howard Neff
Riverside, California

To check valve timing, bring the engine to top dead center (TDC) in the firing position for No. 1 cylinder. With the valve cover off on the No. 1 cylinder side, measure height of the intake and exhaust valve springs. Rotate the crankshaft one revolution until the timing marks indicate TDC 180 degrees out of firing position. Remeasure spring heights and compare with your original measurements. The same differential should exist between the two spring heights. If the intake spring height is less, the cam is advanced. If it is more, the cam is retarded.

Won't Open

I have installed a Holley carburetor on my Ford 390 engine. It seems to work OK in the primary side but I cannot get the secondary barrels to open, no matter how high I rev the engine. I suspect the carburetor is faulty but have no way of checking. Is there a way to check this?

I bought the equipment before reading the facts on converting the 390 to 4-barrel, so I may not have bought the right equipment. The carburetor is a 650 cfm model and the manifold is an aluminum high-rise type with separate chambers for the primary and secondary sides of the carburetor. I have not installed headers and have not done anything to the distributor. I just installed the equipment last weekend and so far do not seem to be getting the power out of this that I should.

E. T. Jackson
Miami, Florida

Unfortunately, you have made several poor choices. The carb you chose is not ideal for your engine, and the manifold is not any more efficient than a stock cast iron 4-barrel manifold. The number of equipment choices available to the RV owner who is attempting to improve performance and mileage is so large that it's easy to make mistakes.

Aside from the fact that the carburetor is not an ideal choice, you'll never get the secondaries to open simply by revving the engine. They are vacuum-operated and respond to engine demand. When the engine demand exceeds the capability of the primary venturi, the secondaries will open automatically. This usually will occur under heavy throttle at about 3000 rpm. The secondaries on your carburetor may never fully open because the carburetor is slightly too large for your engine.

After you get the carb/manifold problems corrected, the distributor should be tuned; headers of the proper size and type should be installed.

Fresh Air Induction

Do you recommend installation of a tube that channels cool air from in front of the radiator to the air cleaner? My van gets very hot under the hood and I would think this would help.

Chester Murray
San Diego, California

Fresh air induction will help in hot weather. Although beneficial, it can produce problems on a van that would not occur on a pickup truck or car. With many vans, the heated air passing through the radiator is restricted and partially retained in the confined engine compartment. The engine ingests a good deal of air and this helps make room for more air to pass through the radiator. When the air for the carburetor is taken from ahead of the radiator, this restricts air movement in the engine compartment and reduces air flow through the radiator, which can compound the problems.

If you decide to try fresh air induction on your van, you might watch your temperature gauge closely during hot weather and see if engine temperature is increased when the air induction is in use. Disconnect it and reconnect it several times to get a good comparison.

While building an induction system, do not simply attach a tube to the snorkel on the air cleaner. If the snorkel is about 2 to 3 inches wide and you attach a single 2- or 3-inch hose to it, restriction will result causing preignition and loss of power.

Installation of dual 3-inch or a single 4-inch hose will work best. If your air cleaner is equipped with a heat tube induction from the exhaust manifold for cold-weather starts, eliminate it for summer use and reconnect it in winter, if needed. Keep the length of the fresh air induction tube to a minimum and avoid sharp bends.

Wrong Equipment

My local speed shop talked me into replacing my stock 2-barrel carburetor with a Holley 3310 carburetor on my Dodge 360 engine, before I began reading your columns about proper choice of carburetors. The carburetor didn't help much.

Werner Hughey
Denver, Colorado

Many people buy incorrect equipment in the attempt to increase engine efficiency. Many engines do not accept replacement equipment with any beneficial results. In your case, a carburetor change does help substantially, but not the carburetor you bought. Some equipment changes, in fact, will produce a loss in low-end power.

Carburetors seem to be the most critical and controversial of the choices you can make because there are so many replacement carburetors to choose from, in various sizes. Generally, carburetors are recommended according to cubic inch displacement of the engine, which is totally incorrect. The carburetor has no way of knowing what size the engine is. The carburetor only produces fuel relative to the velocity of air traveling through its venturi. Different engines in the same cubic inch size will be completely different in volumetric efficiency and will require different carburetors. Operational range, vehicle weight and altitude all enter the selection process, so don't be fooled by the magic sliding scale.

Troubleshooting RV Batteries

32

A discussion of batteries may seem off-target in a book about engine fuel economy and performance. But since auxiliary batteries play a critical role in how well the RV owner can enjoy his home on wheels, and since there is so much misinformation in circulation, it seems appropriate. Also, if the only battery recharge method available during primitive camping is running the engine (no AC generator), battery recharge methods may determine how long one can camp without the need to burn fuel for battery recharging.

Many RV owners encounter battery problems but the trailerist in particular has trouble with rapid loss of power in his trailer (auxiliary) battery. There are several reasons, none of which are very difficult to understand once you examine how batteries and charging systems work. We'll examine those reasons in detail here, and present the information which we hope will help you understand batteries and charging systems in all types of RVs, so you can make more effective use of them.

The trailerist's woes probably can be compared with the situation at an RV rally in which several RVs are hooked to one water source, and he's at the end of the line. The water goes through so many different hoses and interconnections, some of them restrictive, that he only gets a dribble though the pressure at the head of the line is normal.

The 12-volt charging system can be compared to a water system.

Before we get into the reasons for battery problems and what can be done about them, let's talk about the tools needed to troubleshoot 12-volt systems.

In addition to the small hand tools, you need a temperature-corrected hydrometer and a voltmeter. Without those two you will be operating in the dark. The hydrometers with the little floating balls are not sufficiently accurate and should not be used as anything but very rough indicators. The voltmeter should read the usual scale for 12-volt systems—between about 8 and 16 volts.

Multimeters measure DV voltage, plus many other electrical functions and are good investments. They're available from electronics supply stores.

Battery-Charging Misconceptions

The primary misconception most RV owners have is with respect to the function of the voltage regulator under the hood. The voltage regulator is generally believed to shut off the alternator's output to the battery or batteries when they're fully charged. For that reason, most motorists believe that the regulator shuts off the alternator when the starting battery is fully charged, and leaves the auxiliary battery only partially charged. Not so. The auxiliary may be only partially charged, but not for that reason.

The function of the voltage regulator—whether external or built into the alternator—is to limit the alternator's voltage output to a specific level. This level fluctuates a bit due to temperature variations, but it's usually around 14 volts. Why 14 volts if the battery is 12-volt? Back to the water system. If a

pump is attempting to fill a water tank that contains air pressure at the top, the pump pressure must exceed the air pressure or no water will enter. The alternator must have higher "pressure" than that inside the battery, for a charge to occur.

The battery itself determines when, if, and how much charge it will take. If the battery is dead, it will take the full output of the alternator (limited only by wiring inadequacies). If it is nearing full charge, it will accept only a small portion of the alternator output. The alternator can be connected to two batteries and it can be expected to charge both, although at a slower rate because its output will be divided.

The typical situation involves a starting battery and a single auxiliary battery. After camping without hookups for the night, the auxiliary has been depleted, say 50 percent. But the starting battery has been resting all night. When the engine is started, the starting battery will accept a low charge rate for only a few minutes. That hard-working auxiliary needs a recharge; it *will* accept the charge *if* the charge line is adequate and if the battery is in good condition. More on battery condition later.

Back to the water system analogy. The rate at which the water pump fills the tank depends on the pump's output and the size of the pipe. If the pump's output is limited to 14 psi, the next limiting factor is the size of the pipe. A half-inch pipe will deliver much less water than a 1-inch pipe. Since your alternator's output is limited to about 14 volts, the size and length of the charge line to the auxiliary battery has control over the charge rate. *Distance* is critical here. The battery may be 25 feet away from the alternator. As length of the charge line increases, wire size must increase.

Battery charging is complicated by several other factors, but the primary problems are the bottlenecks created by an inadequate wire size and poor connections. The pump can't deliver the water if the pipe is too small or is partially clogged. Battery problems are worse in RVs than in any other automotive battery usage area, due to inadequate charging. Ten-gauge wire is the minimum necessary for positive and negative lines to an auxiliary battery, and if the battery is more than about 15 feet away from the alternator, eight gauge is preferred.

Lack of Maintenance

Even when a proper wire size is used, maintenance may be lacking . . . and it takes only one weak link in the chain to create a restriction. Corrosion at connections will do it. Terminals inside the trailer connector may become corroded. Corrosion under battery lugs is another cause. Don't forget the ground (negative) wire. It must be of the same size as the positive wire. Some hitch shops will use a good-sized positive line and then run a wire about the size of lamp cord as a ground from the trailer connector to the frame. It's OK to use the tow vehicle or motorhome chassis

as the ground circuit but wire size and connections must be equally as good as on the positive side. Paint should be scraped away so the ground connections to the frame have good metal-to-metal contact. Use petroleum jelly or silicone dialectric compound on the connections to retard formation of corrosion. Use TV contact cleaner (available in radio/TV supply stores) on the contacts inside the trailer connector. In other words, keep the pipes clear.

What happens when the pipes are not clear? It's called *voltage drop.* Here's where your voltmeter enters the picture. And your hydrometer.

1.265 sp. gr.	100% charged
1.225 sp. gr.	75% charged
1.190 sp. gr.	50% charged
1.155 sp gr.	25% charged
1.120 sp. gr.	Discharged

The accompanying specific gravity scale offers readings that are necessary to interpret what you see on the hydrometer. The 1.265 level is identified as the full-charge level, and the surprising thing is that your auxiliary battery may *never* see 1.265 specific gravity. In other words, your charging system may never bring the battery up to full charge, due to bottlenecks in the charging system. If so, your battery has been de-rated. Instead of a 105-amp-hour battery, you now may have a 70-amp-hour battery, or whatever the level might be according to your recharging inadequacy. No wonder the battery doesn't seem to last very long under heavy appliance usage!

If the battery has been allowed to remain in a discharged state for an extended period, hard sulfate forms; when that happens, the battery has been permanently de-rated. Many RV purchasers are hamstrung from the outset. Their coaches have been allowed to sit on a dealer's lot for periods ranging from two months to more than a year. Unless the dealer is maintenance-oriented, only the starting battery has been kept in a good state of charge. Your *new* auxiliary battery may have been allowed to sit dead for several months, which is the reason why it doesn't act like a new battery.

Formation of sulfate on the plates occurs naturally when the battery delivers power and the state of charge is reduced. This natural sulfate should not be confused with the formation of *hard* sulfate when the battery sits in a discharged state and the normal soft sulfate coating the plates is allowed to harden with time. It cannot be removed by normal recharge methods. The electrolyte of a fully charged battery contains about 36 percent sulfuric acid (by weight). When a cell is discharged, the sulfuric acid reacts with the active materials of the positive and negative plates to form soft lead sulfate on the plates. The process is reversed during recharging.

In all these cases, the temperature-corrected hydrometer will tell you the story . . . if you read it properly. When you *think* you have driven far enough to fully charge the battery or when you have been connected to an outside power source for at least 24 hours so

your electrical converter supposedly is recharging the battery, check all six cells with the hydrometer. If the specific gravity reading is not at least 1.230, corrective measures are in order. If you see a substantial deviation in the reading on one of the cells compared to the other, you may have a dead cell.

If the specific gravity reading is below 1.230, take the rig to a service station and ask them to recharge the battery to 1.265, making sure the charge rate is not so high that it raises electrolyte temperature above 125 degrees F, which can damage the battery.

When sulfate has hardened on the battery plates, the battery often is permanently de-rated or ruined. But in the case of only partial formation of the hard sulfate, a sustained charge of about 10 amps over a period of several hours sometimes can break the sulfate and bring the battery back as close as possible to the original capacity. It's a shame that new batteries are harmed or ruined by inadequate charging because they're quite expensive.

Checking Voltage

If and when the battery is up to 1.265, you can use your voltmeter (preferably a handheld unit) to determine the voltage reaching the battery or batteries. The voltage at the alternator or converter doesn't mean much because bottlenecks in the charging lines can cause voltage drop and seriously reduce your recharge capability. First, take your voltmeter to your local garage and ask them to compare its readings to those of their larger, more expensive diagnostic equipment. If your meter is off, determine the error and adjust the meter. Then run the engine at about 2000 rpm and check voltage at your auxiliary battery (which you previously have had recharged to 1.265). It should be around 14 volts. It could be as high as 14.5 volts when the engine is cold because the voltage regulation system compensates for temperatures. This is necessary because a battery's ability to receive a charge and to provide power is reduced in cold weather. This is why RV travelers have more battery problems in winter than at other times.

If the voltage level is below 14, check voltage at the alternator. If it's 14 volts or higher, voltage drop is occurring between the alternator and auxiliary battery and this is why your auxiliary battery never is recharged fully. Using your voltmeter, check the charge line at intervals toward the alternator until you find the bottleneck. It could be a loose connection, a poorly operating mechanical battery isolator or simply a length of wire of inadequate size.

One point of caution: When you read voltage between a diode-type (solid state) dual battery isolator and the alternator, voltage will be higher than normal because the isolator induces higher voltage. This will not be the case with a mechanical isolator (relay). If the wire between the alternator and isolator is at least No. 10 in size, and if distance is less than 2 or 3 feet, you can assume no voltage drop between the alternator and isolator. But check con-

nections for corrosion and for tightness. Otherwise, for the purpose of your investigation into possible voltage drop, temporarily bypass your isolator with a length of No. 10 or No. 8 wire.

Connectors should be soldered on the wires. A loose connection can provide that weak link. After the bottleneck is corrected and the battery is recharged to 1.265 specific gravity, subsequent recharges should be routine.

Getting the Right Battery

As a battery ages, its capacity gradually is reduced. How fast this occurs depends to a substantial degree on the type of battery it is.

There are automotive starting batteries and there are deep-cycle batteries designed for the rigors of RV accessories use. An automotive starting battery will lose some of its capacity each time its charge level is reduced to less than 50 percent. The automotive starting battery is designed to offer short bursts of power of more than 200 amps, for engine starting. The deep-cycle battery is built for repeated deep discharging. It will last much longer under RV accessories usage than will the automotive starting battery, hence the usual disclaimer in starting battery warranties which reduces or eliminates coverage when the dealer finds out the battery has been in deep-cycle use.

Batteries, like tanks, have different capacities. The capacity of a tank is obvious from its size, whereas two batteries may look the same but actually

Deep-cycle batteries are superior to automotive starting batteries for RV accessories usage. 12-volt batteries may be used in parallel, or 6-volt batteries may be used with in-series wiring hookup.

have sizable differences in their ability to store electrical energy. Again, like a tank, one cannot get 80 gallons out of a 50-gallon tank nor can one obtain 80 gallons from an 80-gallon tank if it's only half full to start with.

It's important that the buyer choose a battery intended for deep-cycle use. But it's also important to concentrate on power ratings. For example, the number of plates in a battery is not as important as the rating of the battery in terms of reserve capacity or amp hours—the best indicators of performance when the battery will be used for RV appliances. The cold cranking performance rating is the proper measure in selecting a battery for engine starting. Plates have many different

sizes. For example, nine small plates in a cell are no better than seven large plates, in terms of their electrical characteristics.

In past years it has been difficult to find deep-cycle batteries, but no more. Gould is marketing their AP-105 deep-cycle battery nationwide through selected Penney's stores. Sears sells a deep-cycle Die-Hard. And AC-Delco has a battery they call High-Cycle that is somewhere between a starting battery and a deep-cycle; it has high output for engine cranking as well as the ability to withstand RV accessories usage.

Deep-cycle 12-volt batteries may be used in pairs if they are the same rated capacity and about the same age. Two 6-volt batteries can be used simultaneously, since they are connected in series rather than in parallel. In such a connection, the negative post of one battery is connected to the positive post of the other. The remaining positive and negative posts are connected to the appliance load. Thus the batteries are never fully interconnected except when power is being drawn from them.

Maintenance-free (sealed) batteries have grown popular as automotive starting batteries, but most are not suitable for RV deep-cycle usage. The Delco High Cycle is an exception.

The amp-hour rating of a battery indicates what you might expect to get out of it in terms of power. To use the ratings, divide the amp-hour rating of the battery by the average load on the battery; you will get the number of hours the battery will support that load. The figures are approximate. Same goes

A good temperature-corrected hydrometer is a valuable tool in using batteries most effectively.

for reserve capacity, which is listed in minutes. The reserve capacity rating is the number of minutes a particular battery will support a 25-amp load. When you're shopping for deep-cycle batteries, get the highest rating possible. The ratings are based on total depletion; by drawing the battery down to 9 or 10 volts we don't get the full rated capacity of the battery.

A hydrometer is the most accurate indicator when you're trying to determine if your alternator or converter is fully recharging the battery. During our tests, we recorded hydrometer as well as voltmeter readings. During depletion, the hydrometer readings decreased consistently, along with voltage readings. But during recharge tests the hydrometer readings stayed at the bottom of the scale until well after recharge was under way. The hydrometer can be used to measure battery condition in the upper regions of the scale during recharge, but the voltmeter otherwise is the best indicator.

Reading the Hydrometer

When using a hydrometer, it's important to read the instrument correctly. If it's not held or filled properly, erroneous readings can result. The hydrometer bulb should be squeezed to fill the device so the float does not bottom or hit the top. The hydrometer should be lightly thumped, tapped, or shaken to make sure the float is not sticking to the side of the tube. The scale should be read looking straight across the level of fluid in the tube—not from above or below. Temperature correction is important. For example, in 20-degree weather a hydrometer might read 1.250 specific gravity until the temperature factor is employed and it reduces the reading to 1.226—a substantial drop.

In reading a voltmeter for proper charging, you're looking for levels between 13.8 and 14.5. But in reading the meter for battery condition, the load on the battery at the time will affect the readings. For comparative readings, check the voltmeter with the same load on the line. For instance, check it with two interior lights on—nothing else. Never check it with no load because readings will be abnormally high.

Experience will tell you your tolerances—how far your battery is from depletion when you see a particular reading. The built-in battery condition monitors are handy for this, even though they have color-band rather than numerical scales. Soon you'll learn to relate the needle positions in the scales to your own situation. But the portable voltmeter with a numerical scale is best for general use.

Speaking of gauges, if you really want to know what's happening with your auxiliary battery, install a 0-60 amp ammeter on the charge line from the alternator to that battery. In the morning, on the road, you'll see a healthy charge rate—possibly upwards of 40 to 50 amps if you have a 60-amp alternator and are using No. 8 wire—while you might also see a zero charge rate on your factory-installed ammeter for the starting battery. Those widely differing readings prove that the two batteries can effectively be charged in parallel if the wiring hookup is correct.

Winter Problems

Winter is particularly hard on RV batteries. More is expected of them, to operate RV forced-air furnaces.

Most RV batteries are mounted in outside compartments; this is as should be, because a battery emits explosive hydrogen and oxygen gases while being charged. This causes a disadvantage in cold weather because once the battery is down, you have a hell of a time recharging it if the battery internal temperature is only zero—or maybe less.

At zero degrees, your ability to recharge the battery is retarded to less than half the normal rate. The solution is to heat the battery. Either it can be relocated inside a heated area of the coach, preferably adjacent to a furnace hot-air duct, or you can install heat tape designed for plumbing that would automatically go into operation anytime you start your AC generator (if you have one). If the battery is relocated inside the coach, you *must* install a tube in each battery cap vent to channel the gases outside. The plastic tubing used in the passenger earphones on commercial airliners is impervious to battery acid, so it would work for this. The vent cap is drilled just large enough that the tube is press-fitted into it. All six tubes are routed outside and secured. The battery is contained in a plastic battery box and securely anchored to the floor so the battery will not fall out and so acid will be contained in the box in the event of a vehicle turnover. Keeping the battery outside is safer. But with proper precautions, moving the battery inside with the heat from your furnace allows you to keep it at 70 to 80 degrees, —ideal temperature for efficiency.

Battery Isolation

In motorhomes and campers, isolating the starting battery from RV appliances is necessary and most of these coaches are equipped with battery isolators which electrically or electronically separate the starting battery from the auxiliary. Many tow vehicles have these devices, although many owners provide their own isolation simply by unplugging the trailer connector when they stop for the night. Thus the starting battery no longer is connected to the trailer battery. However, there is more to it than meets the eye.

Batteries can be charged in parallel, as described earlier, but the current should be controlled. Simply running a wire from the alternator to the trailer battery creates interconnection between the trailer and the engine starting battery when the trailer connector is plugged in. With the right setup, a parallel charge can occur to both batteries even though the batteries are electronically separated. It would be similar to two water tanks being filled from the same pipe which splits into two legs. Each of the legs has a valve which allows the water to flow in only one direction. Thus, water from one tank can never flow into the other tank if pump pressure ever drops, or if one tank is full and the other is empty. The diodes in a battery isolator are one-way electrical valves.

Another type of isolator is simply a mechanical relay, using contact points to open and close, connecting the starting battery to the auxiliary, when the ignition key is turned on. Both types work well but the top-quality electronic isolator has the edge because it has no mechanical components to wear out or become corroded, causing volt-

age drop. However, an electronic regulator of poor quality can short out internally and cause the alternator to overcharge the starting battery, or it can short to ground, blowing the alternator. This doesn't happen with top-quality units, and it doesn't happen often with any electronic isolator.

The best of batteries and charging systems can provide you with only the amount of capacity your batteries can store, so it's wise to hold appliance usage to a minimum. In coaches where incandescent lights must be used in large numbers, installation of two or three large overhead fluorescent lights could cut power consumption.

After your battery capacity and charging problems have been solved, maintenance will be important to retaining that capacity. Periodically inspect all connections for tightness and corrosion. Coat the battery connections with petroleum jelly and keep the top of the battery clean. Dirt and grime can create conductivity between the positive and negative posts and cause capacity losses. Corrosion at terminals can severely restrict recharge capability. Check electrolyte level monthly (except on maintenance-free batteries); add distilled water when necessary.

Battery problems may seem insurmountable to many RV owners. But the problems are fairly simple to correct if you know where to look. In most cases our battery needs are well within the capability offered by the batteries featured here—even during winter—providing that the batteries are recharged properly.

Index